THE FIREFLY MINI
FRENCH/ENGLISH
VISUAL DICTIONARY

Jean-Claude **Corbeil**
Ariane **Archambault**

FIREFLY BOOKS

A FIREFLY BOOK

Published by Firefly Books Ltd. 2009
Copyright © 2006 QA International

All rights reserved. No part of this publication may be reproduced, stored in a retrieval system or transmitted in any form or by any means, electronic, mechanical, photocopying, recording or otherwise, without the prior written permission of the Publisher.

First printing

Publisher Cataloging-in-Publication Data (U.S.)
Corbeil, Jean-Claude.
  The Firefly mini French English visual dictionary / Jean-Claude Corbeil ; Ariane Archambault.
  [600] p. : col. ill. ; cm.
  Includes index.
  Summary: A comprehensive general reference visual dictionary featuring terms in English and French. Includes sections on astronomy, geography, the animal and vegetable kingdoms, human biology, the home, clothing and accessories, art and architecture, communication, transportation, energy, science, society and sports.
  ISBN-13: 978-1-55407-493-8 (pbk.)
  ISBN-10: 1-55407-493-2 (pbk.)
  1. Picture dictionaries, French. 2. Picture dictionaries, English.
3. French language – Dictionaries – English. 4. English language – Dictionaries – French. I. Archambault, Ariane. II. Title.
  443.21 dc22   PC2629.C6736 2006

Library and Archives Canada Cataloguing in Publication
Corbeil, Jean-Claude, 1932-
  The Firefly mini French/English visual dictionary / Jean-Claude Corbeil, Ariane Archambault.
  Includes index.
  ISBN-13: 978-1-55407-493-8
  ISBN-10: 1-55407-493-2
    1. Picture dictionaries, French. 2. Picture dictionaries, English.
3. English language–Dictionaries–French. 4. French language–Dictionaries–English.
I. Archambault, Ariane, 1936- II. Title.
AG250.C66374 2006   443'.21   C2006-900745-4

Published in the United States by
Firefly Books (U.S.) Inc.
P.O. Box 1338, Ellicott Station
Buffalo, New York 14205

443.21
COR

Published in Canada by
Firefly Books Ltd.
66 Leek Crescent
Richmond Hill, Ontario L4B 1H1

Cover design: Gareth Lind

Printed in Singapore
11 10 9 8 7 6 5 4 3 2   12 11 10 09
Version 3.5.1

ACKNOWLEDGMENTS

Our deepest gratitude to the individuals, institutions, companies and businesses that have provided us with the latest technical documentation for use in preparing *The Firefly Mini French/English Visual Dictionary*.

Arcand, Denys (réalisateur); Association Internationale de Signalisation Maritime; Association canadienne des paiements (Charlie Clarke); Association des banquiers canadiens (Lise Provost); Automobiles Citroën; Automobiles Peugeot; Banque du Canada (Lyse Brousseau); Banque Royale du Canada (Raymond Chouinard, Francine Morel, Carole Trottier); Barrett Xplore inc.; Bazarin, Christine;Bibliothèque du Parlement canadien (Service de renseignements); Bibliothèque nationale du Québec (Jean-François Palomino); Bluechip Kennels (Olga Gagne); Bombardier Aéronautique; Bridgestone-Firestone; Brother (Canada); Canadien National; Casavant Frères ltée; C.O.J.O. ATHENES 2004 (Bureau des Médias Internationaux); Centre Eaton de Montréal; Centre national du Costume (Recherche et de Diffusion); Cetacean Society International (William R. Rossiter); Chagnon, Daniel (architecte D.E.S. – M.E.Q.); Cohen et Rubin Architectes (Maggy Cohen); Commission Scolaire de Montréal (École St-Henri); Compagnie de la Baie d'Hudson (Nunzia Iavarone, Ron Oyama); Corporation d'hébergement du Québec (Céline Drolet); École nationale de théâtre du Canada (Bibliothèque); Élevage Le Grand Saphir (Stéphane Ayotte); Énergie atomique du Canada ltée; Eurocopter; Famous Players; Fédération bancaire française (Védi Hékiman); Fontaine, PierreHenry (biologiste); Future Shop; Garaga; Groupe Jean Coutu; Hôpital du Sacré-Cœur de Montréal; Hôtel Inter-Continental; Hydro-Québec; I.P.I.Q. (Serge Bouchard); IGA Barcelo; International Entomological Society (Dr. Michael Geisthardt); Irisbus; Jérôme, Danielle (O.D.); La Poste (Colette Gouts); Le Groupe Canam Manac inc.; Lévesque, Georges (urgentologue); Lévesque, Robert (chef machiniste); Manutan; Marriot Spring Hill suites; MATRA S.A.; Métro inc.; ministère canadien de la Défense nationale (Affaires publiques); ministère de la Défense, République Française; ministère de la Justice du Québec (Service de la gestion immobilière – Carol Sirois); ministère de l'Éducation du Québec (Direction de l'équipement scolaire- Daniel Chagnon); Muse Productions (Annick Barbery); National Aeronautics and Space Administration; National Oceanic and Atmospheric Administration; Nikon Canada inc.; Normand, Denis (consultant en télécommunications); Office de la langue française du Québec (Chantal Robinson); Paul Demers & Fils inc.; Phillips (France); Pratt & Whitney Canada inc.; Prévost Car inc.; Radio Shack Canada ltée; Réno-Dépôt inc.; Robitaille, Jean-François (Département de biologie, Université Laurentienne); Rocking T Ranch and Poultry Farm (Pete and Justine Theer); RONA inc.; Sears Canada inc.; Secrétariat d'État du Canada : Bureau de la traduction ; Service correctionnel du Canada; Société d'Entomologie Africaine (Alain Drumont); Société des musées québécois (Michel Perron); Société Radio-Canada; Sony du Canada ltée; Sûreté du Québec; Théâtre du Nouveau Monde; Transports Canada (Julie Poirier); Urgences-Santé (Éric Berry); Ville de Longueuil (Direction de la police); Ville de Montréal (Service de la prévention des incendies); Vimont Lexus Toyota; Volvo Bus Corporation; Yamaha Motor Canada Ltd.

QA International wishes to extend a special thank you to the following people for their contribution to *The Firefly Mini French/English Visual Dictionary*:

Jean-Louis Martin, Marc Lalumière, Jacques Perrault, Stéphane Roy, Alice Comtois, Michel Blais, Christiane Beauregard, Mamadou Togola, Annie Maurice, Charles Campeau, Mivil Deschênes, Jonathan Jacques, Martin Lortie, Frédérick Simard, Yan Tremblay, Mathieu Blouin, Sébastien Dallaire, Hoang Khanh Le, Martin Desrosiers, Nicolas Oroc, François Escalmel, Danièle Lemay, Pierre Savoie, Benoit Bourdeau, Marie-Andrée Lemieux, Caroline Soucy, Yves Chabot, Anne-Marie Ouellette, Anne-Marie Villeneuve, Anne-Marie Brault, Nancy Lepage, Daniel Provost, François Vézina, Brad Wilson, Michael Worek, Lionel Koffler, Maraya Raduha, Dave Harvey, Mike Parkes, George Walker, Anna Simmons, Sophie Pellerin, Kien Tang, Guylaine Houle, Tony O'Riley.

The Firefly Mini French/English Visual Dictionary was created and produced by
QA International
329, rue de la Commune Ouest, 3e étage
Montréal (Québec) H2Y 2E1 Canada
T 514.499.3000 F 514.499.3010
www.qa-international.com

EDITORIAL STAFF

Publisher: Jacques Fortin
Authors: Jean-Claude Corbeil and Ariane Archambault
Editorial Director: François Fortin
Editor-in-Chief: Serge D'Amico
Graphic Design: Anne Tremblay

PRODUCTION

Nathalie Fréchette
Cynthia Morneau

TERMINOLOGICAL RESEARCH

Jean Beaumont
Catherine Briand
Nathalie Guillo
Anne Rouleau

ILLUSTRATIONS

Art Direction: Jocelyn Gardner, Anouk Noël
Jean-Yves Ahern
Rielle Lévesque
Alain Lemire
Mélanie Boivin
Yan Bohler
Claude Thivierge
Pascal Bilodeau
Michel Rouleau
Carl Pelletier
Raymond Martin

LAYOUT

Pascal Goyette
Janou-Ève LeGuerrier
Véronique Boisvert
Karine Raymond
Geneviève Théroux Béliveau

DOCUMENTATION

Gilles Vézina
Kathleen Wynd
Stéphane Batigne
Sylvain Robichaud
Jessie Daigle

DATA MANAGEMENT

Programmer: Éric Gagnon
Daniel Beaulieu

REVISION

Marie-Nicole Cimon
Liliane Michaud
Véronica Schami

PREPRESS

Karine Lévesque
François Hénault
Julien Brisebois
Patrick Mercure

Jean-Claude Corbeil is an expert in linguistic planning, with a world-wide reputation in the fields of comparative terminology and socio-linguistics. He serves as a consultant to various international organizations and governments.

Ariane Archambault, a specialist in applied linguistics, has taught foreign languages and is now a terminologist and editor of dictionaries and reference books.

Introduction to
The Firefly Mini French/English Visual Dictionary

A DICTIONARY FOR ONE AND ALL

The Firefly Mini French/English Visual Dictionary uses pictures to define words. With thousands of illustrations and thousands of specialist and general terms, it provides a rich source of knowledge about the world around you.

Designed for the general reader and students of language, *The Firefly Mini French/English Visual Dictionary* responds to the needs of anyone seeking precise, correct terms for a wide range of objects. Using illustrations enables you to "see" immediately the meaning of each term.

You can use *The Firefly Mini French/English Visual Dictionary* in several ways:

By going from an idea to a word. If you are familiar with an object but do not know the correct name for it, you can look up the object in the dictionary and you will find the various parts correctly named.

By going from a word to an idea. If you want to check the meaning of a term, refer to the index where you will find the term and be directed to the appropriate illustration that defines the term.

For sheer pleasure. You can flip from one illustration to another or from one word to another, for the sole purpose of enjoying the illustrations and enriching your knowledge of the world around us.

STRUCTURE

The Firefly Mini French/English Visual Dictionary is divided into THEMES, outlining subjects from astronomy to sports.

More complex subjects are divided into SUB-THEMES; for example, the Animal Kingdom chapter is divided into themes including insects and arachnids, mollusks, and crustaceans.

The TITLES name the object and, at times, the chief members of a class of objects are brought together under the same SUBTITLE.

The ILLUSTRATIONS show an object, a process or a phenomenon, and the most significant details from which they are constructed. It serves as a visual definition for each of the terms presented.

TERMINOLOGY

Each word in *The Firefly Mini French/English Visual Dictionary* has been carefully chosen and verified. Sometimes different words are used to name the same object, and in these cases the word most commonly used was chosen.

TITLE
It is highlighted in English, and the French equivalent is placed underneath in smaller characters. If the title runs over a number of pages, it is printed in gray on the pages subsequent to the first page on which it appears.

SUB-THEME
Most themes are subdivided into sub-themes. The sub-theme is given both in English and in French.

NARROW LINES
These link the word to the item indicated. Where too many lines would make reading difficult, they have been replaced by color codes with captions or, in rare cases, by numbers.

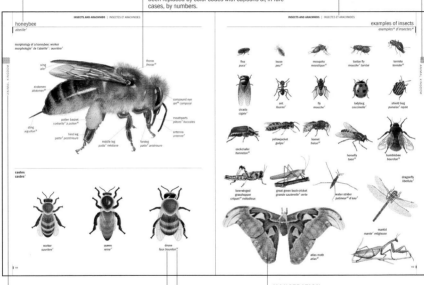

THEME
It is always unilingual, in English.

ILLUSTRATION
It serves as the visual definition for the terms associated with it.

GENDER INDICATION
F: feminine M: masculine N: neuter

The gender of each word in a term is indicated.

TERM
Each term appears in the index with a reference to the pages on which it appears. It is given in both languages, with English as the main index entry.

The characters shown in the dictionary are men or women when the function illustrated can be fulfilled by either. In these cases, the gender assigned to the word depends on the illustration; in fact, the word is either masculine or feminine depending on the sex of the person.

Contents

List of chapters

ASTRONOMY

solar system
système^M solaire

outer planets
planètes^F externes

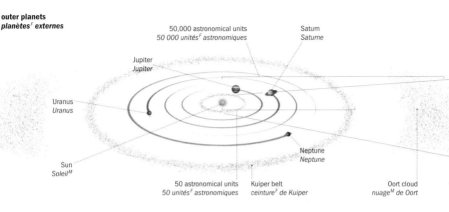

50,000 astronomical units
50 000 unités^F astronomiques

Saturn
Saturne

Jupiter
Jupiter

Uranus
Uranus

Sun
Soleil^M

Neptune
Neptune

50 astronomical units
50 unités^F astronomiques

Kuiper belt
ceinture^F de Kuiper

Oort cloud
nuage^M de Oort

planets and satellites
planètes^F et satellites^M

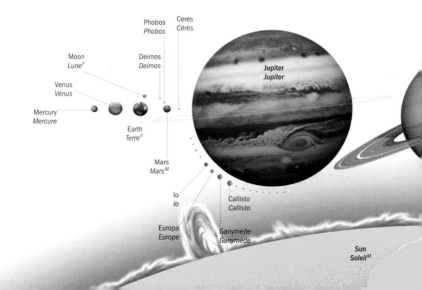

Phobos
Phobos

Ceres
Cérès

Moon
Lune^F

Deimos
Deimos

Venus
Vénus

Jupiter
Jupiter

Mercury
Mercure

Earth
Terre^F

Mars
Mars^M

Io
Io

Callisto
Callisto

Europa
Europe

Ganymede
Ganymède

Sun
Soleil^M

inner planets
planètes^F internes

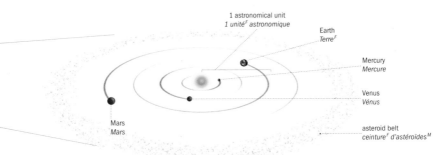

1 astronomical unit
1 unité^F astronomique

Earth
Terre^F

Mercury
Mercure

Venus
Vénus

asteroid belt
ceinture^F d'astéroïdes^M

Mars
Mars

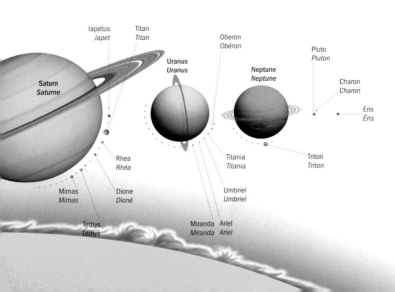

Iapetus
Japet

Titan
Titan

Oberon
Obéron

Pluto
Pluton

Saturn
Saturne

Uranus
Uranus

Neptune
Neptune

Charon
Charon

Eris
Éris

Titania
Titania

Triton
Triton

Rhea
Rhéa

Mimas
Mimas

Dione
Dioné

Umbriel
Umbriel

Tethys
Téthys

Miranda
Miranda

Ariel
Ariel

Sun
Soleil[M]

structure of the Sun
structure[F] *du Soleil*[M]

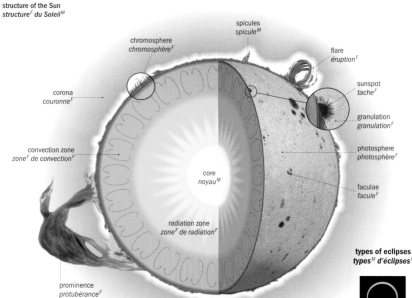

spicules
spicule[M]

chromosphere
chromosphère[F]

flare
éruption[F]

corona
couronne[F]

sunspot
tache[F]

granulation
granulation[F]

convection zone
zone[F] *de convection*[F]

photosphere
photosphère[F]

core
noyau[M]

faculae
facule[F]

radiation zone
zone[F] *de radiation*[F]

prominence
protubérance[F]

types of eclipses
types[M] *d'éclipses*[F]

annular eclipse
éclipse[F] *annulaire*

solar eclipse
éclipse[F] *de Soleil*[M]

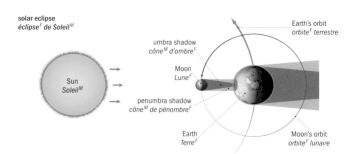

Earth's orbit
orbite[F] *terrestre*

umbra shadow
cône[M] *d'ombre*[F]

Moon
Lune[F]

Sun
Soleil[M]

penumbra shadow
cône[M] *de pénombre*[F]

Earth
Terre[F]

Moon's orbit
orbite[F] *lunaire*

partial eclipse
éclipse[F] *partielle*

total eclipse
éclipse[F] *totale*

Moon
Lune^F

types of eclipses
types^M d'éclipses^F

partial eclipse
éclipse^F partielle

total eclipse
éclipse^F totale

lunar features
relief^M lunaire

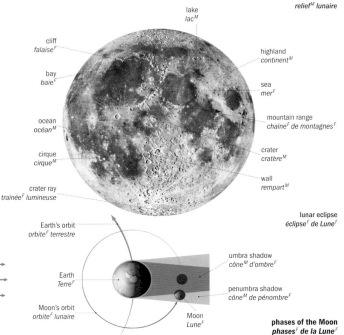

lake
lac^M

cliff
falaise^F

bay
baie^F

ocean
océan^M

cirque
cirque^M

crater ray
trainée^F lumineuse

highland
continent^M

sea
mer^F

mountain range
chaîne^F de montagnes^F

crater
cratère^M

wall
rempart^M

lunar eclipse
éclipse^F de Lune^F

Sun
Soleil^M

Earth's orbit
orbite^F terrestre

Earth
Terre^F

Moon's orbit
orbite^F lunaire

umbra shadow
cône^M d'ombre^F

penumbra shadow
cône^M de pénombre^F

Moon
Lune^F

phases of the Moon
phases^F de la Lune^F

new moon
nouvelle Lune^F

new crescent
premier croissant^M

first quarter
premier quartier^M

waxing gibbous
gibbeuse^F croissante

full moon
pleine Lune^F

waning gibbous
gibbeuse^F décroissante

last quarter
dernier quartier^M

old crescent
dernier croissant^M

ASTRONOMY

galaxy
galaxie^F

Milky Way
Voie^F Lactée

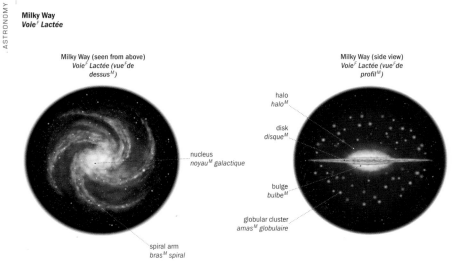

Milky Way (seen from above)
Voie^F Lactée (vue^F de dessus^M)

Milky Way (side view)
Voie^F Lactée (vue^F de profil^M)

nucleus
noyau^M galactique

halo
halo^M

disk
disque^M

bulge
bulbe^M

globular cluster
amas^M globulaire

spiral arm
bras^M spiral

comet
comète^F

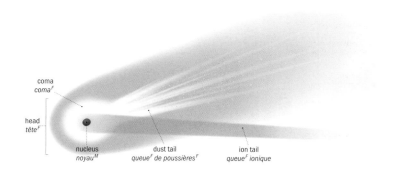

coma
coma^F

head
tête^F

nucleus
noyau^M

dust tail
queue^F de poussières^F

ion tail
queue^F ionique

Hubble space telescope
télescope^M spatial Hubble

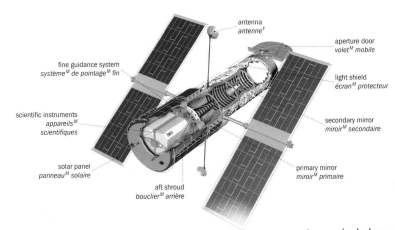

antenna
antenne^F

aperture door
volet^M mobile

fine guidance system
système^M de pointage^M fin

light shield
écran^M protecteur

scientific instruments
appareils^M
scientifiques

secondary mirror
miroir^M secondaire

solar panel
panneau^M solaire

primary mirror
miroir^M primaire

aft shroud
bouclier^M arrière

astronomical observatory
observatoire^M astronomique

cross section of an astronomical observatory
coupe^F d'un observatoire^M astronomique

secondary mirror
miroir^M secondaire

light
lumière^F

observatory
observatoire^M

telescope
télescope^M

dome shutter
cimier^M mobile

rotating dome
coupole^F rotative

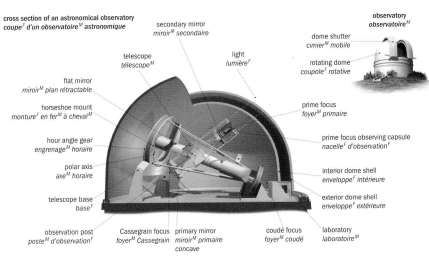

flat mirror
miroir^M plan rétractable

horseshoe mount
monture^F en fer^M à cheval^M

hour angle gear
engrenage^M horaire

polar axis
axe^M horaire

telescope base
base^F

observation post
poste^M d'observation^F

Cassegrain focus
foyer^M Cassegrain

primary mirror
miroir^M primaire
concave

coudé focus
foyer^M coudé

prime focus
foyer^M primaire

prime focus observing capsule
nacelle^F d'observation^F

interior dome shell
enveloppe^F intérieure

exterior dome shell
enveloppe^F extérieure

laboratory
laboratoire^M

ASTRONOMY

refracting telescope
lunette^F astronomique

finderscope
chercheur^M

cradle
bride^F de fixation^F

main tube
tube^M

dew shield
pare-soleil^M

eyepiece
oculaire^M

eyepiece holder
tube^M porte-oculaire^M

star diagonal
oculaire^M coudé

declination setting scale
cercle^M de déclinaison^F

focusing knob
bouton^M de mise^F au point^M

azimuth clamp
vis^F de blocage^M (azimut^M)

azimuth fine adjustment
réglage^M micrométrique (azimut^M)

altitude clamp
vis^F de blocage^M (latitude^F)

altitude fine adjustment
réglage^M micrométrique (latitude^F)

right ascension setting scale
cercle^M d'ascension^F droite

fork
fourche^F

counterweight
contrepoids^M

tripod accessories shelf
plateau^M pour accessoires^M

tripod
trépied^M

cross section of a refracting telescope
coupe^F d'une lunette^F astronomique

light
lumière^F

eyepiece
oculaire^M

objective lens
lentille^F objectif^M

main tube
tube^M

reflecting telescope
télescope^M

finderscope
chercheur^M

eyepiece
oculaire^M

cradle
bride^F *de fixation*^F

support
support^M *de fixation*^F

main tube
tube^M

focusing knob
bouton^M *de mise*^F *au point*^M

declination setting scale
cercle^M *de déclinaison*^F

right ascension setting scale
cercle^M *d'ascension*^F *droite*

azimuth clamp
vis^F *de blocage*^M *(azimut*^M*)*

azimuth fine adjustment
réglage^M *micrométrique (azimut*^M*)*

altitude clamp
vis^F *de blocage*^M *(latitude*^F*)*

altitude fine adjustment
réglage^M *micrométrique (latitude*^F*)*

cross section of a reflecting telescope
coupe^F *d'un télescope*^M

eyepiece
oculaire^M

secondary mirror
miroir^M *secondaire*

concave primary mirror
miroir^M *primaire concave*

light
lumière^F

main tube
tube^M

ASTRONOMY

spacesuit
scaphandre^M spatial

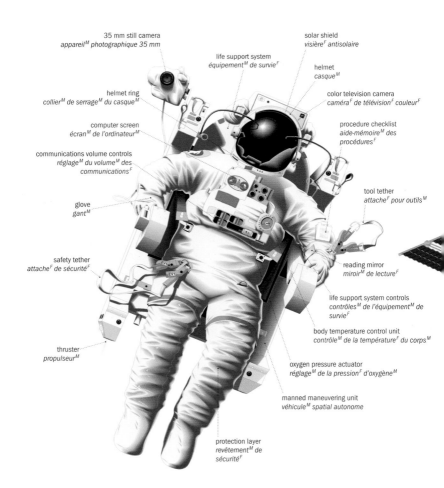

35 mm still camera
appareil^M photographique 35 mm

solar shield
visière^F antisolaire

life support system
équipement^M de survie^F

helmet
casque^M

helmet ring
collier^M de serrage^M du casque^M

color television camera
caméra^F de télévision^F couleur^F

computer screen
écran^M de l'ordinateur^M

procedure checklist
*aide-mémoire^M des
procédures^F*

communications volume controls
*réglage^M du volume^M des
communications^F*

glove
gant^M

tool tether
attache^F pour outils^M

safety tether
attache^F de sécurité^F

reading mirror
miroir^M de lecture^F

life support system controls
*contrôles^M de l'équipement^M de
survie^F*

body temperature control unit
contrôle^M de la température^F du corps^M

thruster
propulseur^M

oxygen pressure actuator
réglage^M de la pression^F d'oxygène^M

manned maneuvering unit
véhicule^M spatial autonome

protection layer
*revêtement^M de
sécurité^F*

international space station
station^F spatiale internationale

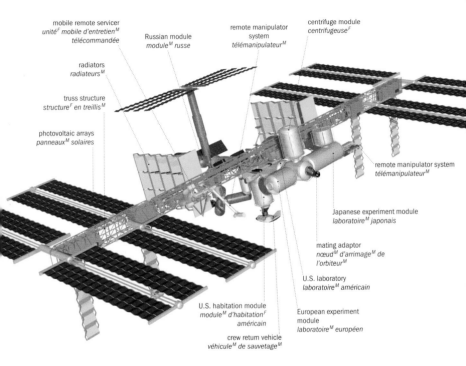

mobile remote servicer
*unité^F mobile d'entretien^M
télécommandée*

remote manipulator
system
télémanipulateur^M

centrifuge module
centrifugeuse^F

Russian module
module^M russe

radiators
radiateurs^M

truss structure
structure^F en treillis^M

photovoltaic arrays
panneaux^M solaires

remote manipulator system
télémanipulateur^M

Japanese experiment module
laboratoire^M japonais

mating adaptor
*nœud^M d'arrimage^M de
l'orbiteur^M*

U.S. laboratory
laboratoire^M américain

U.S. habitation module
*module^M d'habitation^F
américain*

European experiment
module
laboratoire^M européen

crew return vehicle
véhicule^M de sauvetage^M

space shuttle
navette^F spatiale

space shuttle at takeoff
navette^F spatiale au décollage^M

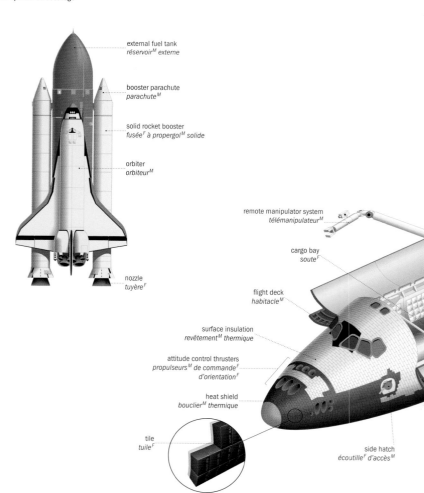

external fuel tank
réservoir^M externe

booster parachute
parachute^M

solid rocket booster
fusée^F à propergol^M solide

orbiter
orbiteur^M

remote manipulator system
télémanipulateur^M

cargo bay
soute^F

flight deck
habitacle^M

nozzle
tuyère^F

surface insulation
revêtement^M thermique

attitude control thrusters
*propulseurs^M de commande^F
d'orientation^F*

heat shield
bouclier^M thermique

tile
tuile^F

side hatch
écoutille^F d'accès^M

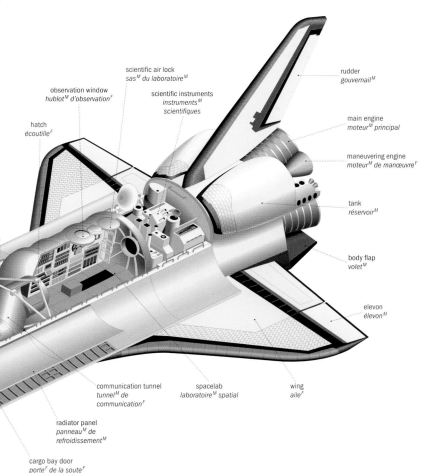

orbiter
orbiteur[M]

scientific air lock
sas[M] *du laboratoire*[M]

observation window
hublot[M] *d'observation*[F]

scientific instruments
instruments[M]
scientifiques

hatch
écoutille[F]

rudder
gouvernail[M]

main engine
moteur[M] *principal*

maneuvering engine
moteur[M] *de manœuvre*[F]

tank
réservoir[M]

body flap
volet[M]

elevon
élevon[M]

communication tunnel
tunnel[M] *de*
communication[F]

spacelab
laboratoire[M] *spatial*

wing
aile[F]

radiator panel
panneau[M] *de*
refroidissement[M]

cargo bay door
porte[F] *de la soute*[F]

configuration of the continents

configuration^F des continents^M

EARTH

planisphere
planisphère^M

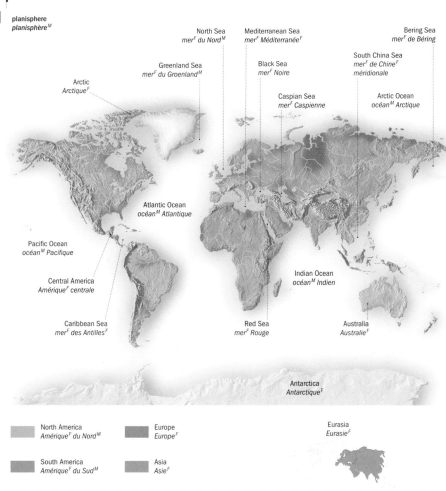

Arctic
Arctique^F

Greenland Sea
mer^F du Groenland^M

North Sea
mer^F du Nord^M

Mediterranean Sea
mer^F Méditerranée^F

Black Sea
mer^F Noire

Caspian Sea
mer^F Caspienne

Bering Sea
mer^F de Béring

South China Sea
*mer^F de Chine^F
méridionale*

Arctic Ocean
océan^M Arctique

Atlantic Ocean
océan^M Atlantique

Pacific Ocean
océan^M Pacifique

Central America
Amérique^F centrale

Indian Ocean
océan^M Indien

Caribbean Sea
mer^F des Antilles^F

Red Sea
mer^F Rouge

Australia
Australie^F

Antarctica
Antarctique^F

North America
Amérique^F du Nord^M

Europe
Europe^F

Eurasia
Eurasie^F

South America
Amérique^F du Sud^M

Asia
Asie^F

Oceania
Océanie^F

Africa
Afrique^F

Antarctica
Antarctique^F

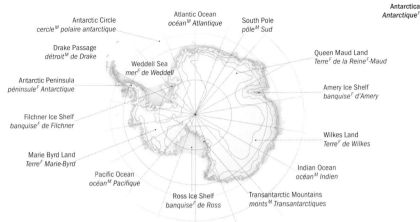

Antarctic Circle
cercle^M polaire antarctique

Atlantic Ocean
océan^M Atlantique

South Pole
pôle^M Sud

Drake Passage
détroit^M de Drake

Weddell Sea
mer^F de Weddell

Queen Maud Land
Terre^F de la Reine^F-Maud

Antarctic Peninsula
péninsule^F Antarctique

Amery Ice Shelf
banquise^F d'Amery

Filchner Ice Shelf
banquise^F de Filchner

Wilkes Land
Terre^F de Wilkes

Marie Byrd Land
Terre^F Marie-Byrd

Indian Ocean
océan^M Indien

Pacific Ocean
océan^M Pacifique

Ross Ice Shelf
banquise^F de Ross

Transantarctic Mountains
monts^M Transantarctiques

Oceania
Océanie^F

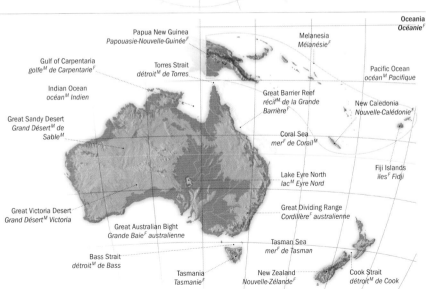

Papua New Guinea
Papouasie-Nouvelle-Guinée^F

Melanesia
Mélanésie^F

Gulf of Carpentaria
golfe^M de Carpentarie^F

Torres Strait
détroit^M de Torres

Pacific Ocean
océan^M Pacifique

Indian Ocean
océan^M Indien

Great Barrier Reef
récif^M de la Grande Barrière^F

New Caledonia
Nouvelle-Calédonie^F

Great Sandy Desert
Grand Désert^M de Sable^M

Coral Sea
mer^F de Corail^M

Fiji Islands
îles^F Fidji

Lake Eyre North
lac^M Eyre Nord

Great Dividing Range
Cordillère^F australienne

Great Victoria Desert
Grand Désert^M Victoria

Great Australian Bight
Grande Baie^F australienne

Tasman Sea
mer^F de Tasman

Bass Strait
détroit^M de Bass

Tasmania
Tasmanie^F

New Zealand
Nouvelle-Zélande^F

Cook Strait
détroit^M de Cook

North America
Amérique^F du Nord^M

Beaufort Sea
mer^F de Beaufort

Mackenzie River
Mackenzie^M

Hudson Bay
baie^F d'Hudson

Baffin Island
Terre^F de Baffin

Bering Strait
détroit^M de Béring

Greenland
Groenland^M

Great Lakes
Grands Lacs^M

Gulf of Alaska
golfe^M d'Alaska

Newfoundland Island
île^F de Terre-Neuve

Aleutian Islands
Îles^F Aléoutiennes

Rocky Mountains
montagnes^F Rocheuses

Saint Lawrence River
Saint-Laurent^M

Grand Canyon
Grand Canyon^M

Appalachian Mountains
Appalaches^F

Mississippi River
Mississippi^M

Gulf of California
golfe^M de Californie^F

Gulf of Mexico
golfe^M du Mexique^M

West Indies
Antilles^F

Yucatan Peninsula
péninsule^F du Yucatan^M

Caribbean Sea
mer^F des Antilles^F

Central America
Amérique^F centrale

Isthmus of Panama
isthme^M de Panama^M

South America
Amérique^F du Sud^M

Orinoco River
Orénoque^M

Amazon River
Amazone^F

Gulf of Panama
golfe^M de Panama^M

Equator
équateur^M

Andes Cordillera
cordillère^F des Andes

Lake Titicaca
lac^M Titicaca

Atacama Desert
désert^M d'Atacama

Paraná River
Paraná^M

Patagonia
Patagonie^F

Falkland Islands
Îles^F Falkland

Tierra del Fuego
Terre^F de Feu^M

Cape Horn
cap^M Horn

Drake Passage
détroit^M de Drake

configuration of the continents

EARTH

Europe
Europe^F

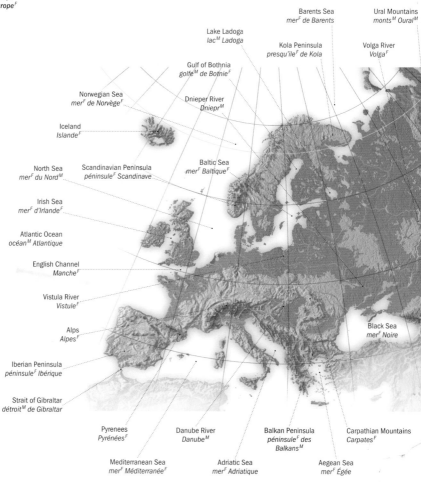

Barents Sea
mer^F *de Barents*

Ural Mountains
monts^M *Oural*^{M}

Lake Ladoga
lac^M *Ladoga*

Kola Peninsula
presqu'île^F *de Kola*

Volga River
Volga^F

Gulf of Bothnia
golfe^M *de Botnie*^{F}

Norwegian Sea
mer^F *de Norvège*^{F}

Dnieper River
Dniepr^M

Iceland
Islande^F

North Sea
mer^F *du Nord*^{M}

Scandinavian Peninsula
péninsule^F *Scandinave*

Baltic Sea
mer^F *Baltique*^{F}

Irish Sea
mer^F *d'Irlande*^{F}

Atlantic Ocean
océan^M *Atlantique*

English Channel
Manche^F

Vistula River
Vistule^F

Alps
Alpes^F

Black Sea
mer^F *Noire*

Iberian Peninsula
péninsule^F *Ibérique*

Strait of Gibraltar
détroit^M *de Gibraltar*

Pyrenees
Pyrénées^F

Danube River
Danube^M

Balkan Peninsula
péninsule^F *des Balkans*^{M}

Carpathian Mountains
Carpates^F

Mediterranean Sea
mer^F *Méditerranée*^{F}

Adriatic Sea
mer^F *Adriatique*

Aegean Sea
mer^F *Égée*

Asia
Asie[F]

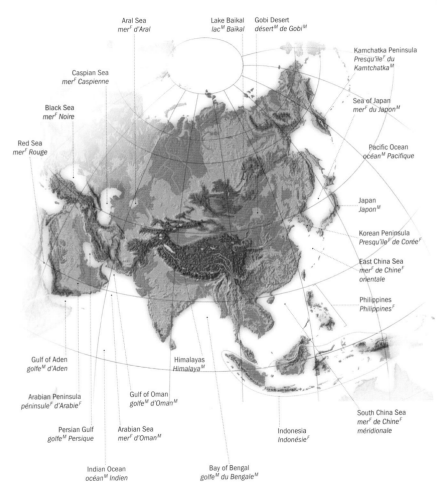

Aral Sea
mer[F] *d'Aral*

Lake Baikal
lac[M] *Baïkal*

Gobi Desert
désert[M] *de Gobi*[M]

Kamchatka Peninsula
Presqu'île[F] *du Kamtchatka*[M]

Caspian Sea
mer[F] *Caspienne*

Sea of Japan
mer[F] *du Japon*[M]

Black Sea
mer[F] *Noire*

Pacific Ocean
océan[M] *Pacifique*

Red Sea
mer[F] *Rouge*

Japan
Japon[M]

Korean Peninsula
Presqu'île[F] *de Corée*[F]

East China Sea
mer[F] *de Chine*[F] *orientale*

Philippines
Philippines[F]

Gulf of Aden
golfe[M] *d'Aden*

Himalayas
Himalaya[M]

Arabian Peninsula
péninsule[F] *d'Arabie*[F]

Gulf of Oman
golfe[M] *d'Oman*[M]

South China Sea
mer[F] *de Chine*[F] *méridionale*

Persian Gulf
golfe[M] *Persique*

Arabian Sea
mer[F] *d'Oman*[M]

Indonesia
Indonésie[F]

Indian Ocean
océan[M] *Indien*

Bay of Bengal
golfe[M] *du Bengale*[M]

Africa
Afrique^F

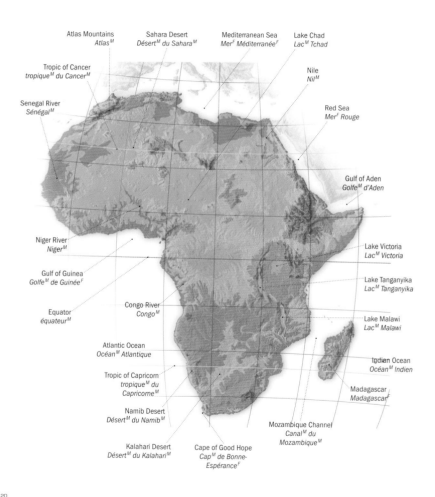

Atlas Mountains
Atlas^M

Sahara Desert
Désert^M *du Sahara*^M

Mediterranean Sea
Mer^F *Méditerranée*^F

Lake Chad
Lac^M *Tchad*

Tropic of Cancer
tropique^M *du Cancer*^M

Nile
Nil^M

Senegal River
Sénégal^M

Red Sea
Mer^F *Rouge*

Gulf of Aden
Golfe^M *d'Aden*

Niger River
Niger^M

Lake Victoria
Lac^M *Victoria*

Gulf of Guinea
Golfe^M *de Guinée*^F

Lake Tanganyika
Lac^M *Tanganyika*

Equator
équateur^M

Congo River
Congo^M

Lake Malawi
Lac^M *Malawi*

Atlantic Ocean
Océan^M *Atlantique*

Indian Ocean
Océan^M *Indien*

Tropic of Capricorn
tropique^M *du Capricorne*^M

Madagascar
Madagascar^F

Namib Desert
Désert^M *du Namib*^M

Mozambique Channel
Canal^M *du Mozambique*^M

Kalahari Desert
Désert^M *du Kalahari*^M

Cape of Good Hope
Cap^M *de Bonne-Espérance*^F

cartography
cartographie[F]

Earth coordinate system
coordonnées[F] *terrestres*

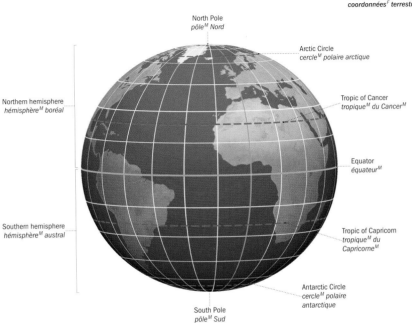

North Pole
pôle[M] *Nord*

Arctic Circle
cercle[M] *polaire arctique*

Tropic of Cancer
tropique[M] *du Cancer*[M]

Northern hemisphere
hémisphère[M] *boréal*

Equator
équateur[M]

Southern hemisphere
hémisphère[M] *austral*

Tropic of Capricorn
tropique[M] *du Capricorne*[M]

Antarctic Circle
cercle[M] *polaire antarctique*

South Pole
pôle[M] *Sud*

hemispheres
hémisphères[M]

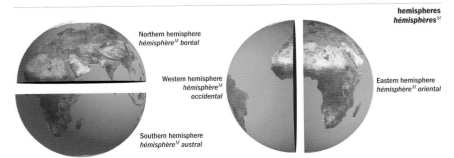

Northern hemisphere
hémisphère[M] *boréal*

Western hemisphere
hémisphère[M]
occidental

Eastern hemisphere
hémisphère[M] *oriental*

Southern hemisphere
hémisphère[M] *austral*

EARTH

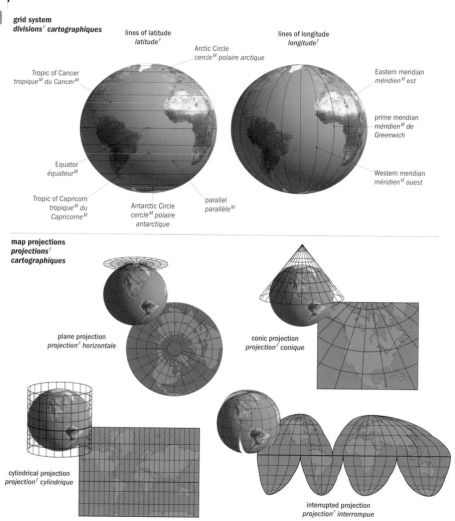

grid system
divisions^F cartographiques

lines of latitude
latitude^F

lines of longitude
longitude^F

Arctic Circle
cercle^M polaire arctique

Tropic of Cancer
tropique^M du Cancer^M

Eastern meridian
méridien^M est

prime meridian
*méridien^M de
Greenwich*

Equator
équateur^M

Western meridian
méridien^M ouest

Tropic of Capricorn
*tropique^M du
Capricorne^M*

Antarctic Circle
*cercle^M polaire
antarctique*

parallel
parallèle^M

map projections
*projections^F
cartographiques*

plane projection
projection^F horizontale

conic projection
projection^F conique

cylindrical projection
projection^F cylindrique

interrupted projection
projection^F interrompue

compass rose
rose^F des vents^M

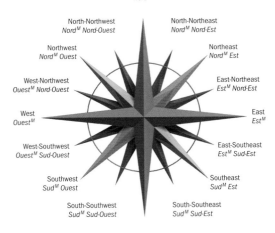

North
Nord^M

North-Northwest
Nord^M Nord-Ouest

North-Northeast
Nord^M Nord-Est

Northwest
Nord^M Ouest

Northeast
Nord^M Est

West-Northwest
Ouest^M Nord-Ouest

East-Northeast
Est^M Nord-Est

West
Ouest^M

East
Est^M

West-Southwest
Ouest^M Sud-Ouest

East-Southeast
Est^M Sud-Est

Southwest
Sud^M Ouest

Southeast
Sud^M Est

South-Southwest
Sud^M Sud-Ouest

South-Southeast
Sud^M Sud-Est

South
Sud^M

political map
carte^F politique

internal boundary
division^F territoriale

province
province^F

city
grande ville^F

international boundary
frontière^F

capital
capitale^F

country
pays^M

state
État^M

CANADA

UNITED STATES

MEXICO

physical map
carte^F *physique*

bay
baie^F

sea
mer^F

strait
détroit^M

mountain range
chaîne^F *de montagnes*^F

island
île^F

ocean
océan^M

prairie
prairie^F

mountain mass
massif^M *montagneux*

river estuary
estuaire^M

lake
lac^M

river
rivière^F

plateau
plateau^M

archipelago
archipel^M

gulf
golfe^M

peninsula
péninsule^F

cape
cap^M

plain
plaine^F

river
fleuve^M

isthmus
isthme^M

urban map
plan^M urbain

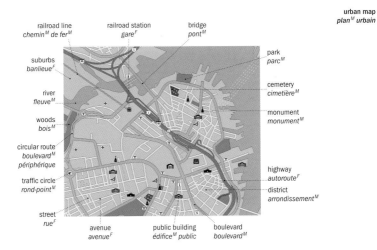

railroad line
chemin^M de fer^M

railroad station
gare^F

bridge
pont^M

park
parc^M

suburbs
banlieue^F

cemetery
cimetière^M

river
fleuve^F

monument
monument^M

woods
bois^M

circular route
boulevard^M
périphérique

highway
autoroute^F

traffic circle
rond-point^M

district
arrondissement^M

street
rue^F

avenue
avenue^F

public building
édifice^M public

boulevard
boulevard^M

road map
carte^F routière

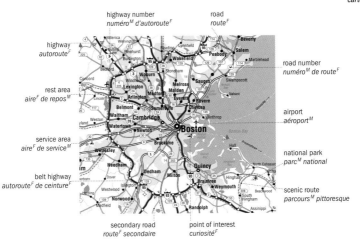

highway number
numéro^M d'autoroute^F

road
route^F

highway
autoroute^F

road number
numéro^M de route^F

rest area
aire^F de repos^M

airport
aéroport^M

service area
aire^F de service^M

national park
parc^M national

belt highway
autoroute^F de ceinture^F

scenic route
parcours^M pittoresque

secondary road
route^F secondaire

point of interest
curiosité^F

section of the Earth's crust
coupe^F de la croûte^F terrestre

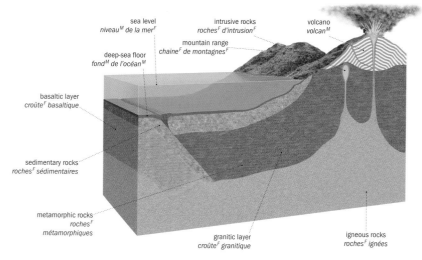

sea level
niveau^M de la mer^F

intrusive rocks
roches^F d'intrusion^F

volcano
volcan^M

mountain range
chaine^F de montagnes^F

deep-sea floor
fond^M de l'océan^M

basaltic layer
croûte^F basaltique

sedimentary rocks
roches^F sédimentaires

metamorphic rocks
roches^F
métamorphiques

granitic layer
croûte^F granitique

igneous rocks
roches^F ignées

structure of the Earth
structure^F de la Terre^F

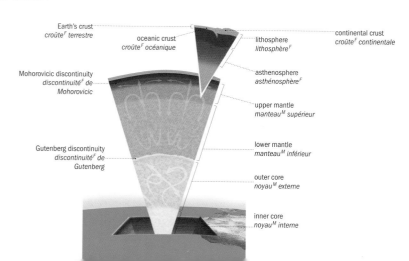

Earth's crust
croûte^F terrestre

oceanic crust
croûte^F océanique

continental crust
croûte^F continentale

lithosphere
lithosphère^F

Mohorovicic discontinuity
discontinuité^F de
Mohorovicic

asthenosphere
asthénosphère^F

upper mantle
manteau^M supérieur

Gutenberg discontinuity
discontinuité^F de
Gutenberg

lower mantle
manteau^M inférieur

outer core
noyau^M externe

inner core
noyau^M interne

tectonic plates
plaques^F tectoniques

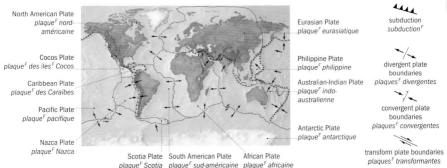

North American Plate
plaque^F nord-américaine

Cocos Plate
plaque^F des îles^F Cocos

Caribbean Plate
plaque^F des Caraïbes

Pacific Plate
plaque^F pacifique

Nazca Plate
plaque^F Nazca

Scotia Plate
plaque^F Scotia

South American Plate
plaque^F sud-américaine

African Plate
plaque^F africaine

Eurasian Plate
plaque^F eurasiatique

Philippine Plate
plaque^F philippine

Australian-Indian Plate
plaque^F indo-australienne

Antarctic Plate
plaque^F antarctique

subduction
subduction^F

divergent plate boundaries
plaques^F divergentes

convergent plate boundaries
plaques^F convergentes

transform plate boundaries
plaques^F transformantes

earthquake
séisme^M

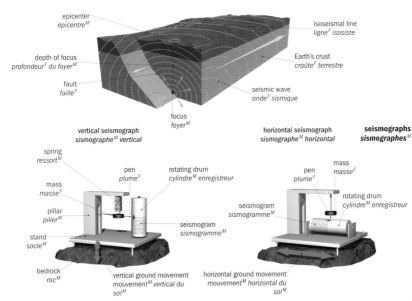

epicenter
épicentre^M

depth of focus
profondeur^F du foyer^M

fault
faille^F

focus
foyer^M

isoseismal line
ligne^F isosiste

Earth's crust
croûte^F terrestre

seismic wave
onde^F sismique

vertical seismograph
sismographe^M vertical

spring
ressort^M

mass
masse^F

pillar
pilier^M

stand
socle^M

pen
plume^F

rotating drum
cylindre^M enregistreur

seismogram
sismogramme^M

bedrock
roc^M

vertical ground movement
mouvement^M vertical du sol^M

horizontal seismograph
sismographe^M horizontal

mass
masse^F

pen
plume^F

rotating drum
cylindre^M enregistreur

seismogram
sismogramme^M

horizontal ground movement
mouvement^M horizontal du sol^M

seismographs
sismographes^M

volcano

volcan^M

volcano during eruption
volcan^M *en éruption*^F

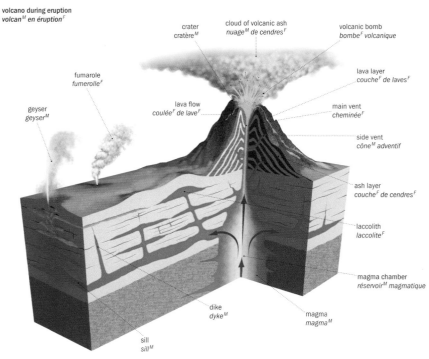

crater
cratère^M

cloud of volcanic ash
nuage^M de cendres^F

volcanic bomb
bombe^F volcanique

fumarole
fumerolle^F

lava layer
couche^F de laves^F

geyser
geyser^M

lava flow
coulée^F de lave^F

main vent
cheminée^F

side vent
cône^M adventif

ash layer
couche^F de cendres^F

laccolith
laccolite^F

magma chamber
réservoir^M magmatique

dike
dyke^M

magma
magma^M

sill
sill^M

examples of volcanoes
exemples^M *de volcans*^M

explosive volcano
volcan^M explosif

effusive volcano
volcan^M effusif

mountain
montagne^F

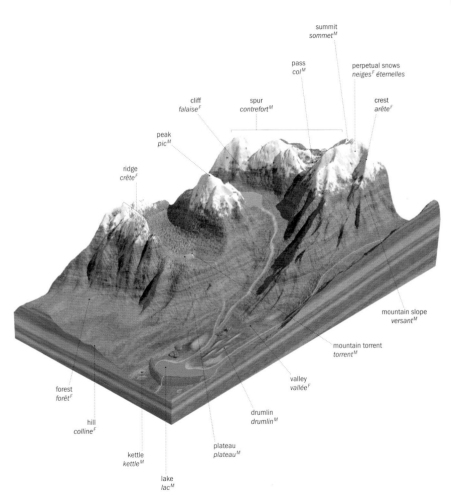

summit
sommet^M

pass
col^M

perpetual snows
neiges^F *éternelles*

cliff
falaise^F

spur
contrefort^M

crest
arête^F

peak
pic^M

ridge
crête^F

mountain slope
versant^M

mountain torrent
torrent^M

valley
vallée^F

forest
forêt^F

hill
colline^F

kettle
kettle^M

drumlin
drumlin^M

plateau
plateau^M

lake
lac^M

glacier

glacier[M]

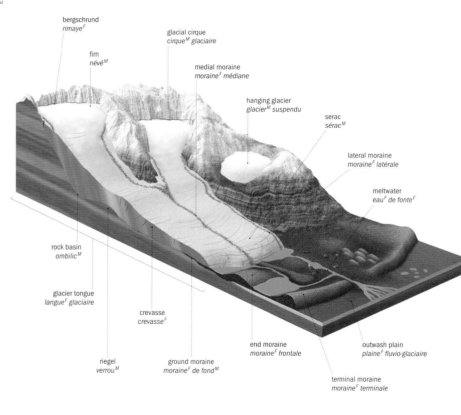

bergschrund
rimaye[F]

glacial cirque
cirque[M] *glaciaire*

firn
névé[M]

medial moraine
moraine[F] *médiane*

hanging glacier
glacier[M] *suspendu*

serac
sérac[M]

lateral moraine
moraine[F] *latérale*

meltwater
eau[F] *de fonte*[F]

rock basin
ombilic[M]

glacier tongue
langue[F] *glaciaire*

crevasse
crevasse[F]

riegel
verrou[M]

ground moraine
moraine[F] *de fond*[M]

end moraine
moraine[F] *frontale*

outwash plain
plaine[F] *fluvio-glaciaire*

terminal moraine
moraine[F] *terminale*

cave
grotte[F]

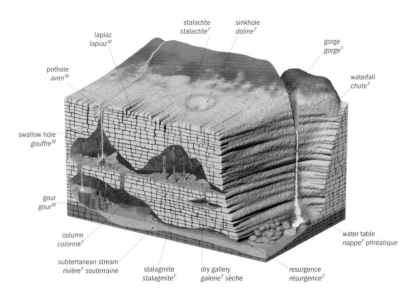

pothole
aven[M]

lapiaz
lapiaz[M]

stalactite
stalactite[F]

sinkhole
doline[F]

gorge
gorge[F]

waterfall
chute[F]

swallow hole
gouffre[M]

gour
gour[M]

column
colonne[F]

subterranean stream
rivière[F] *souterraine*

stalagmite
stalagmite[F]

dry gallery
galerie[F] *sèche*

resurgence
résurgence[F]

water table
nappe[F] *phréatique*

landslides
mouvements[M] *de terrain*[M]

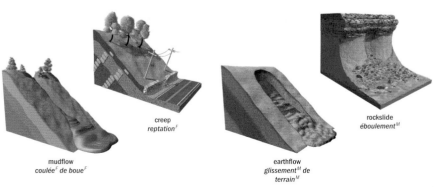

mudflow
coulée[F] *de boue*[F]

creep
reptation[F]

earthflow
glissement[M] *de terrain*[M]

rockslide
éboulement[M]

watercourse

cours^M d'eau^F

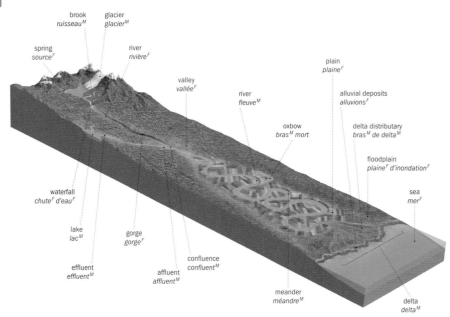

brook
ruisseau^M

glacier
glacier^M

spring
source^F

river
rivière^F

valley
vallée^F

plain
plaine^F

river
fleuve^M

alluvial deposits
alluvions^F

oxbow
bras^M mort

delta distributary
bras^M de delta^M

floodplain
plaine^F d'inondation^F

sea
mer^F

waterfall
chute^F d'eau^F

lake
lac^M

gorge
gorge^F

confluence
confluent^M

effluent
effluent^M

affluent
affluent^M

meander
méandre^M

delta
delta^M

lakes

lacs^M

glacial lake
lac^M d'origine^F
glaciaire

volcanic lake
lac^M d'origine^F
volcanique

tectonic lake
lac^M d'origine^F
tectonique

oxbow lake
lac^M en croissant^M

oasis
oasis^F

artificial lake
lac^M artificiel

wave
vague[F]

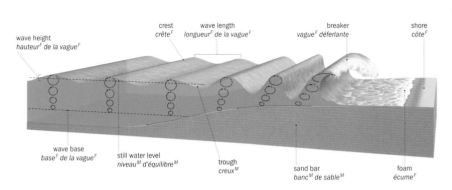

wave height
hauteur[F] *de la vague*[F]

crest
crête[F]

wave length
longueur[F] *de la vague*[F]

breaker
vague[F] *déferlante*

shore
côte[F]

wave base
base[F] *de la vague*[F]

still water level
niveau[M] *d'équilibre*[M]

trough
creux[M]

sand bar
banc[M] *de sable*[M]

foam
écume[F]

ocean floor
fond[M] *de l'océan*[M]

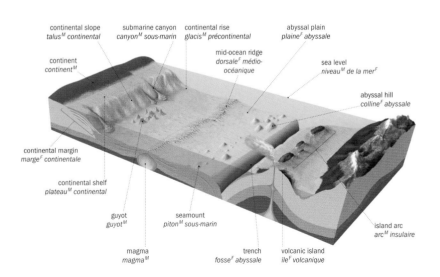

continental slope
talus[M] *continental*

submarine canyon
canyon[M] *sous-marin*

continental rise
glacis[M] *précontinental*

abyssal plain
plaine[F] *abyssale*

continent
continent[M]

mid-ocean ridge
dorsale[F] *médio-océanique*

sea level
niveau[M] *de la mer*[F]

abyssal hill
colline[F] *abyssale*

continental margin
marge[F] *continentale*

continental shelf
plateau[M] *continental*

guyot
guyot[M]

seamount
piton[M] *sous-marin*

island arc
arc[M] *insulaire*

magma
magma[M]

trench
fosse[F] *abyssale*

volcanic island
île[F] *volcanique*

ocean trenches and ridges
fosses[F] *et dorsales*[F] *océaniques*

EARTH

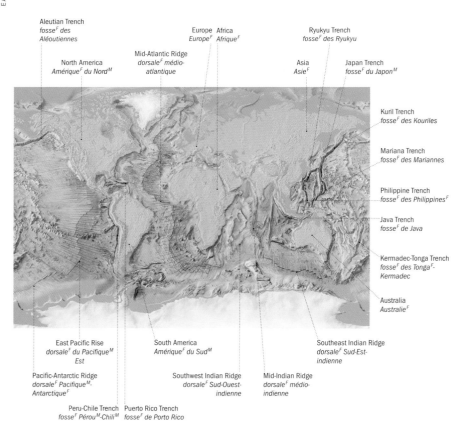

Aleutian Trench
fosse[F] *des
Aléoutiennes*

North America
Amérique[F] *du Nord*[M]

Mid-Atlantic Ridge
dorsale[F] *médio-
atlantique*

Europe
Europe[F]

Africa
Afrique[F]

Ryukyu Trench
fosse[F] *des Ryukyu*

Asia
Asie[F]

Japan Trench
fosse[F] *du Japon*[M]

Kuril Trench
fosse[F] *des Kouriles*

Mariana Trench
fosse[F] *des Mariannes*

Philippine Trench
fosse[F] *des Philippines*[F]

Java Trench
fosse[F] *de Java*

Kermadec-Tonga Trench
fosse[F] *des Tonga*[F]-
Kermadec

Australia
Australie[F]

East Pacific Rise
dorsale[F] *du Pacifique*[M]
Est

Pacific-Antarctic Ridge
dorsale[F] *Pacifique*[M]-
Antarctique[F]

South America
Amérique[F] *du Sud*[M]

Southwest Indian Ridge
dorsale[F] *Sud-Ouest-
indienne*

Mid-Indian Ridge
dorsale[F] *médio-
indienne*

Southeast Indian Ridge
dorsale[F] *Sud-Est-
indienne*

Peru-Chile Trench
fosse[F] *Pérou*[M]-*Chili*[M]

Puerto Rico Trench
fosse[F] *de Porto Rico*

common coastal features
configuration[F] du littoral[M]

EARTH

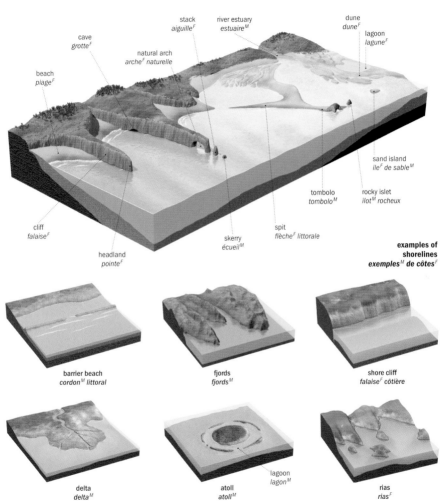

cave
grotte[F]

stack
aiguille[F]

river estuary
estuaire[M]

dune
dune[F]

lagoon
lagune[F]

natural arch
arche[F] naturelle

beach
plage[F]

sand island
ile[F] de sable[M]

tombolo
tombolo[M]

rocky islet
ilot[M] rocheux

cliff
falaise[F]

spit
flèche[F] littorale

skerry
écueil[M]

headland
pointe[F]

**examples of
shorelines
*exemples[M] de côtes[F]***

barrier beach
cordon[M] littoral

fjords
fjords[M]

shore cliff
falaise[F] côtière

delta
delta[M]

atoll
atoll[M]

lagoon
lagon[M]

rias
rias[F]

35

desert
désert^M

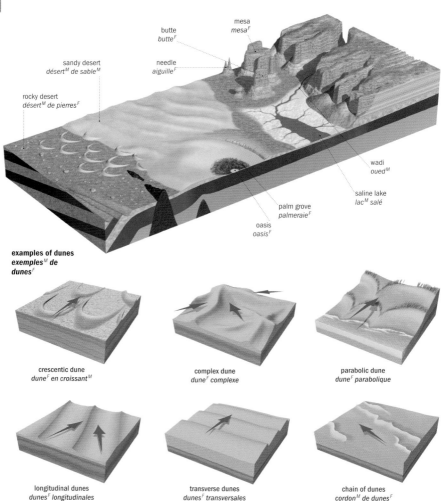

mesa
mesa^F

butte
butte^F

needle
aiguille^F

sandy desert
désert^M *de sable*^M

rocky desert
désert^M *de pierres*^F

wadi
oued^M

saline lake
lac^M *salé*

palm grove
palmeraie^F

oasis
oasis^F

examples of dunes
exemples*^M *de
***dunes*^F**

crescentic dune
dune^F *en croissant*^M

complex dune
dune^F *complexe*

parabolic dune
dune^F *parabolique*

longitudinal dunes
dunes^F *longitudinales*

transverse dunes
dunes^F *transversales*

chain of dunes
cordon^M *de dunes*^F

profile of the Earth's atmosphere
coupe[F] de l'atmosphère[F] terrestre

EARTH

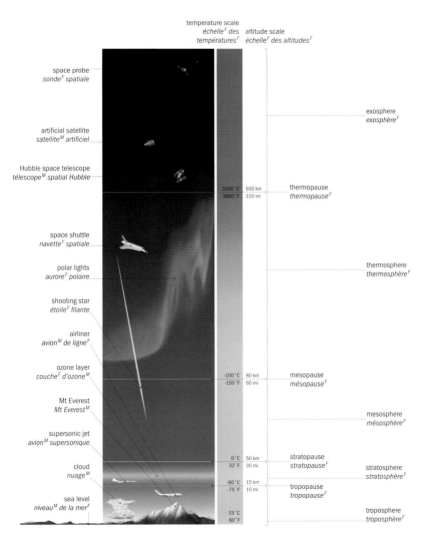

temperature scale
échelle[F] des
températures[F] altitude scale
échelle[F] des altitudes[F]

space probe
sonde[F] spatiale

artificial satellite
satellite[M] artificiel

Hubble space telescope
télescope[M] spatial Hubble

2000°C 500 km thermopause
3600°F 310 mi *thermopause[F]*

space shuttle
navette[F] spatiale

polar lights
aurore[F] polaire

shooting star
étoile[F] filante

airliner
avion[M] de ligne[F]

ozone layer
couche[F] d'ozone[M]

-100°C 80 km mesopause
-150°F 60 mi *mésopause[F]*

Mt Everest
Mt Everest[M]

supersonic jet
avion[M] supersonique

0°C 50 km stratopause
32°F 30 mi *stratopause[F]*

cloud
nuage[M]

-60°C 15 km tropopause
-75°F 10 mi *tropopause[F]*

sea level
niveau[M] de la mer[F]

15°C
60°F

exosphere
exosphère[F]

thermosphere
thermosphère[F]

mesosphere
mésosphère[F]

stratosphere
stratosphère[F]

troposphere
troposphère[F]

EARTH

seasons of the year
cycle^M des saisons^F

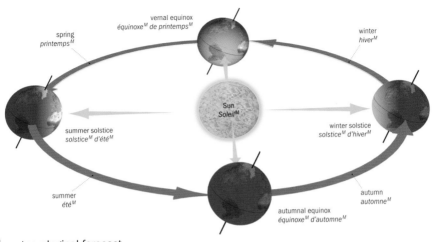

spring
printemps^M

vernal equinox
équinoxe^M de printemps^M

winter
hiver^M

Sun
Soleil^M

summer solstice
solstice^M d'été^M

winter solstice
solstice^M d'hiver^M

summer
été^M

autumn
automne^M

autumnal equinox
équinoxe^M d'automne^M

meteorological forecast
prévision^F météorologique

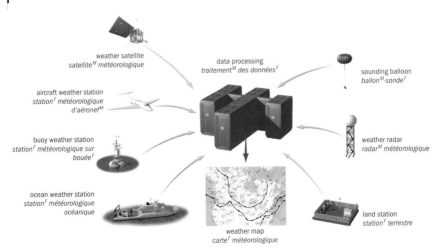

weather satellite
satellite^M météorologique

data processing
traitement^M des données^F

sounding balloon
ballon^M-sonde^F

aircraft weather station
*station^F météorologique
d'aéronef^M*

buoy weather station
*station^F météorologique sur
bouée^F*

weather radar
radar^M météorologique

ocean weather station
*station^F météorologique
océanique*

land station
station^F terrestre

weather map
carte^F météorologique

weather map
carte^F météorologique

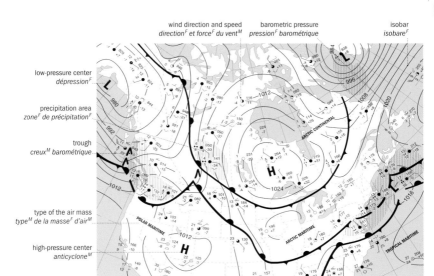

wind direction and speed
direction^F et force^F du vent^M

barometric pressure
pression^F barométrique

isobar
isobare^F

low-pressure center
dépression^F

precipitation area
zone^F de précipitation^F

trough
creux^M barométrique

type of the air mass
type^M de la masse^F d'air^M

high-pressure center
anticyclone^M

ARCTIC CONTINENTAL

POLAR MARITIME

ARCTIC MARITIME

TROPICAL MARITIME

station model
disposition^F des informations^F d'une station^F

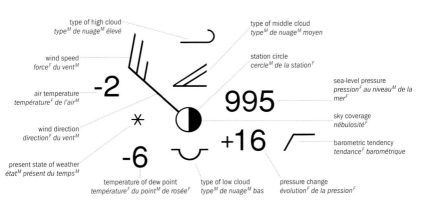

type of high cloud
type^M de nuage^M élevé

type of middle cloud
type^M de nuage^M moyen

wind speed
force^F du vent^M

station circle
cercle^M de la station^F

air temperature
température^F de l'air^M

sea-level pressure
pression^F au niveau^M de la mer^F

wind direction
direction^F du vent^M

sky coverage
nébulosité^F

barometric tendency
tendance^F barométrique

present state of weather
état^M présent du temps^M

temperature of dew point
température^F du point^M de rosée^F

type of low cloud
type^M de nuage^M bas

pressure change
évolution^F de la pression^F

climates of the world
climats^M du monde^M

climats^M du monde^M

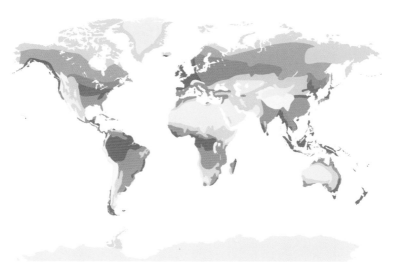

tropical climates
climats*^M *tropicaux

    tropical rain forest
    tropical humide

    tropical wet-and-dry (savanna)
    tropical humide et sec (savane^F*)*

dry climates
climats*^M *arides

    steppe
    steppe^F

    desert
    désert^M

cold temperate climates
climats*^M *tempérés froids

    humid continental—hot summer
    continental humide, à été^M *chaud*

    humid continental—warm summer
    continental humide, à été^M *frais*

    subarctic
    subarctique

warm temperate climates
climats*^M *tempérés chauds

    humid subtropical
    subtropical humide

    Mediterranean subtropical
    méditerranéen

    marine
    océanique

polar climates
climats*^M *polaires

    polar tundra
    toundra^F

    polar ice cap
    calotte^F *glaciaire*

highland climates
***climats*^M *de montagne*^F**

    highland
    climats^M *de montagne*^F

precipitation
précipitations^F

EARTH

winter precipitation
***précipitations*^F
*hivernales***

warm air
air^M *chaud*

cold air
air^M *froid*

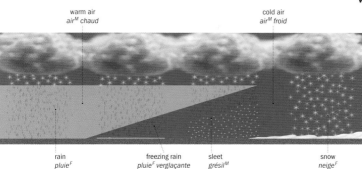

rain
pluie^F

freezing rain
pluie^F *verglaçante*

sleet
grésil^M

snow
neige^F

stormy sky
ciel^M *d'orage*^M

cloud
nuage^M

lightning
éclair^M

rainbow
arc-en-ciel^M

rain
pluie^F

dew
rosée^F

mist
brume^F

fog
brouillard^M

rime
givre^M

frost
verglas^M

clouds
nuages^M

high clouds
***nuages*^M *de haute altitude*^F**

middle clouds
***nuages*^M *de moyenne*
altitude^F**

low clouds
***nuages*^M *de basse*
altitude^F**

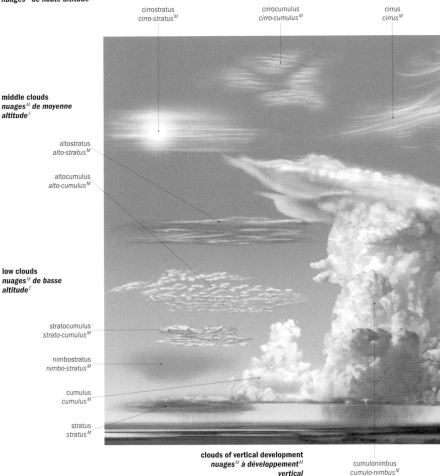

cirrostratus
cirro-stratus^M

cirrocumulus
cirro-cumulus^M

cirrus
cirrus^M

altostratus
alto-stratus^M

altocumulus
alto-cumulus^M

stratocumulus
strato-cumulus^M

nimbostratus
nimbo-stratus^M

cumulus
cumulus^M

stratus
stratus^M

clouds of vertical development
***nuages*^M *à développement*^M
*vertical***

cumulonimbus
cumulo-nimbus^M

tornado and waterspout
tornade^F et trombe^F marine

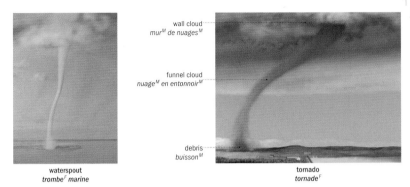

wall cloud
mur^M de nuages^M

funnel cloud
nuage^M en entonnoir^M

debris
buisson^M

waterspout
trombe^F marine

tornado
tornade^F

tropical cyclone
cyclone^M tropical

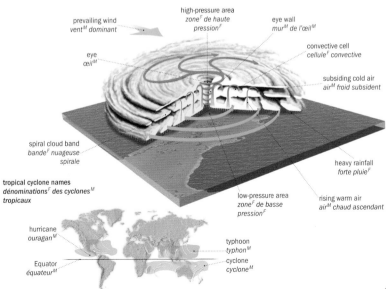

prevailing wind
vent^M dominant

high-pressure area
zone^F de haute pression^F

eye wall
mur^M de l'œil^M

eye
œil^M

convective cell
cellule^F convective

subsiding cold air
air^M froid subsident

spiral cloud band
bande^F nuageuse spirale

heavy rainfall
forte pluie^F

tropical cyclone names
dénominations^F des cyclones^M tropicaux

low-pressure area
zone^F de basse pression^F

rising warm air
air^M chaud ascendant

hurricane
ouragan^M

typhoon
typhon^M

Equator
équateur^M

cyclone
cyclone^M

EARTH

vegetation and biosphere
végétation^F *et biosphère*^F

vegetation regions
distribution*^F *de la
***végétation*^F**

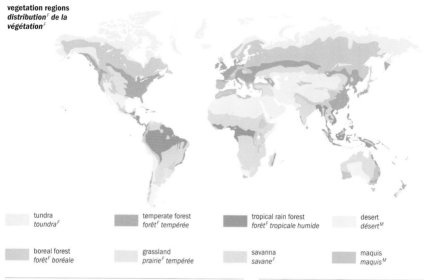

tundra *toundra*^F	temperate forest *forêt*^F *tempérée*	tropical rain forest *forêt*^F *tropicale humide*	desert *désert*^M
boreal forest *forêt*^F *boréale*	grassland *prairie*^F *tempérée*	savanna *savane*^F	maquis *maquis*^M

elevation zones and vegetation
***paysage*^M *végétal selon l'altitude*^F**

structure of the biosphere
***structure*^F *de la biosphère*^F**

glacier
glacier^M

tundra
toundra^F

coniferous forest
forêt^F *de conifères*^M

mixed forest
forêt^F *mixte*

deciduous forest
forêt^F *de feuillus*^M

tropical forest
forêt^F *tropicale*

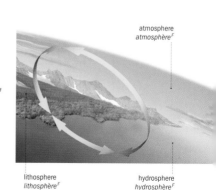

atmosphere
atmosphère^F

lithosphere
lithosphère^F

hydrosphere
hydrosphère^F

food chain
chaine^F alimentaire

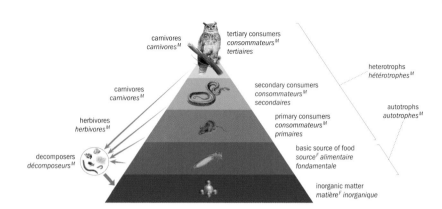

carnivores
carnivores^M

tertiary consumers
*consommateurs^M
tertiaires*

heterotrophs
hétérotrophes^M

carnivores
carnivores^M

secondary consumers
*consommateurs^M
secondaires*

autotrophs
autotrophes^M

herbivores
herbivores^M

primary consumers
*consommateurs^M
primaires*

decomposers
décomposeurs^M

basic source of food
*source^F alimentaire
fondamentale*

inorganic matter
matière^F inorganique

hydrologic cycle
cycle^M de l'eau^F

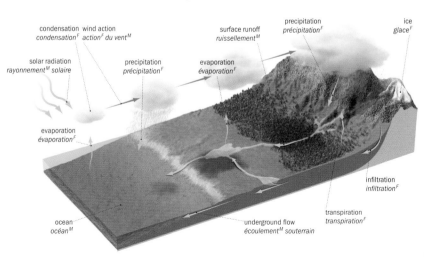

condensation
condensation^F

wind action
action^F du vent^M

surface runoff
ruissellement^M

precipitation
précipitation^F

ice
glace^F

solar radiation
rayonnement^M solaire

precipitation
précipitation^F

evaporation
évaporation^F

evaporation
évaporation^F

infiltration
infiltration^F

ocean
océan^M

underground flow
écoulement^M souterrain

transpiration
transpiration^F

greenhouse effect

effet^M de serre^F

EARTH

natural greenhouse effect
effet^M de serre^F naturel

reflected solar radiation
rayonnement^M solaire réfléchi

heat loss
perte^F de chaleur^F

solar radiation
rayonnement^M solaire

tropopause
tropopause^F

greenhouse gas
gaz^M à effet^M de serre^F

absorbed solar radiation
rayonnement^M solaire absorbé

absorption by clouds
absorption^F par les nuages^M

absorption by Earth's surface
absorption^F par le sol^M

infrared radiation
rayonnement^M infrarouge

heat energy
énergie^F calorifique

enhanced greenhouse effect
augmentation^F de l'effet^M de serre^F

fossil fuel
combustible^M fossile

greenhouse gas concentration
concentration^F des gaz^M à effet^M de serre^F

global warming
réchauffement^M global

air conditioning system
système^M de climatisation^F

intensive husbandry
élevage^M intensif

intensive farming
agriculture^F intensive

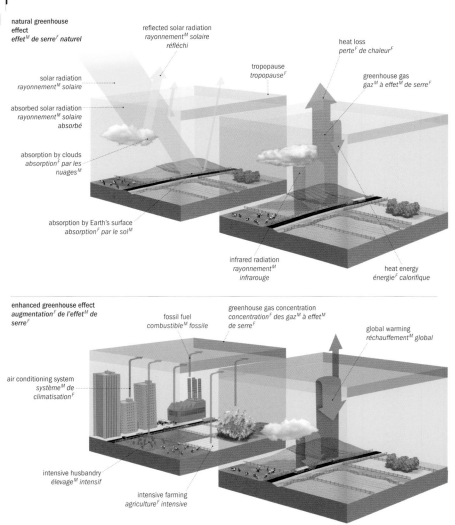

air pollution
pollution^F de l'air^M

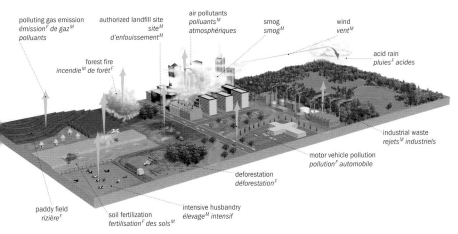

polluting gas emission
émission^F de gaz^M
polluants

authorized landfill site
site^M
d'enfouissement^M

air pollutants
polluants^M
atmosphériques

smog
smog^M

wind
vent^M

acid rain
pluies^F acides

forest fire
incendie^M de forêt^F

industrial waste
rejets^M industriels

motor vehicle pollution
pollution^F automobile

deforestation
déforestation^F

paddy field
rizière^F

soil fertilization
fertilisation^F des sols^M

intensive husbandry
élevage^M intensif

land pollution
pollution^F du sol^M

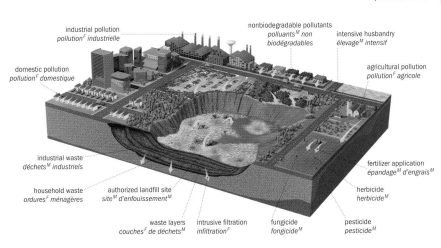

industrial pollution
pollution^F industrielle

nonbiodegradable pollutants
polluants^M non
biodégradables

intensive husbandry
élevage^M intensif

domestic pollution
pollution^F domestique

agricultural pollution
pollution^F agricole

industrial waste
déchets^M industriels

household waste
ordures^F ménagères

authorized landfill site
site^M d'enfouissement^M

waste layers
couches^F de déchets^M

intrusive filtration
infiltration^F

fungicide
fongicide^M

fertilizer application
épandage^M d'engrais^M

herbicide
herbicide^M

pesticide
pesticide^M

water pollution
pollution^F de l'eau^F

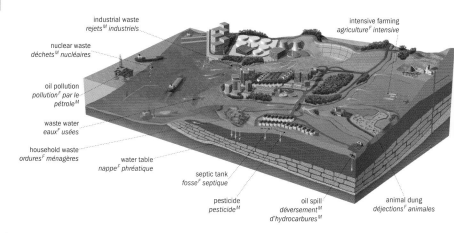

industrial waste
rejets^M industriels

nuclear waste
déchets^M nucléaires

oil pollution
pollution^F par le pétrole^M

waste water
eaux^F usées

household waste
ordures^F ménagères

water table
nappe^F phréatique

septic tank
fosse^F septique

pesticide
pesticide^M

oil spill
déversement^M d'hydrocarbures^M

intensive farming
agriculture^F intensive

animal dung
déjections^F animales

acid rain
pluies^F acides

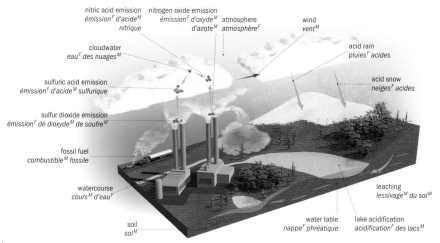

nitric acid emission
émission^F d'acide^M nitrique

nitrogen oxide emission
émission^F d'oxyde^M d'azote^M

atmosphere
atmosphère^F

wind
vent^M

cloudwater
eau^F des nuages^M

acid rain
pluies^F acides

sulfuric acid emission
émission^F d'acide^M sulfurique

acid snow
neiges^F acides

sulfur dioxide emission
émission^F de dioxyde^M de soufre^M

fossil fuel
combustible^M fossile

watercourse
cours^M d'eau^F

leaching
lessivage^M du sol^M

soil
sol^M

water table
nappe^F phréatique

lake acidification
acidification^F des lacs^M

selective sorting of waste
tri^M sélectif des déchets^M

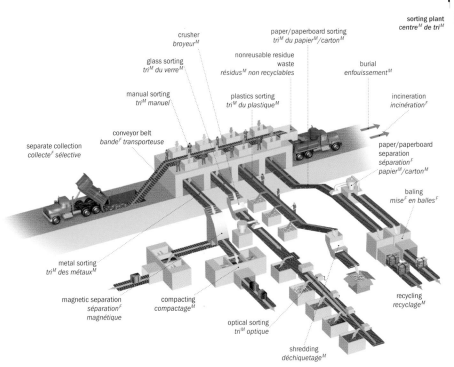

sorting plant
centre^M de tri^M

crusher
broyeur^M

paper/paperboard sorting
tri^M du papier^M/carton^M

nonreusable residue
waste
résidus^M non recyclables

burial
enfouissement^M

glass sorting
tri^M du verre^M

manual sorting
tri^M manuel

plastics sorting
tri^M du plastique^M

incineration
incinération^F

conveyor belt
bande^F transporteuse

separate collection
collecte^F sélective

paper/paperboard
separation
*séparation^F
papier^M/carton^M*

baling
mise^F en balles^F

metal sorting
tri^M des métaux^M

recycling
recyclage^M

magnetic separation
*séparation^F
magnétique*

compacting
compactage^M

optical sorting
tri^M optique

shredding
déchiquetage^M

recycling containers
*conteneurs^M de collecte^F
sélective*

paper recycling container
conteneur^M à papier^M

aluminum recycling container
*conteneur^M à boites^F
métalliques*

glass collection unit
*colonne^F de collecte^F du
verre^M*

glass recycling container
conteneur^M à verre^M

paper collection unit
*colonne^F de collecte^F du
papier^M*

recycling bin
bac^M de recyclage^M

plant cell

cellule[F] *végétale*

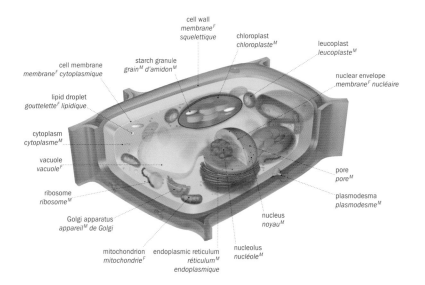

cell wall
membrane[F]
squelettique

chloroplast
chloroplaste[M]

leucoplast
leucoplaste[M]

cell membrane
membrane[F] *cytoplasmique*

starch granule
grain[M] *d'amidon*[M]

nuclear envelope
membrane[F] *nucléaire*

lipid droplet
gouttelette[F] *lipidique*

cytoplasm
cytoplasme[M]

vacuole
vacuole[F]

pore
pore[M]

ribosome
ribosome[M]

plasmodesma
plasmodesme[M]

Golgi apparatus
appareil[M] *de Golgi*

nucleus
noyau[M]

mitochondrion
mitochondrie[F]

endoplasmic reticulum
réticulum[M]
endoplasmique

nucleolus
nucléole[M]

lichen

lichen[M]

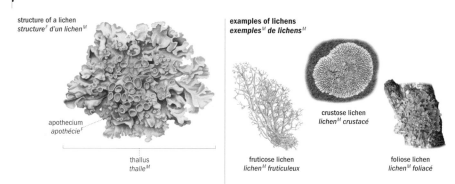

structure of a lichen
structure[F] *d'un lichen*[M]

examples of lichens
exemples[M] **de lichens**[M]

apothecium
apothécie[F]

thallus
thalle[M]

crustose lichen
lichen[M] *crustacé*

fruticose lichen
lichen[M] *fruticuleux*

foliose lichen
lichen[M] *foliacé*

structure of a moss
structure[F] *d'une mousse*[F]

examples of mosses
exemples[M] **de mousses**[F]

capsule
capsule[F]

stalk
pédicelle[M]

leaf
feuille[F]

stem
tige[F]

rhizoid
rhizoïde[M]

prickly sphagnum
sphaigne[F] *squarreuse*

common hair cap moss
polytric[M] *commun*

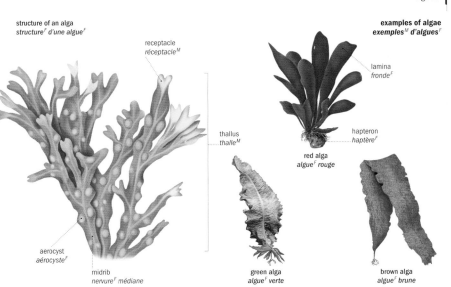

structure of an alga
structure[F] *d'une algue*[F]

examples of algae
exemples[M] **d'algues**[F]

receptacle
réceptacle[M]

lamina
fronde[F]

thallus
thalle[M]

hapteron
haptère[F]

red alga
algue[F] *rouge*

aerocyst
aérocyste[F]

midrib
nervure[F] *médiane*

green alga
algue[F] *verte*

brown alga
algue[F] *brune*

mushroom

champignon M

structure of a mushroom
structure F *d'un champignon* M

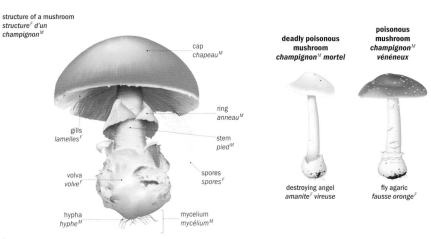

cap
chapeau M

ring
anneau M

gills
lamelles F

stem
pied M

volva
volve F

spores
spores F

hypha
hyphe M

mycelium
mycélium M

deadly poisonous mushroom
champignon M *mortel*

destroying angel
amanite F *vireuse*

poisonous mushroom
champignon M *vénéneux*

fly agaric
fausse oronge F

fern

fougère F

structure of a fern
structure F *d'une fougère* F

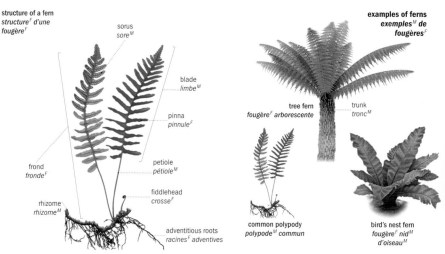

sorus
sore M

blade
limbe M

pinna
pinnule F

petiole
pétiole M

fiddlehead
crosse F

frond
fronde F

rhizome
rhizome M

adventitious roots
racines F *adventives*

examples of ferns
exemples M *de fougères* F

tree fern
fougère F *arborescente*

trunk
tronc M

common polypody
polypode M *commun*

bird's nest fern
fougère F *nid* M *d'oiseau* M

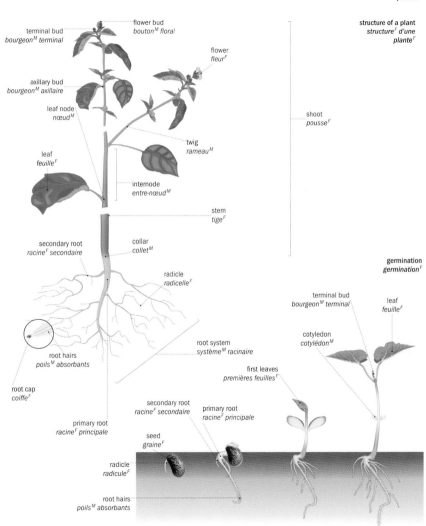

structure of a plant
structure^F *d'une plante*^F

flower bud
bouton^M *floral*

terminal bud
bourgeon^M *terminal*

flower
fleur^F

axillary bud
bourgeon^M *axillaire*

leaf node
nœud^M

shoot
pousse^F

twig
rameau^M

leaf
feuille^F

internode
entre-nœud^M

stem
tige^F

secondary root
racine^F *secondaire*

collar
collet^M

radicle
radicelle^F

germination
germination^F

terminal bud
bourgeon^M *terminal*

leaf
feuille^F

root system
système^M *racinaire*

cotyledon
cotylédon^M

root hairs
poils^M *absorbants*

first leaves
premières feuilles^F

root cap
coiffe^F

secondary root
racine^F *secondaire*

primary root
racine^F *principale*

primary root
racine^F *principale*

seed
graine^F

radicle
radicule^F

root hairs
poils^M *absorbants*

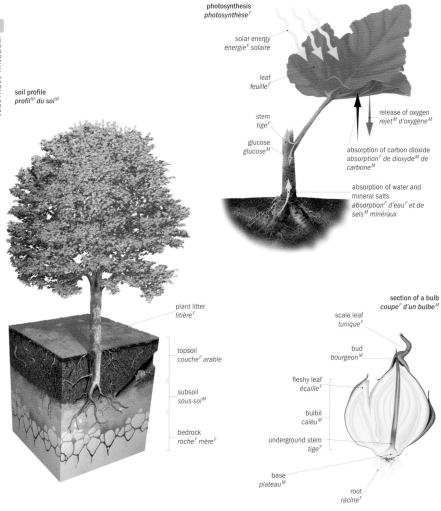

photosynthesis
photosynthèse[F]

solar energy
énergie[F] *solaire*

leaf
feuille[F]

stem
tige[F]

glucose
glucose[M]

release of oxygen
rejet[M] *d'oxygène*[M]

absorption of carbon dioxide
absorption[F] *de dioxyde*[M] *de
carbone*[M]

absorption of water and
mineral salts
absorption[F] *d'eau*[F] *et de
sels*[M] *minéraux*

soil profile
profil[M] *du sol*[M]

plant litter
litière[F]

topsoil
couche[F] *arable*

subsoil
sous-sol[M]

bedrock
roche[F] *mère*[F]

section of a bulb
coupe[F] *d'un bulbe*[M]

scale leaf
tunique[F]

bud
bourgeon[M]

fleshy leaf
écaille[F]

bulbil
caïeu[M]

underground stem
tige[F]

base
plateau[M]

root
racine[F]

simple leaves
feuilles[F] simples

reniform
réniforme

cordate
cordée

orbiculate
arrondie

spatulate
spatulée

linear
linéaire

hastate
hastée

ovate
ovoide

lanceolate
lancéolée

peltate
peltée

structure of a leaf
structure[F] d'une feuille[F]

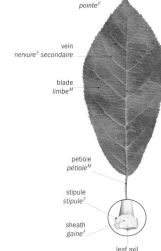
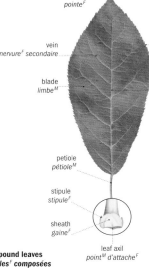
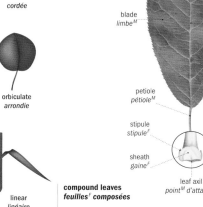

tip
pointe[F]

vein
nervure[F] secondaire

margin
bord[M]

blade
limbe[M]

midrib
nervure[F] principale

petiole
pétiole[M]

stipule
stipule[F]

sheath
gaine[F]

leaf axil
point[M] d'attache[F]

compound leaves
feuilles[F] composées

trifoliolate
trifoliée

pinnatifid
pennée

palmate
palmée

abruptly pinnate
paripennée

odd pinnate
imparipennée

leaf margins
bord[M] d'une feuille[F]

dentate
denté

doubly dentate
doublement denté

crenate
crénelé

ciliate
cilié

entire
entier

lobate
lobé

flower
fleur^F

VEGETABLE KINGDOM

structure of a flower
structure^F *d'une fleur*^F

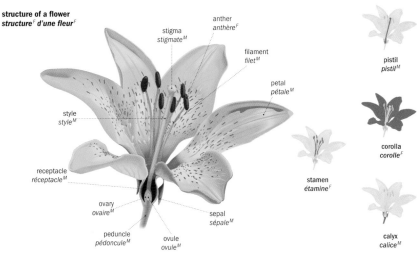

stigma
stigmate^M

anther
anthère^F

filament
filet^M

petal
pétale^M

style
style^M

receptacle
réceptacle^M

ovary
ovaire^M

peduncle
pédoncule^M

ovule
ovule^M

sepal
sépale^M

pistil
pistil^M

corolla
corolle^F

stamen
étamine^F

calyx
calice^M

examples of flowers
exemples^M *de fleurs*^F

orchid
orchidée^F

daffodil
jonquille^F

poppy
coquelicot^M

tulip
tulipe^F

lily of the valley
muguet^M

carnation
œillet^M

rose
rose^F

begonia
bégonia^M

lily
lis^M

violet
violette^F

crocus
crocus^M

sunflower
tournesol^M

types of inflorescences
modes^M d'inflorescence^F

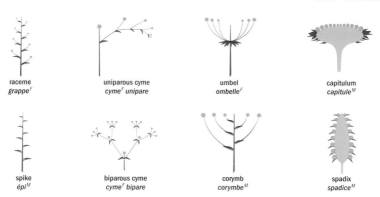

raceme
grappe^F

uniparous cyme
cyme^F unipare

umbel
ombelle^F

capitulum
capitule^M

spike
épi^M

biparous cyme
cyme^F bipare

corymb
corymbe^M

spadix
spadice^M

fruit
fruits^M

fleshy fruit: stone fruit
fruit^M charnu à noyau^M

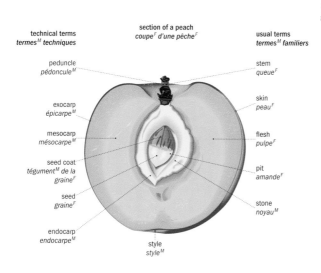

technical terms
termes^M techniques

section of a peach
coupe^F d'une pêche^F

usual terms
termes^M familiers

peduncle
pédoncule^M

exocarp
épicarpe^M

mesocarp
mésocarpe^M

seed coat
tégument^M de la graine^F

seed
graine^F

endocarp
endocarpe^M

style
style^M

stem
queue^F

skin
peau^F

flesh
pulpe^F

pit
amande^F

stone
noyau^M

fleshy fruit: pome fruit
fruit^M charnu à pépins^M

section of an apple
coupe^F d'une pomme^F

technical terms
termes^M techniques

usual terms
termes^M familiers

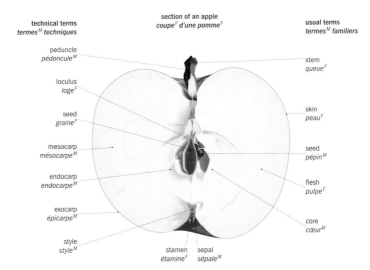

peduncle
pédoncule^M

loculus
loge^F

seed
graine^F

mesocarp
mésocarpe^M

endocarp
endocarpe^M

exocarp
épicarpe^M

style
style^M

stamen
étamine^F

sepal
sépale^M

stem
queue^F

skin
peau^F

seed
pépin^M

flesh
pulpe^F

core
cœur^M

fleshy fruit: citrus fruit
fruit^M charnu : agrume^M

section of an orange
coupe^F d'une orange^F

technical terms
termes^M techniques

usual terms
termes^M familiers

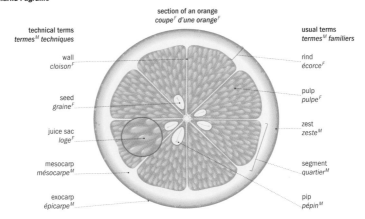

wall
cloison^F

seed
graine^F

juice sac
loge^F

mesocarp
mésocarpe^M

exocarp
épicarpe^M

rind
écorce^F

pulp
pulpe^F

zest
zeste^M

segment
quartier^M

pip
pépin^M

VEGETABLE KINGDOM

technical terms
termes^M techniques

section of a grape
coupe^F d'un raisin^M

usual terms
termes^M familiers

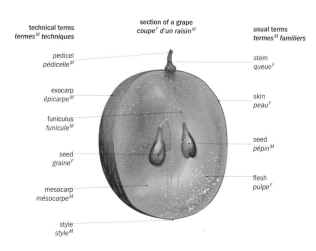

pedicel
pédicelle^M

exocarp
épicarpe^M

funiculus
funicule^M

seed
graine^F

mesocarp
mésocarpe^M

style
style^M

stem
queue^F

skin
peau^F

seed
pépin^M

flesh
pulpe^F

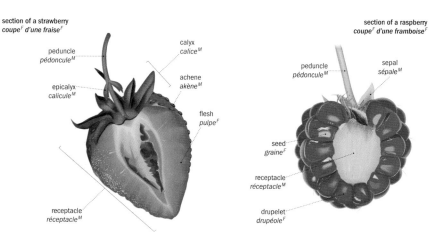

section of a strawberry
coupe^F d'une fraise^F

peduncle
pédoncule^M

epicalyx
calicule^M

calyx
calice^M

achene
akène^M

flesh
pulpe^F

receptacle
réceptacle^M

section of a raspberry
coupe^F d'une framboise^F

peduncle
pédoncule^M

sepal
sépale^M

seed
graine^F

receptacle
réceptacle^M

drupelet
drupéole^F

dry fruits
fruits^M **secs**

section of a follicle: star anise
coupe^F *d'un follicule*^{M} : *anis*^{M} *étoilé*

section of a silique: mustard
coupe^F *d'une silique*^{F} : *moutarde*^{F}

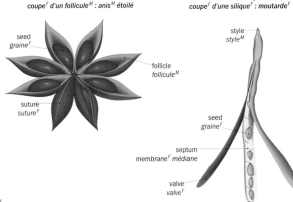

seed
graine^F

follicle
follicule^M

suture
suture^F

style
style^M

seed
graine^F

septum
membrane^F *médiane*

valve
valve^F

husk
brou^M

section of a hazelnut
coupe^F *d'une noisette*^{F}

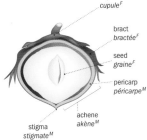

cupule
cupule^F

bract
bractée^F

seed
graine^F

pericarp
péricarpe^M

achene
akène^M

stigma
stigmate^M

section of a legume: pea
coupe^F *d'une gousse*^{F} :
pois^M

section of a capsule: poppy
coupe^F *d'une capsule*^{F} :
pavot^M

calyx
calice^M

midrib
nervure^F *principale*

pea
pois^M

funiculus
funicule^M

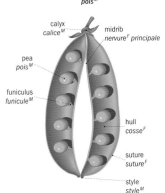

hull
cosse^F

suture
suture^F

style
style^M

pore
pore^M

seed
graine^F

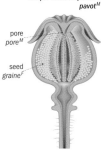

section of a walnut
coupe^F *d'une noix*^{F}

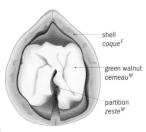

shell
coque^F

green walnut
cerneau^M

partition
zeste^M

VEGETABLE KINGDOM

buckwheat
sarrasin^M

buckwheat: raceme
sarrasin^M : *grappe*^F

wheat
blé^M

wheat: spike
blé^M : *épi*^M

section of a grain of wheat
coupe^F *d'un grain*^M *de
blé*^M

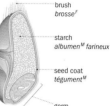

brush
brosse^F

starch
albumen^M *farineux*

seed coat
tégument^M

germ
germe^M

barley
orge^F

barley: spike
orge^F : *épi*^M

rice
riz^M

rice: panicle
riz^M : *panicule*^F

oats
avoine^F

oats: panicle
avoine^F : *panicule*^F

sorghum
sorgho^M

sorghum: panicle
sorgho^M : *panicule*^F

rye
seigle^M

rye: spike
seigle^M : *épi*^M

millet
millet^M

millet: spike
millet^M : *épi*^M

corn
maïs^M

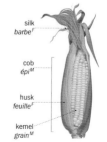

silk
barbe^F

cob
épi^M

husk
feuille^F

kernel
grain^M

corn: cob
maïs^M : *épi*^M

grape
vigne^F

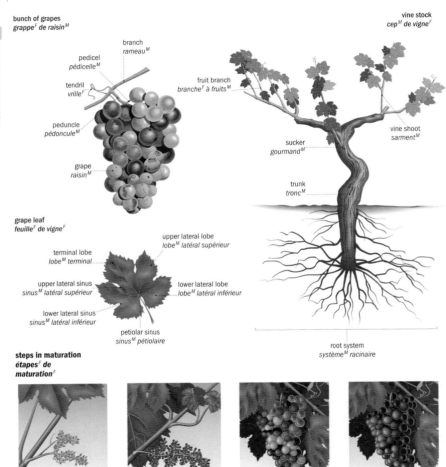

bunch of grapes
grappe^F *de raisin*^M

vine stock
cep^M *de vigne*^F

branch
rameau^M

pedicel
pédicelle^M

tendril
vrille^F

fruit branch
branche^F *à fruits*^M

peduncle
pédoncule^M

grape
raisin^M

vine shoot
sarment^M

sucker
gourmand^M

trunk
tronc^M

grape leaf
feuille^F *de vigne*^F

upper lateral lobe
lobe^M *latéral supérieur*

terminal lobe
lobe^M *terminal*

upper lateral sinus
sinus^M *latéral supérieur*

lower lateral lobe
lobe^M *latéral inférieur*

lower lateral sinus
sinus^M *latéral inférieur*

petiolar sinus
sinus^M *pétiolaire*

root system
système^M *racinaire*

steps in maturation
étapes^F *de maturation*^F

flowering
floraison^F

fruition
nouaison^F

ripening
véraison^F

ripeness
maturité^F

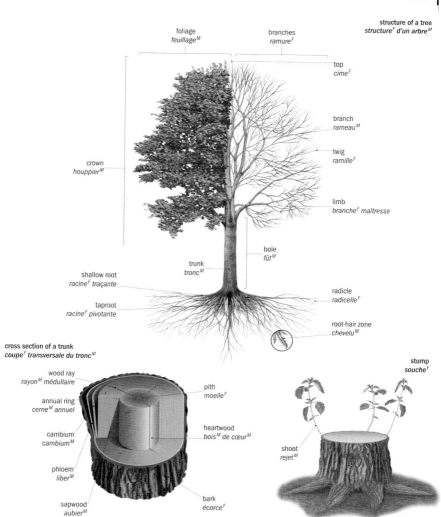

structure of a tree
structure^F *d'un arbre*^M

foliage
feuillage^M

branches
ramure^F

top
cime^F

branch
rameau^M

twig
ramille^F

limb
branche^F *maîtresse*

crown
houppier^M

bole
fût^M

trunk
tronc^M

shallow root
racine^F *traçante*

radicle
radicelle^F

taproot
racine^F *pivotante*

root-hair zone
chevelu^M

cross section of a trunk
coupe^F *transversale du tronc*^M

wood ray
rayon^M *médullaire*

pith
moelle^F

annual ring
cerne^M *annuel*

cambium
cambium^M

heartwood
bois^M *de cœur*^M

phloem
liber^M

sapwood
aubier^M

bark
écorce^F

stump
souche^F

shoot
rejet^M

63

examples of broadleaved trees
exemples^M d'arbres^M feuillus

oak
chêne^M

birch
bouleau^M

weeping willow
saule^M pleureur

poplar
peuplier^M

palm tree
palmier^M

maple
érable^M

beech
hêtre^M

walnut
noyer^M

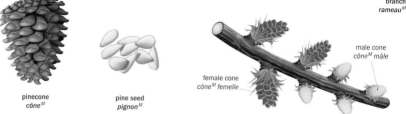

branch
rameau^M

male cone
cône^M *mâle*

female cone
cône^M *femelle*

pinecone
cône^M

pine seed
pignon^M

examples of leaves
exemples^M **de**
feuilles^F

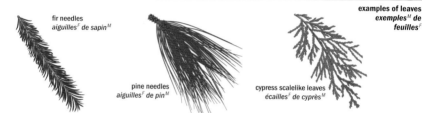

fir needles
aiguilles^F *de sapin*^M

pine needles
aiguilles^F *de pin*^M

cypress scalelike leaves
écailles^F *de cyprès*^M

examples of conifers
exemples^M **de conifères**^M

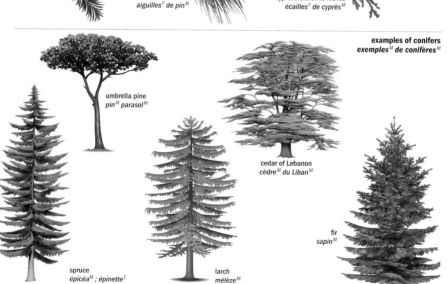

umbrella pine
pin^M *parasol*^M

cedar of Lebanon
cèdre^M *du Liban*^M

fir
sapin^M

spruce
épicéa^M ; *épinette*^F

larch
mélèze^M

animal cell
cellule^F animale

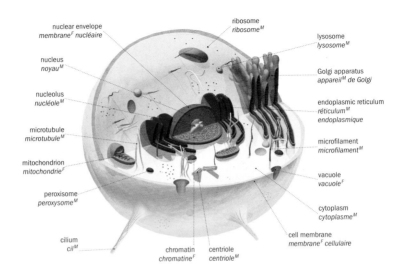

nuclear envelope
membrane^F nucléaire

ribosome
ribosome^M

lysosome
lysosome^M

nucleus
noyau^M

Golgi apparatus
appareil^M de Golgi

nucleolus
nucléole^M

endoplasmic reticulum
réticulum^M endoplasmique

microtubule
microtubule^M

microfilament
microfilament^M

mitochondrion
mitochondrie^F

vacuole
vacuole^F

peroxisome
peroxysome^M

cytoplasm
cytoplasme^M

cilium
cil^M

cell membrane
membrane^F cellulaire

chromatin
chromatine^F

centriole
centriole^M

unicellulars
unicellulaires^M

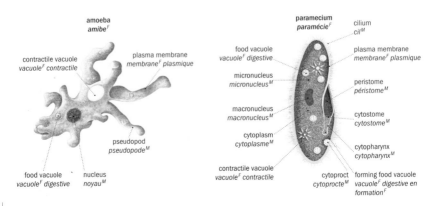

amoeba
amibe^F

paramecium
paramécie^F

cilium
cil^M

contractile vacuole
vacuole^F contractile

plasma membrane
membrane^F plasmique

food vacuole
vacuole^F digestive

plasma membrane
membrane^F plasmique

micronucleus
micronucleus^M

peristome
péristome^M

macronucleus
macronucleus^M

cytostome
cytostome^M

cytoplasm
cytoplasme^M

cytopharynx
cytopharynx^M

pseudopod
pseudopode^M

contractile vacuole
vacuole^F contractile

cytoproct
cytoprocte^M

forming food vacuole
vacuole^F digestive en formation^F

food vacuole
vacuole^F digestive

nucleus
noyau^M

butterfly
papillon[M]

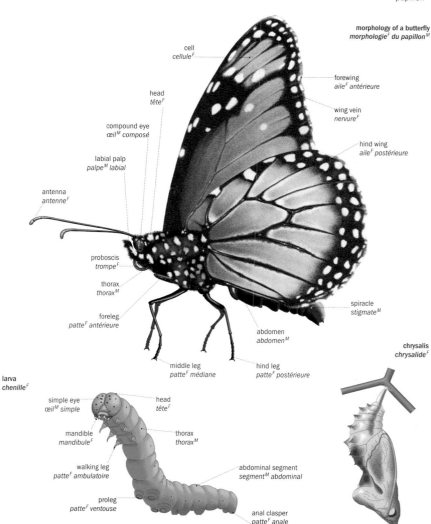

morphology of a butterfly
morphologie[F] *du papillon*[M]

cell
cellule[F]

forewing
aile[F] *antérieure*

wing vein
nervure[F]

head
tête[F]

hind wing
aile[F] *postérieure*

compound eye
œil[M] *composé*

labial palp
palpe[M] *labial*

antenna
antenne[F]

proboscis
trompe[F]

thorax
thorax[M]

spiracle
stigmate[M]

foreleg
patte[F] *antérieure*

abdomen
abdomen[M]

middle leg
patte[F] *médiane*

hind leg
patte[F] *postérieure*

chrysalis
chrysalide[F]

larva
chenille[F]

simple eye
œil[M] *simple*

head
tête[F]

mandible
mandibule[F]

thorax
thorax[M]

walking leg
patte[F] *ambulatoire*

abdominal segment
segment[M] *abdominal*

proleg
patte[F] *ventouse*

anal clasper
patte[F] *anale*

honeybee
abeille^F

morphology of a honeybee: worker
morphologie^F *de l'abeille*^F *: ouvrière*^F

wing
aile^F

thorax
thorax^M

abdomen
abdomen^M

compound eye
œil^M *composé*

pollen basket
corbeille^F *à pollen*^M

mouthparts
pièces^F *buccales*

sting
aiguillon^M

hind leg
patte^F *postérieure*

antenna
antenne^F

middle leg
patte^F *médiane*

foreleg
patte^F *antérieure*

castes
castes^F

worker
ouvrière^F

queen
reine^F

drone
faux bourdon^M

examples of insects
exemples^M d'insectes^M

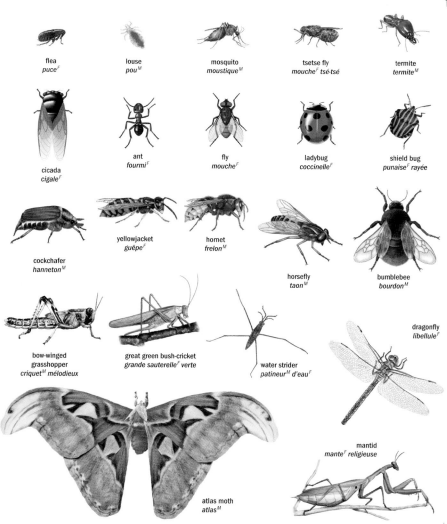

flea
puce^F

louse
pou^M

mosquito
moustique^M

tsetse fly
mouche^F tsé-tsé

termite
termite^M

cicada
cigale^F

ant
fourmi^F

fly
mouche^F

ladybug
coccinelle^F

shield bug
punaise^F rayée

cockchafer
hanneton^M

yellowjacket
guêpe^F

hornet
frelon^M

horsefly
taon^M

bumblebee
bourdon^M

bow-winged
grasshopper
criquet^M mélodieux

great green bush-cricket
grande sauterelle^F verte

water strider
patineur^M d'eau^F

dragonfly
libellule^F

atlas moth
atlas^M

mantid
mante^F religieuse

spider
araignée[F]

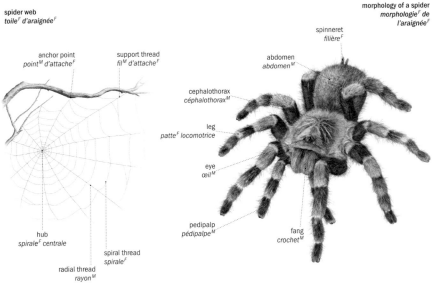

spider web
toile[F] *d'araignée*[F]

morphology of a spider
morphologie[F] *de*
l'araignée[F]

spinneret
filière[F]

anchor point
point[M] *d'attache*[F]

support thread
fil[M] *d'attache*[F]

abdomen
abdomen[M]

cephalothorax
céphalothorax[M]

leg
patte[F] *locomotrice*

eye
œil[M]

hub
spirale[F] *centrale*

spiral thread
spirale[F]

radial thread
rayon[M]

pedipalp
pédipalpe[M]

fang
crochet[M]

examples of arachnids
exemples[M] *d'arachnides*[M]

crab spider
araignée[F]-*crabe*[M]

garden spider
épeire[F]

scorpion
scorpion[M]

tick
tique[F]

water spider
argyronète[F]

red-kneed tarantula
mygale[F] *du Mexique*[M]

lobster
homard[M]

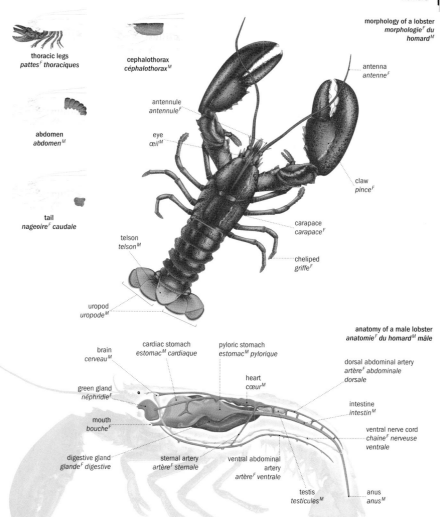

thoracic legs
pattes[F] *thoraciques*

abdomen
abdomen[M]

tail
nageoire[F] *caudale*

cephalothorax
céphalothorax[M]

morphology of a lobster
morphologie[F] *du homard*[M]

antenna
antenne[F]

antennule
antennule[F]

eye
œil[M]

claw
pince[F]

carapace
carapace[F]

telson
telson[M]

cheliped
griffe[F]

uropod
uropode[M]

anatomy of a male lobster
anatomie[F] *du homard*[M] *mâle*

brain
cerveau[M]

cardiac stomach
estomac[M] *cardiaque*

pyloric stomach
estomac[M] *pylorique*

heart
cœur[M]

dorsal abdominal artery
artère[F] *abdominale dorsale*

green gland
néphridie[F]

mouth
bouche[F]

intestine
intestin[M]

ventral nerve cord
chaîne[F] *nerveuse ventrale*

digestive gland
glande[F] *digestive*

sternal artery
artère[F] *sternale*

ventral abdominal artery
artère[F] *ventrale*

testis
testicules[M]

anus
anus[M]

ANIMAL KINGDOM

snail
escargot^M

morphology of a snail
morphologie^F *de l'escargot*^M

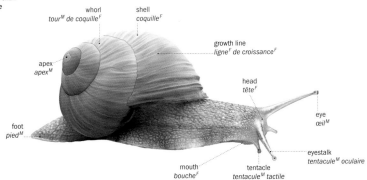

whorl
tour^M *de coquille*^F

shell
coquille^F

growth line
ligne^F *de croissance*^F

apex
apex^M

head
tête^F

eye
œil^M

foot
pied^M

eyestalk
tentacule^M *oculaire*

mouth
bouche^F

tentacle
tentacule^M *tactile*

octopus
pieuvre^F

morphology of an octopus
morphologie^F *de la pieuvre*^F

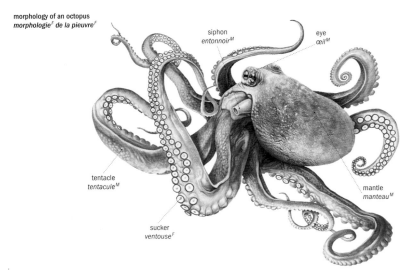

siphon
entonnoir^M

eye
œil^M

tentacle
tentacule^M

mantle
manteau^M

sucker
ventouse^F

univalve shell
coquillage^M univalve

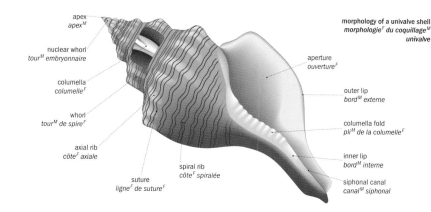

apex
apex^M

nuclear whorl
tour^M embryonnaire

columella
columelle^F

whorl
tour^M de spire^F

axial rib
côte^F axiale

suture
ligne^F de suture^F

spiral rib
côte^F spiralée

morphology of a univalve shell
morphologie^F du coquillage^M univalve

aperture
ouverture^F

outer lip
bord^M externe

columella fold
pli^M de la columelle^F

inner lip
bord^M interne

siphonal canal
canal^M siphonal

ANIMAL KINGDOM

bivalve shell
coquillage^M bivalve

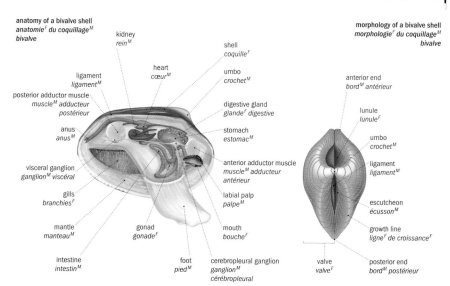

anatomy of a bivalve shell
anatomie^F du coquillage^M bivalve

kidney
rein^M

heart
cœur^M

ligament
ligament^M

posterior adductor muscle
muscle^M adducteur postérieur

anus
anus^M

visceral ganglion
ganglion^M viscéral

gills
branchies^F

mantle
manteau^M

intestine
intestin^M

gonad
gonade^F

foot
pied^M

shell
coquille^F

umbo
crochet^M

digestive gland
glande^F digestive

stomach
estomac^M

anterior adductor muscle
muscle^M adducteur antérieur

labial palp
palpe^M

mouth
bouche^F

cerebropleural ganglion
ganglion^M cérébropleural

morphology of a bivalve shell
morphologie^F du coquillage^M bivalve

anterior end
bord^M antérieur

lunule
lunule^F

umbo
crochet^M

ligament
ligament^M

escutcheon
écusson^M

growth line
ligne^F de croissance^F

valve
valve^F

posterior end
bord^M postérieur

ANIMAL KINGDOM

cartilaginous fish
poisson^M cartilagineux

morphology of a female shark
morphologie^F du requin^M femelle

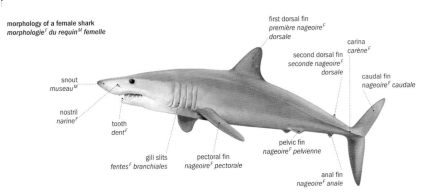

first dorsal fin
*première nageoire^F
dorsale*

carina
carène^F

second dorsal fin
*seconde nageoire^F
dorsale*

caudal fin
nageoire^F caudale

snout
museau^M

nostril
narine^F

tooth
dent^F

gill slits
fentes^F branchiales

pectoral fin
nageoire^F pectorale

pelvic fin
nageoire^F pelvienne

anal fin
nageoire^F anale

bony fish
poisson^M osseux

morphology of a perch
morphologie^F de la perche^F;
morphologie^F de la perchaude^F

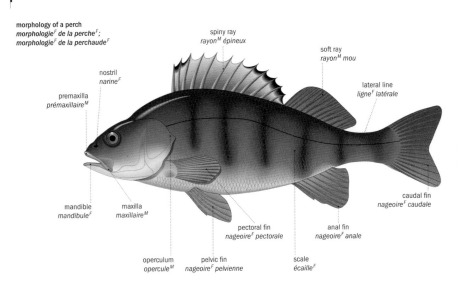

spiny ray
rayon^M épineux

soft ray
rayon^M mou

lateral line
ligne^F latérale

nostril
narine^F

premaxilla
prémaxillaire^M

mandible
mandibule^F

maxilla
maxillaire^M

operculum
opercule^M

pelvic fin
nageoire^F pelvienne

pectoral fin
nageoire^F pectorale

anal fin
nageoire^F anale

scale
écaille^F

caudal fin
nageoire^F caudale

frog
grenouille^F

morphology of a frog
morphologie^F *de la grenouille*^F

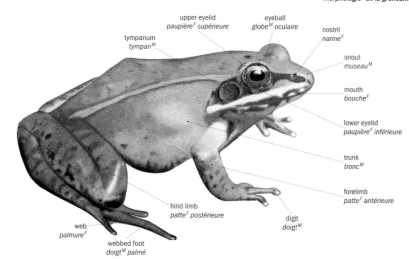

upper eyelid
paupière^F *supérieure*

eyeball
globe^M *oculaire*

nostril
narine^F

tympanum
tympan^M

snout
museau^M

mouth
bouche^F

lower eyelid
paupière^F *inférieure*

trunk
tronc^M

forelimb
patte^F *antérieure*

hind limb
patte^F *postérieure*

digit
doigt^M

web
palmure^F

webbed foot
doigt^M *palmé*

examples of amphibians
exemples^M *d'amphibiens*^M

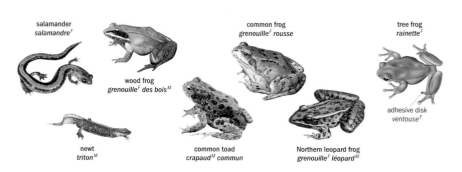

salamander
salamandre^F

wood frog
grenouille^F *des bois*^M

common frog
grenouille^F *rousse*

tree frog
rainette^F

adhesive disk
ventouse^F

newt
triton^M

common toad
crapaud^M *commun*

Northern leopard frog
grenouille^F *léopard*^M

snake

serpent[M]

morphology of a venomous snake: head
morphologie[F] du serpent[M] venimeux : tête[F]

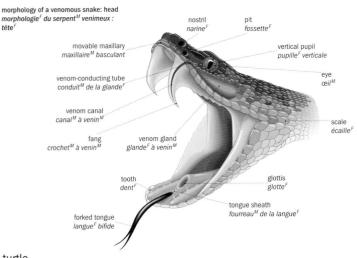

nostril
narine[F]

pit
fossette[F]

movable maxillary
maxillaire[M] basculant

vertical pupil
pupille[F] verticale

venom-conducting tube
conduit[M] de la glande[F]

eye
œil[M]

venom canal
canal[M] à venin[M]

scale
écaille[F]

fang
crochet[M] à venin[M]

venom gland
glande[F] à venin[M]

tooth
dent[F]

glottis
glotte[F]

forked tongue
langue[F] bifide

tongue sheath
fourreau[M] de la langue[F]

turtle

tortue[F]

morphology of a turtle
morphologie[F] de la tortue[F]

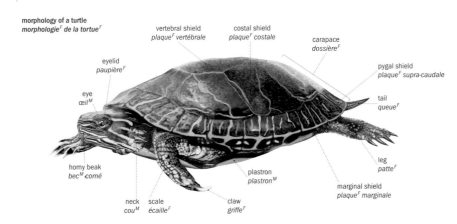

vertebral shield
plaque[F] vertébrale

costal shield
plaque[F] costale

carapace
dossière[F]

eyelid
paupière[F]

pygal shield
plaque[F] supra-caudale

eye
œil[M]

tail
queue[F]

horny beak
bec[M] corné

leg
patte[F]

neck
cou[M]

scale
écaille[F]

plastron
plastron[M]

claw
griffe[F]

marginal shield
plaque[F] marginale

examples of reptiles
exemples^M de reptiles^M

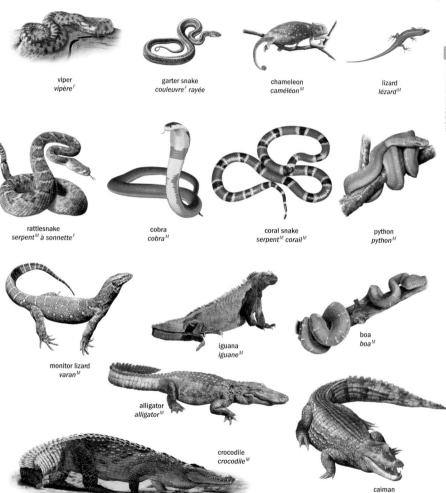

viper
vipère^F

garter snake
couleuvre^F rayée

chameleon
caméléon^M

lizard
lézard^M

rattlesnake
serpent^M à sonnette^F

cobra
cobra^M

coral snake
serpent^M corail^M

python
python^M

monitor lizard
varan^M

iguana
iguane^M

boa
boa^M

alligator
alligator^M

crocodile
crocodile^M

caiman
caïman^M

bird

oiseau^M

ANIMAL KINGDOM

morphology of a bird
morphologie^F *de l'oiseau*^M

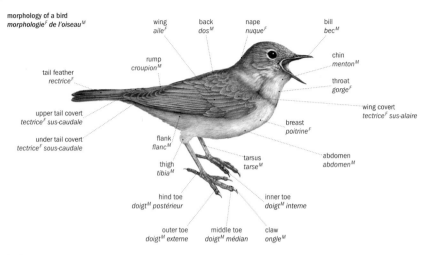

wing
aile^F

back
dos^M

nape
nuque^F

bill
bec^M

rump
croupion^M

chin
menton^M

throat
gorge^F

tail feather
rectrice^F

wing covert
tectrice^F *sus-alaire*

upper tail covert
tectrice^F *sus-caudale*

breast
poitrine^F

under tail covert
tectrice^F *sous-caudale*

flank
flanc^M

abdomen
abdomen^M

thigh
tibia^M

tarsus
tarse^M

hind toe
doigt^M *postérieur*

inner toe
doigt^M *interne*

outer toe
doigt^M *externe*

middle toe
doigt^M *médian*

claw
ongle^M

head
tête^F

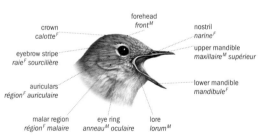

forehead
front^M

crown
calotte^F

nostril
narine^F

eyebrow stripe
raie^F *sourcilière*

upper mandible
maxillaire^M *supérieur*

auriculars
région^F *auriculaire*

lower mandible
mandibule^F

malar region
région^F *malaire*

eye ring
anneau^M *oculaire*

lore
lorum^M

wing
aile^F

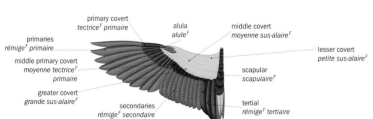

primary covert
tectrice^F *primaire*

alula
alule^F

middle covert
moyenne sus-alaire^F

primaries
rémige^F *primaire*

lesser covert
petite sus-alaire^F

middle primary covert
moyenne tectrice^F
primaire

scapular
scapulaire^F

greater covert
grande sus-alaire^F

secondaries
rémige^F *secondaire*

tertial
rémige^F *tertiaire*

ANIMAL KINGDOM

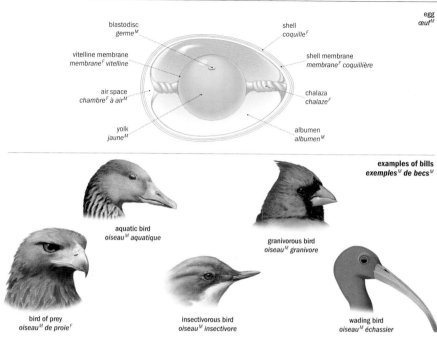

egg
œuf^M

blastodisc
germe^M

shell
coquille^F

vitelline membrane
membrane^F vitelline

shell membrane
membrane^F coquillière

air space
chambre^F à air^M

chalaza
chalaze^F

yolk
jaune^M

albumen
albumen^M

examples of bills
exemples^M de becs^M

aquatic bird
oiseau^M aquatique

granivorous bird
oiseau^M granivore

bird of prey
oiseau^M de proie^F

insectivorous bird
oiseau^M insectivore

wading bird
oiseau^M échassier

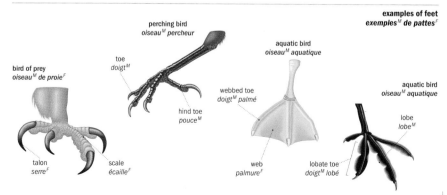

examples of feet
exemples^M de pattes^F

perching bird
oiseau^M percheur

aquatic bird
oiseau^M aquatique

bird of prey
oiseau^M de proie^F

toe
doigt^M

aquatic bird
oiseau^M aquatique

webbed toe
doigt^M palmé

hind toe
pouce^M

lobe
lobe^M

talon
serre^F

scale
écaille^F

web
palmure^F

lobate toe
doigt^M lobé

examples of birds

exemples^M d'oiseaux^M

ANIMAL KINGDOM

hummingbird
colibri^M

European robin
rouge-gorge^M

finch
pinson^M

kingfisher
martin-pêcheur^M

nightingale
rossignol^M

sparrow
moineau^M

swallow
hirondelle^F

starling
étourneau^M

jay
geai^M

cardinal
cardinal^M

swift
martinet^M

partridge
perdrix^F

condor
condor^M

macaw
ara^M

woodpecker
pic^M

raven
corbeau^M

toucan
toucan^M

vulture
vautour^M

penguin
manchot^M

albatross
albatros^M

heron
héron^M

pelican
pélican^M

stork
cigogne^F

ANIMAL KINGDOM

pheasant
faisan^M

great horned owl
grand duc^M
d'Amérique^F

falcon
faucon^M

quail
caille^F

eagle
aigle^M

duck
canard^M

pigeon
pigeon^M

hen
poule^F

turkey
dindon^M

guinea fowl
pintade^F

goose
oie^F

rooster
coq^M

ostrich
autruche^F

peacock
paon^M

flamingo
flamant^M

ANIMAL KINGDOM

rodent
rongeur^M

morphology of a rat
morphologie^F *du rat*^M

pinna
pavillon^M

whisker
vibrisse^F

nose
nez^M

digit
doigt^M

claw
griffe^F

fur
pelage^M

tail
queue^F

examples of rodents
exemples^M *de mammifères*^M *rongeurs*^M

field mouse
mulot^M

chipmunk
tamia^M

jerboa
gerboise^F

hamster
hamster^M

squirrel
écureuil^M

rat
rat^M

guinea pig
cochon^M *d'Inde*

porcupine
porc-épic^M

groundhog
marmotte^F

beaver
castor^M

examples of lagomorphs
exemples^M *de mammifères*^M *lagomorphes*^M

pika
pika^M

rabbit
lapin^M

hare
lièvre^M

horse
cheval^M

morphology of a horse
morphologie^F *du cheval*^M

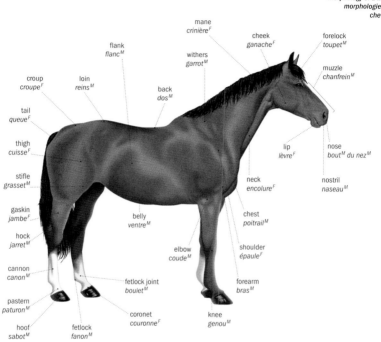

mane
crinière^F

cheek
ganache^F

forelock
toupet^M

flank
flanc^M

withers
garrot^M

muzzle
chanfrein^M

croup
croupe^F

loin
reins^M

back
dos^M

tail
queue^F

thigh
cuisse^F

lip
lèvre^F

nose
bout^M *du nez*^M

stifle
grasset^M

neck
encolure^F

nostril
naseau^M

gaskin
jambe^F

belly
ventre^M

chest
poitrail^M

hock
jarret^M

elbow
coude^M

shoulder
épaule^F

cannon
canon^M

fetlock joint
boulet^M

forearm
bras^M

pastern
paturon^M

coronet
couronne^F

knee
genou^M

hoof
sabot^M

fetlock
fanon^M

gaits
allures^F

walk
pas^M

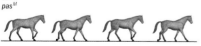

pace
amble^M

trot
trot^M

canter
galop^M

examples of ungulate mammals
exemples^M de mammifères^M ongulés

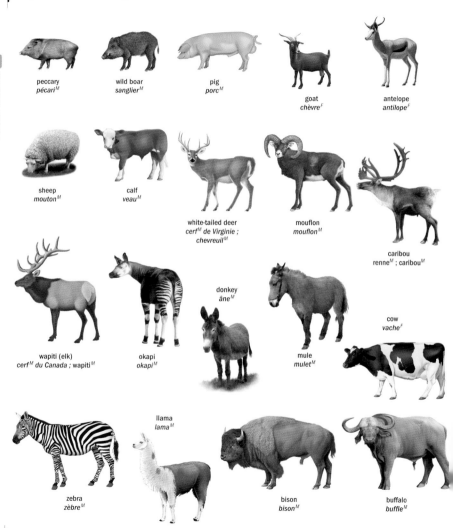

peccary
pécari^M

wild boar
sanglier^M

pig
porc^M

goat
chèvre^F

antelope
antilope^F

sheep
mouton^M

calf
veau^M

white-tailed deer
*cerf^M de Virginie ;
chevreuil^M*

mouflon
mouflon^M

caribou
renne^M ; caribou^M

wapiti (elk)
cerf^M du Canada ; wapiti^M

okapi
okapi^M

donkey
âne^M

mule
mulet^M

cow
vache^F

zebra
zèbre^M

llama
lama^M

bison
bison^M

buffalo
buffle^M

ox
bœuf^M

yak
yack^M

horse
cheval^M

moose
élan^M ; *orignal*^M

bactrian camel
chameau^M

dromedary camel
dromadaire^M

rhinoceros
rhinocéros^M

hippopotamus
hippopotame^M

giraffe
girafe^F

elephant
éléphant^M

dog
chien M

morphology of a dog
morphologie F *du chien* M

stop
stop M

muzzle
museau M

cheek
joue F

flews
babines F

withers
garrot M

back
dos M

thigh
cuisse F

shoulder
épaule F

elbow
coude M

forearm
avant-bras M

knee
genou M

tail
queue F

wrist
poignet M

hock
jarret M

toe
orteil M

examples of dog breeds
races F *de chiens* M

bulldog
bouledogue M

collie
colley M

Dalmatian
dalmatien M

poodle
caniche M

schnauzer
schnauzer M

Great Dane
danois M

German shepherd
berger M *allemand*

Saint Bernard
saint-bernard M

cat
chat^M

ANIMAL KINGDOM

cat's head
tête^F

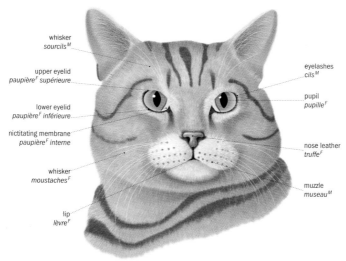

whisker
sourcils^M

upper eyelid
paupière^F *supérieure*

lower eyelid
paupière^F *inférieure*

nictitating membrane
paupière^F *interne*

whisker
moustaches^F

lip
lèvre^F

eyelashes
cils^M

pupil
pupille^F

nose leather
truffe^F

muzzle
museau^M

examples of cat breeds
races^F *de chats*^M

Siamese
siamois^M

Abyssinian
abyssin^M

Persian
persan^M

Maine coon
Maine coon^M

Manx
chat^M *de l'île*^F *de Man*

examples of carnivorous mammals

exemples^M de mammifères^M carnivores

ANIMAL KINGDOM

weasel
belette^F

mink
vison^M

stone marten
fouine^F

marten
martre^F

fox
renard^M

raccoon
raton^M *laveur*

fennec
fennec^M

river otter
loutre^F *de rivière*^F

mongoose
mangouste^F

badger
blaireau^M

skunk
moufette^F

hyena
hyène^F

lynx
lynx^M

wolf
loup^M

cougar
puma^M

cheetah
guépard^M

leopard
léopard^M

lion
lion^M

jaguar
jaguar^M

tiger
tigre^M

polar bear
ours^M *polaire*

black bear
ours^M *noir*

dolphin
dauphin^M

morphology of a dolphin
morphologie^F *du dauphin*^M

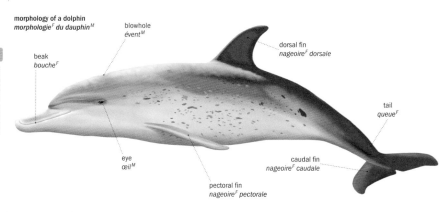

blowhole
évent^M

beak
bouche^F

dorsal fin
nageoire^F *dorsale*

tail
queue^F

eye
œil^M

caudal fin
nageoire^F *caudale*

pectoral fin
nageoire^F *pectorale*

examples of marine mammals
exemples^M *de mammifères*^M *marins*

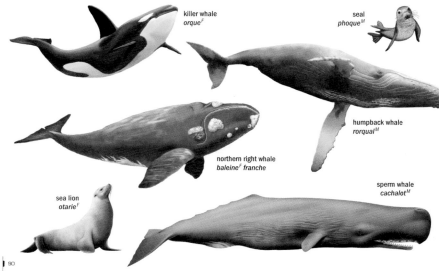

killer whale
orque^F

seal
phoque^M

humpback whale
rorqual^M

northern right whale
baleine^F *franche*

sperm whale
cachalot^M

sea lion
otarie^F

gorilla
gorille^M

morphology of a gorilla
morphologie^F *du gorille*^M

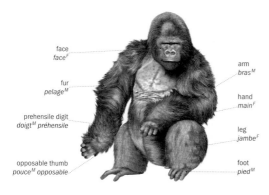

face
face^F

fur
pelage^M

prehensile digit
doigt^M *préhensile*

opposable thumb
pouce^M *opposable*

arm
bras^M

hand
main^F

leg
jambe^F

foot
pied^M

examples of primates
exemples^M *de mammifères*^M *primates*^M

tamarin
tamarin^M

marmoset
ouistiti^M

baboon
babouin^M

macaque
macaque^M

orangutan
orang-outan^M

chimpanzee
chimpanzé^M

lemur
lémurien^M

gibbon
gibbon^M

man
homme^M

anterior view
face^F *antérieure*

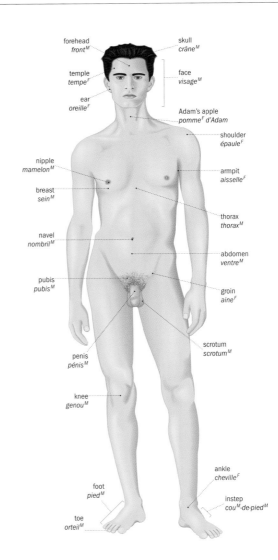

forehead
front^M

skull
crâne^M

temple
tempe^F

face
visage^M

ear
oreille^F

Adam's apple
pomme^F *d'Adam*

shoulder
épaule^F

nipple
mamelon^M

armpit
aisselle^F

breast
sein^M

thorax
thorax^M

navel
nombril^M

abdomen
ventre^M

pubis
pubis^M

groin
aine^F

scrotum
scrotum^M

penis
pénis^M

knee
genou^M

ankle
cheville^F

foot
pied^M

instep
cou^M*-de-pied*^M

toe
orteil^M

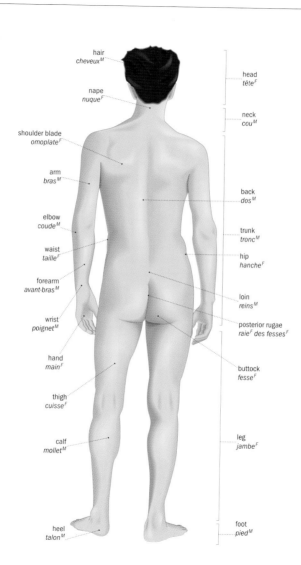

posterior view
face^F postérieure

hair
cheveux^M

nape
nuque^F

shoulder blade
omoplate^F

arm
bras^M

elbow
coude^M

waist
taille^F

forearm
avant-bras^M

wrist
poignet^M

hand
main^F

thigh
cuisse^F

calf
mollet^M

heel
talon^M

head
tête^F

neck
cou^M

back
dos^M

trunk
tronc^M

hip
hanche^F

loin
reins^M

posterior rugae
raie^F des fesses^F

buttock
fesse^F

leg
jambe^F

foot
pied^M

HUMAN BEING

woman

femme^F

anterior view
face^F *antérieure*

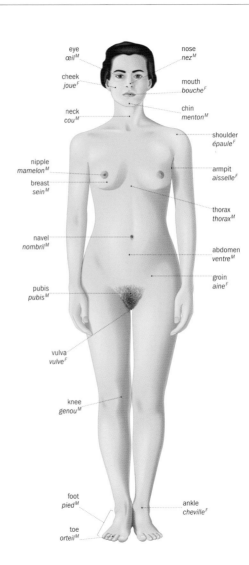

eye
œil^M

nose
nez^M

cheek
joue^F

mouth
bouche^F

neck
cou^M

chin
menton^M

shoulder
épaule^F

nipple
mamelon^M

armpit
aisselle^F

breast
sein^M

thorax
thorax^M

navel
nombril^M

abdomen
ventre^M

groin
aine^F

pubis
pubis^M

vulva
vulve^F

knee
genou^M

foot
pied^M

ankle
cheville^F

toe
orteil^M

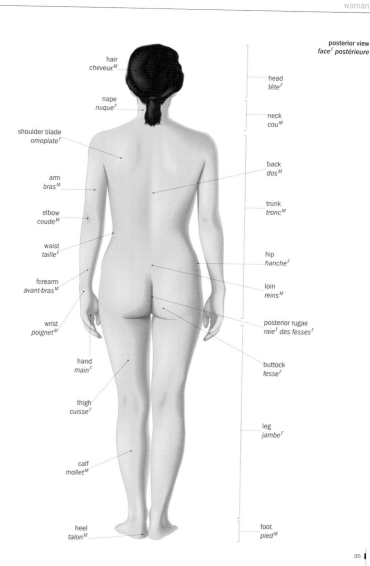

posterior view
face^F postérieure

hair
cheveux^M

head
tête^F

nape
nuque^F

neck
cou^M

shoulder blade
omoplate^F

back
dos^M

arm
bras^M

trunk
tronc^M

elbow
coude^M

waist
taille^F

hip
hanche^F

forearm
avant-bras^M

loin
reins^M

wrist
poignet^M

posterior rugae
raie^F des fesses^F

hand
main^F

buttock
fesse^F

thigh
cuisse^F

leg
jambe^F

calf
mollet^M

heel
talon^M

foot
pied^M

HUMAN BEING

95

muscles
muscles^M

HUMAN BEING

anterior view
face^F *antérieure*

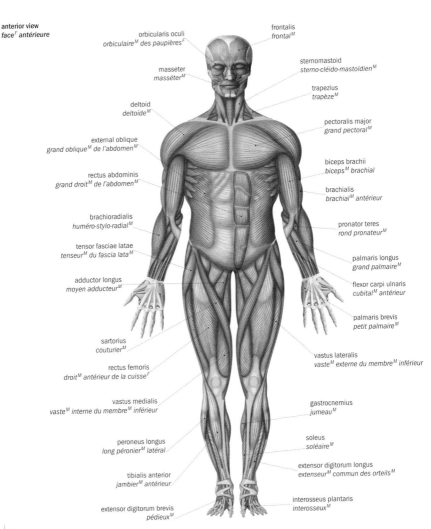

orbicularis oculi
orbiculaire^M *des paupières*^F

frontalis
frontal^M

masseter
masséter^M

sternomastoid
sterno-cléido-mastoïdien^M

trapezius
trapèze^M

deltoid
deltoïde^M

pectoralis major
grand pectoral^M

external oblique
grand oblique^M *de l'abdomen*^M

biceps brachii
biceps^M *brachial*

rectus abdominis
grand droit^M *de l'abdomen*^M

brachialis
brachial^M *antérieur*

brachioradialis
huméro-stylo-radial^M

pronator teres
rond pronateur^M

tensor fasciae latae
tenseur^M *du fascia lata*^M

palmaris longus
grand palmaire^M

adductor longus
moyen adducteur^M

flexor carpi ulnaris
cubital^M *antérieur*

palmaris brevis
petit palmaire^M

sartorius
couturier^M

vastus lateralis
vaste^M *externe du membre*^M *inférieur*

rectus femoris
droit^M *antérieur de la cuisse*^F

vastus medialis
vaste^M *interne du membre*^M *inférieur*

gastrocnemius
jumeau^M

peroneus longus
long péronier^M *latéral*

soleus
soléaire^M

extensor digitorum longus
extenseur^M *commun des orteils*^M

tibialis anterior
jambier^M *antérieur*

interosseus plantaris
interosseux^M

extensor digitorum brevis
pédieux^M

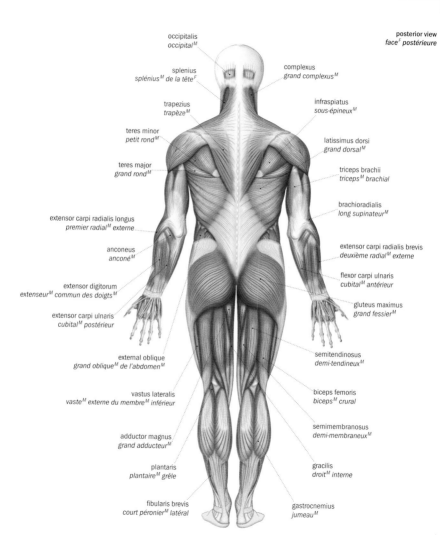

occipitalis
occipital^M

splenius
splénius^M de la tête^F

trapezius
trapèze^M

teres minor
petit rond^M

teres major
grand rond^M

extensor carpi radialis longus
premier radial^M externe

anconeus
anconé^M

extensor digitorum
extenseur^M commun des doigts^M

extensor carpi ulnaris
cubital^M postérieur

external oblique
grand oblique^M de l'abdomen^M

vastus lateralis
vaste^M externe du membre^M inférieur

adductor magnus
grand adducteur^M

plantaris
plantaire^M grêle

fibularis brevis
court péronier^M latéral

complexus
grand complexus^M

infraspiatus
sous-épineux^M

latissimus dorsi
grand dorsal^M

triceps brachii
triceps^M brachial

brachioradialis
long supinateur^M

extensor carpi radialis brevis
deuxième radial^M externe

flexor carpi ulnaris
cubital^M antérieur

gluteus maximus
grand fessier^M

semitendinosus
demi-tendineux^M

biceps femoris
biceps^M crural

semimembranosus
demi-membraneux^M

gracilis
droit^M interne

gastrocnemius
jumeau^M

skeleton

squelette^M

HUMAN BEING

anterior view
vue^F *antérieure*

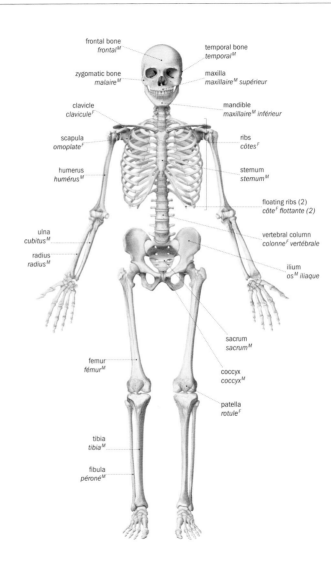

frontal bone
frontal^M

temporal bone
temporal^M

zygomatic bone
malaire^M

maxilla
maxillaire^M *supérieur*

clavicle
clavicule^F

mandible
maxillaire^M *inférieur*

scapula
omoplate^F

ribs
côtes^F

humerus
humérus^M

sternum
sternum^M

floating ribs (2)
côte^F *flottante (2)*

ulna
cubitus^M

radius
radius^M

vertebral column
colonne^F *vertébrale*

ilium
os^M *iliaque*

sacrum
sacrum^M

femur
fémur^M

coccyx
coccyx^M

patella
rotule^F

tibia
tibia^M

fibula
péroné^M

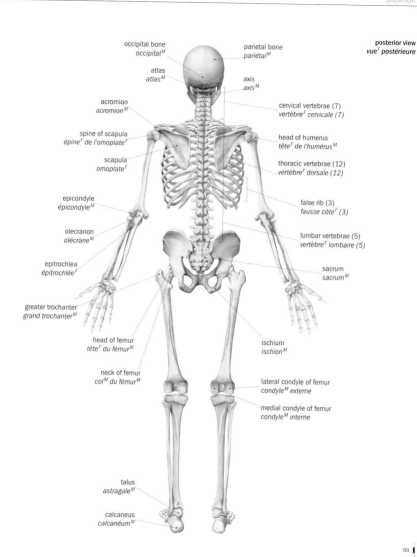

occipital bone
occipital^M

parietal bone
pariétal^M

posterior view
vue^F *postérieure*

atlas
atlas^M

axis
axis^M

acromion
acromion^M

cervical vertebrae (7)
vertèbre^F *cervicale (7)*

spine of scapula
épine^F *de l'omoplate*^F

head of humerus
tête^F *de l'humérus*^M

scapula
omoplate^F

thoracic vertebrae (12)
vertèbre^F *dorsale (12)*

epicondyle
épicondyle^M

false rib (3)
fausse côte^F *(3)*

olecranon
olécrane^M

lumbar vertebrae (5)
vertèbre^F *lombaire (5)*

epitrochlea
épitrochlée^F

sacrum
sacrum^M

greater trochanter
grand trochanter^M

head of femur
tête^F *du fémur*^M

ischium
ischion^M

neck of femur
col^M *du fémur*^M

lateral condyle of femur
condyle^M *externe*

medial condyle of femur
condyle^M *interne*

talus
astragale^M

calcaneus
calcanéum^M

skeleton

HUMAN BEING

lateral view of adult skull
vue^F latérale du crâne^M
adulte

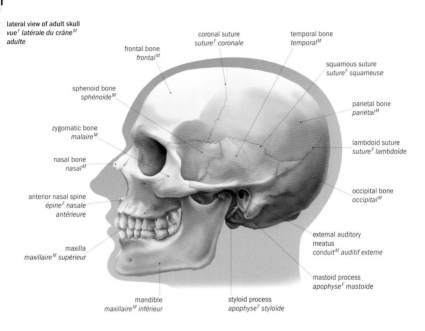

coronal suture
suture^F coronale

temporal bone
temporal^M

frontal bone
frontal^M

squamous suture
suture^F squameuse

sphenoid bone
sphénoïde^M

parietal bone
pariétal^M

zygomatic bone
malaire^M

lambdoid suture
suture^F lambdoïde

nasal bone
nasal^M

anterior nasal spine
épine^F nasale antérieure

occipital bone
occipital^M

external auditory meatus
conduit^M auditif externe

maxilla
maxillaire^M supérieur

mastoid process
apophyse^F mastoïde

mandible
maxillaire^M inférieur

styloid process
apophyse^F styloïde

lateral view of child's skull
vue^F latérale du crâne^M
d'enfant^M

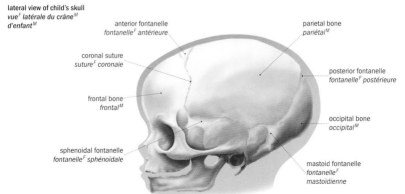

anterior fontanelle
fontanelle^F antérieure

parietal bone
pariétal^M

coronal suture
suture^F coronale

posterior fontanelle
fontanelle^F postérieure

frontal bone
frontal^M

occipital bone
occipital^M

sphenoidal fontanelle
fontanelle^F sphénoïdale

mastoid fontanelle
fontanelle^F mastoïdienne

teeth
dents^F

human denture
denture^F *humaine*

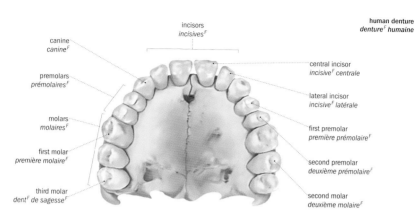

incisors
incisives^F

canine
canine^F

premolars
prémolaires^F

molars
molaires^F

first molar
première molaire^F

third molar
dent^F *de sagesse*^F

central incisor
incisive^F *centrale*

lateral incisor
incisive^F *latérale*

first premolar
première prémolaire^F

second premolar
deuxième prémolaire^F

second molar
deuxième molaire^F

cross section of a molar
coupe^F *d'une molaire*^F

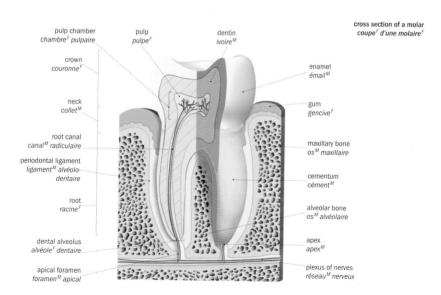

pulp chamber
chambre^F *pulpaire*

pulp
pulpe^F

dentin
ivoire^M

crown
couronne^F

neck
collet^M

root canal
canal^M *radiculaire*

periodontal ligament
ligament^M *alvéolo-
dentaire*

root
racine^F

dental alveolus
alvéole^F *dentaire*

apical foramen
foramen^M *apical*

enamel
émail^M

gum
gencive^F

maxillary bone
os^M *maxillaire*

cementum
cément^M

alveolar bone
os^M *alvéolaire*

apex
apex^M

plexus of nerves
réseau^M *nerveux*

blood circulation
circulation^F sanguine

principal veins and arteries
*principales veines^F et
artères^F*

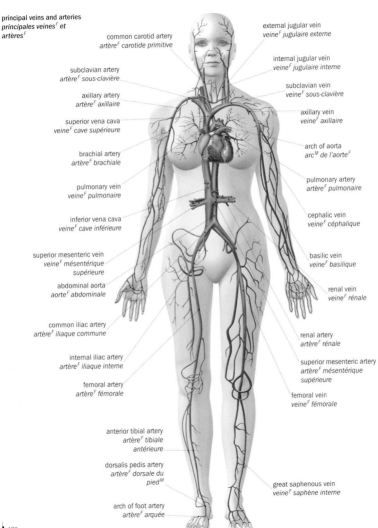

common carotid artery
artère^F carotide primitive

external jugular vein
veine^F jugulaire externe

internal jugular vein
veine^F jugulaire interne

subclavian artery
artère^F sous-clavière

subclavian vein
veine^F sous-clavière

axillary artery
artère^F axillaire

axillary vein
veine^F axillaire

superior vena cava
veine^F cave supérieure

arch of aorta
arc^M de l'aorte^F

brachial artery
artère^F brachiale

pulmonary artery
artère^F pulmonaire

pulmonary vein
veine^F pulmonaire

cephalic vein
veine^F céphalique

inferior vena cava
veine^F cave inférieure

superior mesenteric vein
*veine^F mésentérique
supérieure*

basilic vein
veine^F basilique

abdominal aorta
aorte^F abdominale

renal vein
veine^F rénale

common iliac artery
artère^F iliaque commune

renal artery
artère^F rénale

internal iliac artery
artère^F iliaque interne

superior mesenteric artery
*artère^F mésentérique
supérieure*

femoral artery
artère^F fémorale

femoral vein
veine^F fémorale

anterior tibial artery
*artère^F tibiale
antérieure*

dorsalis pedis artery
*artère^F dorsale du
pied^M*

great saphenous vein
veine^F saphène interne

arch of foot artery
artère^F arquée

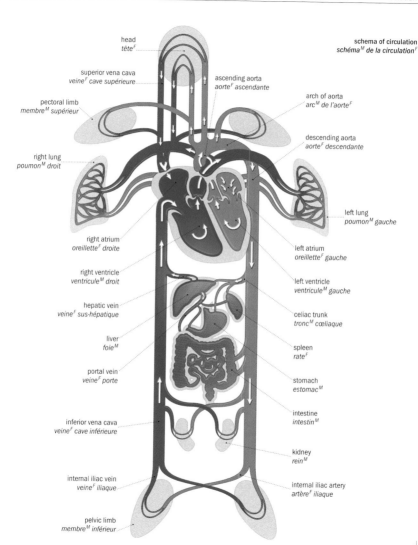

schema of circulation
schéma^M de la circulation^F

head
tête^F

superior vena cava
veine^F cave supérieure

ascending aorta
aorte^F ascendante

arch of aorta
arc^M de l'aorte^F

pectoral limb
membre^M supérieur

descending aorta
aorte^F descendante

right lung
poumon^M droit

left lung
poumon^M gauche

right atrium
oreillette^F droite

left atrium
oreillette^F gauche

right ventricle
ventricule^M droit

left ventricle
ventricule^M gauche

hepatic vein
veine^F sus-hépatique

celiac trunk
tronc^M cœliaque

liver
foie^M

spleen
rate^F

portal vein
veine^F porte

stomach
estomac^M

intestine
intestin^M

inferior vena cava
veine^F cave inférieure

kidney
rein^M

internal iliac vein
veine^F iliaque

internal iliac artery
artère^F iliaque

pelvic limb
membre^M inférieur

blood circulation

HUMAN BEING

composition of the blood
composition^F du sang^M

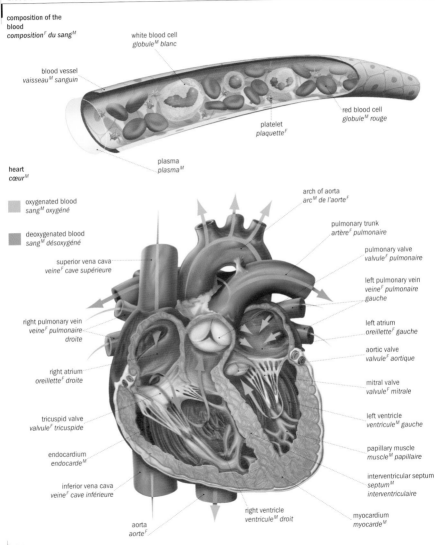

white blood cell
globule^M blanc

blood vessel
vaisseau^M sanguin

red blood cell
globule^M rouge

platelet
plaquette^F

plasma
plasma^M

heart
cœur^M

oxygenated blood
sang^M oxygéné

deoxygenated blood
sang^M désoxygéné

arch of aorta
arc^M de l'aorte^F

pulmonary trunk
artère^F pulmonaire

pulmonary valve
valvule^F pulmonaire

superior vena cava
veine^F cave supérieure

left pulmonary vein
veine^F pulmonaire gauche

right pulmonary vein
veine^F pulmonaire droite

left atrium
oreillette^F gauche

aortic valve
valvule^F aortique

right atrium
oreillette^F droite

mitral valve
valvule^F mitrale

tricuspid valve
valvule^F tricuspide

left ventricle
ventricule^M gauche

endocardium
endocarde^M

papillary muscle
muscle^M papillaire

inferior vena cava
veine^F cave inférieure

interventricular septum
septum^M interventriculaire

aorta
aorte^F

right ventricle
ventricule^M droit

myocardium
myocarde^M

respiratory system
appareil^M respiratoire

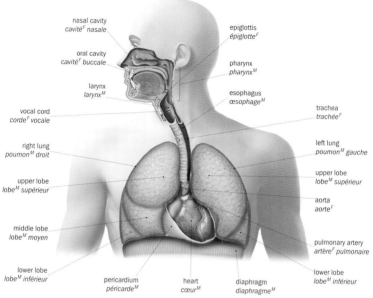

nasal cavity
cavité^F nasale

oral cavity
cavité^F buccale

larynx
larynx^M

vocal cord
corde^F vocale

right lung
poumon^M droit

upper lobe
lobe^M supérieur

middle lobe
lobe^M moyen

lower lobe
lobe^M inférieur

pericardium
péricarde^M

heart
cœur^M

diaphragm
diaphragme^M

epiglottis
épiglotte^F

pharynx
pharynx^M

esophagus
œsophage^M

trachea
trachée^F

left lung
poumon^M gauche

upper lobe
lobe^M supérieur

aorta
aorte^F

pulmonary artery
artère^F pulmonaire

lower lobe
lobe^M inférieur

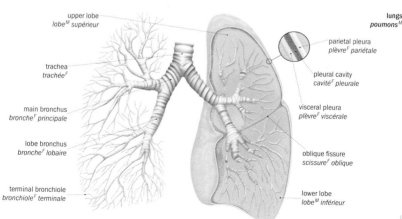

upper lobe
lobe^M supérieur

trachea
trachée^F

main bronchus
bronche^F principale

lobe bronchus
bronche^F lobaire

terminal bronchiole
bronchiole^F terminale

lungs
poumons^M

parietal pleura
plèvre^F pariétale

pleural cavity
cavité^F pleurale

visceral pleura
plèvre^F viscérale

oblique fissure
scissure^F oblique

lower lobe
lobe^M inférieur

digestive system
appareil^M digestif

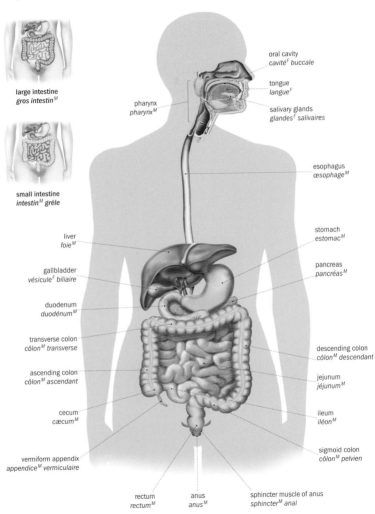

large intestine
gros intestin^M

small intestine
intestin^M grêle

oral cavity
cavité^F buccale

tongue
langue^F

pharynx
pharynx^M

salivary glands
glandes^F salivaires

esophagus
œsophage^M

stomach
estomac^M

liver
foie^M

pancreas
pancréas^M

gallbladder
vésicule^F biliaire

duodenum
duodénum^M

transverse colon
côlon^M transverse

descending colon
côlon^M descendant

ascending colon
côlon^M ascendant

jejunum
jéjunum^M

cecum
cæcum^M

ileum
iléon^M

vermiform appendix
appendice^M vermiculaire

sigmoid colon
côlon^M pelvien

rectum
rectum^M

anus
anus^M

sphincter muscle of anus
sphincter^M anal

urinary system
appareil^M urinaire

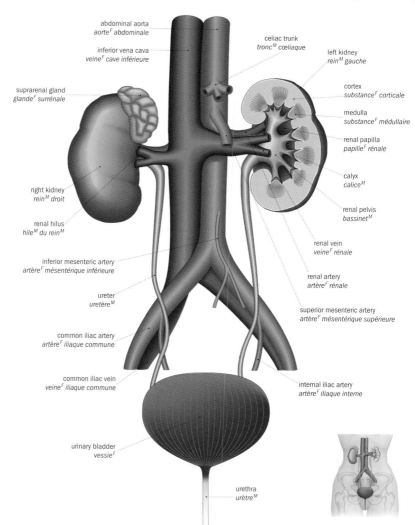

abdominal aorta
aorte^F abdominale

inferior vena cava
veine^F cave inférieure

celiac trunk
tronc^M cœliaque

left kidney
rein^M gauche

cortex
substance^F corticale

suprarenal gland
glande^F surrénale

medulla
substance^F médullaire

renal papilla
papilie^F rénale

right kidney
rein^M droit

calyx
calice^M

renal hilus
hile^M du rein^M

renal pelvis
bassinet^M

renal vein
veine^F rénale

inferior mesenteric artery
artère^F mésentérique inférieure

renal artery
artère^F rénale

ureter
uretère^M

superior mesenteric artery
artère^F mésentérique supérieure

common iliac artery
artère^F iliaque commune

common iliac vein
veine^F iliaque commune

internal iliac artery
artère^F iliaque interne

urinary bladder
vessie^F

urethra
urètre^M

nervous system

système^M nerveux

HUMAN BEING

peripheral nervous system
système^M nerveux périphérique

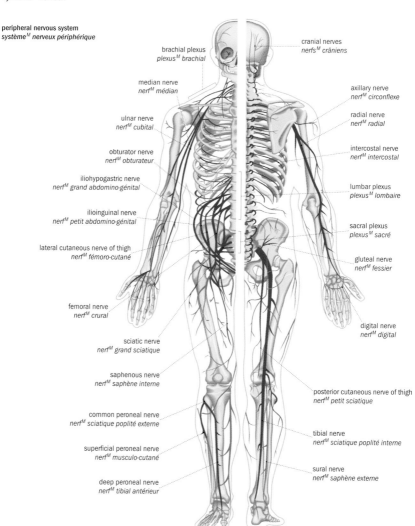

brachial plexus
plexus^M brachial

cranial nerves
nerfs^M crâniens

median nerve
nerf^M médian

axillary nerve
nerf^M circonflexe

ulnar nerve
nerf^M cubital

radial nerve
nerf^M radial

obturator nerve
nerf^M obturateur

intercostal nerve
nerf^M intercostal

iliohypogastric nerve
nerf^M grand abdomino-génital

lumbar plexus
plexus^M lombaire

ilioinguinal nerve
nerf^M petit abdomino-génital

sacral plexus
plexus^M sacré

lateral cutaneous nerve of thigh
nerf^M fémoro-cutané

gluteal nerve
nerf^M fessier

femoral nerve
nerf^M crural

digital nerve
nerf^M digital

sciatic nerve
nerf^M grand sciatique

saphenous nerve
nerf^M saphène interne

posterior cutaneous nerve of thigh
nerf^M petit sciatique

common peroneal nerve
nerf^M sciatique poplité externe

tibial nerve
nerf^M sciatique poplité interne

superficial peroneal nerve
nerf^M musculo-cutané

sural nerve
nerf^M saphène externe

deep peroneal nerve
nerf^M tibial antérieur

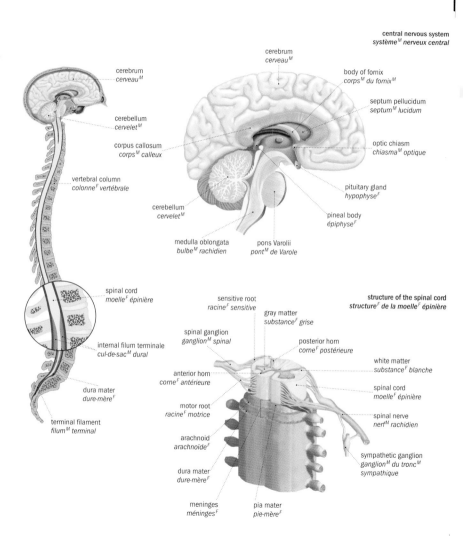

central nervous system
système^M nerveux central

cerebrum
cerveau^M

cerebrum
cerveau^M

body of fornix
corps^M du fornix^M

septum pellucidum
septum^M lucidum

cerebellum
cervelet^M

corpus callosum
corps^M calleux

optic chiasm
chiasma^M optique

vertebral column
colonne^F vertébrale

cerebellum
cervelet^M

pituitary gland
hypophyse^F

pineal body
épiphyse^F

medulla oblongata
bulbe^M rachidien

pons Varolii
pont^M de Varole

spinal cord
moelle^F épinière

structure of the spinal cord
structure^F de la moelle^F épinière

sensitive root
racine^F sensitive

gray matter
substance^F grise

spinal ganglion
ganglion^M spinal

posterior horn
corne^F postérieure

internal filum terminale
cul-de-sac^M dural

white matter
substance^F blanche

anterior horn
corne^F antérieure

spinal cord
moelle^F épinière

dura mater
dure-mère^F

motor root
racine^F motrice

spinal nerve
nerf^M rachidien

terminal filament
filum^M terminal

arachnoid
arachnoïde^F

sympathetic ganglion
*ganglion^M du tronc^M
sympathique*

dura mater
dure-mère^F

meninges
méninges^F

pia mater
pie-mère^F

HUMAN BEING

chain of neurons
chaîne^F de neurones^M

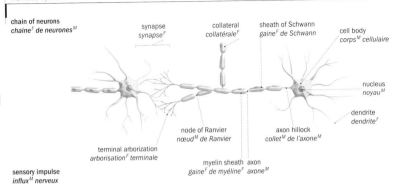

synapse
synapse^F

collateral
collatérale^F

sheath of Schwann
gaine^F de Schwann

cell body
corps^M cellulaire

nucleus
noyau^M

dendrite
dendrite^F

axon hillock
collet^M de l'axone^M

node of Ranvier
nœud^M de Ranvier

terminal arborization
arborisation^F terminale

myelin sheath
gaine^F de myéline

axon
axone^M

sensory impulse
influx^M nerveux

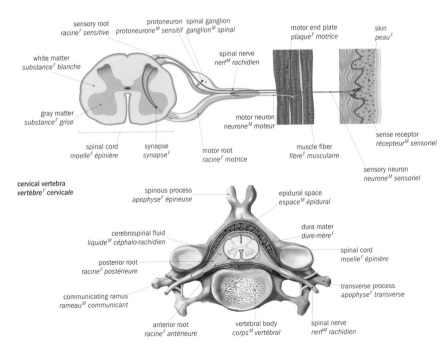

sensory root
racine^F sensitive

protoneuron
protoneurone^M sensitif

spinal ganglion
ganglion^M spinal

motor end plate
plaque^F motrice

skin
peau^F

white matter
substance^F blanche

spinal nerve
nerf^M rachidien

gray matter
substance^F grise

motor neuron
neurone^M moteur

spinal cord
moelle^F épinière

synapse
synapse^F

motor root
racine^F motrice

muscle fiber
fibre^F musculaire

sense receptor
récepteur^M sensoriel

sensory neuron
neurone^M sensoriel

cervical vertebra
vertèbre^F cervicale

spinous process
apophyse^F épineuse

epidural space
espace^M épidural

cerebrospinal fluid
liquide^M céphalo-rachidien

dura mater
dure-mère^F

posterior root
racine^F postérieure

spinal cord
moelle^F épinière

communicating ramus
rameau^M communicant

transverse process
apophyse^F transverse

anterior root
racine^F antérieure

vertebral body
corps^M vertébral

spinal nerve
nerf^M rachidien

male reproductive organs
organes^M génitaux masculins

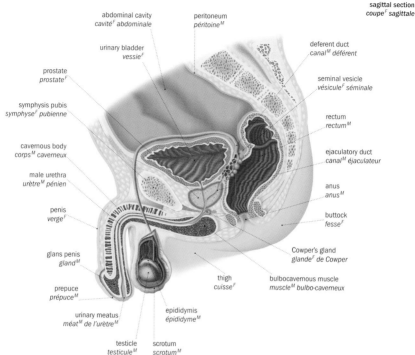

sagittal section
coupe^F sagittale

abdominal cavity
cavité^F abdominale

peritoneum
péritoine^M

urinary bladder
vessie^F

deferent duct
canal^M déférent

prostate
prostate^F

seminal vesicle
vésicule^F séminale

symphysis pubis
symphyse^F pubienne

rectum
rectum^M

cavernous body
corps^M caverneux

ejaculatory duct
canal^M éjaculateur

male urethra
urètre^M pénien

anus
anus^M

penis
verge^F

buttock
fesse^F

glans penis
gland^M

Cowper's gland
glande^F de Cowper

prepuce
prépuce^M

thigh
cuisse^F

bulbocavernous muscle
muscle^M bulbo-caverneux

urinary meatus
méat^M de l'urètre^M

epididymis
épididyme^M

testicle
testicule^M

scrotum
scrotum^M

spermatozoon
spermatozoïde^M

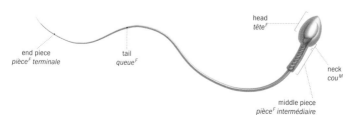

head
tête^F

end piece
pièce^F terminale

tail
queue^F

neck
cou^M

middle piece
pièce^F intermédiaire

female reproductive organs
organes^M génitaux féminins

sagittal section
coupe^F sagittale

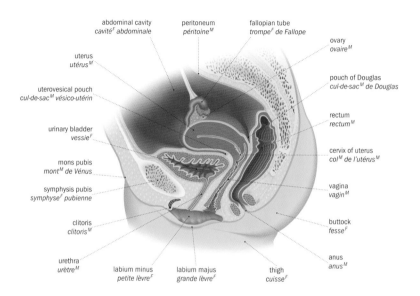

abdominal cavity
cavité^F abdominale

peritoneum
péritoine^M

fallopian tube
trompe^F de Fallope

ovary
ovaire^M

uterus
utérus^M

pouch of Douglas
cul-de-sac^M de Douglas

uterovesical pouch
cul-de-sac^M vésico-utérin

rectum
rectum^M

urinary bladder
vessie^F

cervix of uterus
col^M de l'utérus^M

mons pubis
mont^M de Vénus

vagina
vagin^M

symphysis pubis
symphyse^F pubienne

buttock
fesse^F

clitoris
clitoris^M

anus
anus^M

urethra
urètre^M

labium minus
petite lèvre^F

labium majus
grande lèvre^F

thigh
cuisse^F

egg
ovule^M

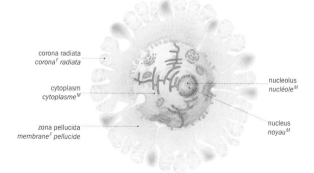

corona radiata
corona^F radiata

nucleolus
nucléole^M

cytoplasm
cytoplasme^M

zona pellucida
membrane^F pellucide

nucleus
noyau^M

ampulla of fallopian tube
ampoule^F de la trompe^F utérine

isthmus of fallopian tube
isthme^M de la trompe^F utérine

infundibulum of fallopian tube
pavillon^M de la trompe^F utérine

uterus
utérus^M

ovary
ovaire^M

fallopian tubes
trompes^F de Fallope

broad ligament of uterus
ligament^M large de l'utérus^M

labium minus
petite lèvre^F

vulva
vulve^F

vagina
vagin^M

labium majus
grande lèvre^F

breast
sein^M

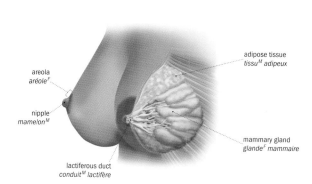

areola
aréole^F

adipose tissue
tissu^M adipeux

nipple
mamelon^M

mammary gland
glande^F mammaire

lactiferous duct
conduit^M lactifère

touch
toucher^M

skin
peau^F

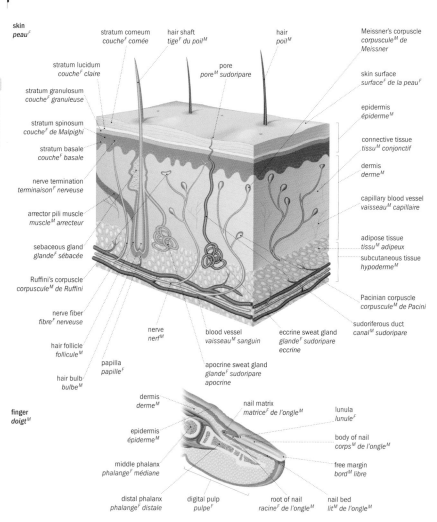

stratum corneum
couche^F *cornée*

hair shaft
tige^F *du poil*^M

pore
pore^M *sudoripare*

hair
poil^M

Meissner's corpuscle
corpuscule^M *de Meissner*

stratum lucidum
couche^F *claire*

skin surface
surface^F *de la peau*^F

stratum granulosum
couche^F *granuleuse*

epidermis
épiderme^M

stratum spinosum
couche^F *de Malpighi*

connective tissue
tissu^M *conjonctif*

stratum basale
couche^F *basale*

dermis
derme^M

nerve termination
terminaison^F *nerveuse*

capillary blood vessel
vaisseau^M *capillaire*

arrector pili muscle
muscle^M *arrecteur*

adipose tissue
tissu^M *adipeux*

sebaceous gland
glande^F *sébacée*

subcutaneous tissue
hypoderme^M

Ruffini's corpuscle
corpuscule^M *de Ruffini*

Pacinian corpuscle
corpuscule^M *de Pacini*

nerve fiber
fibre^F *nerveuse*

nerve
nerf^M

blood vessel
vaisseau^M *sanguin*

eccrine sweat gland
glande^F *sudoripare eccrine*

sudoriferous duct
canal^M *sudoripare*

hair follicle
follicule^M

papilla
papille^F

apocrine sweat gland
glande^F *sudoripare apocrine*

hair bulb
bulbe^M

finger
doigt^M

dermis
derme^M

nail matrix
matrice^F *de l'ongle*^M

lunula
lunule^F

epidermis
épiderme^M

body of nail
corps^M *de l'ongle*^M

middle phalanx
phalange^F *médiane*

free margin
bord^M *libre*

distal phalanx
phalange^F *distale*

digital pulp
pulpe^F

root of nail
racine^F *de l'ongle*^M

nail bed
lit^M *de l'ongle*^M

touch

hand
main[F]

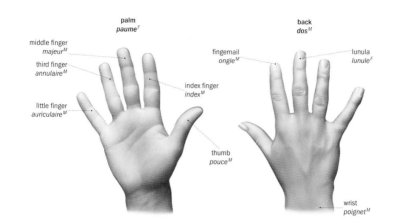

palm
paume[F]

back
dos[M]

middle finger
majeur[M]

third finger
annulaire[M]

index finger
index[M]

little finger
auriculaire[M]

thumb
pouce[M]

fingernail
ongle[M]

lunula
lunule[F]

wrist
poignet[M]

HUMAN BEING

hearing
ouïe[F]

auricle
pavillon[M]

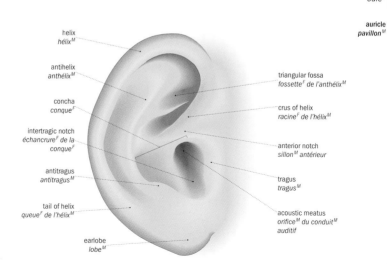

helix
hélix[M]

antihelix
anthélix[M]

concha
conque[F]

intertragic notch
échancrure[F] *de la*
conque[F]

antitragus
antitragus[M]

tail of helix
queue[F] *de l'hélix*[M]

earlobe
lobe[M]

triangular fossa
fossette[F] *de l'anthélix*[M]

crus of helix
racine[F] *de l'hélix*[M]

anterior notch
sillon[M] *antérieur*

tragus
tragus[M]

acoustic meatus
orifice[M] *du conduit*[M]
auditif

HUMAN BEING

structure of the ear
structure^F de l'oreille^F

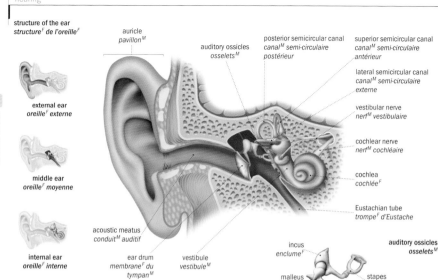

external ear
oreille^F externe

middle ear
oreille^F moyenne

internal ear
oreille^F interne

auricle
pavillon^M

auditory ossicles
osselets^M

posterior semicircular canal
canal^M semi-circulaire postérieur

superior semicircular canal
canal^M semi-circulaire antérieur

lateral semicircular canal
canal^M semi-circulaire externe

vestibular nerve
nerf^M vestibulaire

cochlear nerve
nerf^M cochléaire

cochlea
cochlée^F

Eustachian tube
trompe^F d'Eustache

acoustic meatus
conduit^M auditif

ear drum
membrane^F du tympan^M

vestibule
vestibule^M

incus
enclume^F

malleus
marteau^M

stapes
étrier^M

auditory ossicles
osselets^M

smell and taste
odorat^M et goût^M

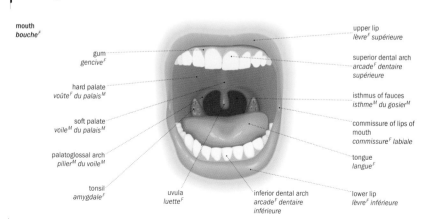

mouth
bouche^F

gum
gencive^F

hard palate
voûte^F du palais^M

soft palate
voile^M du palais^M

palatoglossal arch
pilier^M du voile^M

tonsil
amygdale^F

uvula
luette^F

inferior dental arch
arcade^F dentaire inférieure

upper lip
lèvre^F supérieure

superior dental arch
arcade^F dentaire supérieure

isthmus of fauces
isthme^M du gosier^M

commissure of lips of mouth
commissure^F labiale

tongue
langue^F

lower lip
lèvre^F inférieure

smell and taste

external nose
parties^F *externes du nez*^M

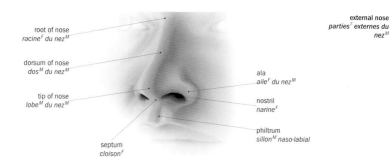

root of nose
racine^F *du nez*^M

dorsum of nose
dos^M *du nez*^M

tip of nose
lobe^M *du nez*^M

septum
cloison^F

ala
aile^F *du nez*^M

nostril
narine^F

philtrum
sillon^M *naso-labial*

nasal fossae
fosses^F *nasales*

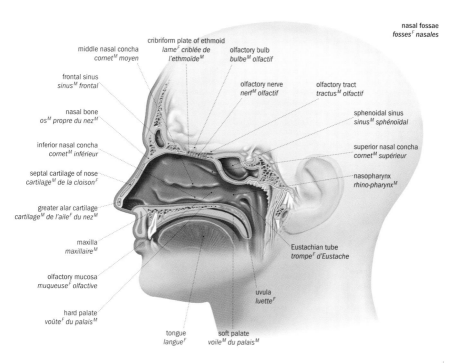

middle nasal concha
cornet^M *moyen*

cribriform plate of ethmoid
lame^F *criblée de l'ethmoïde*^M

olfactory bulb
bulbe^M *olfactif*

frontal sinus
sinus^M *frontal*

olfactory nerve
nerf^M *olfactif*

olfactory tract
tractus^M *olfactif*

nasal bone
os^M *propre du nez*^M

sphenoidal sinus
sinus^M *sphénoïdal*

inferior nasal concha
cornet^M *inférieur*

superior nasal concha
cornet^M *supérieur*

septal cartilage of nose
cartilage^M *de la cloison*^F

nasopharynx
rhino-pharynx^M

greater alar cartilage
cartilage^M *de l'aile*^F *du nez*^M

maxilla
maxillaire^M

Eustachian tube
trompe^F *d'Eustache*

olfactory mucosa
muqueuse^F *olfactive*

hard palate
voûte^F *du palais*^M

uvula
luette^F

tongue
langue^F

soft palate
voile^M *du palais*^M

dorsum of tongue
dos^M de la langue^F

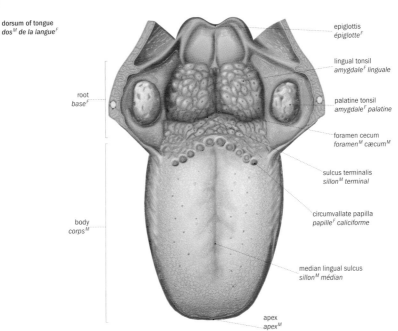

epiglottis
épiglotte^F

lingual tonsil
amygdale^F linguale

palatine tonsil
amygdale^F palatine

root
base^F

foramen cecum
foramen^M cæcum^M

sulcus terminalis
sillon^M terminal

circumvallate papilla
papille^F caliciforme

body
corps^M

median lingual sulcus
sillon^M médian

apex
apex^M

taste receptors
récepteurs^M du goût^M

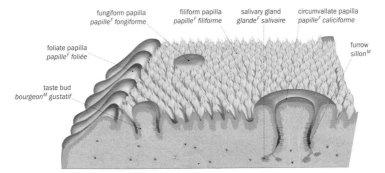

fungiform papilla
papille^F fongiforme

filiform papilla
papille^F filiforme

salivary gland
glande^F salivaire

circumvallate papilla
papille^F caliciforme

foliate papilla
papille^F foliée

furrow
sillon^M

taste bud
bourgeon^M gustatif

sight
vue[F]

eye
œil[M]

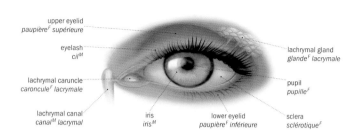

upper eyelid
paupière[F] *supérieure*

eyelash
cil[M]

lachrymal caruncle
caroncule[F] *lacrymale*

lachrymal canal
canal[M] *lacrymal*

iris
iris[M]

lower eyelid
paupière[F] *inférieure*

lachrymal gland
glande[F] *lacrymale*

pupil
pupille[F]

sclera
sclérotique[F]

eyeball
globe[M] *oculaire*

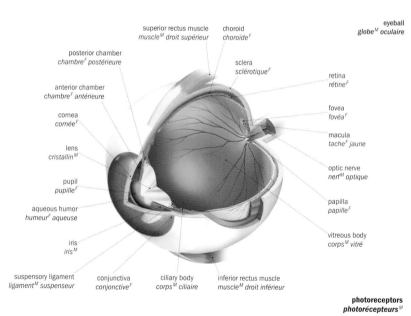

superior rectus muscle
muscle[M] *droit supérieur*

choroid
choroïde[F]

posterior chamber
chambre[F] *postérieure*

sclera
sclérotique[F]

anterior chamber
chambre[F] *antérieure*

retina
rétine[F]

cornea
cornée[F]

fovea
fovéa[F]

lens
cristallin[M]

macula
tache[F] *jaune*

pupil
pupille[F]

optic nerve
nerf[M] *optique*

aqueous humor
humeur[F] *aqueuse*

papilla
papille[F]

iris
iris[M]

vitreous body
corps[M] *vitré*

suspensory ligament
ligament[M] *suspenseur*

conjunctiva
conjonctive[F]

ciliary body
corps[M] *ciliaire*

inferior rectus muscle
muscle[M] *droit inférieur*

photoreceptors
photorécepteurs[M]

cone
cône[M]

rod
bâtonnet[M]

supermarket
supermarché^M

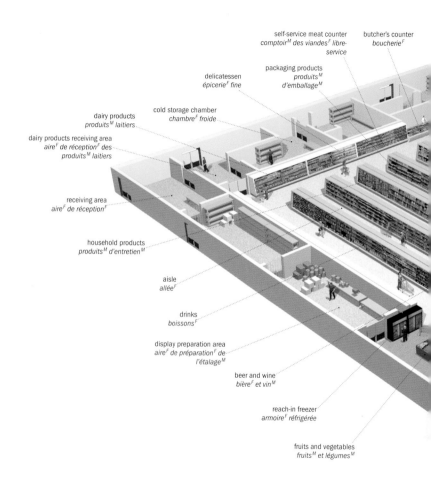

self-service meat counter
comptoir^M *des viandes*^F *libre-service*

butcher's counter
boucherie^F

packaging products
produits^M *d'emballage*^M

delicatessen
épicerie^F *fine*

cold storage chamber
chambre^F *froide*

dairy products
produits^M *laitiers*

dairy products receiving area
aire^F *de réception*^F *des produits*^M *laitiers*

receiving area
aire^F *de réception*^F

household products
produits^M *d'entretien*^M

aisle
allée^F

drinks
boissons^F

display preparation area
aire^F *de préparation*^F *de l'étalage*^M

beer and wine
bière^F *et vin*^M

reach-in freezer
armoire^F *réfrigérée*

fruits and vegetables
fruits^M *et légumes*^M

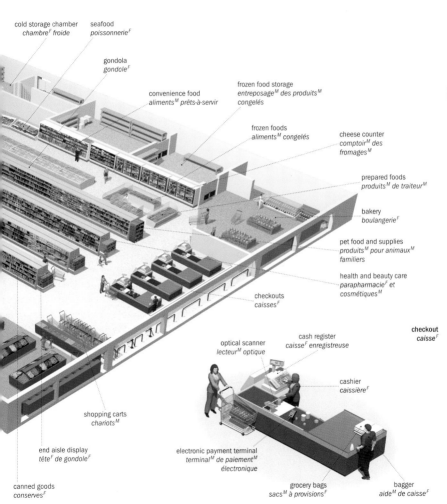

cold storage chamber
chambre^F froide

seafood
poissonnerie^F

gondola
gondole^F

convenience food
aliments^M prêts-à-servir

frozen food storage
entreposage^M des produits^M
congelés

frozen foods
aliments^M congelés

cheese counter
comptoir^M des
fromages^M

prepared foods
produits^M de traiteur^M

bakery
boulangerie^F

pet food and supplies
produits^M pour animaux^M
familiers

health and beauty care
parapharmacie^F et
cosmétiques^M

checkouts
caisses^F

checkout
caisse^F

cash register
caisse^F enregistreuse

optical scanner
lecteur^M optique

cashier
caissière^F

shopping carts
chariots^M

end aisle display
tête^F de gondole^F

electronic payment terminal
terminal^M de paiement^M
électronique

canned goods
conserves^F

grocery bags
sacs^M à provisions^F

bagger
aide^M de caisse^F

farmstead

ferme^F

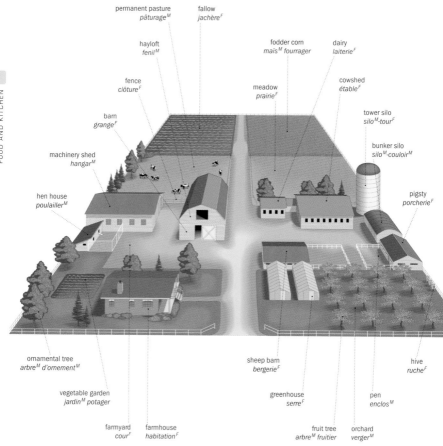

permanent pasture
pâturage^M

fallow
jachère^F

hayloft
fenil^M

fodder corn
maïs^M fourrager

dairy
laiterie^F

fence
clôture^F

meadow
prairie^F

cowshed
étable^F

barn
grange^F

tower silo
silo^M-tour^F

bunker silo
silo^M-couloir^M

machinery shed
hangar^M

hen house
poulailler^M

pigsty
porcherie^F

ornamental tree
arbre^M d'ornement^M

sheep barn
bergerie^F

hive
ruche^F

vegetable garden
jardin^M potager

greenhouse
serre^F

pen
enclos^M

farmyard
cour^F

farmhouse
habitation^F

fruit tree
arbre^M fruitier

orchard
verger^M

mushrooms
champignons[M]

truffle
truffe[F]

wood ear
oreille-de-Judas[F]

royal agaric
oronge[F] *vraie*

delicious lactarius
lactaire[M] *délicieux*

enoki
collybie[F] *à pied*[M]
velouté

oyster
pleurote[M] *en forme*[F]
d'huître[F]

cultivated mushrooms
champignon[M] *de couche*[F]

green russula
russule[F] *verdoyante*

morels
morille[F]

edible boletus
cèpe[M]

shitake
shiitake[M]

chanterelles
chanterelle[F] *commune*

seaweed
algues[F]

arame
aramé[M]

wakame
wakamé[M]

kombu
kombu[M]

spirulina
spiruline[F]

Irish moss
mousse[F] *d'Irlande*[F]

hijiki
hijiki[M]

sea lettuce
laitue[F] *de mer*[F]

agar-agar
agar-agar[M]

nori
nori[M]

dulse
rhodyménie[M] *palmé*

FOOD AND KITCHEN

vegetables
légumes^M

bulb vegetables
légumes^M **bulbes**^M

shallot
échalote^F

water chestnut
châtaigne^F *d'eau*^F

green onion
oignon^M *vert*

scallion
ciboule^F

garlic
ail^M

chives
ciboulette^F

leeks
poireaux^M

yellow onion
oignon^M *jaune*

red onion
oignon^M *rouge*

white onion
oignon^M *blanc*

pickling onions
oignons^M *à mariner*

tuber vegetables
légumes^M **tubercules**^M

cassava
manioc^M

crosne
crosne^M

taro
taro^M

jicama
jicama^M

tropical yam
igname^F

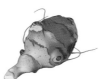
Jerusalem artichoke
topinambour^M

sweet potato
patate^F

potatoes
pommes^F *de terre*^F

stalk vegetables
légumes^M tiges^F

asparagus
asperge^F

tip
pointe^F

spear
turion^M

bundle
botte^F

Swiss chard
bette^F à carde^F

leaf
feuille^F

rib
carde^F

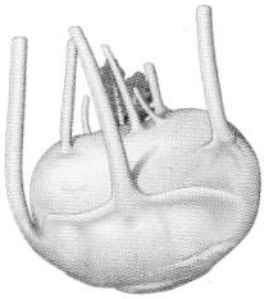

kohlrabi
chou^M-rave^F

cardoon
cardon^M

fennel
fenouil^M

stalk
tige^F

bulb
bulbe^M

bamboo shoot
pousse^F de bambou^M

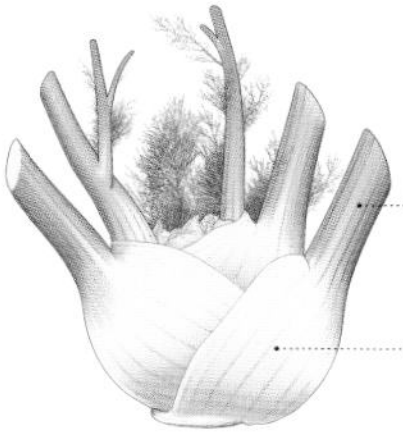

celery
céleri^M

branch
branche^F

fiddleheads
crosses^F de fougère^F

head
pied^M

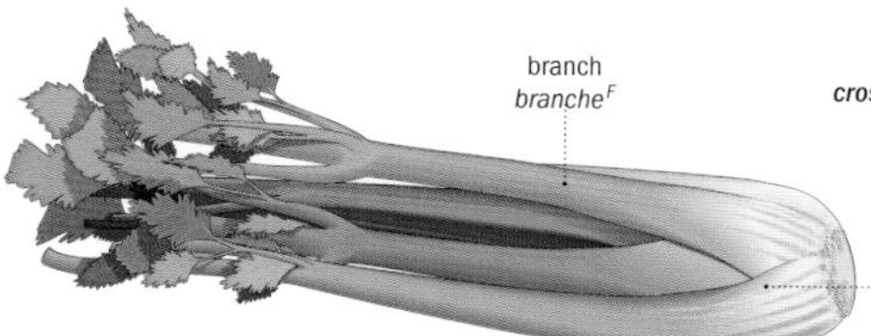

rhubarb
rhubarbe^F

vegetables

leaf vegetables
légumes^M feuilles^F

leaf lettuce
laitue^F frisée

romaine lettuce
romaine^F

celtuce
laitue^F asperge^F

sea kale
chou^M marin

collards
chou^M cavalier^M

escarole
scarole^F

butter lettuce
laitue^F pommée

iceberg lettuce
laitue^F iceberg^M

radicchio
chicorée^F de Trévise

ornamental kale
chou^M laitue^F

curly kale
chou^M frisé

grape leaves
feuille^F de vigne^F

brussels sprouts
choux^M de Bruxelles

red cabbage
chou^M pommé rouge

white cabbage
chou^M pommé blanc

savoy cabbage
chou^M de Milan

green cabbage
chou^M pommé vert

pe-tsai
pe-tsai^M

bok choy
pak-choi^M

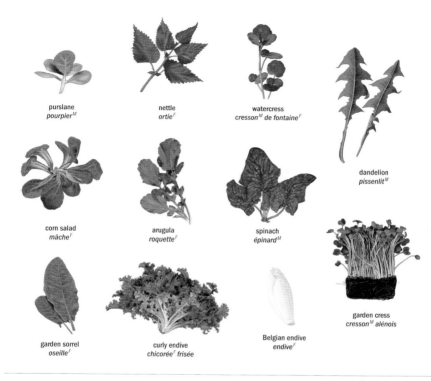

purslane
pourpier^M

nettle
ortie^F

watercress
cresson^M *de fontaine*^F

dandelion
pissenlit^M

corn salad
mâche^F

arugula
roquette^F

spinach
épinard^M

garden sorrel
oseille^F

curly endive
chicorée^F *frisée*

Belgian endive
endive^F

garden cress
cresson^M *alénois*

inflorescent vegetables
légumes^M *fleurs*^F

cauliflower
chou^M-*fleur*^F

broccoli
brocoli^M

Gai-lohn
Gai lon^M

broccoli rabe
brocoli^M *italien*

artichoke
artichaut^M

fruit vegetables
légumes^M fruits^M

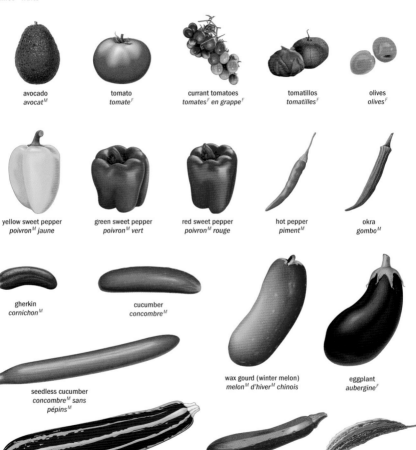

avocado
avocat^M

tomato
tomate^F

currant tomatoes
tomates^F en grappe^F

tomatillos
tomatilles^F

olives
olives^F t

yellow sweet pepper
poivron^M jaune

green sweet pepper
poivron^M vert

red sweet pepper
poivron^M rouge

hot pepper
piment^M

okra
gombo^M

gherkin
cornichon^M

cucumber
concombre^M

seedless cucumber
*concombre^M sans
pépins^M*

wax gourd (winter melon)
melon^M d'hiver^M chinois

eggplant
aubergine^F

summer squash
courge^F

zucchini
courgette^F

bitter melon
margose^F

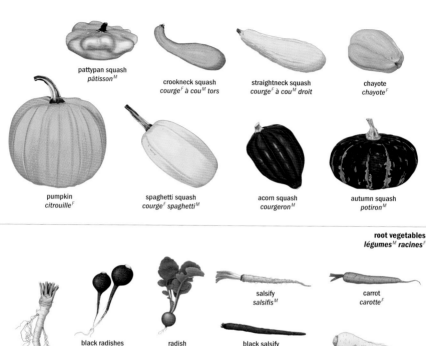

pattypan squash
pâtisson^M

crookneck squash
courge^F *à cou*^{M} *tors*

straightneck squash
courge^F *à cou*^{M} *droit*

chayote
chayote^F

pumpkin
citrouille^F

spaghetti squash
courge^F *spaghetti*^{M}

acorn squash
courgeron^M

autumn squash
potiron^M

root vegetables
légumes^M *racines*^{F}

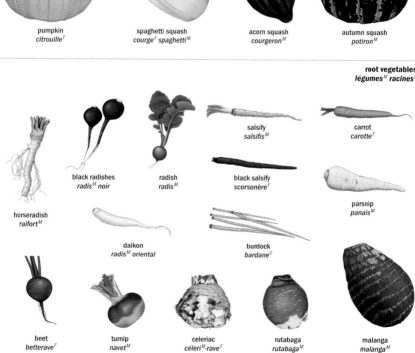

horseradish
raifort^M

black radishes
radis^M *noir*

radish
radis^M

salsify
salsifis^M

black salsify
scorsonère^F

carrot
carotte^F

parsnip
panais^M

daikon
radis^M *oriental*

burdock
bardane^F

beet
betterave^F

turnip
navet^M

celeriac
céleri^M-*rave*^{F}

rutabaga
rutabaga^M

malanga
malanga^M

FOOD AND KITCHEN

legumes
légumineuses^F

alfalfa sprouts
luzerne^F

lupines
lupin^M

peanut
arachide^F

lentils
lentilles^F

broad beans
fèves^F

peas
pois^M

dolichos beans
doliques^M

chick peas
pois^M *chiches*

split peas
pois^M *cassés*

black-eyed peas
dolique^M *à œil*^M *noir*

lablab beans
dolique^M *d'Égypte*^F

green peas
petits pois^M

snow peas
pois^M *mange-tout*^M

yard-long beans
dolique^M *asperge*^F

legumes

FOOD AND KITCHEN

beans
haricots^M

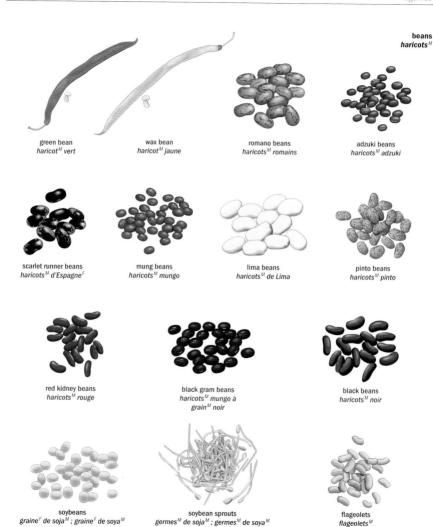

green bean
haricot^M *vert*

wax bean
haricot^M *jaune*

romano beans
haricots^M *romains*

adzuki beans
haricots^M *adzuki*

scarlet runner beans
haricots^M *d'Espagne*^F

mung beans
haricots^M *mungo*

lima beans
haricots^M *de Lima*

pinto beans
haricots^M *pinto*

red kidney beans
haricots^M *rouge*

black gram beans
haricots^M *mungo à*
grain^M *noir*

black beans
haricots^M *noir*

soybeans
graine^F *de soja*^M ; *graine*^F *de soya*^M

soybean sprouts
germes^M *de soja*^M ; *germes*^M *de soya*^M

flageolets
flageolets^M

fruits
fruits^M

berries
baies^F

currants
groseilles^F *à grappes*^F *;*
gadelle^F

black currants
cassis^M

gooseberries
groseilles^F *à maquereau*^M

grapes
raisins^M

blueberries
bleuets^M

bilberries
myrtilles^F

red whortleberries
airelles^F

alkekengi
alkékenge^M

cranberries
canneberges^F *; atoca*^M

raspberries
framboises^F

blackberries
mûres^F

strawberries
fraises^F

stone fruits
fruits^M *à noyau*^M

plums
prunes^F

peach
pêche^F

nectarine
nectarine^F

apricot
abricot^M

cherries
cerises^F

dates
dattes^F

dry fruits
fruits^M *secs*

macadamia nuts
noix^F *de macadamia*^M

ginkgo nuts
noix^F *de ginkgo*^M

pistachio nuts
pistaches^F

pine nuts
pignons^M

cola nuts
noix^F *de cola*^M

pecan nuts
noix^F *de pacane*^F

cashews
noix^F *de cajou*^M

almonds
amandes^F

hazelnuts
noisettes^F

walnut
noix^F

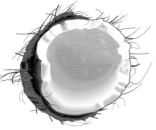

coconut
noix^F *de coco*^M

chestnuts
marrons^M

beechnut
faîne^F

Brazil nuts
noix^F *du Brésil*^M

pome fruits
fruits^M *à pépins*^M

pear
poire^F

quince
coing^M

apple
pomme^F

Japanese plums
nèfles^F *du Japon*^M

citrus fruits
agrumes^M

FOOD AND KITCHEN

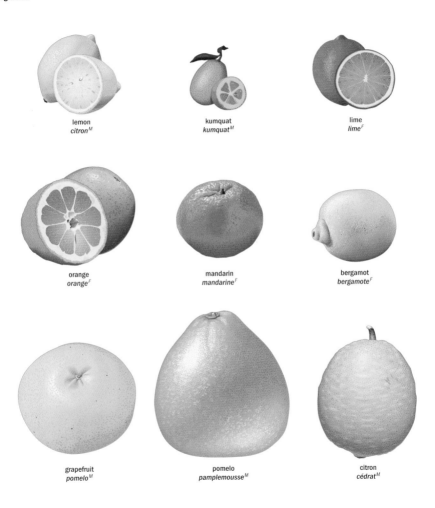

lemon
citron^M

kumquat
kumquat^M

lime
lime^F

orange
orange^F

mandarin
mandarine^F

bergamot
bergamote^F

grapefruit
pomelo^M

pomelo
pamplemousse^M

citron
cédrat^M

cantaloupe
cantaloup^M

casaba melon
melon^M *Casaba*

honeydew melon
melon^M *miel*^M

muskmelon
melon^M *brodé*

canary melon
melon^M *brésilien*

watermelon
pastèque^F

Ogen melon
melon^M *d'Ogen*

tropical fruits
fruits^M tropicaux

plantain
banane^F plantain^M

banana
banane^F

longan
longane^M

tamarillo
tamarillo^M

passion fruit
fruit^M de la Passion^F

horned melon
melon^M à cornes^F

mangosteen
mangoustan^M

kiwi
kiwi^M

pomegranate
grenade^F

cherimoya
chérimole^F

jackfruit
jaque^M

pineapple
ananas^M

jaboticabas
jaboticaba^M

litchi
litchi^M

fig
figue^F

Chinese dates
jujube^M

sapodilla
sapotille^F

guava
goyave^F

rambutan
ramboutan^M

Japanese persimmon
kaki^M

prickly pear
figue^F *de Barbarie*

carambola
carambole^F

Asian pear
pomme^F *poire*^F

mango
mangue^F

durian
durian^M

papaya
papaye^F

pepino
pepino^M

feijoa
feijoa^M

spices
épices^F

juniper berries
baies^F *de genièvre*^M

cloves
clou^M *de girofle*^M

allspice
piment^M *de la Jamaique*^F

white mustard
moutarde^F *blanche*

black mustard
moutarde^F *noire*

black pepper
poivre^M *noir*

white pepper
poivre^M *blanc*

pink pepper
poivre^M *rose*

green pepper
poivre^M *vert*

nutmeg
noix^F *de muscade*^F

caraway
carvi^M

cardamom
cardamome^F

cinnamon
cannelle^F

saffron
safran^M

cumin
cumin^M

curry
curry^M

turmeric
curcuma^M

fenugreek
fenugrec^M

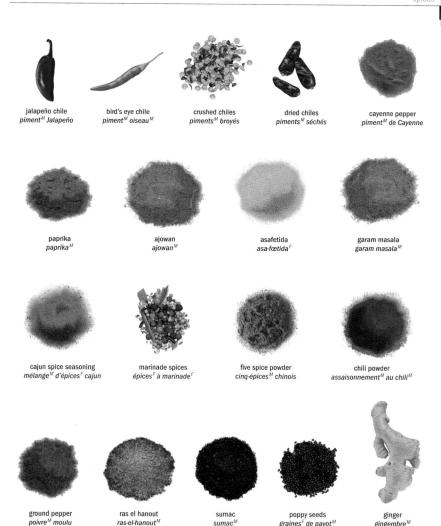

jalapeño chile
piment^M Jalapeño

bird's eye chile
piment^M oiseau^M

crushed chiles
piments^M broyés

dried chiles
piments^M séchés

cayenne pepper
piment^M de Cayenne

paprika
paprika^M

ajowan
ajowan^M

asafetida
asa-fœtida^F

garam masala
garam masala^M

cajun spice seasoning
mélange^M d'épices^F cajun

marinade spices
épices^F à marinade^F

five spice powder
cinq-épices^M chinois

chili powder
assaisonnement^M au chili^M

ground pepper
poivre^M moulu

ras el hanout
ras-el-hanout^M

sumac
sumac^M

poppy seeds
graines^F de pavot^M

ginger
gingembre^M

condiments
condiments ^M

Tabasco® sauce
sauce^F Tabasco®M

Worcestershire sauce
sauce^F Worcestershire

tamarind paste
pâte^F de tamarin^M

vanilla extract
extrait^M de vanille^F

tomato paste
concentré^M de tomate^F

tomato sauce
coulis^M de tomate^F

hummus
hoummos^M

tahini
tahini^M

hoisin sauce
sauce^F hoisin

soy sauce
sauce^F soja^M ; sauce^F soya^M

powdered mustard
moutarde^F en poudre^F

wholegrain mustard
moutarde^F à l'ancienne^F

Dijon mustard
moutarde^F de Dijon

German mustard
moutarde^F allemande

English mustard
moutarde^F anglaise

American mustard
moutarde^F américaine

plum sauce
sauce^F aux prunes^F

mango chutney
chutney^M à la mangue^F

harissa
harissa^F

sambal oelek
sambal oelek^M

ketchup
ketchup^M

wasabi
wasabi^M

table salt
sel^M fin

coarse salt
gros sel^M

sea salt
sel^M marin

balsamic vinegar
vinaigre^M balsamique

rice vinegar
vinaigre^M de riz^M

apple cider vinegar
vinaigre^M de cidre^M

malt vinegar
vinaigre^M de malt^M

wine vinegar
vinaigre^M de vin^M

herbs
fines herbes^F

dill
aneth^M

anise
anis^M

sweet bay
laurier^M

oregano
origan^M

tarragon
estragon^M

basil
basilic^M

sage
sauge^F

thyme
thym^M

mint
menthe^F

parsley
persil^M

chervil
cerfeuil^M

coriander
coriandre^F

rosemary
romarin^M

hyssop
hysope^F

borage
bourrache^F

lovage
livèche^F

savory
sarriette^F

lemon balm
mélisse^F

cereal
céréales^F

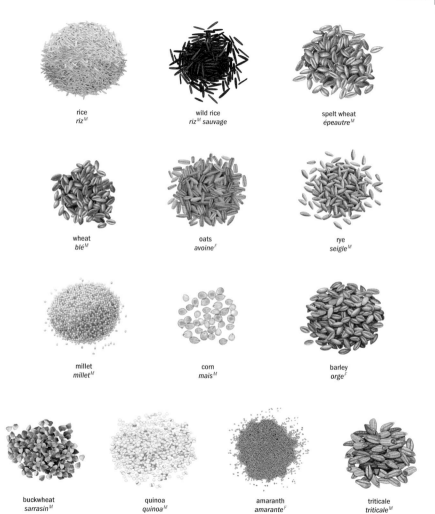

rice
riz^M

wild rice
riz^M *sauvage*

spelt wheat
épeautre^M

wheat
blé^M

oats
avoine^F

rye
seigle^M

millet
millet^M

corn
maïs^M

barley
orge^F

buckwheat
sarrasin^M

quinoa
quinoa^M

amaranth
amarante^F

triticale
triticale^M

cereal products
produits^M *céréaliers*

flour and semolina
farine^F **et semoule**^F

semolina
semoule^F

whole-wheat flour
farine^F *de blé*^M *complet ; farine*^F *de blé*^M *entier*

couscous
couscous^M

all-purpose flour
farine^F *tout usage*^M

unbleached flour
farine^F *non blanchie*

oat flour
farine^F *d'avoine*^F

corn flour
farine^F *de maïs*^M

bread
pain^M

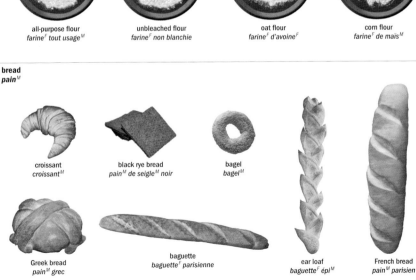

croissant
croissant^M

black rye bread
pain^M *de seigle*^M *noir*

bagel
bagel^M

Greek bread
pain^M *grec*

baguette
baguette^F *parisienne*

ear loaf
baguette^F *épi*^M

French bread
pain^M *parisien*

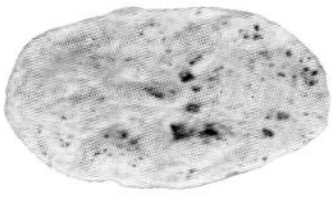

cereal products

chapati
pain^M chapati indien

tortillas
tortillas^F

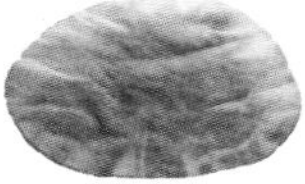

pita bread
pain^M pita

naan
pain^M naan indien

unleavened bread
pain^M azyme

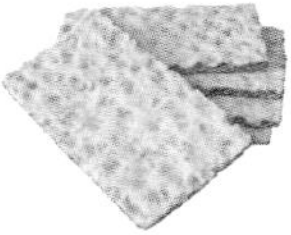

cracked rye bread
cracker^M de seigle^M

Scandinavian cracked bread
cracker^M scandinave

phyllo dough
pâte^F phyllo^F

Danish rye bread
pain^M de seigle^M danois

American corn bread
pain^M de maïs^M américain

multigrain bread
pain^M multicéréales

Russian pumpernickel
pain^M noir russe

German rye bread
pain^M de seigle^M allemand

challah
pain^M tchallah juif

white bread
pain^M blanc

wholemeal bread
pain^M complet

farmhouse bread
pain^M de campagne^F

Irish soda bread
pain^M irlandais

English loaf
pain^M de mie^F

cereal products

pasta
pâtes^F *alimentaires*

rigatoni
rigatoni^M

rotini
rotini^M

conchiglie
conchiglie^F

fusilli
fusilli^M

spaghetti
spaghetti^M

ditali
ditali^M

gnocchi
gnocchi^M

tortellini
tortellini^M

spaghettini
spaghettini^M

elbows
coudes^M

penne
penne^M

cannelloni
cannelloni^M

spaghettini
spaghettini^M

lasagna
lasagne^F

ravioli
ravioli^M

spinach tagliatelle
tagliatelle^M *aux épinards*^M

fettucine
fettucine^M

Asian noodles
nouilles^F asiatiques

soba noodles
nouilles^F soba

somen noodles
nouilles^F somen

udon noodles
nouilles^F udon

rice paper
galettes^F de riz^M

rice noodles
nouilles^F de riz^M

bean thread cellophane noodles
nouilles^F de haricots^M mungo

egg noodles
nouilles^F aux œufs^M

rice vermicelli
vermicelles^M de riz^M

won ton skins
pâtes^F won-ton

rice
riz^M

white rice
riz^M blanc

brown rice
riz^M complet

parboiled rice
riz^M étuvé

basmati rice
riz^M basmati

FOOD AND KITCHEN

coffee and infusions
café^M et infusions^F

coffee
café^M

green coffee beans
grains^M de café^M verts

roasted coffee beans
grains^M de café^M torréfiés

herbal teas
tisanes^F

linden
tilleul^M

chamomile
camomille^F

verbena
verveine^F

tea
thé^M

green tea
thé^M vert

black tea
thé^M noir

oolong tea
thé^M oolong

tea bag
thé^M en sachet^M

chocolate
chocolat^M

dark chocolate
chocolat^M noir

milk chocolate
chocolat^M au lait^M

cocoa
cacao^M

white chocolate
chocolat^M blanc

sugar
sucre^M

granulated sugar
sucre^M granulé

powdered sugar
sucre^M glace^F

brown sugar
cassonade^F

rock candy
sucre^M candi

molasses
mélasse^F

corn syrup
sirop^M de maïs^M

maple syrup
sirop^M d'érable^M

honey
miel^M

fats and oils
huiles^F et matières^F grasses

corn oil
huile^F de maïs^M

olive oil
huile^F d'olive^F

sunflower-seed oil
huile^F de tournesol^M

peanut oil
huile^F d'arachide^F

sesame oil
huile^F de sésame^M

shortening
saindoux^M

lard
lard^M

margarine
margarine^F

dairy products
produits^M laitiers

yogurt
yaourt^M ; yogourt^M

ghee
ghee^M

butter
beurre^M

whipping cream
crème^F épaisse ; crème^F à fouetter

sour cream
crème^F aigre ; crème^F sure

milk
lait^M

homogenized milk
lait^M homogénéisé

goat's milk
lait^M de chèvre^F

evaporated milk
lait^M concentré

buttermilk
babeurre^M

powdered milk
lait^M en poudre^F

fresh cheeses
fromages^M frais

cottage cheese
cottage^M

mozzarella
mozzarella^F

ricotta
ricotta^F

cream cheese
fromage^M à la crème^F

goat's-milk cheeses
fromages^M de chèvre^F

chèvre cheese
chèvre^M frais

Crottin de Chavignol
crottin^M de Chavignol

pressed cheeses
fromages^M *à pâte*^F *pressée*

Jarlsberg
jarlsberg^M

Emmenthal
emmenthal^M

raclette
raclette^F

Parmesan
parmesan^M

Gruyère
gruyère^M

Romano
romano^M

blue-veined cheeses
fromages^M *à pâte*^F *persillée*

Roquefort
roquefort^M

Stilton
stilton^M

Gorgonzola
gorgonzola^M

Danish Blue
bleu^M *danois*

soft cheeses
fromages^M *à pâte*^F *molle*

Pont-l'Évêque
pont-l'évêque^M

Coulommiers
coulommiers^M

Camembert
camembert^M

Brie
brie^M

Munster
munster^M

FOOD AND KITCHEN

meat
viande^F

FOOD AND KITCHEN

cuts of beef
découpes^F *de bœuf*^M

steak
bifteck^M

beef cubes
cubes^M *de bœuf*^M

ground beef
bœuf^M *haché*

shank
jarret^M

tenderloin roast
filet^M *de bœuf*^M

rib roast
rôti^M *de côtes*^F

back ribs
côtes^F *levées de dos*^M

cuts of veal
découpes^F *de veau*^M

veal cubes
cubes^M *de veau*^M

ground veal
veau^M *haché*

shank
jarret^M

roast
rôti^M

steak
bifteck^M

chop
côte^F

cuts of lamb
découpes^F d'agneau^M

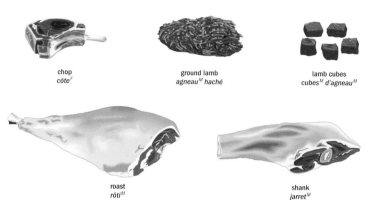

chop
côte^F

ground lamb
agneau^M haché

lamb cubes
cubes^M d'agneau^M

roast
rôti^M

shank
jarret^M

cuts of pork
découpes^F de porc^M

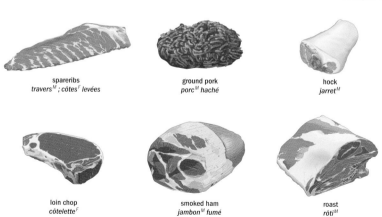

spareribs
travers^M ; côtes^F levées

ground pork
porc^M haché

hock
jarret^M

loin chop
côtelette^F

smoked ham
jambon^M fumé

roast
rôti^M

organ meat
abats^M

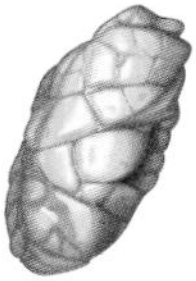

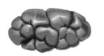

sweetbreads
ris^M

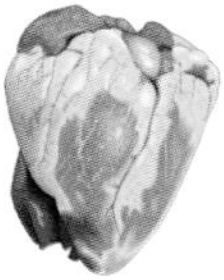

heart
cœur^M

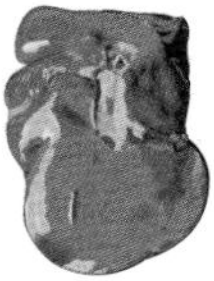

liver
foie^M

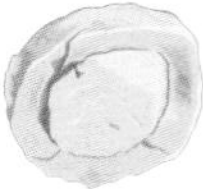

marrow
moelle^F

tongue
langue^F

kidney
rognons^M

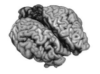

brains
cervelle^F

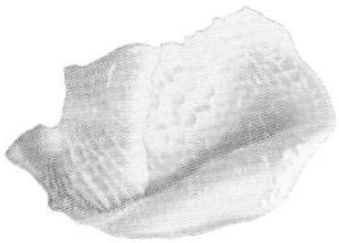

tripe
tripes^F

game
gibier^M

quail
caille^F

pigeon
pigeon^M

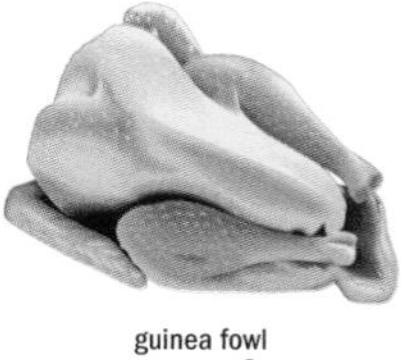

hare
lièvre^M

guinea fowl
pintade^F

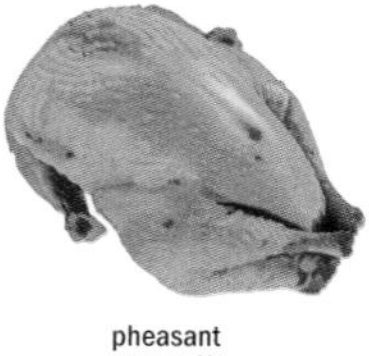

pheasant
faisan^M

rabbit
lapin^M

poultry
volaille^F

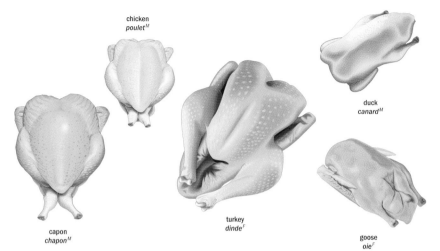

chicken
poulet^M

duck
canard^M

capon
chapon^M

turkey
dinde^F

goose
oie^F

eggs
œufs^M

ostrich egg
œuf^M *d'autruche*^F

goose egg
œuf^M *d'oie*^F

quail egg
œuf^M *de caille*^F

pheasant egg
œuf^M *de faisane*^F

duck egg
œuf^M *de cane*^F

hen egg
œuf^M *de poule*^F

delicatessen
charcuterie^F

rillettes
rillettes^F

foie gras
foie^M *gras*

prosciutto
prosciutto^M

kielbasa sausage
saucisson^M *kielbasa*

mortadella
mortadelle^F

blood sausage
boudin^M

chorizo
chorizo^M

pepperoni
pepperoni^M

Genoa salami
salami^M *de Gênes*

German salami
salami^M *allemand*

Toulouse sausages
saucisse^F *de Toulouse*

merguez sausages
merguez^F

andouillette
andouillette^F

chipolata sausage
chipolata^F

frankfurters
saucisse^F *de Francfort*

pancetta
pancetta^F

cooked ham
jambon^M *cuit*

American bacon
bacon^M *américain*

Canadian bacon
bacon^M *canadien*

mollusks
mollusques^M

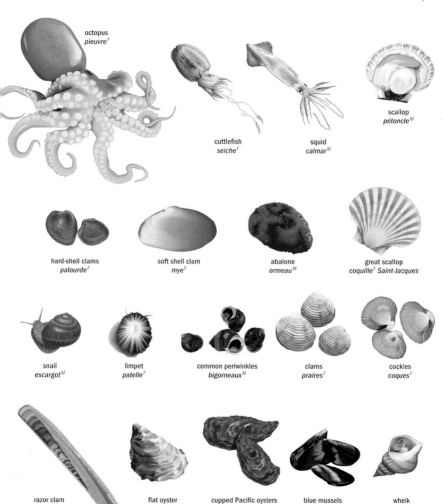

octopus
pieuvre^F

cuttlefish
seiche^F

squid
calmar^M

scallop
pétoncle^M

hard-shell clams
palourde^F

soft shell clam
mye^F

abalone
ormeau^M

great scallop
coquille^F *Saint-Jacques*

snail
escargot^M

limpet
patelle^F

common periwinkles
bigorneaux^M

clams
praires^F

cockles
coques^F

razor clam
couteau^M

flat oyster
huître^F *plate*

cupped Pacific oysters
huîtres^F *creuses du Pacifique*^M

blue mussels
moules^F

whelk
buccin^M

crustaceans
crustacés^M

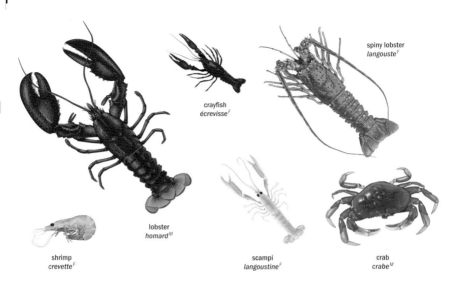

crayfish
écrevisse^F

spiny lobster
langouste^F

lobster
homard^M

shrimp
crevette^F

scampi
langoustine^F

crab
crabe^M

cartilaginous fishes
poissons^M *cartilagineux*

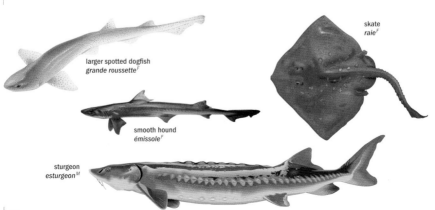

skate
raie^F

larger spotted dogfish
grande roussette^F

smooth hound
émissole^F

sturgeon
esturgeon^M

bony fishes
poissons^M osseux

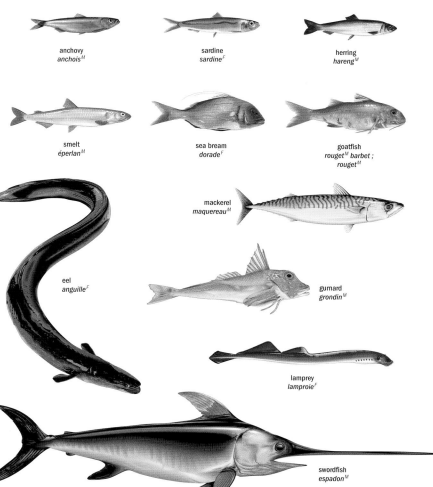

anchovy
anchois^M

sardine
sardine^F

herring
hareng^M

smelt
éperlan^M

sea bream
dorade^F

goatfish
rouget^M barbet ;
rouget^M

mackerel
maquereau^M

eel
anguille^F

gurnard
grondin^M

lamprey
lamproie^F

swordfish
espadon^M

bony fishes

bass
*perche^F truitée ;
achigan^M*

mullet
mulet^M

carp
carpe^F

perch
perche^F ; perchaude^F

shad
alose^F

pike
brochet^M

pike perch
sandre^M ; doré^M

bluefish
tassergal^M

sea bass
bar^M commun

monkfish
baudroie^F

tuna
thon^M

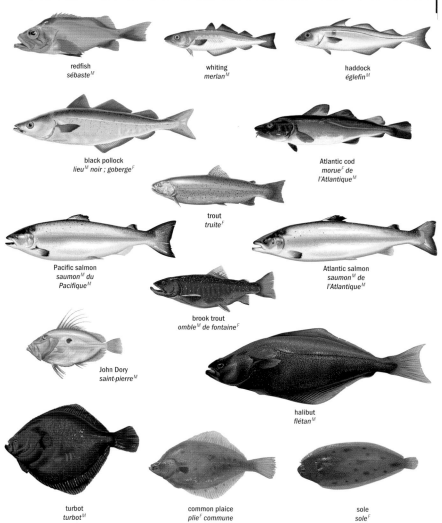

redfish
sébaste^M

whiting
merlan^M

haddock
églefin^M

black pollock
lieu^M *noir ; goberge*^F

Atlantic cod
morue^F *de
l'Atlantique*^M

trout
truite^F

Pacific salmon
saumon^M *du
Pacifique*^M

Atlantic salmon
saumon^M *de
l'Atlantique*^M

brook trout
omble^M *de fontaine*^F

John Dory
saint-pierre^M

halibut
flétan^M

turbot
turbot^M

common plaice
plie^F *commune*

sole
sole^F

packaging
emballage^M

pouch
sachet^M

parchment paper
papier^M sulfurisé

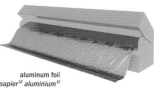

aluminum foil
papier^M aluminium^M

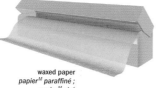

waxed paper
*papier^M paraffiné ;
papier^M ciré*

plastic film
(cellophane)
pellicule^F plastique

freezer bag
sac^M de congélation^F

egg carton
boîte^F à œufs^M

mesh bag
sac^M-filet^M

canisters
boîtes^F alimentaires

food tray
barquette^F

small crate
caissette^F

small open crate
cageot^M

FOOD AND KITCHEN

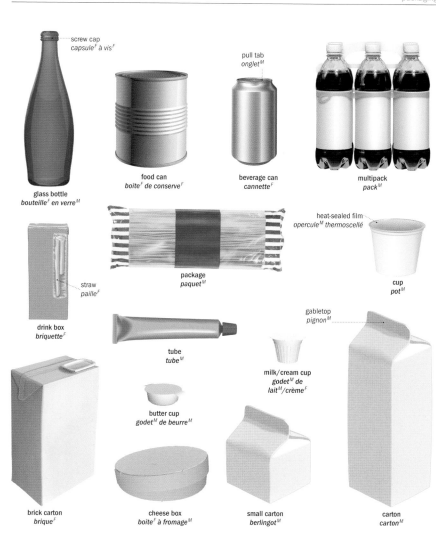

screw cap
capsule^F à vis^F

glass bottle
bouteille^F en verre^M

food can
boîte^F de conserve^F

pull tab
onglet^M

beverage can
cannette^F

multipack
pack^M

package
paquet^M

heat-sealed film
opercule^M thermoscellé

cup
pot^M

straw
paille^F

drink box
briquette^F

tube
tube^M

gabletop
pignon^M

milk/cream cup
*godet^M de
lait^M/crème^F*

butter cup
godet^M de beurre^M

brick carton
brique^F

cheese box
boîte^F à fromage^M

small carton
berlingot^M

carton
carton^M

kitchen
cuisine^F

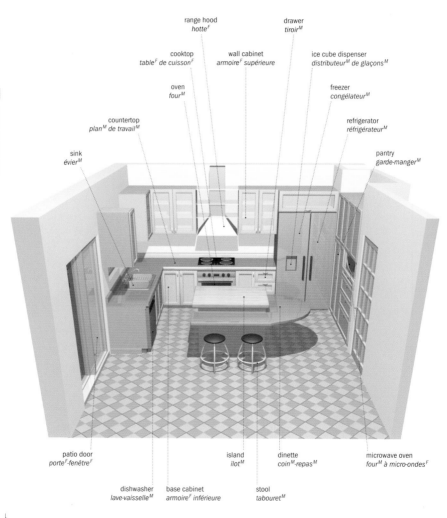

range hood
hotte^F

drawer
tiroir^M

cooktop
table^F *de cuisson*^F

wall cabinet
armoire^F *supérieure*

ice cube dispenser
distributeur^M *de glaçons*^M

oven
four^M

freezer
congélateur^M

countertop
plan^M *de travail*^M

refrigerator
réfrigérateur^M

sink
évier^M

pantry
garde-manger^M

patio door
porte^F-*fenêtre*^F

island
îlot^M

dinette
coin^M-*repas*^M

microwave oven
four^M *à micro-ondes*^F

dishwasher
lave-vaisselle^M

base cabinet
armoire^F *inférieure*

stool
tabouret^M

glassware
verres M

liqueur glass
verre M *à liqueur* F

port glass
verre M *à porto* M

sparkling wine glass
coupe F *à mousseux* M

brandy snifter
verre M *à cognac* M

Alsace glass
verre M *à vin* M *d'Alsace* F

burgundy glass
verre M *à bourgogne* M

bordeaux glass
verre M *à bordeaux* M

white wine glass
verre M *à vin* M *blanc*

water goblet
verre M *à eau* F

cocktail glass
verre M *à cocktail* M

highball glass
verre M *à gin* M

old-fashioned glass
verre M *à whisky* M

beer mug
chope F *à bière* F

champagne flute
flûte F *à champagne* M

small decanter
carafon M

decanter
carafe F

dinnerware

vaisselle[F]

demitasse
tasse[F] *à café*[M]

cup
tasse[F] *à thé*[M]

coffee mug
chope[F] *à café*[M]

creamer
crémier[M]

sugar bowl
sucrier[M]

salt shaker
salière[F]

pepper shaker
poivrière[F]

gravy boat
saucière[F]

butter dish
beurrier[M]

ramekin
ramequin[M]

soup bowl
bol[M]

rim soup bowl
assiette[F] *creuse*

dinner plate
assiette[F] *plate*

salad plate
assiette[F] *à salade*[F]

bread and butter plate
assiette[F] *à dessert*[M]

teapot
théière[F]

platter
plat[M] *ovale*

vegetable bowl
légumier[M]

fish platter
plat[M] *à poisson*[M]

hors d'oeuvre dish
ravier[M]

water pitcher
pichet[M]

salad bowl
saladier[M]

salad dish
bol[M] *à salade*[F]

soup tureen
soupière[F]

silverware
couvert^M

knife
couteau ^M

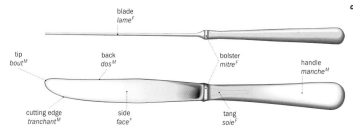

blade
lame^F

tip
bout^M

back
dos^M

bolster
mitre^F

handle
manche^M

cutting edge
tranchant^M

side
face^F

tang
soie^F

fork
fourchette ^F

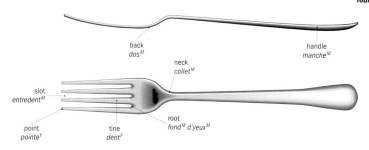

back
dos^M

handle
manche^M

neck
collet^M

slot
entredent^M

point
pointe^F

tine
dent^F

root
fond^M *d'yeux*^M

spoon
cuiller ^F

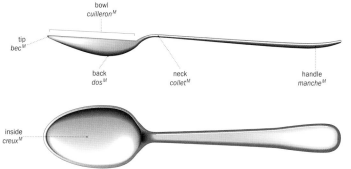

bowl
cuilleron^M

tip
bec^M

back
dos^M

neck
collet^M

handle
manche^M

inside
creux^M

silverware

examples of forks
exemples^M de fourchettes^F

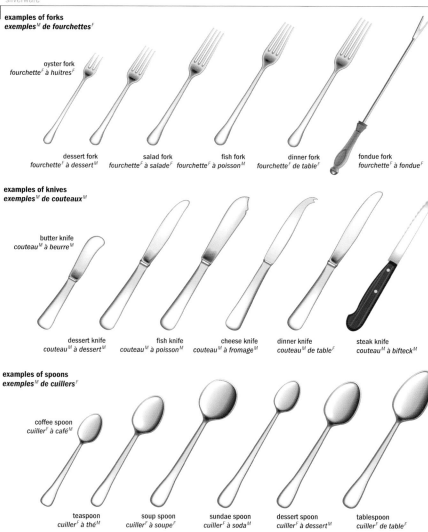

oyster fork
fourchette^F à huîtres^F

dessert fork
fourchette^F à dessert^M

salad fork
fourchette^F à salade^F

fish fork
fourchette^F à poisson^M

dinner fork
fourchette^F de table^F

fondue fork
fourchette^F à fondue^F

examples of knives
exemples^M de couteaux^M

butter knife
couteau^M à beurre^M

dessert knife
couteau^M à dessert^M

fish knife
couteau^M à poisson^M

cheese knife
couteau^M à fromage^M

dinner knife
couteau^M de table^F

steak knife
couteau^M à bifteck^M

examples of spoons
exemples^M de cuillers^F

coffee spoon
cuiller^F à café^M

teaspoon
cuiller^F à thé^M

soup spoon
cuiller^F à soupe^F

sundae spoon
cuiller^F à soda^M

dessert spoon
cuiller^F à dessert^M

tablespoon
cuiller^F de table^F

FOOD AND KITCHEN

kitchen utensils
ustensiles^M *de cuisine*^F

kitchen knife
couteau^M *de cuisine*^F

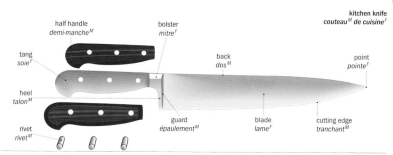

half handle
demi-manche^M

bolster
mitre^F

tang
soie^F

back
dos^M

point
pointe^F

heel
talon^M

rivet
rivet^M

guard
épaulement^M

blade
lame^F

cutting edge
tranchant^M

examples of utensils for cutting
exemples^M *de couteaux*^M *de cuisine*^F

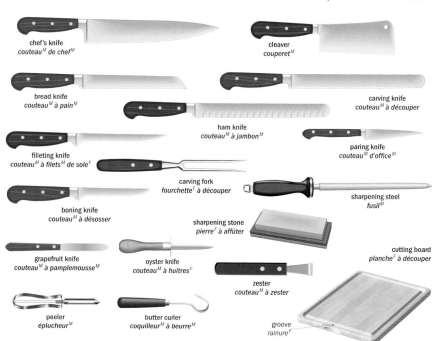

chef's knife
couteau^M *de chef*^M

cleaver
couperet^M

bread knife
couteau^M *à pain*^M

carving knife
couteau^M *à découper*

ham knife
couteau^M *à jambon*^M

paring knife
couteau^M *d'office*^M

filleting knife
couteau^M *à filets*^M *de sole*^F

carving fork
fourchette^F *à découper*

sharpening steel
fusil^M

boning knife
couteau^M *à désosser*

sharpening stone
pierre^F *à affûter*

grapefruit knife
couteau^M *à pamplemousse*^M

oyster knife
couteau^M *à huitres*^F

zester
couteau^M *à zester*

cutting board
planche^F *à découper*

peeler
éplucheur^M

butter curler
coquilleur^M *à beurre*^M

groove
rainure^F

kitchen utensils

for opening
pour ouvrir

can opener
ouvre-boîtes[M]

bottle opener
décapsuleur[M]

waiter's corkscrew
tire-bouchon[M] *de sommelier*[M]

lever corkscrew
tire-bouchon[M] *à levier*[M]

for grinding and grating
pour broyer et râper

nutcracker
casse-noix[M]

mortar
mortier[M]

pestle
pilon[M]

meat grinder
hachoir[M]

garlic press
presse-ail[M]

citrus juicer
presse-agrumes[M]

nutmeg grater
râpe[F] *à muscade*[F]

grater
râpe[F]

rotary cheese grater
râpe[F] *à fromage*[M]
cylindrique

pusher
poussoir[M]

crank
manivelle[F]

drum
tambour[M]

handle
poignée[F]

pasta maker
machine[F] *à faire les pâtes*[F]

food mill
moulin[M] *à légumes*[M]

mandoline
mandoline[F]

FOOD AND KITCHEN

for measuring
pour mesurer

measuring spoons
cuillers^F doseuses

measuring cups
mesures^F

candy thermometer
thermomètre^M à sucre^M

measuring cup
tasse^F à mesurer

meat thermometer
thermomètre^M à viande^F

oven thermometer
thermomètre^M de four^M

instant-read thermometer
thermomètre^M à mesure^F instantanée

measuring beaker
verre^M à mesurer

kitchen timer
minuteur^M

egg timer
sablier^M

kitchen scale
balance^F de cuisine^F

for straining and draining
pour passer et égoutter

mesh strainer
passoire^F fine

muslin
mousseline^F

chinois
chinois^M

funnel
entonnoir^M

colander
passoire^F

fry basket
panier^M à friture^F

sieve
tamis^M

salad spinner
essoreuse^F à salade^F

FOOD AND KITCHEN

baking utensils
pour la pâtisserie^F

icing syringe
piston^M *à décorer*

pastry cutting wheel
roulette^F *de pâtissier*^M

pastry brush
pinceau^M *à pâtisserie*^F

egg beater
batteur^M *à œufs*^M

whisk
fouet^M

sifter
tamis^M *à farine*^F

cookie cutters
emporte-pièces^M

dredger
saupoudreuse^F

pastry blender
mélangeur^M *à
pâtisserie*^F

pastry bag and nozzles
poche^F *à douilles*^F

mixing bowls
bols^M *à mélanger*

rolling pin
rouleau^M *à pâtisserie*^F

baking sheet
plaque^F *à pâtisserie*^F

muffin pan
moule^M *à muffins*^M

soufflé dish
moule^M *à soufflé*^M

charlotte mold
moule^M *à charlotte*^F

spring-form pan
moule^M *à fond*^M *amovible*

pie pan
moule^M *à tarte*^F

quiche plate
moule^M *à quiche*^F

cake pan
moule^M *à gâteau*^M

set of utensils
jeu^M d'ustensiles^M

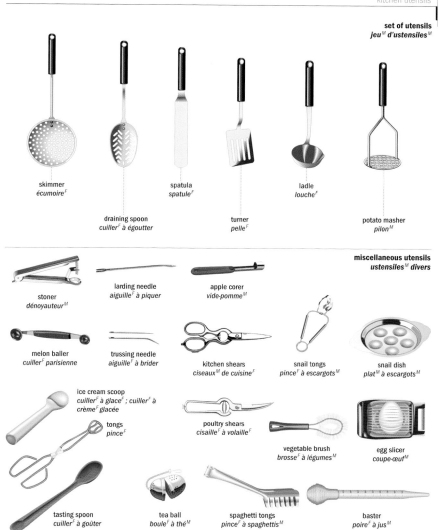

skimmer
écumoire^F

draining spoon
cuiller^F à égoutter

spatula
spatule^F

turner
pelle^F

ladle
louche^F

potato masher
pilon^M

miscellaneous utensils
ustensiles^M divers

stoner
dénoyauteur^M

larding needle
aiguille^F à piquer

apple corer
vide-pomme^M

melon baller
cuiller^F parisienne

trussing needle
aiguille^F à brider

kitchen shears
ciseaux^M de cuisine^F

snail tongs
pince^F à escargots^M

snail dish
plat^M à escargots^M

ice cream scoop
*cuiller^F à glace^F ; cuiller^F à
crème^F glacée*

tongs
pince^F

poultry shears
cisaille^F à volaille^F

vegetable brush
brosse^F à légumes^M

egg slicer
coupe-œuf^M

tasting spoon
cuiller^F à goûter

tea ball
boule^F à thé^M

spaghetti tongs
pince^F à spaghettis^M

baster
poire^F à jus^M

cooking utensils

batterie^F de cuisine^F

wok set
wok^M

lid
couvercle^M

rack
grille^F

wok
wok^M

burner ring
collier^M

tagine
tajine^M

fondue set
service^M à fondue^F

fondue pot
caquelon^M

stand
support^M

burner
réchaud^M

fish poacher
poissonnière^F

rack
grille^F

lid
couvercle^M

dripping pan
lèchefrite^F

terrine
terrine^F

roasting pans
plats^M à rôtir

pressure cooker
autocuiseur^M

pressure regulator
régulateur^M de pression^F

safety valve
soupape^F

Dutch oven
faitout^M

stock pot
marmite^F

couscous kettle
couscoussier^M

frying pan
poêle^F *à frire*

steamer
cuit-vapeur^M

egg poacher
pocheuse^F

sauté pan
sauteuse^F

small saucepan
poêlon^M

diable
diable^M

crêpe pan
poêle^F *à crêpes*^F

steamer basket
panier^M *cuit-vapeur*^M

double boiler
bain-marie^M

saucepan
casserole^F

domestic appliances
appareils^M électroménagers

FOOD AND KITCHEN

for mixing and blending
pour mélanger et battre

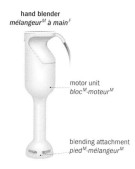

hand blender
mélangeur^M à main^F

motor unit
bloc^M-moteur^M

blending attachment
pied^M-mélangeur^M

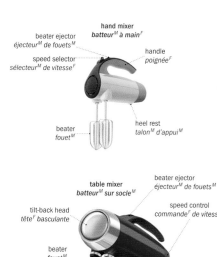

hand mixer
batteur^M à main^F

beater ejector
éjecteur^M de fouets^M

speed selector
sélecteur^M de vitesse^F

handle
poignée^F

beater
fouet^M

heel rest
talon^M d'appui^M

blender
mélangeur^M

cap
bouchon^M

container
récipient^M

cutting blade
couteau^M

motor unit
bloc^M-moteur^M

control button
touche^F de commande^F

table mixer
batteur^M sur socle^M

beater ejector
éjecteur^M de fouets^M

tilt-back head
tête^F basculante

speed control
commande^F de vitesse^F

beater
fouet^M

mixing bowl
bol^M

turntable
plateau^M tournant

stand
socle^M

beaters
fouets^M

four blade beater
fouet^M quatre pales^F

spiral beater
fouet^M en spirale^F

wire beater
fouet^M à fil^M

dough hook
crochet^M pétrisseur

domestic appliances

food processor
robot^M de cuisine^F

for cutting
pour couper

feed tube
entonnoir^M

lid
couvercle^M

bowl
bol^M

spindle
arbre^M

blade
couteau^M

handle
poignée^F

disks
disques^M

motor unit
bloc^M-moteur^M

for juicing
pour presser

electric knife
couteau^M électrique

power cord
cordon^M d'alimentation^F

blade
lame^F

on-off switch
interrupteur^M

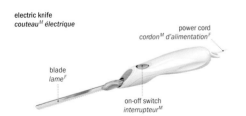

citrus juicer
presse-agrumes^M

reamer
toupie^F

strainer
passoire^F

bowl with serving spout
bol^M verseur

motor unit
bloc^M-moteur^M

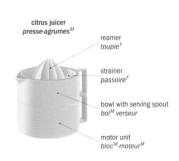

domestic appliances

for cooking
pour cuire

microwave oven
four^M à micro-ondes^F

door
porte^F

window
hublot^M

clock timer
horloge^F programmatrice

control panel
tableau^M de commande^F

latch
loquet^M

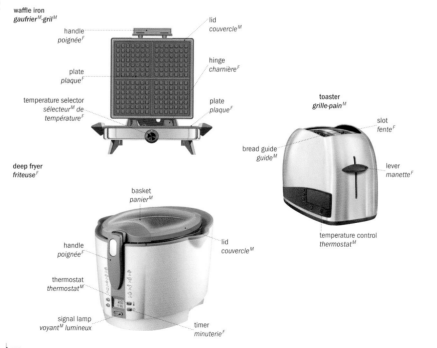

waffle iron
gaufrier^M-gril^M

handle
poignée^F

lid
couvercle^M

plate
plaque^F

hinge
charnière^F

temperature selector
sélecteur^M de température^F

plate
plaque^F

toaster
grille-pain^M

slot
fente^F

bread guide
guide^M

lever
manette^F

deep fryer
friteuse^F

basket
panier^M

handle
poignée^F

lid
couvercle^M

thermostat
thermostat^M

temperature control
thermostat^M

signal lamp
voyant^M lumineux

timer
minuterie^F

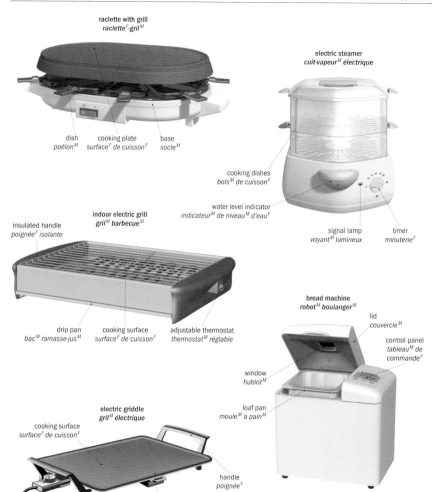

raclette with grill
raclette^F-gril^M

electric steamer
cuit-vapeur^M électique

dish
poêlon^M

cooking plate
surface^F de cuisson^F

base
socle^M

cooking dishes
bols^M de cuisson^F

water level indicator
indicateur^M de niveau^M d'eau^F

signal lamp
voyant^M lumineux

timer
minuterie^F

indoor electric grill
gril^M barbecue^M

insulated handle
poignée^F isolante

drip pan
bac^M ramasse-jus^M

cooking surface
surface^F de cuisson^F

adjustable thermostat
thermostat^M réglable

bread machine
robot^M boulanger^M

lid
couvercle^M

control panel
tableau^M de commande^F

window
hublot^M

loaf pan
moule^M à pain^M

electric griddle
gril^M électrique

cooking surface
surface^F de cuisson^F

handle
poignée^F

detachable control
commande^F amovible

grease well
collecteur^M de graisse^F

FOOD AND KITCHEN

179

miscellaneous domestic appliances
appareils^M électroménagers divers

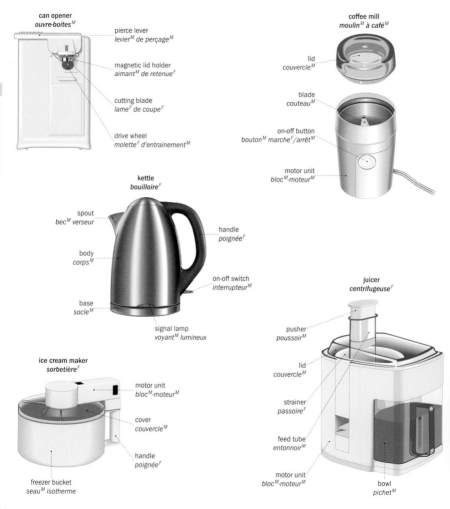

can opener
ouvre-boîtes^M

pierce lever
levier^M de perçage^M

magnetic lid holder
aimant^M de retenue^F

cutting blade
lame^F de coupe^F

drive wheel
molette^F d'entraînement^M

coffee mill
moulin^M à café^M

lid
couvercle^M

blade
couteau^M

on-off button
bouton^M marche^F/arrêt^M

motor unit
bloc^M-moteur^M

kettle
bouilloire^F

spout
bec^M verseur

handle
poignée^F

body
corps^M

on-off switch
interrupteur^M

base
socle^M

signal lamp
voyant^M lumineux

juicer
centrifugeuse^F

pusher
poussoir^M

lid
couvercle^M

strainer
passoire^F

feed tube
entonnoir^M

motor unit
bloc^M-moteur^M

bowl
pichet^M

ice cream maker
sorbetière^F

motor unit
bloc^M-moteur^M

cover
couvercle^M

handle
poignée^F

freezer bucket
seau^M isotherme

coffee makers
cafetières^F

automatic drip coffee maker
cafetière^F *filtre*^M

reservoir
réservoir^M

water level
niveau^M *d'eau*^F

signal lamp
voyant^M *lumineux*

on-off switch
interrupteur^M

lid
couvercle^M

basket
panier^M

carafe
verseuse^F

warming plate
plaque^F *chauffante*

Neapolitan coffee maker
cafetière^F *napolitaine*

espresso machine
machine^F *à espresso*^M

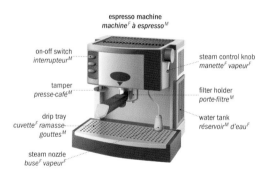

on-off switch
interrupteur^M

tamper
presse-café^M

drip tray
cuvette^F *ramasse-gouttes*^M

steam nozzle
buse^F *vapeur*^F

steam control knob
manette^F *vapeur*^F

filter holder
porte-filtre^M

water tank
réservoir^M *d'eau*^F

vacuum coffee maker
cafetière^F *à infusion*^F

upper bowl
tulipe^F

stem
tige^F

lower bowl
ballon^M

French press
cafetière^F *à piston*^M

espresso maker
cafetière^F *espresso*^M

percolator
percolateur^M

spout
bec^M *verseur*

signal light
voyant^M *lumineux*

exterior of a house

extérieur^M d'une maison^F

HOUSE

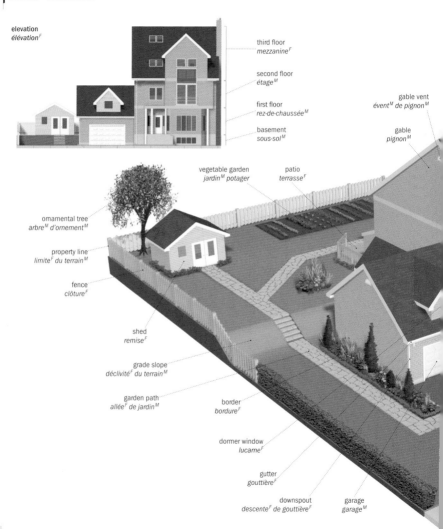

elevation
élévation^F

third floor
mezzanine^F

second floor
étage^M

first floor
rez-de-chaussée^M

basement
sous-sol^M

gable vent
évent^M de pignon^M

gable
pignon^M

vegetable garden
jardin^M potager

patio
terrasse^F

ornamental tree
arbre^M d'ornement^M

property line
limite^F du terrain^M

fence
clôture^F

shed
remise^F

grade slope
déclivité^F du terrain^M

garden path
allée^F de jardin^M

border
bordure^F

dormer window
lucarne^F

gutter
gouttière^F

downspout
descente^F de gouttière^F

garage
garage^M

skylight
lanterneau^M

lightning rod
paratonnerre^M

chimney pot
mitron^M

chimney
cheminée^F

roof
toit^M

cornice
corniche^F

steps
perron^M

basement window
fenêtre^F *de sous-sol*^M

hedge
haie^F

lawn
pelouse^F

flower bed
massif^M

sidewalk
trottoir^M

porch
porche^M

driveway
entrée^F *de garage*^M

site plan
plan^M *du terrain*^M

HOUSE

pool
piscine F

hot tub
spa M

above-ground swimming pool
piscine F *hors sol* M

skimmer
skimmer M ; *écumeur* M *de
surface* F

filter
filtre M

pump
pompe F

upright
montant M

wall
mur M

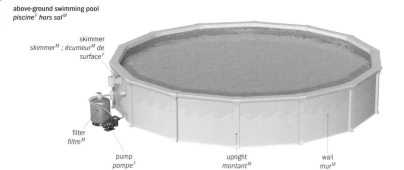

in-ground swimming pool
piscine F *enterrée ; piscine* F *creusée*

underwater light
projecteur M *sous-marin*

main drain
bonde F *de fond* M

diving board
tremplin M

discharge outlet
buse F *de refoulement* M

ladder
échelle F

steps
escalier M

deep end
fosse F *à plonger*

skimmer
skimmer M ; *écumeur* M *de surface* F

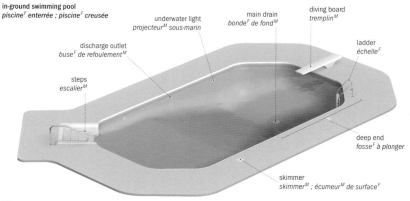

exterior door
porte^F extérieure

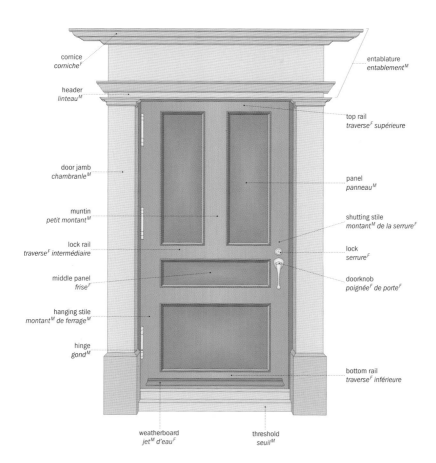

cornice
corniche^F

entablature
entablement^M

header
linteau^M

top rail
traverse^F supérieure

door jamb
chambranle^M

panel
panneau^M

muntin
petit montant^M

shutting stile
montant^M de la serrure^F

lock rail
traverse^F intermédiaire

lock
serrure^F

middle panel
frise^F

doorknob
poignée^F de porte^F

hanging stile
montant^M de ferrage^M

hinge
gond^M

bottom rail
traverse^F inférieure

weatherboard
jet^M d'eau^F

threshold
seuil^M

lock
serrure^F

general view
vue^F **d'ensemble**^M

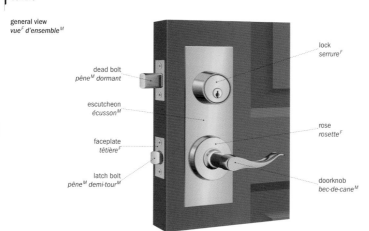

lock
serrure^F

dead bolt
pêne^M *dormant*

escutcheon
écusson^M

rose
rosette^F

faceplate
têtière^F

latch bolt
pêne^M *demi-tour*^M

doorknob
bec-de-cane^M

window
fenêtre^F

structure
structure^F

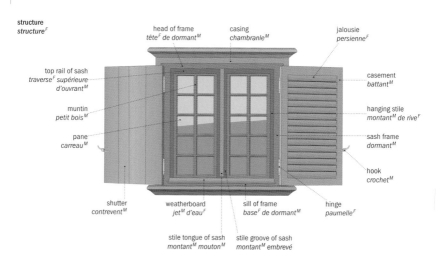

head of frame
tête^F *de dormant*^M

casing
chambranle^M

jalousie
persienne^F

top rail of sash
traverse^F *supérieure*
d'ouvrant^M

casement
battant^M

muntin
petit bois^M

hanging stile
montant^M *de rive*^F

pane
carreau^M

sash frame
dormant^M

hook
crochet^M

shutter
contrevent^M

weatherboard
jet^M *d'eau*^F

sill of frame
base^F *de dormant*^M

hinge
paumelle^F

stile tongue of sash
montant^M *mouton*^M

stile groove of sash
montant^M *embrevé*

frame
charpente[F]

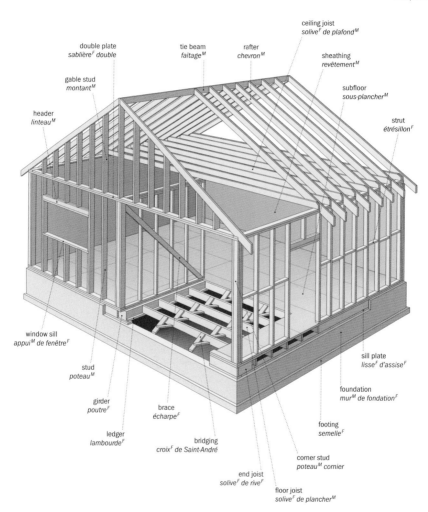

ceiling joist
solive[F] *de plafond*[M]

double plate
sablière[F] *double*

tie beam
faitage[M]

rafter
chevron[M]

sheathing
revêtement[M]

gable stud
montant[M]

subfloor
sous-plancher[M]

header
linteau[M]

strut
étrésillon[F]

window sill
appui[M] *de fenêtre*[F]

sill plate
lisse[F] *d'assise*[F]

stud
poteau[M]

foundation
mur[M] *de fondation*[F]

girder
poutre[F]

brace
écharpe[F]

footing
semelle[F]

ledger
lambourde[F]

bridging
croix[F] *de Saint-André*

corner stud
poteau[M] *cornier*

end joist
solive[F] *de rive*[F]

floor joist
solive[F] *de plancher*[M]

main rooms
principales pièces^F d'une maison^F

first floor
rez-de-chaussée^M

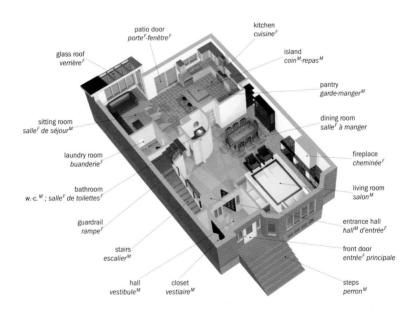

patio door
porte^F-fenêtre^F

kitchen
cuisine^F

glass roof
verrière^F

island
coin^M-repas^M

pantry
garde-manger^M

sitting room
salle^F de séjour^M

dining room
salle^F à manger

laundry room
buanderie^F

fireplace
cheminée^F

bathroom
w.-c.^M ; salle^F de toilettes^F

living room
salon^M

guardrail
rampe^F

entrance hall
hall^M d'entrée^F

stairs
escalier^M

front door
entrée^F principale

hall
vestibule^M

closet
vestiaire^M

steps
perron^M

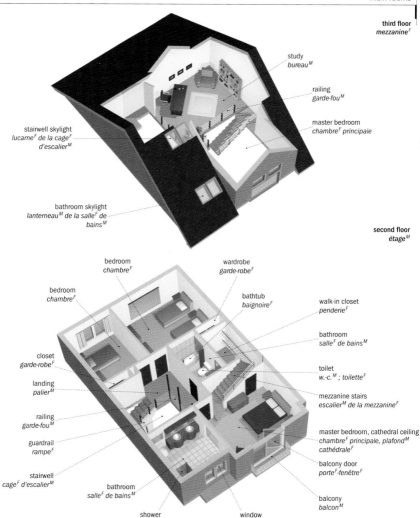

third floor
mezzanine^F

study
bureau^M

railing
garde-fou^M

stairwell skylight
lucarne^F de la cage^F
d'escalier^M

master bedroom
chambre^F principale

bathroom skylight
lanterneau^M de la salle^F de
bains^M

second floor
étage^M

bedroom
chambre^F

wardrobe
garde-robe^F

bedroom
chambre^F

bathtub
baignoire^F

walk-in closet
penderie^F

bathroom
salle^F de bains^M

closet
garde-robe^F

toilet
w.-c.^M ; toilette^F

landing
palier^M

mezzanine stairs
escalier^M de la mezzanine^F

railing
garde-fou^M

master bedroom, cathedral ceiling
chambre^F principale, plafond^M
cathédrale^F

guardrail
rampe^F

balcony door
porte^F-fenêtre^F

stairwell
cage^F d'escalier^M

bathroom
salle^F de bains^M

balcony
balcon^M

shower
douche^F

window
fenêtre^F

HOUSE

wood flooring
parquet[M]

HOUSE

wood flooring on cement screed
parquet[M] *sur chape*[F] *de ciment*[M]

floorboard
lamelle[F]

insulating material
isolant[M]

cement screed
chape[F]

glue
colle[F]

wood flooring on wooden structure
parquet[M] *sur ossature*[F] *de bois*[M]

floorboard
lame[F]

subfloor
sous-plancher[M]

joist
solive[F]

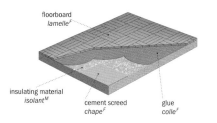
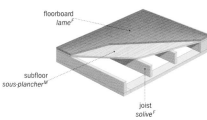

wood flooring arrangements
***arrangements*[M] *des parquets*[M]**

overlay flooring
parquet[M] *à coupe*[F] *perdue*

strip flooring with alternate joints
parquet[M] *à coupe*[F] *de pierre*[F]

herringbone parquet
parquet[M] *à bâtons*[M] *rompus*

herringbone pattern
parquet[M] *en chevrons*[M]

inlaid parquet
parquet[M] *mosaïque*[F]

basket weave pattern
parquet[M] *en vannerie*[F]

Arenberg parquet
parquet[M] *d'Arenberg*

Chantilly parquet
parquet[M] *Chantilly*

Versailles parquet
parquet[M] *Versailles*

textile floor coverings
revêtements[M] *de sol*[M] *textiles*

rug
tapis[M]

pile carpet
moquette[F]

pile
velours[M]

underlay
sous-couche[F]

tackless strip
bande[F] *d'ancrage*[M]

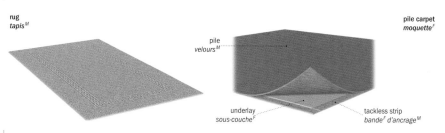

stairs
escalier^M

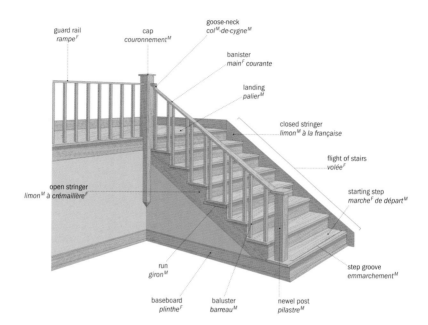

guard rail
rampe^F

cap
couronnement^M

goose-neck
col^M-de-cygne^M

banister
main^F courante

landing
palier^M

closed stringer
limon^M à la française

flight of stairs
volée^F

open stringer
limon^M à crémaillère^F

starting step
marche^F de départ^M

run
giron^M

step groove
emmarchement^M

baseboard
plinthe^F

baluster
barreau^M

newel post
pilastre^M

step
marche^F

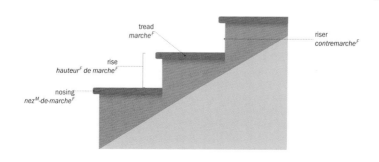

tread
marche^F

riser
contremarche^F

rise
hauteur^F de marche^F

nosing
nez^M-de-marche^F

wood burning
chauffage^M au bois^M

HOUSE

fireplace
cheminée^F à foyer^M
ouvert

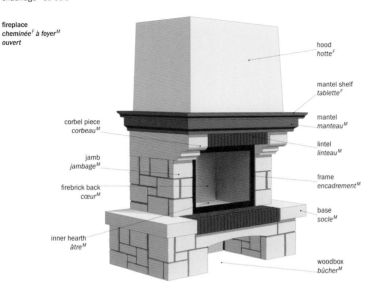

hood
hotte^F

mantel shelf
tablette^F

corbel piece
corbeau^M

mantel
manteau^M

jamb
jambage^M

lintel
linteau^M

firebrick back
cœur^M

frame
encadrement^M

base
socle^M

inner hearth
âtre^M

woodbox
bûcher^M

slow-burning wood stove
poêle^M à combustion^F lente

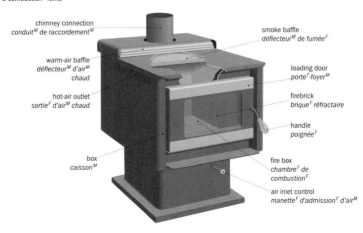

chimney connection
conduit^M de raccordement^M

smoke baffle
déflecteur^M de fumée^F

warm-air baffle
déflecteur^M d'air^M chaud

loading door
porte^F-foyer^M

hot-air outlet
sortie^F d'air^M chaud

firebrick
brique^F réfractaire

handle
poignée^F

box
caisson^M

fire box
chambre^F de combustion^F

air inlet control
manette^F d'admission^F d'air^M

HOUSE

chimney
cheminée^F

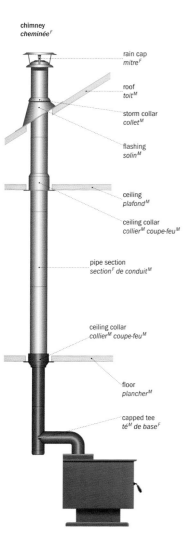

rain cap
mitre^F

roof
toit^M

storm collar
collet^M

flashing
solin^M

ceiling
plafond^M

ceiling collar
collier^M *coupe-feu*^M

pipe section
section^F *de conduit*^M

ceiling collar
collier^M *coupe-feu*^M

floor
plancher^M

capped tee
té^M *de base*^F

fire irons
accessoires^M *de foyer*^M

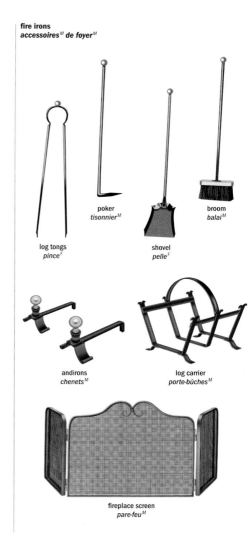

poker
tisonnier^M

broom
balai^M

log tongs
pince^F

shovel
pelle^F

andirons
chenets^M

log carrier
porte-bûches^M

fireplace screen
pare-feu^M

plumbing system
circuit^M *de plomberie*^F

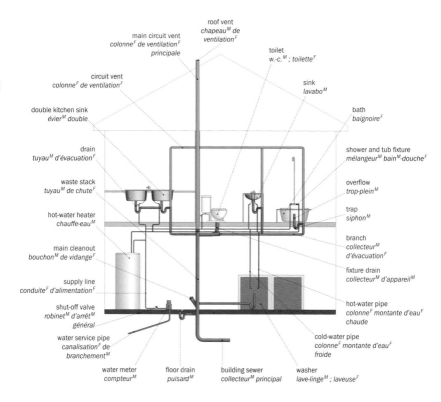

roof vent
chapeau^M *de ventilation*^F

main circuit vent
colonne^F *de ventilation*^F *principale*

toilet
w.-c.^M *; toilette*^F

circuit vent
colonne^F *de ventilation*^F

sink
lavabo^M

double kitchen sink
évier^M *double*

bath
baignoire^F

drain
tuyau^M *d'évacuation*^F

shower and tub fixture
mélangeur^M *bain*^M*-douche*^F

waste stack
tuyau^M *de chute*^F

overflow
trop-plein^M

hot-water heater
chauffe-eau^M

trap
siphon^M

main cleanout
bouchon^M *de vidange*^F

branch
collecteur^M *d'évacuation*^F

supply line
conduite^F *d'alimentation*^F

fixture drain
collecteur^M *d'appareil*^M

shut-off valve
robinet^M *d'arrêt*^M *général*

hot-water pipe
colonne^F *montante d'eau*^F *chaude*

water service pipe
canalisation^F *de branchement*^M

cold-water pipe
colonne^F *montante d'eau*^F *froide*

water meter
compteur^M

floor drain
puisard^M

building sewer
collecteur^M *principal*

washer
lave-linge^M *; laveuse*^F

 ventilating circuit
circuit^M *de ventilation*^F

 draining circuit
circuit^M *d'évacuation*^F

 cold-water circuit
circuit^M *d'eau*^F *froide*

 hot-water circuit
circuit^M *d'eau*^F *chaude*

bathroom
salle^F de bains^M

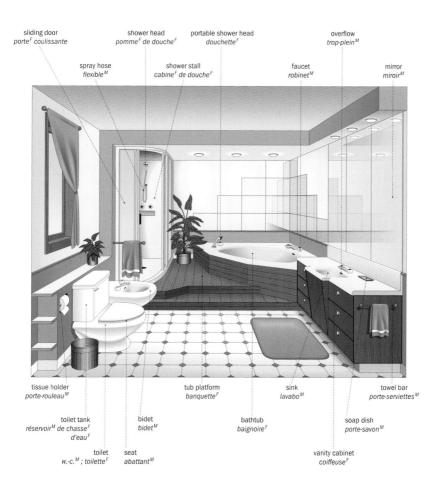

sliding door
porte^F coulissante

spray hose
flexible^M

shower head
pomme^F de douche^F

shower stall
cabine^F de douche^F

portable shower head
douchette^F

faucet
robinet^M

overflow
trop-plein^M

mirror
miroir^M

tissue holder
porte-rouleau^M

toilet tank
*réservoir^M de chasse^F
d'eau^F*

toilet
w.-c.^M ; toilette^F

seat
abattant^M

bidet
bidet^M

tub platform
banquette^F

bathtub
baignoire^F

sink
lavabo^M

soap dish
porte-savon^M

vanity cabinet
coiffeuse^F

towel bar
porte-serviettes^M

toilet

W.-C.^M ; toilette^F

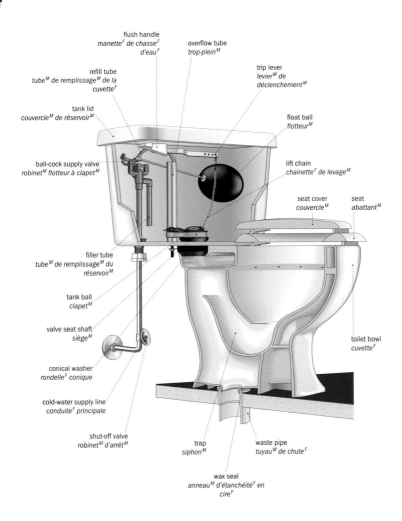

flush handle
*manette^F de chasse^F
d'eau^F*

overflow tube
trop-plein^M

refill tube
*tube^M de remplissage^M de la
cuvette^F*

trip lever
*levier^M de
déclenchement^M*

tank lid
couvercle^M de réservoir^M

float ball
flotteur^M

ball-cock supply valve
robinet^M flotteur à clapet^M

lift chain
chaînette^F de levage^M

seat cover
couvercle^M

seat
abattant^M

filler tube
*tube^M de remplissage^M du
réservoir^M*

tank ball
clapet^M

valve seat shaft
siège^M

toilet bowl
cuvette^F

conical washer
rondelle^F conique

cold-water supply line
conduite^F principale

shut-off valve
robinet^M d'arrêt^M

trap
siphon^M

waste pipe
tuyau^M de chute^F

wax seal
*anneau^M d'étanchéité^F en
cire^F*

examples of branching
exemples^M de branchement^M

garbage disposal sink
évier^M-broyeur^M

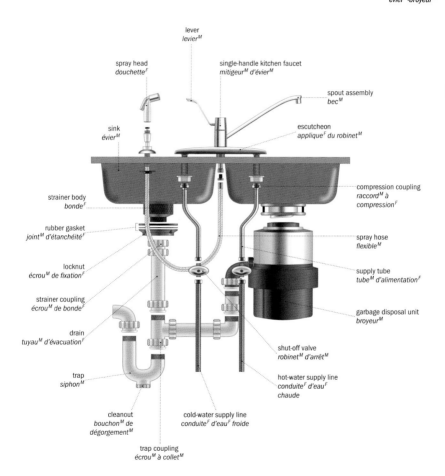

lever
levier^M

spray head
douchette^F

single-handle kitchen faucet
mitigeur^M d'évier^M

spout assembly
bec^M

sink
évier^M

escutcheon
applique^F du robinet^M

strainer body
bonde^F

compression coupling
raccord^M à compression^F

rubber gasket
joint^M d'étanchéité^F

spray hose
flexible^M

locknut
écrou^M de fixation^F

supply tube
tube^M d'alimentation^F

strainer coupling
écrou^M de bonde^F

garbage disposal unit
broyeur^M

drain
tuyau^M d'évacuation^F

shut-off valve
robinet^M d'arrêt^M

trap
siphon^M

hot-water supply line
conduite^F d'eau^F chaude

cleanout
bouchon^M de dégorgement^M

cold-water supply line
conduite^F d'eau^F froide

trap coupling
écrou^M à collet^M

network connection
branchement^M au réseau^M

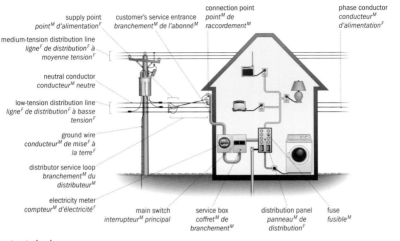

supply point
point^M d'alimentation^F

customer's service entrance
branchement^M de l'abonné^M

connection point
point^M de raccordement^M

phase conductor
conducteur^M d'alimentation^F

medium-tension distribution line
ligne^F de distribution^F à moyenne tension^F

neutral conductor
conducteur^M neutre

low-tension distribution line
ligne^F de distribution^F à basse tension^F

ground wire
conducteur^M de mise^F à la terre^F

distributor service loop
branchement^M du distributeur^M

electricity meter
compteur^M d'électricité^F

main switch
interrupteur^M principal

service box
coffret^M de branchement^M

distribution panel
panneau^M de distribution^F

fuse
fusible^M

contact devices
dispositifs^M de contact^M

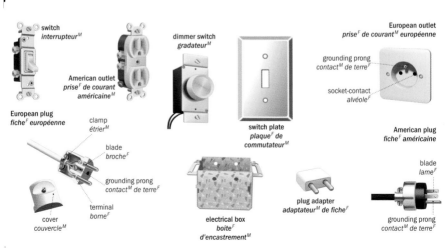

switch
interrupteur^M

dimmer switch
gradateur^M

European outlet
prise^F de courant^M européenne

American outlet
prise^F de courant américaine^M

grounding prong
contact^M de terre^F

socket-contact
alvéole^F

European plug
fiche^F européenne

clamp
étrier^M

blade
broche^F

grounding prong
contact^M de terre^F

terminal
borne^F

cover
couvercle^M

switch plate
plaque^F de commutateur^M

American plug
fiche^F américaine

blade
lame^F

electrical box
boite^F d'encastrement^M

plug adapter
adaptateur^M de fiche^F

grounding prong
contact^M de terre^F

lighting
éclairage^M

incandescent lightbulb
lampe^F à incandescence^F

inert gas
gaz^M inerte

filament
filament^M

button
bouton^M

support
support^M

lead-in wire
entrée^F de courant^M

stem
pied^M

heat deflecting disc
déflecteur^M de chaleur^F

pinch
pincement^M

exhaust tube
queusot^M

base
culot^M

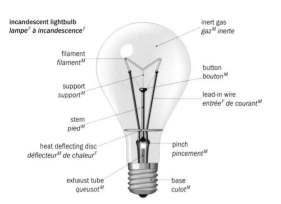

bulb
ampoule^F

lamp socket
douille^F de lampe^F

energy-saving bulb
*lampe^F à économie^F
d'énergie^F*

fluorescent tube
tube^M fluorescent

bulb
ampoule^F

tube retention clip
attache^F du tube^M

mounting plate
plaque^F de montage^M

electronic ballast
ballast^M électronique

housing
boîtier^M

base
culot^M

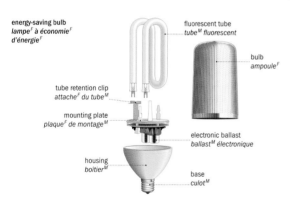

screw base
culot^M à vis^F

bayonet base
culot^M à baïonnette^F

tungsten-halogen lamp
lampe^F à halogène^M

fluorescent tube
tube^M fluorescent

phosphorescent coating
couche^F fluorescente

pin base
culot^M à broches^F

bulb
tube^M

pin
broche^F

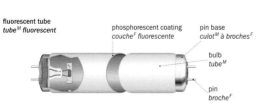

pin
broche^F

HOUSE

armchair
fauteuil^M

HOUSE

parts
parties^F

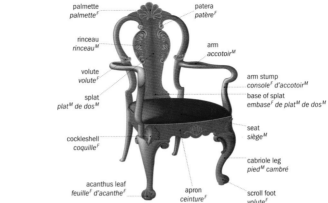

palmette
palmette^F

patera
patère^F

rinceau
rinceau^M

arm
accotoir^M

volute
volute^F

arm stump
console^F d'accotoir^M

splat
plat^M de dos^M

base of splat
embase^F de plat^M de dos^M

cockleshell
coquille^F

seat
siège^M

cabriole leg
pied^M cambré

acanthus leaf
feuille^F d'acanthe^F

apron
ceinture^F

scroll foot
volute^F

examples of armchairs
exemples^M de fauteuils^M

Wassily chair
fauteuil^M Wassily

director's chair
fauteuil^M metteur^M en scène^F

rocking chair
berceuse^F

cabriolet
cabriolet^M

méridienne
méridienne^F

récamier
récamier^M

club chair
fauteuil^M club^M

bergère
bergère^F

sofa
canapé^M

love seat
causeuse^F

chesterfield
canapé^M capitonné

side chair
chaise[F]

parts
parties[F]

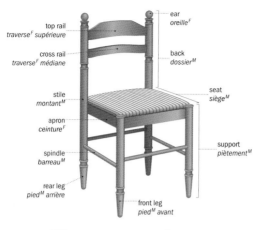

ear
oreille[F]

top rail
traverse[F] *supérieure*

cross rail
traverse[F] *médiane*

back
dossier[M]

stile
montant[M]

seat
siège[M]

apron
ceinture[F]

spindle
barreau[M]

support
piètement[M]

rear leg
pied[M] *arrière*

front leg
pied[M] *avant*

examples of chairs
exemples[M] *de chaises*[F]

rocking chair
chaise[F] *berçante*

stacking chairs
chaises[F] *empilables*

folding chairs
chaises[F] *pliantes*

chaise longue
chaise[F] *longue*

seats
sièges[M]

ottoman
pouf[M]

bench
banc[M]

banquette
banquette[F]

bean bag chair
fauteuil[M]-*sac*[M]

step chair
chaise[F]-*escabeau*[M]

footstool
tabouret[M]

bar stool
tabouret[M]-*bar*[M]

table
table^F

HOUSE

gate-leg table
table^F *à abattants*^M

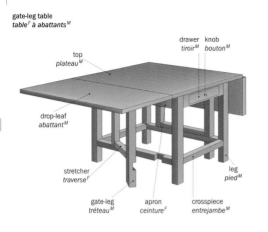

drawer
tiroir^M

knob
bouton^M

top
plateau^M

drop-leaf
abattant^M

stretcher
traverse^F

gate-leg
tréteau^M

apron
ceinture^F

crosspiece
entrejambe^M

leg
pied^M

examples of tables
exemples^M *de tables*^F

extension table
table^F *à rallonges*^F

top
plateau^M

extension
rallonge^F

nest of tables
tables^F *gigognes*

serving cart
desserte^F

storage furniture
meubles^M *de rangement*^M

armoire
armoire^F

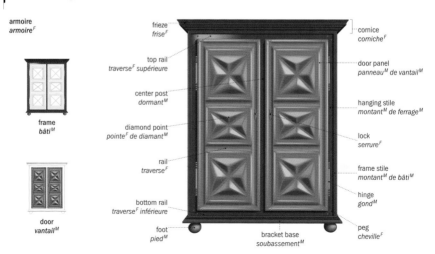

frieze
frise^F

top rail
traverse^F *supérieure*

center post
dormant^M

diamond point
pointe^F *de diamant*^M

rail
traverse^F

bottom rail
traverse^F *inférieure*

foot
pied^M

frame
bâti^M

door
vantail^M

cornice
corniche^F

door panel
panneau^M *de vantail*^M

hanging stile
montant^M *de ferrage*^M

lock
serrure^F

frame stile
montant^M *de bâti*^M

hinge
gond^M

peg
cheville^F

bracket base
soubassement^M

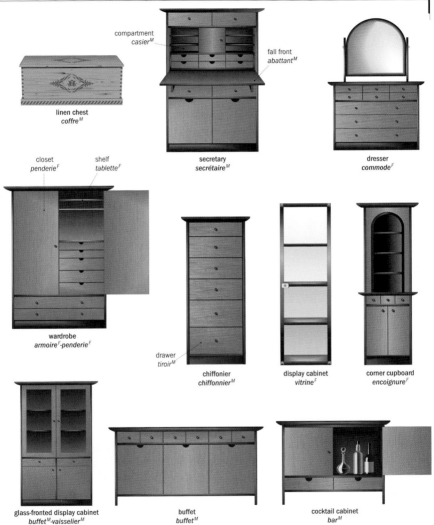

compartment
casier^M

fall front
abattant^M

linen chest
coffre^M

secretary
secrétaire^M

dresser
commode^F

closet
penderie^F

shelf
tablette^F

wardrobe
armoire^F-*penderie*^F

drawer
tiroir^M

chiffonier
chiffonnier^M

display cabinet
vitrine^F

corner cupboard
encoignure^F

glass-fronted display cabinet
buffet^M-*vaisselier*^M

buffet
buffet^M

cocktail cabinet
bar^M

HOUSE

bed
lit^M

HOUSE

sofa bed
canapé^M convertible

futon
futon^M

frame
cadre^M

parts
parties^F

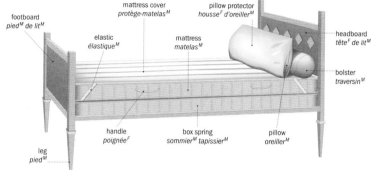

footboard
pied^M de lit^M

mattress cover
protège-matelas^M

pillow protector
housse^F d'oreiller^M

elastic
élastique^M

mattress
matelas^M

headboard
tête^F de lit^M

bolster
traversin^M

handle
poignée^F

box spring
sommier^M tapissier^M

pillow
oreiller^M

leg
pied^M

linen
literie^F

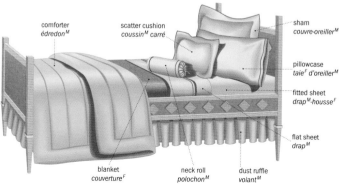

comforter
édredon^M

scatter cushion
coussin^M carré

sham
couvre-oreiller^M

pillowcase
taie^F d'oreiller^M

fitted sheet
drap^M-housse^F

flat sheet
drap^M

blanket
couverture^F

neck roll
polochon^M

dust ruffle
volant^M

children's furniture
meubles^M d'enfants^M

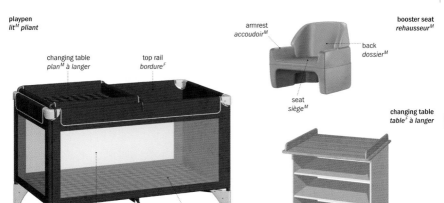

playpen
lit^M pliant

changing table
plan^M à langer

top rail
bordure^F

mesh
filet^M

mattress
matelas^M

booster seat
rehausseur^M

armrest
accoudoir^M

back
dossier^M

seat
siège^M

changing table
table^F à langer

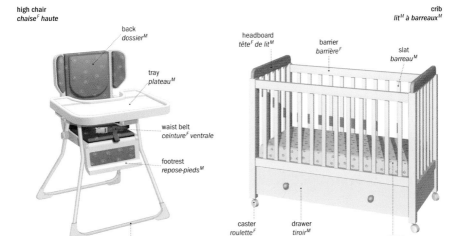

high chair
chaise^F haute

back
dossier^M

tray
plateau^M

waist belt
ceinture^F ventrale

footrest
repose-pieds^M

leg
pied^M

crib
lit^M à barreaux^M

headboard
tête^F de lit^M

barrier
barrière^F

slat
barreau^M

caster
roulette^F

drawer
tiroir^M

mattress
matelas^M

lights
luminaires[M]

ceiling fixture
plafonnier[M]

clamp spotlight
spot[M] *à pince*[F]

halogen desk lamp
lampe[F] *de bureau*[M]
halogène

hanging pendant
suspension[F]

arm
bras[M]

adjustable lamp
lampe[F] *d'architecte*[M]

base
socle[M]

on-off switch
interrupteur[M]

arm
bras[M]

shade
abat-jour[M]

reading lamp
lampe[F] *liseuse*

spring
ressort[M]

adjustable clamp
support[M] *de fixation*[F]

shade
abat-jour[M]

base
socle[M]

stand
pied[M]

floor lamp
lampadaire[M]

table lamp
lampe[F] *de table*[F]

desk lamp
lampe[F] *de bureau*[M]

chandelier
lustre^M

bobeche
coupelle^F

crystal drop
pendeloque^F

crystal button
pampille^F

column
fût^M

track lighting
rail^M *d'éclairage*^{M}

bar frame
gouttière^F

transformer
transformateur^M

contact lever
manette^F *de contact*^{M}

spot
spot^M

wall lantern
lanterne^F *murale*

swivel wall lamp
applique^F *orientable*

wall sconce
applique^F

strip lights
rampe^F *d'éclairage*^{M}

post lantern
lanterne^F *de pied*^{M}

domestic appliances
appareils^M électroménagers

HOUSE

steam iron
fer^M à vapeur^F

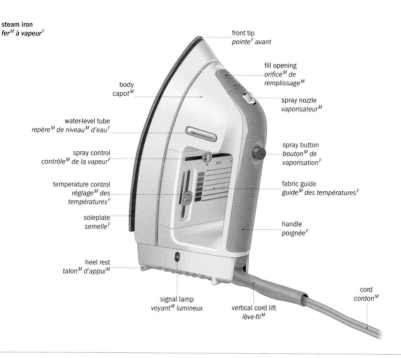

front tip
pointe^F avant

fill opening
orifice^M de remplissage^M

body
capot^M

spray nozzle
vaporisateur^M

water-level tube
repère^M de niveau^M d'eau^F

spray button
bouton^M de vaporisation^F

spray control
contrôle^M de la vapeur^F

temperature control
réglage^M des températures^F

fabric guide
guide^M des températures^F

soleplate
semelle^F

handle
poignée^F

heel rest
talon^M d'appui^M

cord
cordon^M

signal lamp
voyant^M lumineux

vertical cord lift
lève-fil^M

hand held vacuum cleaner
aspirateur^M à main^F

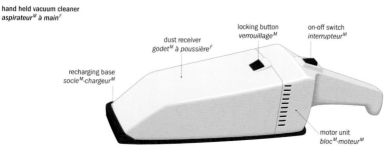

locking button
verrouillage^M

on-off switch
interrupteur^M

dust receiver
godet^M à poussière^F

recharging base
socle^M-chargeur^M

motor unit
bloc^M-moteur^M

HOUSE

upright vacuum cleaner
aspirateur^M-balai^M

on-off switch
interrupteur^M

cylinder vacuum cleaner
aspirateur^M-traineau^M

attachment storage area
compartiment^M d'accessoires^M

hose
tuyau^M flexible

locking device
système^M de verrouillage^M

bag compartment
compartiment^M de sac^M

pipe
tube^M droit

cleaner height adjustment knob
sélecteur^M de hauteur^F

flexible hose
tuyau^M flexible

ventilating grille
grille^F de ventilation^F

on-off switch
interrupteur^M

bumper
pare-chocs^M

brush
brosse^F

attachments
accessoires^M

caster
roulette^F

extension pipe
rallonge^F

cord
cordon^M

handle
poignée^F

rug and floor brush
suceur^M à tapis^M et planchers^M

hood
capot^M

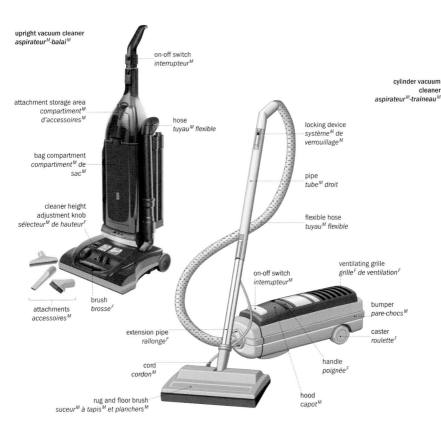

vacuum cleaner attachments
accessoires^M

upholstery nozzle
suceur^M triangulaire à tissus^M

dusting brush
brosse^F à épousseter

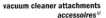

crevice tool
suceur^M plat

floor brush
brosse^F à planchers^M

domestic appliances

HOUSE

range hood
hotte^F

electric range
cuisinière^F *électrique*

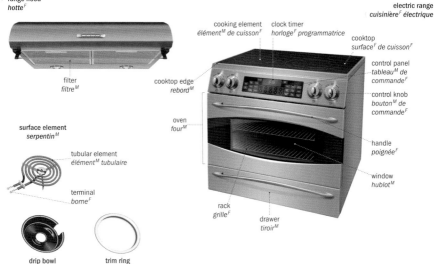

cooking element
élément^M *de cuisson*^F

clock timer
horloge^F *programmatrice*

cooktop
surface^F *de cuisson*^F

control panel
tableau^M *de commande*^F

control knob
bouton^M *de commande*^F

handle
poignée^F

window
hublot^M

filter
filtre^M

cooktop edge
rebord^M

oven
four^M

rack
grille^F

drawer
tiroir^M

surface element
serpentin^M

tubular element
élément^M *tubulaire*

terminal
borne^F

drip bowl
cuvette^F

trim ring
anneau^M

grate
grille^F

burner
brûleur^M

gas range
cuisinière^F *à gaz*^M

burner control knobs
robinets^M

cooktop
table^F *de travail*^M

control panel
tableau^M *de commande*^F

oven
four^M

handle
poignée^F

rack
grille^F

window
hublot^M

door
porte^F

domestic appliances

chest freezer
congélateur^M *coffre*^M

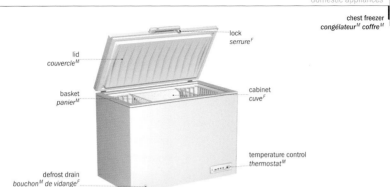

lock
serrure^F

lid
couvercle^M

basket
panier^M

cabinet
cuve^F

temperature control
thermostat^M

defrost drain
bouchon^M *de vidange*^F

HOUSE

refrigerator
réfrigérateur^M

switch
interrupteur^M

door stop
butée^F *de porte*^F

magnetic gasket
joint^M *magnétique*

butter compartment
casier^M *à beurre*^M

shelf
clayette^F

handle
poignée^F

meat keeper
bac^M *à viande*^F

water dispenser
distributeur^M *d'eau*^F

shelf channel
crémaillère^F

refrigerator compartment
réfrigérateur^M

freezer compartment
congélateur^M

storage door
porte^F *étagère*^F

guard rail
barre^F *de retenue*^F

dairy compartment
casier^M *laitier*

crisper
bac^M *à légumes*^M

domestic appliances

HOUSE

front-loading washer
lave-linge^M *à chargement*^{M} *frontal ;*
laveuse^F *à chargement*^{M} *frontal*

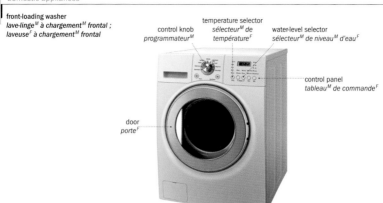

temperature selector
sélecteur^M *de*
température^F

control knob
programmateur^M

water-level selector
sélecteur^M *de niveau*^{M} *d'eau*^{F}

control panel
tableau^M *de commande*^{F}

door
porte^F

top-loading washer
lave-linge^M *à chargement*^{M} *vertical ;*
laveuse^F *à chargement*^{M} *vertical*

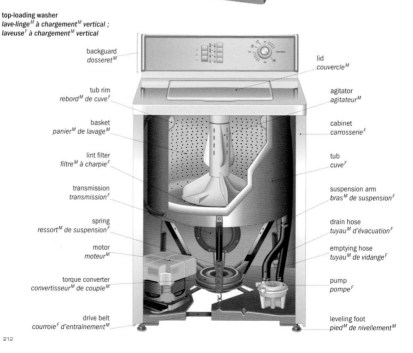

backguard
dosseret^M

lid
couvercle^M

tub rim
rebord^M *de cuve*^{F}

agitator
agitateur^M

basket
panier^M *de lavage*^{M}

cabinet
carrosserie^F

lint filter
filtre^M *à charpie*^{F}

tub
cuve^F

transmission
transmission^F

suspension arm
bras^M *de suspension*^{F}

spring
ressort^M *de suspension*^{F}

drain hose
tuyau^M *d'évacuation*^{F}

motor
moteur^M

emptying hose
tuyau^M *de vidange*^{F}

torque converter
convertisseur^M *de couple*^{M}

pump
pompe^F

drive belt
courroie^F *d'entraînement*^{M}

leveling foot
pied^M *de nivellement*^{M}

domestic appliances

dryer
sèche-linge^M *électrique ; sécheuse*^F

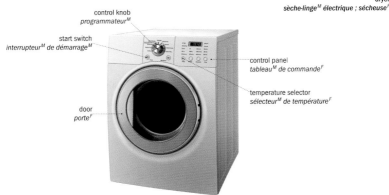

control knob
programmateur^M

start switch
interrupteur^M *de démarrage*^M

control panel
tableau^M *de commande*^F

temperature selector
sélecteur^M *de température*^F

door
porte^F

HOUSE

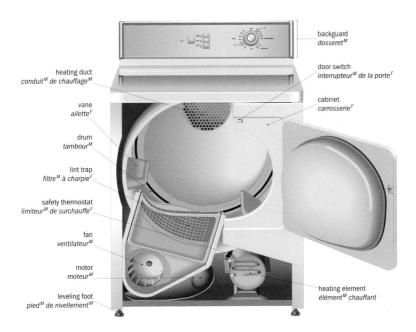

backguard
dosseret^M

heating duct
conduit^M *de chauffage*^M

door switch
interrupteur^M *de la porte*^F

vane
ailette^F

cabinet
carrosserie^F

drum
tambour^M

lint trap
filtre^M *à charpie*^F

safety thermostat
limiteur^M *de surchauffe*^F

fan
ventilateur^M

motor
moteur^M

leveling foot
pied^M *de nivellement*^M

heating element
élément^M *chauffant*

domestic appliances

HOUSE

control panel: dishwasher
tableau^M de commande^F

control buttons
boutons^M de
commande^F

signal lamp
voyant^M lumineux

air vent
grille^F d'aération^F

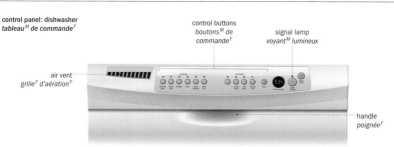

handle
poignée^F

dishwasher
lave-vaisselle^M

rack
panier^M

wash tower
tourelle^F

spray arm
bras^M gicleur^M

overflow protection switch
dispositif^M antidébordement^M

hinge
charnière^F

detergent dispenser
distributeur^M de détergent^M

insulating material
isolant^M

tub
cuve^F

slide
glissière^F

water hose
conduite^F d'eau^F

heating element
élément^M chauffant

drain hose
tuyau^M de vidange^F

pump
pompe^F

leveling foot
pied^M de nivellement^M

gasket
joint^M

rinse-aid dispenser
distributeur^M de produit^M de
rinçage^M

cutlery basket
panier^M à couverts^M

motor
moteur^M

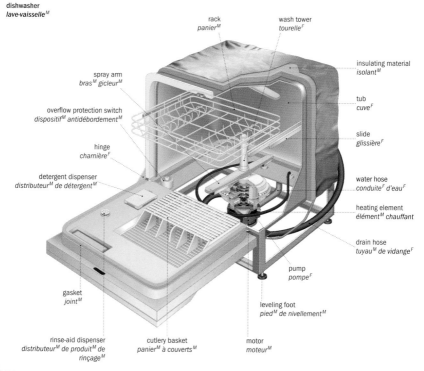

household equipment
articles^M ménagers

tea towel
torchon^M

dustpan
pelle^F à poussière^F ; porte-poussière^M

broom
balai^M

mop
balai^M à franges^F ; vadrouille^F

scouring pad
éponge^F à récurer

brush
brosse^F

block
monture^F

fibers
fibres^F

garbage can
poubelle^F

handle
manche^M

lid
couvercle^M

handle
poignée^F

fibers
fibres^F

pail
seau^M

pouring spout
bec^M verseur

handle
anse^F

plumbing tools
plomberie^F : outils^M

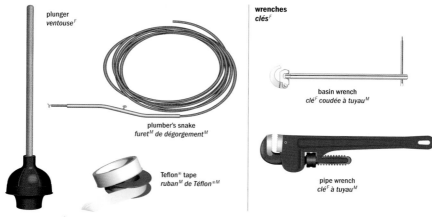

plunger
ventouse^F

plumber's snake
furet^M de dégorgement^M

Teflon® tape
ruban^M de Téflon®^M

wrenches
clés^F

basin wrench
clé^F coudée à tuyau^M

pipe wrench
clé^F à tuyau^M

masonry tools
maçonnerie^F : outils^M

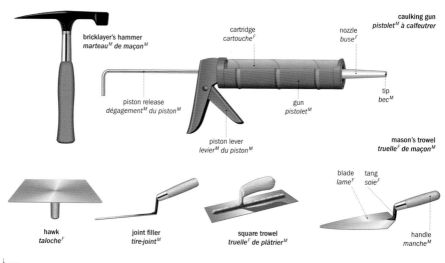

bricklayer's hammer
marteau^M de maçon^M

caulking gun
pistolet^M à calfeutrer

cartridge
cartouche^F

nozzle
buse^F

piston release
dégagement^M du piston^M

gun
pistolet^M

tip
bec^M

piston lever
levier^M du piston^M

mason's trowel
truelle^F de maçon^M

blade
lame^F

tang
soie^F

hawk
taloche^F

joint filler
tire-joint^M

square trowel
truelle^F de plâtrier^M

handle
manche^M

electricity tools
électricité^F : outils^M

drop light
baladeuse^F

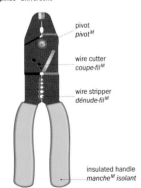

hook
crochet^M

reflector
réflecteur^M

bulb
lampe^F

guard
grillage^M de protection^F

convenience outlet
prise^F de courant^M

handle
manche^M

cord
cordon^M

neon tester
vérificateur^M de circuit^M

wire nut
capuchon^M de connexion^F

receptacle analyzer
*vérificateur^M de prise^F de
courant^M*

voltage tester
vérificateur^M de tension^F

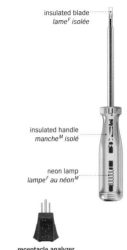

insulated blade
lame^F isolée

insulated handle
manche^M isolé

neon lamp
lampe^F au néon^M

multipurpose tool
pince^F universelle

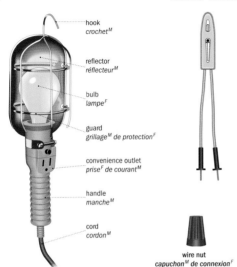

pivot
pivot^M

wire cutter
coupe-fil^M

wire stripper
dénude-fil^M

insulated handle
manche^M isolant

needle-nose pliers
pince^F à long bec^M

lineman's pliers
pince^F d'électricien^M

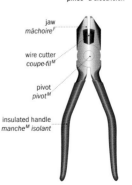

jaw
mâchoire^F

wire cutter
coupe-fil^M

pivot
pivot^M

insulated handle
manche^M isolant

soldering and welding tools
soudage^M : outils^M

DO-IT-YOURSELF AND GARDENING

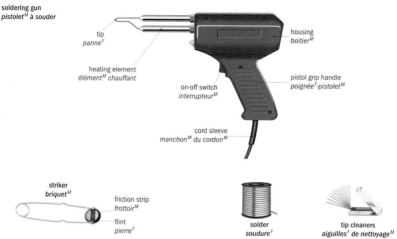

soldering gun
pistolet^M à souder

tip
panne^F

housing
boîtier^M

heating element
élément^M chauffant

pistol grip handle
poignée^F-pistolet^M

on-off switch
interrupteur^M

cord sleeve
manchon^M du cordon^M

striker
briquet^M

friction strip
frottoir^M

flint
pierre^F

solder
soudure^F

tip cleaners
aiguilles^F de nettoyage^M

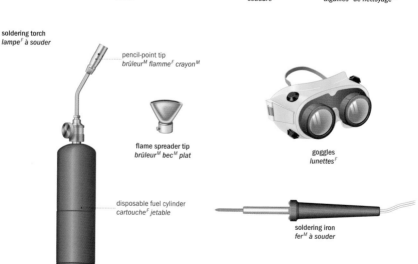

soldering torch
lampe^F à souder

pencil-point tip
brûleur^M flamme^F crayon^M

flame spreader tip
brûleur^M bec^M plat

goggles
lunettes^F

disposable fuel cylinder
cartouche^F jetable

soldering iron
fer^M à souder

painting
peinture^F d'entretien^M

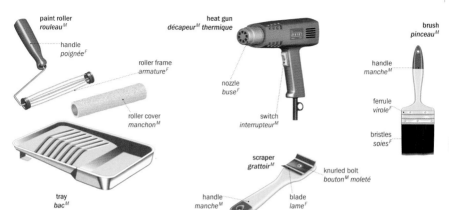

paint roller
rouleau^M

handle
poignée^F

roller frame
armature^F

roller cover
manchon^M

tray
bac^M

heat gun
décapeur^M thermique

nozzle
buse^F

switch
interrupteur^M

scraper
grattoir^M

knurled bolt
bouton^M moleté

handle
manche^M

blade
lame^F

brush
pinceau^M

handle
manche^M

ferrule
virole^F

bristles
soies^F

ladders and stepladders
échelles^F et escabeaux^M

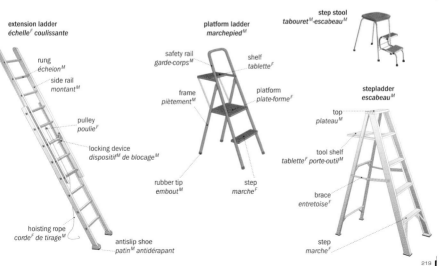

extension ladder
échelle^F coulissante

rung
écheion^M

side rail
montant^M

pulley
poulie^F

locking device
dispositif^M de blocage^M

hoisting rope
corde^F de tirage^M

antislip shoe
patin^M antidérapant

platform ladder
marchepied^M

safety rail
garde-corps^M

shelf
tablette^F

frame
piètement^M

platform
plate-forme^F

rubber tip
embout^M

step
marche^F

step stool
tabouret^M-escabeau^M

stepladder
escabeau^M

top
plateau^M

tool shelf
tablette^F porte-outil^M

brace
entretoise^F

step
marche^F

carpentry: nailing tools
menuiserie^F : outils^M pour clouer

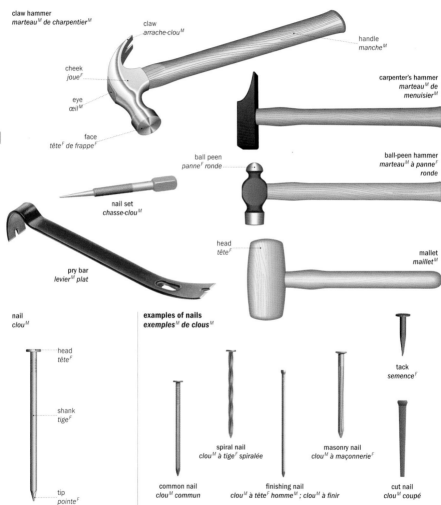

claw hammer
marteau^M de charpentier^M

claw
arrache-clou^M

handle
manche^M

cheek
joue^F

eye
œil^M

face
tête^F de frappe^F

carpenter's hammer
marteau^M de menuisier^M

ball peen
panne^F ronde

ball-peen hammer
marteau^M à panne^F ronde

nail set
chasse-clou^M

head
tête^F

pry bar
levier^M plat

mallet
maillet^M

nail
clou^M

head
tête^F

shank
tige^F

tip
pointe^F

examples of nails
exemples^M de clous^M

tack
semence^F

spiral nail
clou^M à tige^F spiralée

masonry nail
clou^M à maçonnerie^F

common nail
clou^M commun

finishing nail
clou^M à tête^F homme^M ; clou^M à finir

cut nail
clou^M coupé

carpentry: screw-driving tools
menuiserie^F : outils^M pour visser

screwdriver
tournevis^M

tip
pointe^F

shank
tige^F

handle
manche^M

blade
lame^F

examples of tips
exemples^M de pointes^F

square-headed tip
pointe^F carrée

cross-headed tip
pointe^F cruciforme

flat tip
pointe^F plate

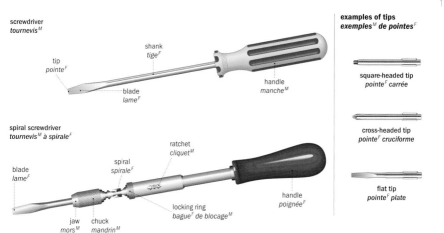

spiral screwdriver
tournevis^M à spirale^F

ratchet
cliquet^M

spiral
spirale^F

blade
lame^F

jaw
mors^M

chuck
mandrin^M

locking ring
bague^F de blocage^M

handle
poignée^F

cordless screwdriver
tournevis^M sans fil^M

bit
embout^M

handle
poignée^F

tip
pointe^F

reversing switch
inverseur^M de marche^F

battery
batterie^F

spring wing
ailette^F à ressort^M

toggle bolt
boulon^M à ailettes^F

expansion bolt
boulon^M à gaine^F d'expansion^F

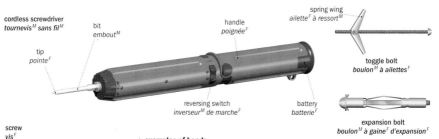

screw
vis^F

head
tête^F

slot
fente^F

shank
fût^M

thread
filet^M

examples of heads
exemples^M de têtes^F

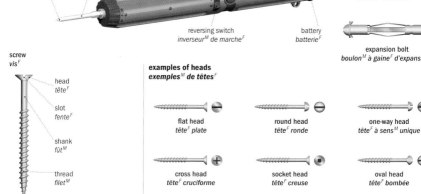

flat head
tête^F plate

round head
tête^F ronde

one-way head
tête^F à sens^M unique

cross head
tête^F cruciforme

socket head
tête^F creuse

oval head
tête^F bombée

carpentry: gripping and tightening tools

menuiserie^F : outils^M pour serrer

pliers
pinces^F

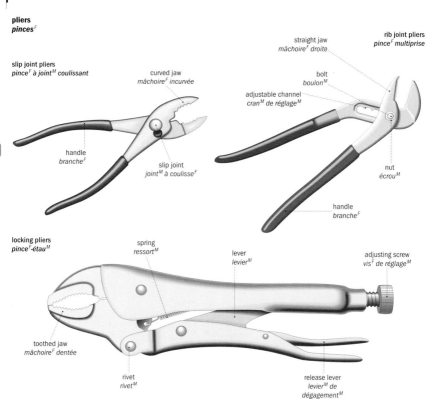

slip joint pliers
pince^F à joint^M coulissant

straight jaw
mâchoire^F droite

curved jaw
mâchoire^F incurvée

rib joint pliers
pince^F multiprise

bolt
boulon^M

adjustable channel
cran^M de réglage^M

handle
branche^F

slip joint
joint^M à coulisse^F

nut
écrou^M

handle
branche^F

locking pliers
pince^F-étau^M

spring
ressort^M

lever
levier^M

adjusting screw
vis^F de réglage^M

toothed jaw
mâchoire^F dentée

rivet
rivet^M

release lever
levier^M de dégagement^M

washers
rondelles^F

flat washer
rondelle^F plate

lock washer
rondelle^F à ressort^M

external tooth lock washer
rondelle^F à denture^F extérieure

internal tooth lock washer
rondelle^F à denture^F intérieure

wrenches
clés F

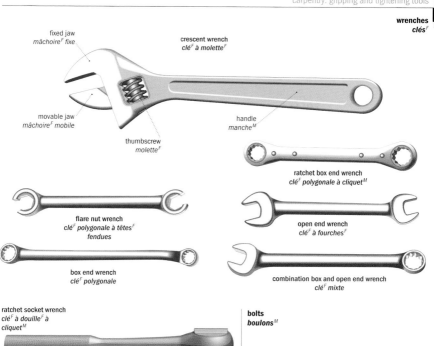

fixed jaw
mâchoire F *fixe*

crescent wrench
clé F *à molette* F

movable jaw
mâchoire F *mobile*

handle
manche M

thumbscrew
molette F

ratchet box end wrench
clé F *polygonale à cliquet* M

flare nut wrench
clé F *polygonale à têtes* F
fendues

open end wrench
clé F *à fourches* F

box end wrench
clé F *polygonale*

combination box and open end wrench
clé F *mixte*

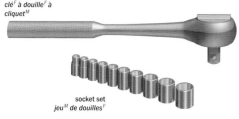

ratchet socket wrench
clé F *à douille* F *à*
cliquet M

socket set
jeu M *de douilles* F

bolts
boulons M

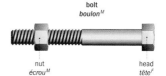

bolt
boulon M

nut
écrou M

head
tête F

shoulder bolt
boulon M *à épaulement* M

threaded rod
tige F *filetée*

shoulder
épaulement M

nuts
écrous M

hexagon nut
écrou M *hexagonal*

acorn nut
écrou M *borgne*

wing nut
écrou M *à oreilles* F

DO-IT-YOURSELF AND GARDENING

carpentry: gripping and tightening tools

C-clamp
serre-joint^M

vise
étau^M

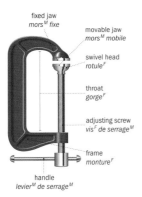

fixed jaw
mors^M *fixe*

movable jaw
mors^M *mobile*

swivel head
rotule^F

throat
gorge^F

adjusting screw
vis^F *de serrage*^M

frame
monture^F

handle
levier^M *de serrage*^M

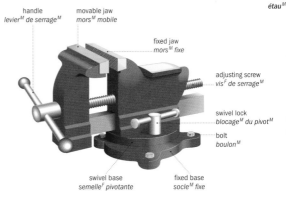

handle
levier^M *de serrage*^M

movable jaw
mors^M *mobile*

fixed jaw
mors^M *fixe*

adjusting screw
vis^F *de serrage*^M

swivel lock
blocage^M *du pivot*^M

bolt
boulon^M

swivel base
semelle^F *pivotante*

fixed base
socle^M *fixe*

pipe clamp
serre-joint^M *à tuyau*^M

handle
levier^M *de serrage*^M

clamping screw
vis^F *de serrage*^M

jaw
mâchoire^F

pipe
tuyau^M

tail stop
sabot^M

locking lever
levier^M *de blocage*^M

work bench and vise
établi^M *étau*^M

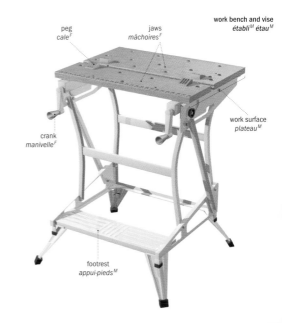

peg
cale^F

jaws
mâchoires^F

work surface
plateau^M

crank
manivelle^F

footrest
appui-pieds^M

carpentry: measuring and marking tools
menuiserieF : instrumentsM de traçageM et de mesureF

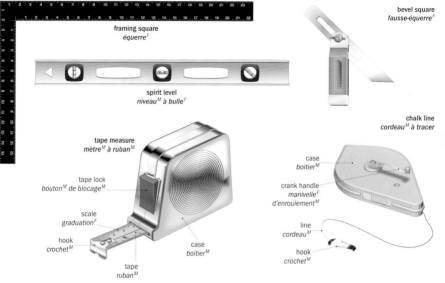

framing square
équerreF

bevel square
fausse-équerreF

spirit level
niveauM à bulleF

chalk line
cordeauM à tracer

tape measure
mètreM à rubanM

tape lock
boutonM de blocageM

case
boîtierM

crank handle
*manivelleF
d'enroulementM*

scale
graduationF

hook
crochetM

case
boitierM

line
cordeauM

hook
crochetM

tape
rubanM

carpentry: miscellaneous material
menuiserieF : matérielM divers

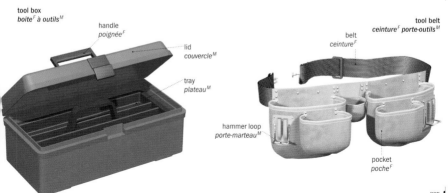

tool box
boîteF à outilsM

handle
poignéeF

lid
couvercleM

tray
plateauM

hammer loop
porte-marteauM

tool belt
ceintureF porte-outilsM

belt
ceintureF

pocket
pocheF

carpentry: sawing tools
menuiserie^F : outils^M pour scier

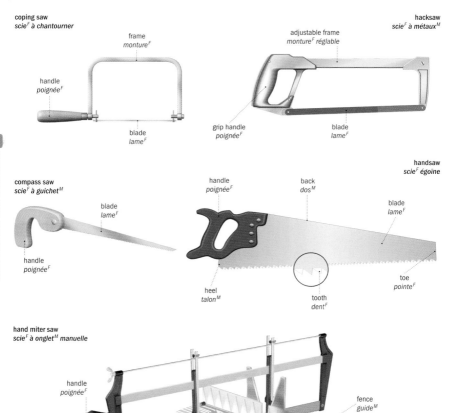

coping saw
scie^F à chantourner

frame
monture^F

handle
poignée^F

blade
lame^F

hacksaw
scie^F à métaux^M

adjustable frame
monture^F réglable

grip handle
poignée^F

blade
lame^F

compass saw
scie^F à guichet^M

blade
lame^F

handle
poignée^F

handsaw
scie^F égoine

handle
poignée^F

back
dos^M

blade
lame^F

heel
talon^M

tooth
dent^F

toe
pointe^F

hand miter saw
scie^F à onglet^M manuelle

handle
poignée^F

fence
guide^M

miter box
boite^F à onglets^M

end stop
butée^F

blade
lame^F

miter latch
verrou^M d'onglet^M

miter scale
échelle^F d'onglet^M

clamp
serre-joint^M

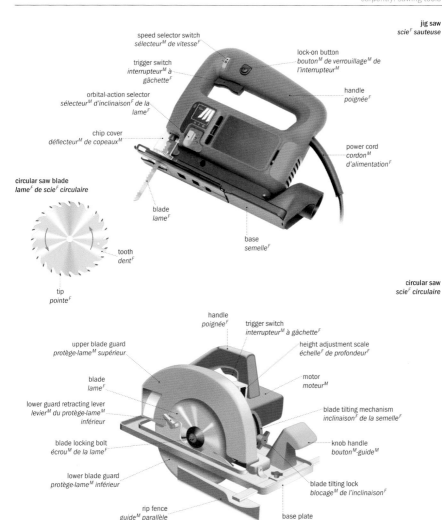

jig saw
scie^F *sauteuse*

speed selector switch
sélecteur^M *de vitesse*^F

trigger switch
interrupteur^M *à*
gâchette^F

lock-on button
bouton^M *de verrouillage*^M *de*
l'interrupteur^M

orbital-action selector
sélecteur^M *d'inclinaison*^F *de la*
lame^F

handle
poignée^F

chip cover
déflecteur^M *de copeaux*^M

power cord
cordon^M
d'alimentation^F

circular saw blade
lame^F *de scie*^F *circulaire*

blade
lame^F

base
semelle^F

tooth
dent^F

tip
pointe^F

circular saw
scie^F *circulaire*

handle
poignée^F

trigger switch
interrupteur^M *à gâchette*^F

upper blade guard
protège-lame^M *supérieur*

height adjustment scale
échelle^F *de profondeur*^F

blade
lame^F

motor
moteur^M

lower guard retracting lever
levier^M *du protège-lame*^M
inférieur

blade tilting mechanism
inclinaison^F *de la semelle*^F

blade locking bolt
écrou^M *de la lame*^F

knob handle
bouton^M*-guide*^M

lower blade guard
protège-lame^M *inférieur*

blade tilting lock
blocage^M *de l'inclinaison*^F

rip fence
guide^M *parallèle*

base plate
semelle^F

carpentry: drilling tools
menuiserie^F : outils^M pour percer

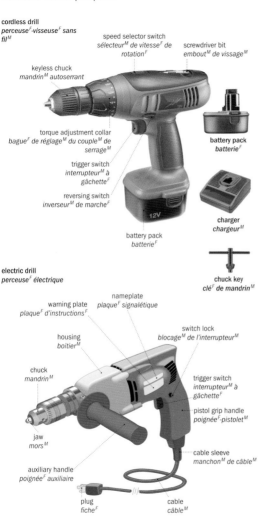

cordless drill
perceuse^F-visseuse^F sans fil^M

speed selector switch
sélecteur^M de vitesse^F de rotation^F

screwdriver bit
embout^M de vissage^M

keyless chuck
mandrin^M autoserrant

torque adjustment collar
bague^F de réglage^M du couple^M de serrage^M

trigger switch
interrupteur^M à gâchette^F

reversing switch
inverseur^M de marche^F

battery pack
batterie^F

battery pack
batterie^F

charger
chargeur^M

chuck key
clé^F de mandrin^M

electric drill
perceuse^F électrique

nameplate
plaque^F signalétique

warning plate
plaque^F d'instructions^F

switch lock
blocage^M de l'interrupteur^M

housing
boîtier^M

chuck
mandrin^M

trigger switch
interrupteur^M à gâchette^F

pistol grip handle
poignée^F-pistolet^M

jaw
mors^M

auxiliary handle
poignée^F auxiliaire

cable sleeve
manchon^M de câble^M

plug
fiche^F

cable
câble^M

examples of bits and drills
exemples^M de mèches^F et de forets^M

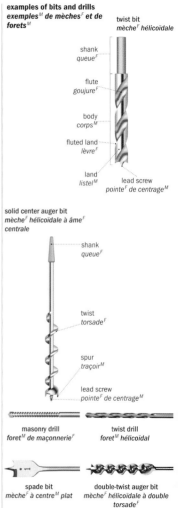

twist bit
mèche^F hélicoïdale

shank
queue^F

flute
goujure^F

body
corps^M

fluted land
lèvre^F

land
listel^M

lead screw
pointe^F de centrage^M

solid center auger bit
mèche^F hélicoïdale à âme^F centrale

shank
queue^F

twist
torsade^F

spur
traçoir^M

lead screw
pointe^F de centrage^M

masonry drill
foret^M de maçonnerie^F

twist drill
foret^M hélicoïdal

spade bit
mèche^F à centre^M plat

double-twist auger bit
mèche^F hélicoïdale à double torsade^F

carpentry: shaping tools
menuiserie^F : outils^M pour façonner

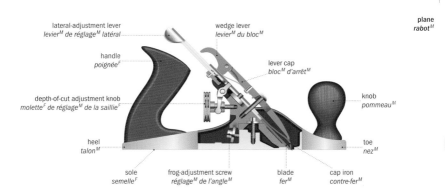

plane
rabot^M

lateral-adjustment lever
levier^M de réglage^M latéral

wedge lever
levier^M du bloc^M

handle
poignée^F

lever cap
bloc^M d'arrêt^M

depth-of-cut adjustment knob
molette^F de réglage^M de la saillie^F

knob
pommeau^M

heel
talon^M

toe
nez^M

sole
semelle^F

frog-adjustment screw
réglage^M de l'angle^M

blade
fer^M

cap iron
contre-fer^M

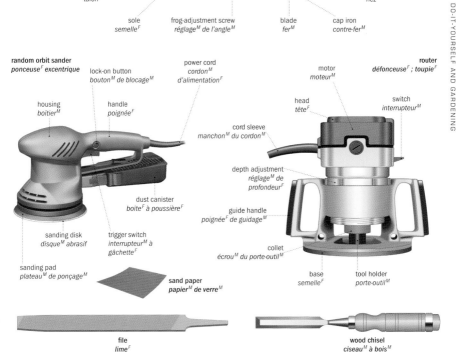

random orbit sander
ponceuse^F excentrique

lock-on button
bouton^M de blocage^M

power cord
cordon^M d'alimentation^F

router
défonceuse^F ; toupie^F

housing
boîtier^M

handle
poignée^F

motor
moteur^M

switch
interrupteur^M

head
tête^F

cord sleeve
manchon^M du cordon^M

depth adjustment
réglage^M de profondeur^F

guide handle
poignée^F de guidage^M

dust canister
boîte^F à poussière^F

collet
écrou^M du porte-outil^M

sanding disk
disque^M abrasif

trigger switch
interrupteur^M à gâchette^F

base
semelle^F

tool holder
porte-outil^M

sanding pad
plateau^M de ponçage^M

sand paper
papier^M de verre^M

file
lime^F

wood chisel
ciseau^M à bois^M

pleasure garden
jardin^M *d'agrément*^M

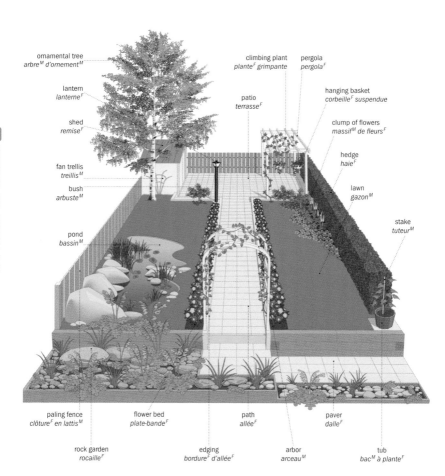

ornamental tree
arbre^M *d'ornement*^M

lantern
lanterne^F

shed
remise^F

fan trellis
treillis^M

bush
arbuste^M

pond
bassin^M

climbing plant
plante^F *grimpante*

patio
terrasse^F

pergola
pergola^F

hanging basket
corbeille^F *suspendue*

clump of flowers
massif^M *de fleurs*^F

hedge
haie^F

lawn
gazon^M

stake
tuteur^M

paling fence
clôture^F *en lattis*^M

flower bed
plate-bande^F

path
allée^F

paver
dalle^F

rock garden
rocaille^F

edging
bordure^F *d'allée*^F

arbor
arceau^M

tub
bac^M *à plante*^F

miscellaneous equipment
équipement^M divers

compost bin
bac^M à compost^M

wheelbarrow
brouette^F

tray
caisse^F

handle
brancard^M

leg
pied^M

wheel
roue^F

seeding and planting tools
outils^M pour semer et planter

garden line
cordeau^M

dibble
plantoir^M

stakes
tuteurs^M

bulb dibble
plantoir^M à bulbes^M

seeder
semoir^M à main^F

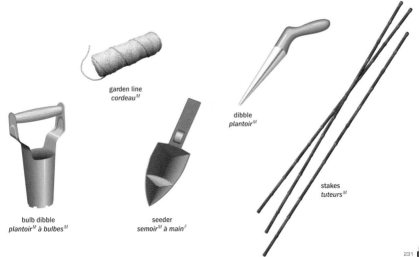

hand tools
jeu^M de petits outils^M

small hand cultivator
griffe^F à fleurs^F

trowel
transplantoir^M

weeder
tire-racine^M

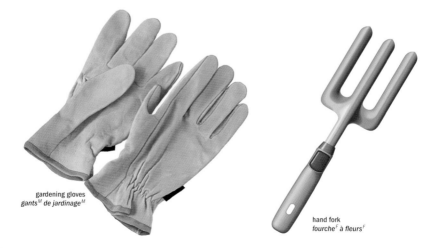

gardening gloves
gants^M de jardinage^M

hand fork
fourche^F à fleurs^F

tools for loosening the earth
outils^M pour remuer la terre^F

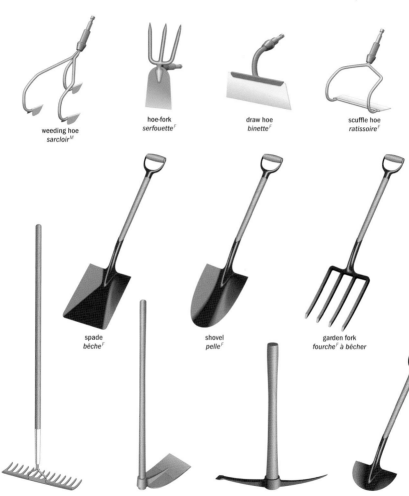

weeding hoe
sarcloir^M

hoe-fork
serfouette^F

draw hoe
binette^F

scuffle hoe
ratissoire^F

rake
râteau^M

spade
bêche^F

shovel
pelle^F

garden fork
fourche^F à bêcher

hoe
houe^F

pick
pioche^F

lawn edger
coupe-bordures^M

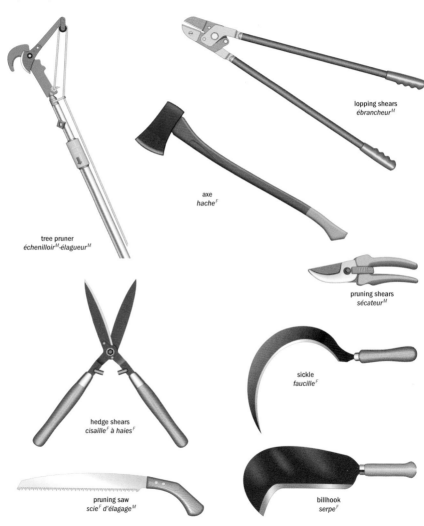

pruning and cutting tools
outils^M *pour couper*

lopping shears
ébrancheur^M

axe
hache^F

tree pruner
échenilloir^M*-élagueur*^M

pruning shears
sécateur^M

hedge shears
cisaille^F *à haies*^F

sickle
faucille^F

pruning saw
scie^F *d'élagage*^M

billhook
serpe^F

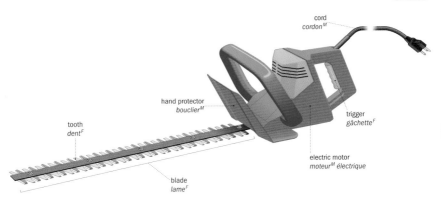

hedge trimmer
taille-haies^M

cord
cordon^M

hand protector
bouclier^M

tooth
dent^F

trigger
gâchette^F

electric motor
moteur^M *électrique*

blade
lame^F

chainsaw
tronçonneuse^F

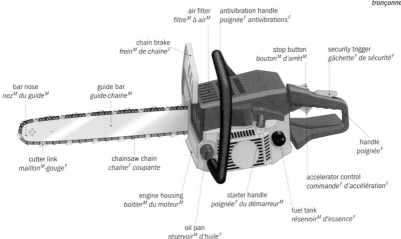

air filter
filtre^M *à air*^M

antivibration handle
poignée^F *antivibrations*^F

chain brake
frein^M *de chaine*^F

stop button
bouton^M *d'arrêt*^M

security trigger
gâchette^F *de sécurité*^F

bar nose
nez^M *du guide*^M

guide bar
guide-chaîne^M

handle
poignée^F

cutter link
maillon^M-*gouge*^F

chainsaw chain
chaîne^F *coupante*

accelerator control
commande^F *d'accélération*^F

engine housing
boitier^M *du moteur*^M

starter handle
poignée^F *du démarreur*^M

fuel tank
réservoir^M *d'essence*^F

oil pan
réservoir^M *d'huile*^F

watering tools
outils^M pour arroser

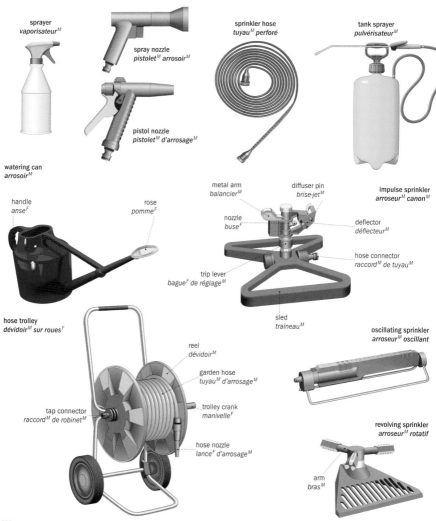

sprayer
vaporisateur^M

spray nozzle
pistolet^M arrosoir^M

pistol nozzle
pistolet^M d'arrosage^M

sprinkler hose
tuyau^M perforé

tank sprayer
pulvérisateur^M

watering can
arrosoir^M

handle
anse^F

rose
pomme^F

metal arm
balancier^M

diffuser pin
brise-jet^M

impulse sprinkler
arroseur^M canon^M

nozzle
buse^F

deflector
déflecteur^M

hose connector
raccord^M de tuyau^M

trip lever
bague^F de réglage^M

sled
traineau^M

hose trolley
dévidoir^M sur roues^F

reel
dévidoir^M

garden hose
tuyau^M d'arrosage^M

trolley crank
manivelle^F

tap connector
raccord^M de robinet^M

hose nozzle
lance^F d'arrosage^M

oscillating sprinkler
arroseur^M oscillant

revolving sprinkler
arroseur^M rotatif

arm
bras^M

lawn care
soins^M de la pelouse^F

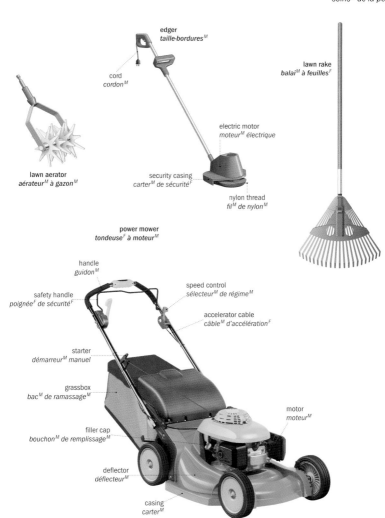

edger
taille-bordures^M

cord
cordon^M

lawn rake
balai^M à feuilles^F

electric motor
moteur^M électrique

lawn aerator
aérateur^M à gazon^M

security casing
carter^M de sécurité^F

nylon thread
fil^M de nylon^M

power mower
tondeuse^F à moteur^M

handle
guidon^M

speed control
sélecteur^M de régime^M

safety handle
poignée^F de sécurité^F

accelerator cable
câble^M d'accélération^F

starter
démarreur^M manuel

grassbox
bac^M de ramassage^M

motor
moteur^M

filler cap
bouchon^M de remplissage^M

deflector
déflecteur^M

casing
carter^M

headgear

coiffure^F

men's headgear
coiffures^F **d'homme**^M

felt hat
chapeau^M *de feutre*^M

hatband
bourdalou^M

binding
galon^M

crown
calotte^F

brim
bord^M

bow
nœud^M *plat*

boater
canotier^M

skullcap
calotte^F

derby
melon^M

garrison cap
calot^M

top hat
haut-de-forme^M

shapka
chapska^M

hunting cap
casquette^F
norvégienne

ear flap
cache-oreilles^M
abattant

cap
casquette^F

panama
panama^M

peak
visière^F

CLOTHING

pillbox hat
tambourin^M

cartwheel hat
capeline^F

cloche
cloche^F

toque
toque^F

gob hat
bob^M

crown
calotte^F

sou'wester
suroit^M

brim
bord^M

turban
turban^M

CLOTHING

balaclava
cagoule^F

peak
visière^F

beret
béret^M

stocking cap
bonnet^M *pompon*^M ;
tuque^F

felt hat
chapeau^M *de feutre*^M

shoes
chaussures^F

men's shoes
chaussures^F d'homme^M

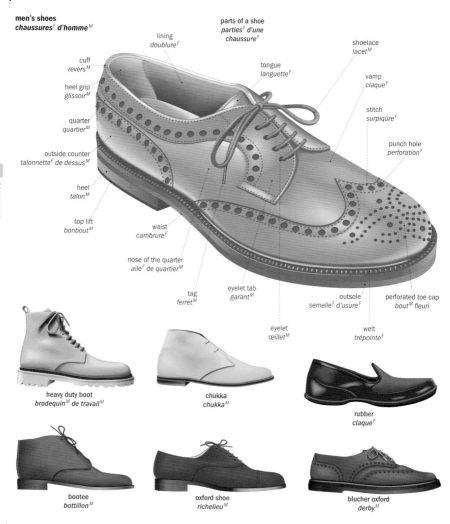

parts of a shoe
parties^F d'une chaussure^F

lining
doublure^F

cuff
revers^M

heel grip
glissoir^M

quarter
quartier^M

outside counter
talonnette^F de dessus^M

heel
talon^M

top lift
bonbout^M

waist
cambrure^F

nose of the quarter
aile^F de quartier^M

tag
ferret^M

tongue
languette^F

shoelace
lacet^M

vamp
claque^F

stitch
surpiqûre^F

punch hole
perforation^F

eyelet tab
garant^M

eyelet
œillet^M

outsole
semelle^F d'usure^F

welt
trépointe^F

perforated toe cap
bout^M fleuri

heavy duty boot
brodequin^M de travail^M

chukka
chukka^M

rubber
claque^F

bootee
bottillon^M

oxford shoe
richelieu^M

blucher oxford
derby^M

women's shoes
chaussures^F *de femme*^F

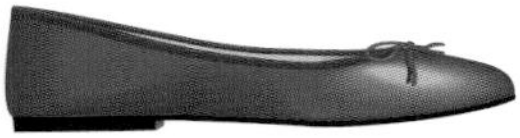

ballerina slipper
ballerine^F

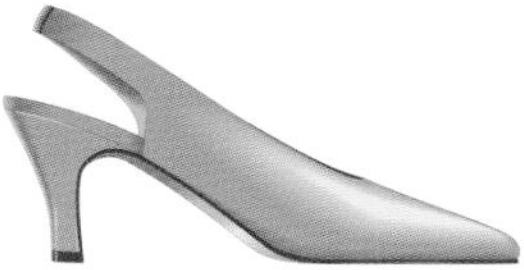

sandal
sandale^F

sling back shoe
escarpin^M-*sandale*^F

pump
escarpin^M

one-bar shoe
Charles IX^M

T-strap shoe
salomé^M

casual shoe
trotteur^M

thigh-boot
cuissarde^F

boot
botte^F

ankle boot
bottine^F

CLOTHING

unisex shoes
chaussuresF unisexes

mule
muleF

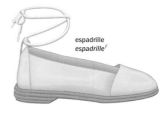

espadrille
espadrilleF

tennis shoe
tennisM

loafer
loaferM ; flâneurM

sandal
nu-piedM

moccasin
mocassinM

thong
tongM

clog
socqueM

sandal
sandaletteF

hiking boot
brodequinM de randonnéeF

men's gloves
gants^M **d'homme**^M

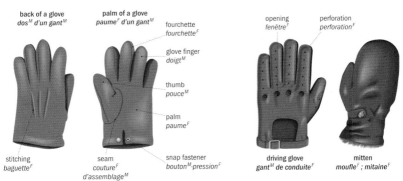

back of a glove
dos^M *d'un gant*^M

palm of a glove
paume^F *d'un gant*^M

fourchette
fourchette^F

glove finger
doigt^M

thumb
pouce^M

palm
paume^F

stitching
baguette^F

seam
couture^F
d'assemblage^M

snap fastener
bouton^M*-pression*^F

opening
fenêtre^F

perforation
perforation^F

driving glove
gant^M *de conduite*^F

mitten
moufle^F ; *mitaine*^F

women's gloves
gants^M **de femme**^F

short glove
gant^M *court*

gauntlet
gant^M *à crispin*^M

evening glove
gant^M *long*

mitt
mitaine^F

wrist-length glove
gant^M *saxe*

gauntlet
rebras^M

men's clothing
vêtements^M d'homme^M

jackets
veston^M et veste^F

double-breasted jacket
veston^M croisé

collar
col^M

peaked lapel
revers^M à cran^M aigu

lining
doublure^F

breast welt pocket
pochette^F

sleeve
manche^F

flap
rabat^M

outside ticket pocket
poche^F-ticket^M

patch pocket
poche^F plaquée

side back vent
fente^F latérale

vest
gilet^M

V-neck
encolure^F en V

lining
doublure^F

welt
patte^F

front
devant^M

welt pocket
poche^F gilet^M

seam
découpe^F

adjustable waist tab
tirant^M de réglage^M

single-breasted jacket
veste^F droite

lapel
revers^M

front
devant^M

notch
cran^M

lining
doublure^F

pocket handkerchief
pochette^F

flap pocket
poche^F tiroir^M

back
dos^M

sleeve
manche^F

center back vent
fente^F médiane

CLOTHING

shirt
chemise^F

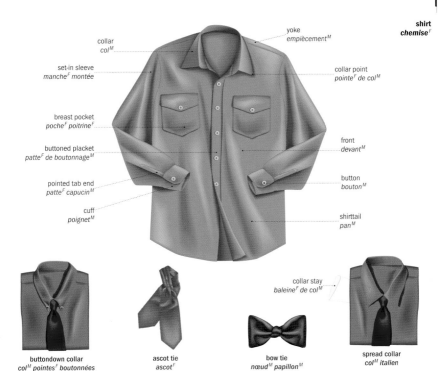

yoke
empiècement^M

collar
col^M

set-in sleeve
manche^F montée

collar point
pointe^F de col^M

breast pocket
poche^F poitrine^F

front
devant^M

buttoned placket
patte^F de boutonnage^M

pointed tab end
patte^F capucin^M

button
bouton^M

cuff
poignet^M

shirttail
pan^M

collar stay
baleine^F de col^M

buttondown collar
col^M pointes^F boutonnées

ascot tie
ascot^F

bow tie
nœud^M papillon^M

spread collar
col^M italien

necktie
cravate^F

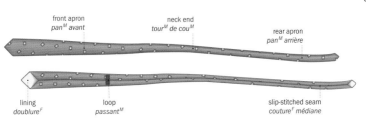

front apron
pan^M avant

neck end
tour^M de cou^M

rear apron
pan^M arrière

lining
doublure^F

loop
passant^M

slip-stitched seam
couture^F médiane

CLOTHING

CLOTHING

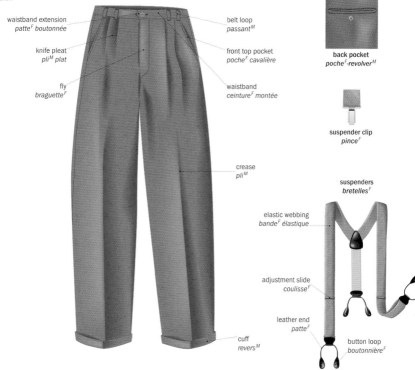

pants
pantalon^M

waistband extension
patte^F *boutonnée*

knife pleat
pli^M *plat*

fly
braguette^F

belt loop
passant^M

front top pocket
poche^F *cavalière*

waistband
ceinture^F *montée*

crease
pli^M

cuff
revers^M

back pocket
poche^F-*revolver*^M

suspender clip
pince^F

suspenders
bretelles^F

elastic webbing
bande^F *élastique*

adjustment slide
coulisse^F

leather end
patte^F

button loop
boutonnière^F

belt
ceinture^F

top stitching
surpiqûre^F

panel
croûte^F *de cuir*^M

tip
pointe^F

punch hole
cran^M

belt loop
passant^M

tongue
ardillon^M

buckle
boucle^F

CLOTHING

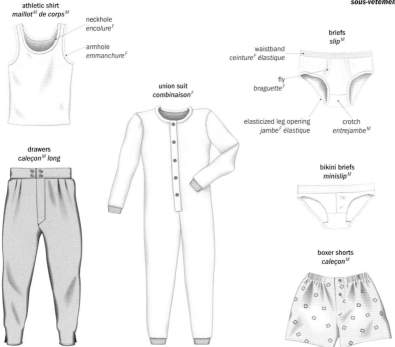

athletic shirt
maillot ^M *de corps* ^M

neckhole
encolure ^F

armhole
emmanchure ^F

briefs
slip ^M

waistband
ceinture ^F *élastique*

fly
braguette ^F

elasticized leg opening
jambe ^F *élastique*

crotch
entrejambe ^M

union suit
combinaison ^F

drawers
caleçon ^M *long*

bikini briefs
minislip ^M

boxer shorts
caleçon ^M

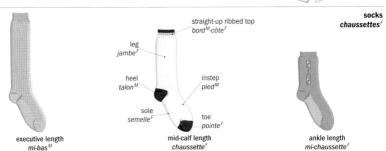

socks
chaussettes ^F

straight-up ribbed top
bord ^M-*côte* ^F

leg
jambe ^F

heel
talon ^M

instep
pied ^M

sole
semelle ^F

toe
pointe ^F

executive length
mi-bas ^M

mid-calf length
chaussette ^F

ankle length
mi-chaussette ^F

CLOTHING

coats
manteaux^M *et blousons*^M

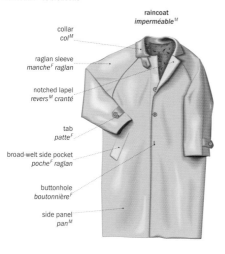

raincoat
imperméable^M

collar
col^M

raglan sleeve
manche^F *raglan*

notched lapel
revers^M *cranté*

tab
patte^F

broad-welt side pocket
poche^F *raglan*

buttonhole
boutonnière^F

side panel
pan^M

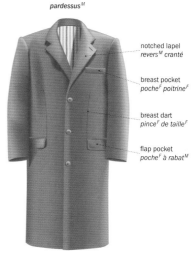

overcoat
pardessus^M

notched lapel
revers^M *cranté*

breast pocket
poche^F *poitrine*^F

breast dart
pince^F *de taille*^F

flap pocket
poche^F *à rabat*^M

trench coat
trench^M

two-way collar
col^M *transformable*

gun flap
bavolet^M

double-breasted
buttoning
double boutonnage^M

belt
ceinture^F

belt loop
passant^M

frame
boucle^F *de ceinture*^F

epaulet
patte^F *d'épaule*^F

raglan sleeve
manche^F *raglan*

sleeve strap loop
passant^M

sleeve strap
patte^F *de serrage*^M

broad-welt side pocket
poche^F *raglan*

three-quarter coat
paletot^M

parka
parka^F ; parka^M

snap-fastening tab
patte^F à boutons^M-pression^F

zipper
fermeture^F à glissière^F

sheepskin jacket
canadienne^F

duffle coat
*duffle-coat^M ;
canadienne^F*

hood
capuchon^M

yoke
empiècement^M

frog
brandebourg^M

patch pocket
poche^F plaquée

toggle fastening
bûchette^F

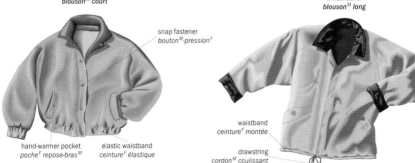

jacket
blouson^M court

snap fastener
bouton^M-pression^F

windbreaker
blouson^M long

hand-warmer pocket
poche^F repose-bras^M

elastic waistband
ceinture^F élastique

waistband
ceinture^F montée

drawstring
cordon^M coulissant

sweaters

tricots^M

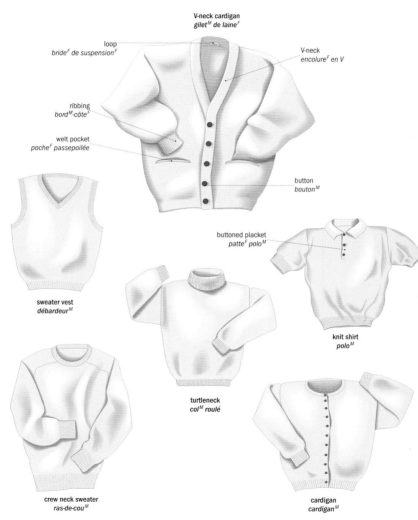

V-neck cardigan
gilet^M *de laine*^F

loop
bride^F *de suspension*^F

V-neck
encolure^F *en V*

ribbing
bord^M*-côte*^F

welt pocket
poche^F *passepoilée*

button
bouton^M

buttoned placket
patte^F *polo*^M

sweater vest
débardeur^M

knit shirt
polo^M

turtleneck
col^M *roulé*

crew neck sweater
ras-de-cou^M

cardigan
cardigan^M

suit
tailleur^M

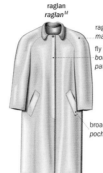

jacket
veste^F

skirt
jupe^F

raglan
raglan^M

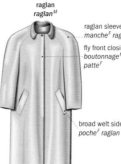

raglan sleeve
manche^F raglan

fly front closing
boutonnage^M sous patte^F

broad welt side pocket
poche^F raglan

coats
manteaux^M

top coat
redingote^F

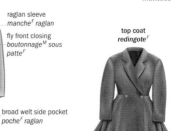

pelerine
pèlerine^F

pelerine
pèlerine^F

seam pocket
poche^F prise dans une couture^F

cape
cape^F

arm slit
passe-bras^M

pea jacket
caban^M

tailored collar
col^M tailleur^M

hand-warmer pocket
poche^F repose-bras^M

mock pocket
fausse poche^F

overcoat
manteau^M

car coat
paletot^M

jacket
veste^F

poncho
poncho^M

CLOTHING

examples of dresses
exemples^M *de robes*^F

sheath dress
robe^F *fourreau*^M

princess-seamed dress
robe^F *princesse*^F

coat dress
robe^F*-manteau*^M

polo dress
robe^F*-polo*^M

housedress
robe^F *de maison*^F

shirtwaist dress
robe^F *chemisier*^M

drop-waist dress
robe^F *taille*^F *basse*

trapeze dress
robe^F *trapèze*^M

sundress
robe^F *bain*^M*-de-soleil*^M

wraparound dress
robe^F *enveloppe*^F

tunic dress
robe^F *tunique*^F

jumper
chasuble^F

examples of skirts
exemples^M de jupes^F

gored skirt
jupe^F à lés^M

kilt
kilt^M

sarong
paréo^M

wraparound skirt
jupe^F portefeuille^M

sheath skirt
jupe^F fourreau^M

ruffled skirt
jupe^F à volants^M étagés

straight skirt
jupe^F droite

yoked skirt
jupe^F à empiècement^M

gathered skirt
jupe^F froncée

culottes
jupe^F-culotte^F

CLOTHING

examples of pleats
exemples^M de plis^M

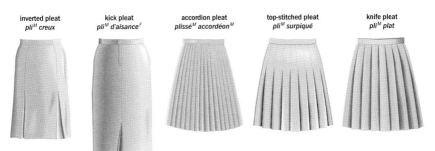

inverted pleat
pli^M creux

kick pleat
pli^M d'aisance^F

accordion pleat
plissé^M accordéon^M

top-stitched pleat
pli^M surpiqué

knife pleat
pli^M plat

examples of pants
exemples^M *de pantalons*^M

shorts
short^M

Bermuda shorts
bermuda^M

knickers
knicker^M

pedal pushers
corsaire^M

jeans
jean^M

ski pants
fuseau^M

footstrap
sous-pied^M

jumpsuit
combinaison^F-
pantalon^M

overalls
salopette^F

bell bottoms
pantalon^M *pattes*^F *d'éléphant*^M

jackets, vest and sweaters
vestes^F *et pulls*^M

bolero
boléro^M

spencer
spencer^M

blazer
blazer^M

safari jacket
saharienne[F]

vest
gilet[M]

twin-set
tandem[M]

crew neck sweater
ras-de-cou[M]

cardigan
cardigan[M]

gusset pocket
poche[F] *soufflet*[M]

examples of shirts
exemples[M] *de corsages*[M]

body suit
corsage[M]*-culotte*[F]

middy
marinière[F]

crotch piece
patte[F] *d'entrejambe*[M]

yoke
empiècement[M]

gather
fronce[F]

shirttail
pan[M]

oversized shirt
liquette[F]

classic blouse
chemisier[M] *classique*

smock
tablier[M]*-blouse*[F]

tunic
tunique[F]

wrapover top
cache-cœur[M]

polo shirt
polo[M]

over-blouse
casaque[F]

CLOTHING

nightwear
vêtements^M **de nuit**^{F}

nightgown
chemise^F de nuit^F

baby doll
nuisette^F

kimono
kimono^M

bathrobe
peignoir^M

pajamas
pyjama^M

negligee
déshabillé^M

hose
bas^M

knee-high sock
mi-bas^M

sock
chaussette^F

ankle sock
mi-chaussette^F

short sock
socquette^F

CLOTHING

panty hose
collant^M

stocking
bas^M

thigh-high stocking
bas^M*-cuissarde*^F

fish net stocking
bas^M *résille*^F

CLOTHING

underwear
sous-vêtements^M

corselette
combiné^M

camisole
caraco^M *; camisole*^F

teddy
teddy^M *; combinaison*^M*-culotte*^M

body suit
body^M *; combiné*^M*-slip*^M

panty corselette
combiné^M*-culotte*^F

half-slip
jupon^M

princess seams
découpe^F *princesse*^F

foundation slip
fond^M *de robe*^F

slip
combinaison^F*-jupon*^M

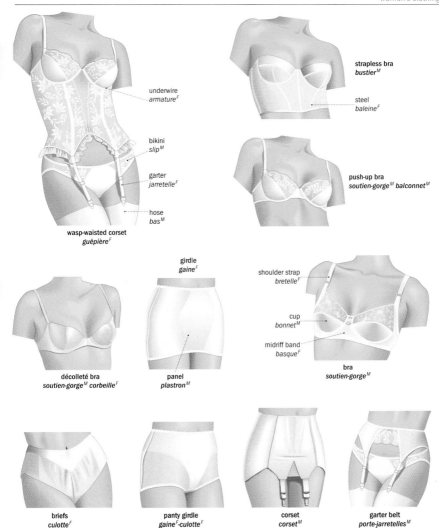

underwire
armature[F]

strapless bra
bustier[M]

steel
baleine[F]

bikini
slip[M]

garter
jarretelle[F]

hose
bas[M]

push-up bra
soutien-gorge[M] *balconnet*[M]

wasp-waisted corset
guêpière[F]

girdle
gaine[F]

shoulder strap
bretelle[F]

cup
bonnet[M]

midriff band
basque[F]

décolleté bra
soutien-gorge[M] *corbeille*[F]

panel
plastron[M]

bra
soutien-gorge[M]

briefs
culotte[F]

panty girdle
gaine[F]-*culotte*[F]

corset
corset[M]

garter belt
porte-jarretelles[M]

newborn children's clothing

vêtements^M de nouveau-né^M

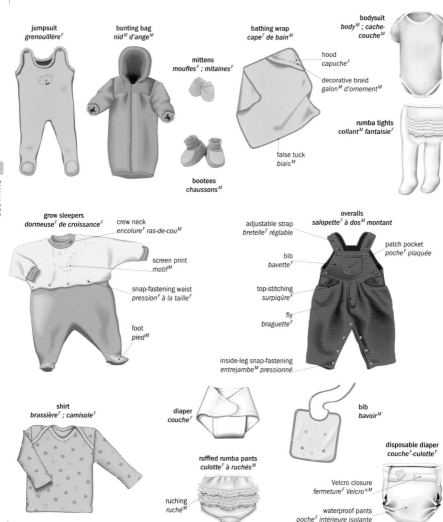

jumpsuit
grenouillère^F

bunting bag
nid^M d'ange^M

mittens
moufles^F ; mitaines^F

bathing wrap
cape^F de bain^M

hood
capuche^F

decorative braid
galon^M d'ornement^M

false tuck
biais^M

bootees
chaussons^M

bodysuit
body^M ; cache-couche^M

rumba tights
collant^M fantaisie^F

grow sleepers
dormeuse^F de croissance^F

crew neck
encolure^F ras-de-cou^M

screen print
motif^M

snap-fastening waist
pression^F à la taille^F

foot
pied^M

overalls
salopette^F à dos^M montant

adjustable strap
bretelle^F réglable

patch pocket
poche^F plaquée

bib
bavette^F

top-stitching
surpiqûre^F

fly
braguette^F

inside-leg snap-fastening
entrejambe^M pressionné

shirt
brassière^F ; camisole^F

diaper
couche^F

bib
bavoir^M

ruffled rumba pants
culotte^F à ruchés^M

ruching
ruché^M

disposable diaper
couche^F-culotte^F

Velcro closure
fermeture^F Velcro®^M

waterproof pants
poche^F intérieure isolante

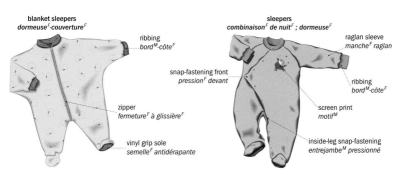

blanket sleepers
dormeuse^F-couverture^F

ribbing
bord^M-côte^F

snap-fastening front
pression^F devant

zipper
fermeture^F à glissière^F

vinyl grip sole
semelle^F antidérapante

sleepers
combinaison^F de nuit^F ; dormeuse^F

raglan sleeve
manche^F raglan

ribbing
bord^M-côte^F

screen print
motif^M

inside-leg snap-fastening
entrejambe^M pressionné

children's clothing
vêtements^M d'enfant^M

CLOTHING

overalls
salopette^F à bretelles^F croisées

button strap
bretelle^F boutonnée

bib
bavette^F

snowsuit
habit^M de neige^F

hood
capuchon^M

overalls
salopette^F

pajamas
polojama^M

T-shirt dress
robe^F tee-shirt^M

rompers
barboteuse^F

training set
tenue^F d'exercice^M

tank top
débardeur^M

shorts
short^M

jumpsuit
combinaison^F

sportswear

tenue^F d'exercice^M

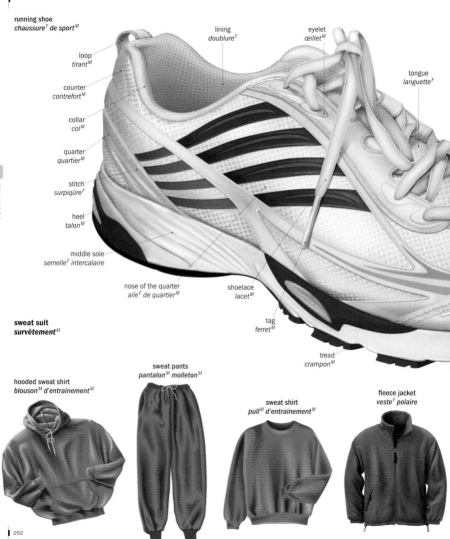

running shoe
chaussure^F de sport^M

loop
tirant^M

counter
contrefort^M

collar
col^M

quarter
quartier^M

stitch
surpiqûre^F

heel
talon^M

middle sole
semelle^F intercalaire

nose of the quarter
aile^F de quartier^M

lining
doublure^F

eyelet
œillet^M

tongue
languette^F

shoelace
lacet^M

tag
ferret^M

tread
crampon^M

sweat suit
survêtement^M

hooded sweat shirt
blouson^M d'entraînement^M

sweat pants
pantalon^M molleton^M

sweat shirt
pull^M d'entraînement^M

fleece jacket
veste^F polaire

CLOTHING

swimming trunks
slip^M *de bain*^M

swimsuit
maillot^M *de bain*^M

leotard
justaucorps^M

footless tights
collant^M *sans pieds*^M

vamp
claque^F

punch hole
perforation^F

outsole
semelle^F *d'usure*^F

tank top
débardeur^M

T-shirt
T-shirt^M

leg-warmer
jambière^F

CLOTHING

pants
pantalon^M

anorak
anorak^M

boxer shorts
short^M *boxeur*^M

shorts
cuissard^M

jewelry
bijouterie^F

earrings
boucles^F **d'oreille**^F

clip earrings
boucles^F *d'oreille*^F *à pince*^F

screw earring
boucles^F *d'oreille*^F *à vis*^F

pierced earrings
boucles^F *d'oreille*^F *à tige*^F

drop earrings
pendants^M *d'oreille*^F

hoop earrings
anneaux^M

necklaces
colliers^M

matinee-length necklace
collier^M *de perles*^F, *longueur*^F *matinée*^F

velvet-band choker
collier^M*-de-chien*^M

pendant
pendentif^M

rope necklace
sautoir^M

opera-length necklace
sautoir^M, *longueur*^F *opéra*^M

bib necklace
collier^M *de soirée*^F

choker
ras-de-cou^M

locket
médaillon^M

bracelets
bracelets^M

identification bracelet
gourmette^F *d'identité*^F

charm bracelet
gourmette^F

bangle
bracelet^M *tubulaire*

rings
bagues^F

band ring
jonc^M

signet ring
chevalière^F

solitaire ring
bague^F *solitaire*^M

engagement ring
bague^F *de fiançailles*^F

wedding ring
alliance^F

nail care
manucure^F

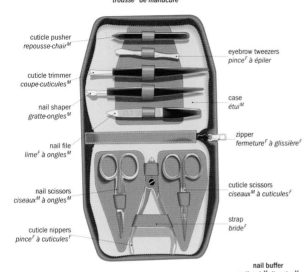

manicure set
trousse^F de manucure^F

cuticle pusher
repousse-chair^M

cuticle trimmer
coupe-cuticules^M

nail shaper
gratte-ongles^M

nail file
lime^F à ongles^M

nail scissors
ciseaux^M à ongles^M

cuticle nippers
pince^F à cuticules^F

eyebrow tweezers
pince^F à épiler

case
étui^M

zipper
fermeture^F à glissière^F

cuticle scissors
ciseaux^M à cuticules^F

strap
bride^F

nail enamel
vernis^M à ongles^M

safety scissors
ciseaux^M de sûreté^F

nail buffer
polissoir^M d'ongles^M

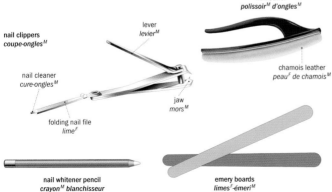

nail clippers
coupe-ongles^M

lever
levier^M

nail cleaner
cure-ongles^M

folding nail file
lime^F

jaw
mors^M

chamois leather
peau^F de chamois^M

toenail scissors
ciseaux^M de pédicure^F

nail whitener pencil
crayon^M blanchisseur d'ongles^M

emery boards
limes^F-émeri^M

makeup

maquillage^M

facial makeup

maquillage^M

fan brush
pinceau^M éventail^M

powder puff
houppette^F

synthetic sponge
éponge^F synthétique

powder blusher
*fard^M à joues^F en
poudre^F*

blusher brush
*pinceau^M pour fard^M à
joues^F*

loose powder
poudre^F libre

loose powder brush
*pinceau^M pour poudre^F
libre*

compact
poudrier^M

pressed powder
poudre^F pressée

liquid foundation
fond^M de teint^M liquide

eye makeup
maquillage^M **des yeux**^M

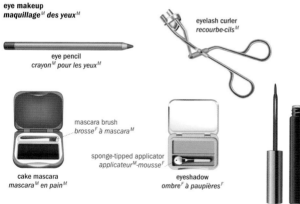

eye pencil
crayon^M pour les yeux^M

eyelash curler
recourbe-cils^M

brow brush and lash comb
brosse^F-peigne^M pour cils^M et sourcils^M

mascara brush
brosse^F à mascara^M

sponge-tipped applicator
applicateur^M-mousse^F

cake mascara
mascara^M en pain^M

eyeshadow
ombre^F à paupières^F

liquid eyeliner
*eye-liner^M liquide ;
ligneur^M*

liquid mascara
mascara^M liquide

lip makeup
maquillage^M **des lèvres**^F

lip brush
pinceau^M à lèvres^F

lipliner
*crayon^M contour^M des
lèvres^F*

lipstick
rouge^M à lèvres^F

body care
soins^M du corps^M

stopper
bouchon^M

bottle
flacon^M

eau de parfum
eau^F de parfum^M

toilet soap
savon^M de toilette^F

hair conditioner
revitalisant^M capillaire

shampoo
shampooing^M

haircolor
colorant^M capillaire

bubble bath
bain^M moussant

eau de toilette
eau^F de toilette^F

deodorant
déodorant^M

washcloth
gant^M de toilette^F

washcloth
débarbouillette^F

massage glove
gant^M de crin^M

vegetable sponge
éponge^F végétale

bath sheet
drap^M de bain^M

bath towel
serviette^F de toilette^F

bath brush
brosse^F pour le bain^M

natural sponge
éponge^F de mer^F

back brush
brosse^F pour le dos^M

hairdressing
coiffure[F]

hairbrushes
brosses[F] *à cheveux*[M]

flat-back brush
brosse[F] *pneumatique*

round brush
brosse[F] *ronde*

quill brush
brosse[F] *anglaise*

vent brush
brosse[F]-*araignée*[F]

combs
peignes[M]

Afro pick
peigne[M] *afro*

teaser comb
peigne[M] *à crêper*

tail comb
peigne[M] *à tige*[F]

barber comb
peigne[M] *de coiffeur*[M]

pitchfork comb
combiné[M] *2 dans 1*

rake comb
démêloir[M]

hair roller
bigoudi[M]

roller
rouleau[M]

hair roller pin
épingle[F] *à bigoudi*[M]

wave clip
pince[F] *à boucles*[F] *de cheveux*[M]

hairpin
épingle[F] *à cheveux*[M]

hair clip
pince[F] *de mise*[F] *en plis*[M]

bobby pin
pince[F] *à cheveux*[M]

barrette
barrette[F]

hairdressing

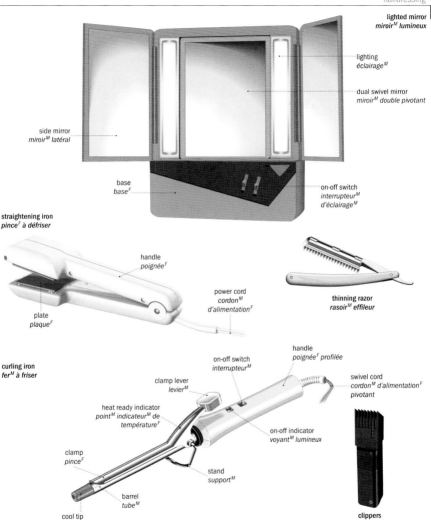

lighted mirror
miroir^M *lumineux*

lighting
éclairage^M

dual swivel mirror
miroir^M *double pivotant*

side mirror
miroir^M *latéral*

base
base^F

on-off switch
interrupteur^M
d'éclairage^M

straightening iron
pince^F *à défriser*

handle
poignée^F

power cord
cordon^M
d'alimentation^F

plate
plaque^F

thinning razor
rasoir^M *effileur*

handle
poignée^F *profilée*

curling iron
fer^M *à friser*

on-off switch
interrupteur^M

swivel cord
cordon^M *d'alimentation*^F
pivotant

clamp lever
levier^M

heat ready indicator
point^M *indicateur*^M *de*
température^F

on-off indicator
voyant^M *lumineux*

clamp
pince^F

stand
support^M

barrel
tube^M

cool tip
embout^M *isolant*

clippers
tondeuse^F

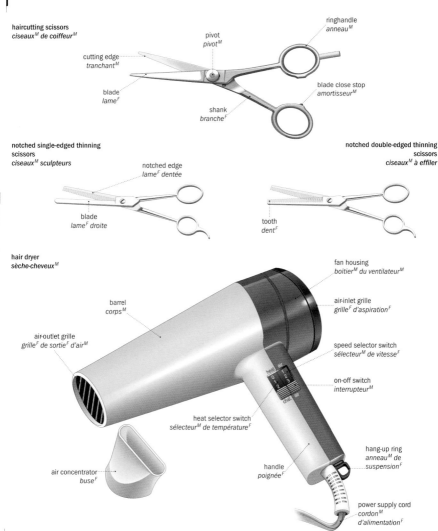

haircutting scissors
ciseaux^M de coiffeur^M

ringhandle
anneau^M

pivot
pivot^M

cutting edge
tranchant^M

blade close stop
amortisseur^M

blade
lame^F

shank
branche^F

notched single-edged thinning scissors
ciseaux^M sculpteurs

notched double-edged thinning scissors
ciseaux^M à effiler

notched edge
lame^F dentée

blade
lame^F droite

tooth
dent^F

hair dryer
sèche-cheveux^M

fan housing
boitier^M du ventilateur^M

barrel
corps^M

air-inlet grille
grille^F d'aspiration^F

air-outlet grille
grille^F de sortie^F d'air^M

speed selector switch
sélecteur^M de vitesse^F

on-off switch
interrupteur^M

heat selector switch
sélecteur^M de température^F

air concentrator
buse^F

hang-up ring
anneau^M de suspension^F

handle
poignée^F

power supply cord
cordon^M d'alimentation^F

shaving
rasage^M

electric razor
rasoir^M *électrique*

floating head
tête^F *flottante*

screen
grille^F

trimmer
tondeuse^F

closeness setting
sélecteur^M *de coupe*^F

housing
boîtier^M

cleaning brush
brosse^F *de nettoyage*^M

charge indicator
indicateur^M *de charge*^F

charging light
voyant^M *de charge*^F

on-off switch
interrupteur^M

charging plug
prise^F *de charge*^F

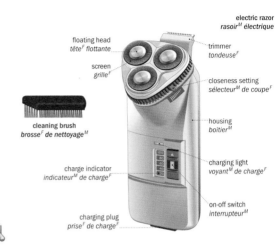

shaving foam
mousse^F *à raser*

power cord
cordon^M
d'alimentation^F

shaving brush
blaireau^M

bristle
soie^F

plug adapter
adaptateur^M *de fiche*^F

aftershave
après-rasage^M

straight razor
rasoir^M *à manche*^M

blade
lame^F

handle
manche^M

pivot
pivot^M

blade injector
distributeur^M *de lames*^F

double-edged razor
rasoir^M *à double*
tranchant^M

head
tête^F

collar
anneau^M

handle
manche^M

disposable razor
rasoir^M *jetable*

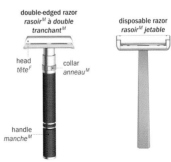

shaving mug
bol^M *à raser*

double-edged blade
lame^F *à double*
tranchant^M

dental care

hygiène^F dentaire

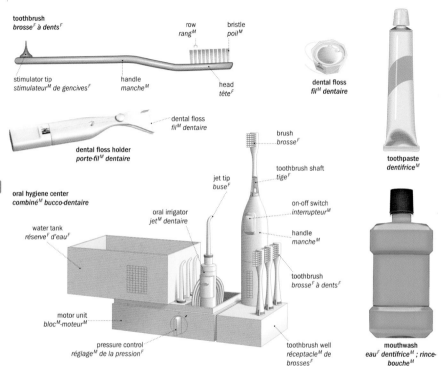

toothbrush
brosse^F à dents^F

row
rang^M

bristle
poil^M

stimulator tip
stimulateur^M de gencives^F

handle
manche^M

head
tête^F

dental floss
fil^M dentaire

dental floss
fil^M dentaire

dental floss holder
porte-fil^M dentaire

brush
brosse^F

toothbrush shaft
tige^F

on-off switch
interrupteur^M

handle
manche^M

jet tip
buse^F

oral hygiene center
combiné^M bucco-dentaire

oral irrigator
jet^M dentaire

water tank
réserve^F d'eau^F

toothbrush
brosse^F à dents^F

motor unit
bloc^M-moteur^M

pressure control
réglage^M de la pression^F

toothbrush well
réceptacle^M de brosses^F

toothpaste
dentifrice^M

mouthwash
eau^F dentifrice^M ; rince-bouche^M

contact lenses

lentilles^F de contact^M

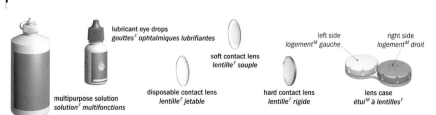

lubricant eye drops
gouttes^F ophtalmiques lubrifiantes

soft contact lens
lentille^F souple

left side
logement^M gauche

right side
logement^M droit

multipurpose solution
solution^F multifonctions

disposable contact lens
lentille^F jetable

hard contact lens
lentille^F rigide

lens case
étui^M à lentilles^F

eyeglasses
lunettes^F

eyeglasses parts
parties^F *des lunettes*^F

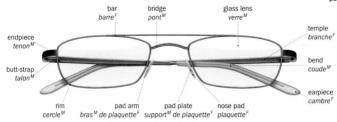

bar
barre^F

bridge
pont^M

glass lens
verre^M

endpiece
tenon^M

temple
branche^F

butt-strap
talon^M

bend
coude^M

earpiece
cambre^F

rim
cercle^M

pad arm
bras^M *de plaquette*^F

pad plate
support^M *de plaquette*^F

nose pad
plaquette^F

examples of eyeglasses
exemples^M *de lunettes*^F

opera glasses
lorgnette^F

sunglasses
lunettes^F *de soleil*^M

half-glasses
demi-lune^F

umbrellas and stick
parapluies^M *et canne*^F

umbrellas
parapluies^M

umbrella stand
porte-parapluies^M

walking stick
canne^F

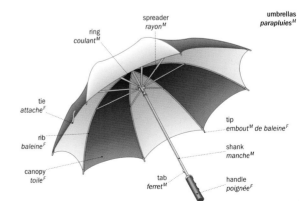

spreader
rayon^M

ring
coulant^M

tie
attache^F

rib
baleine^F

canopy
toile^F

tab
ferret^M

tip
embout^M *de baleine*^F

shank
manche^M

handle
poignée^F

leather goods
articles^M de maroquinerie^F

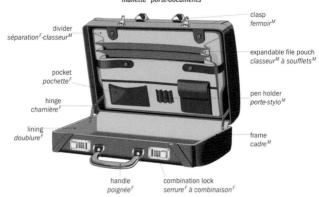

attaché case
mallette^F porte-documents^M

divider
séparation^F-classeur^M

pocket
pochette^F

hinge
charnière^F

lining
doublure^F

clasp
fermoir^M

expandable file pouch
classeur^M à soufflets^M

pen holder
porte-stylo^M

frame
cadre^M

handle
poignée^F

combination lock
serrure^F à combinaison^F

bottom-fold portfolio
porte-documents^M à soufflet^M

retractable handle
poignée^F rentrante

exterior pocket
poche^F extérieure

gusset
soufflet^M

briefcase
serviette^F

tab
patte^F

key lock
serrure^F à clé^F

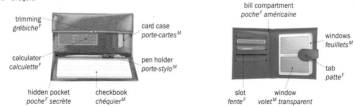

checkbook/secretary clutch
portefeuille^M chéquier^M

trimming
grébiche^F

calculator
calculette^F

hidden pocket
poche^F secrète

card case
porte-cartes^M

pen holder
porte-stylo^M

checkbook
chéquier^M

card case
porte-cartes^M

bill compartment
poche^F américaine

windows
feuillets^M

tab
patte^F

slot
fente^F

window
volet^M transparent

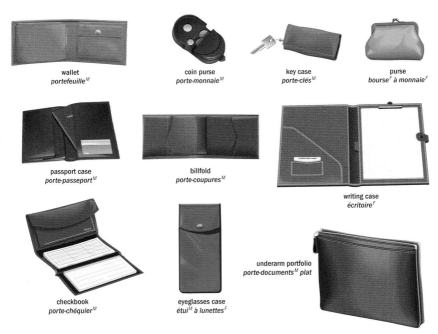

wallet
portefeuille[M]

coin purse
porte-monnaie[M]

key case
porte-clés[M]

purse
bourse[F] *à monnaie*[F]

passport case
porte-passeport[M]

billfold
porte-coupures[M]

writing case
écritoire[F]

checkbook
porte-chéquier[M]

eyeglasses case
étui[M] *à lunettes*[F]

underarm portfolio
porte-documents[M] *plat*

handbags
sacs[M] *à main*[F]

drawstring bag
sac[M] *seau*[M]

satchel bag
sac[M] *cartable*[M]

eyelet
œillet[M]

drawstring
lacet[M] *de serrage*[M]

front pocket
poche[F] *frontale*

handle
poignée[F]

flap
rabat[M]

clasp
fermoir[M]

lock
serrure[F]

handbags

box bag
sac^M *boîte*^F

drawstring bag
balluchon^M

shoulder bag
sac^M *à bandoulière*^F

buckle
boucle^F

shoulder strap
bandoulière^F

muff
manchon^M

hobo bag
sac^M *besace*^F

accordion bag
sac^M *accordéon*^M

tote bag
sac^M *fourre-tout*^M

men's bag
pochette^F *d'homme*^M

gusset
soufflet^M

sea bag
sac^M *marin*^M

duffel bag
sac^M *polochon*^M

carrier bag
sac^M *à provisions*^F

shopping bag
cabas^M

luggage
bagages^M

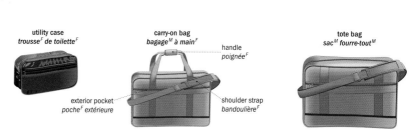

utility case
trousse^F *de toilette*^F

carry-on bag
bagage^M *à main*^F

handle
poignée^F

tote bag
sac^M *fourre-tout*^M

exterior pocket
poche^F *extérieure*

shoulder strap
bandoulière^F

garment bag
housse^F à vêtements^M

luggage carrier
porte-bagages^M

backpack
sac^M à dos^M

frame
armature^F

luggage elastic
sangle^F élastique

stand
béquille^F

zipper
fermeture^F à glissière^F

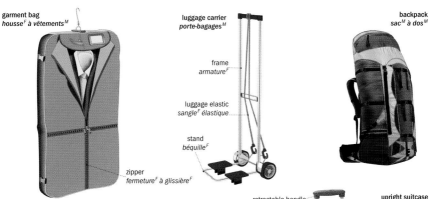

retractable handle
poignée^F escamotable

upright suitcase
valise^F verticale

Pullman case
valise^F pullman^M

handle
poignée^F

identification tag
porte-adresse^M

frame
cadre^M

pull strap
dragonne^F

trim
garniture^F

wheel
roulette^F

weekender
valise^F fin^F de semaine^F

hasp
moraillon^M

interior pocket
poche^F intérieure

trunk
malle^F

tray
plateau^M

curtain
panneau^M de séparation^F

latch
crampon^M de fermeture^F

garment strap
sangle^F serre-vêtements^M

cornerpiece
cantonnière^F

lock
serrure^F

fittings
ferrure^F

handle
poignée^F

shell
coque^F

pyramid
pyramide^F

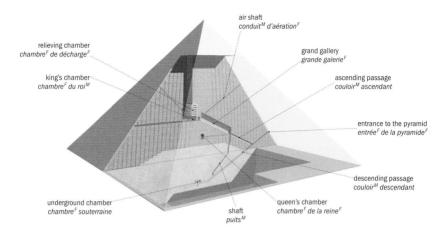

air shaft
conduit^M d'aération^F

relieving chamber
chambre^F de décharge^F

grand gallery
grande galerie^F

king's chamber
chambre^F du roi^M

ascending passage
couloir^M ascendant

entrance to the pyramid
entrée^F de la pyramide^F

descending passage
couloir^M descendant

underground chamber
chambre^F souterraine

shaft
puits^M

queen's chamber
chambre^F de la reine^F

Greek theater
théâtre^M grec

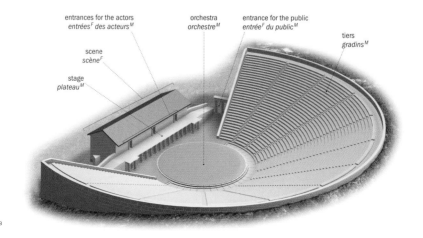

entrances for the actors
entrées^F des acteurs^M

orchestra
orchestre^M

entrance for the public
entrée^F du public^M

tiers
gradins^M

scene
scène^F

stage
plateau^M

Greek temple
temple^M grec

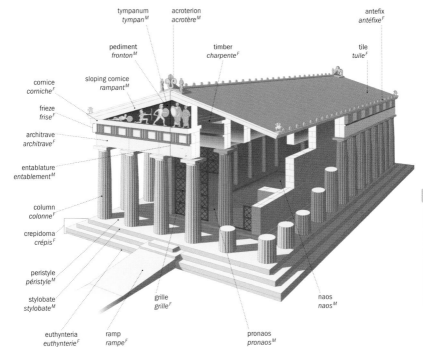

tympanum
tympan^M

acroterion
acrotère^M

timber
charpente^F

antefix
antéfixe^F

tile
tuile^F

pediment
fronton^M

cornice
corniche^F

sloping cornice
rampant^M

frieze
frise^F

architrave
architrave^F

entablature
entablement^M

column
colonne^F

crepidoma
crépis^F

peristyle
péristyle^M

stylobate
stylobate^M

euthynteria
euthynterie^F

ramp
rampe^F

grille
grille^F

pronaos
pronaos^M

naos
naos^M

ARTS AND ARCHITECTURE

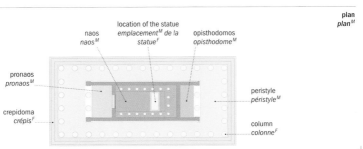

plan
plan^M

naos
naos^M

location of the statue
emplacement^M de la statue^F

opisthodomos
opisthodome^M

pronaos
pronaos^M

crepidoma
crépis^F

peristyle
péristyle^M

column
colonne^F

Roman house

maison^F romaine

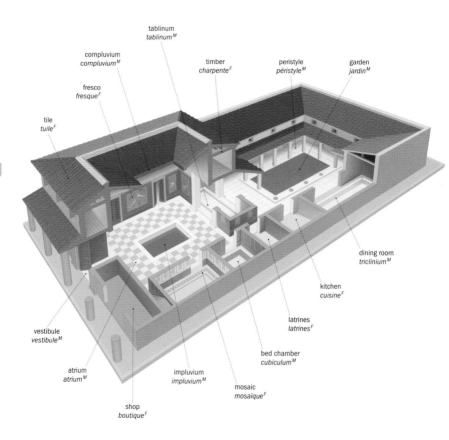

tablinum
tablinum^M

compluvium
compluvium^M

timber
charpente^F

peristyle
péristyle^M

garden
jardin^M

fresco
fresque^F

tile
tuile^F

dining room
triclinium^M

kitchen
cuisine^F

latrines
latrines^F

vestibule
vestibule^M

bed chamber
cubiculum^M

atrium
atrium^M

impluvium
impluvium^M

mosaic
mosaïque^F

shop
boutique^F

Roman amphitheater
amphithéâtre^M romain

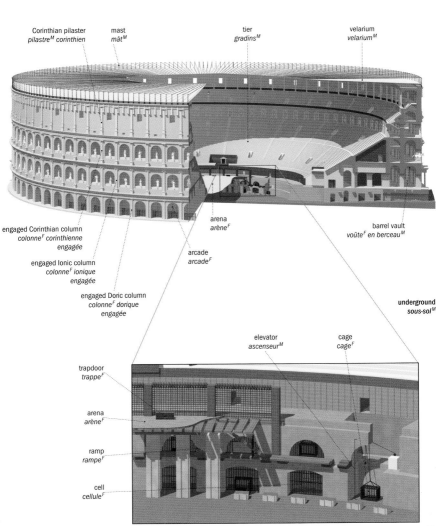

Corinthian pilaster
pilastre^M corinthien

mast
mât^M

tier
gradins^M

velarium
velarium^M

engaged Corinthian column
*colonne^F corinthienne
engagée*

engaged Ionic column
*colonne^F ionique
engagée*

engaged Doric column
*colonne^F dorique
engagée*

arena
arène^F

arcade
arcade^F

barrel vault
voûte^F en berceau^M

underground
sous-sol^M

elevator
ascenseur^M

cage
cage^F

trapdoor
trappe^F

arena
arène^F

ramp
rampe^F

cell
cellule^F

castle
château^M fort

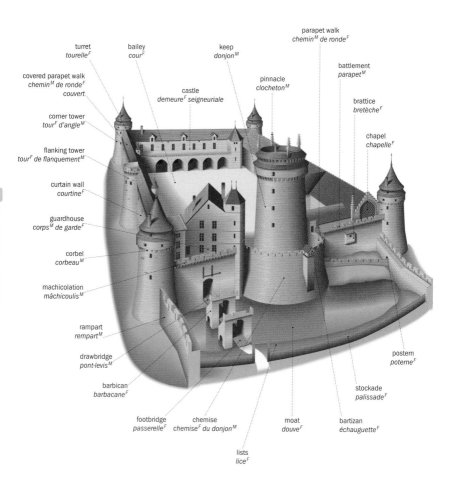

parapet walk
chemin^M de ronde^F

turret
tourelle^F

bailey
cour^F

keep
donjon^M

battlement
parapet^M

covered parapet walk
chemin^M de ronde^F
couvert

pinnacle
clocheton^M

castle
demeure^F seigneuriale

brattice
bretèche^F

corner tower
tour^F d'angle^M

chapel
chapelle^F

flanking tower
tour^F de flanquement^M

curtain wall
courtine^F

guardhouse
corps^M de garde^F

corbel
corbeau^M

machicolation
mâchicoulis^M

rampart
rempart^M

postern
poterne^F

drawbridge
pont-levis^M

barbican
barbacane^F

stockade
palissade^F

footbridge
passerelle^F

chemise
chemise^F du donjon^M

moat
douve^F

bartizan
échauguette^F

lists
lice^F

pagoda
pagode^F

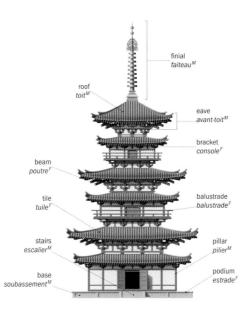

finial
faîteau^M

roof
toit^M

eave
avant-toit^M

bracket
console^F

beam
poutre^F

balustrade
balustrade^F

tile
tuile^F

stairs
escalier^M

pillar
pilier^M

base
soubassement^M

podium
estrade^F

Aztec temple
temple^M aztèque

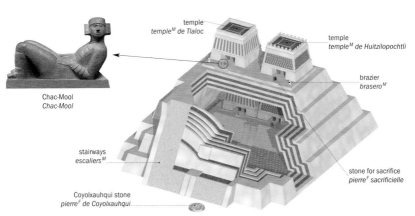

temple
temple^M de Tlaloc

temple
temple^M de Huitzilopochtli

brazier
brasero^M

Chac-Mool
Chac-Mool

stairways
escaliers^M

stone for sacrifice
pierre^F sacrificielle

Coyolxauhqui stone
pierre^F de Coyolxauhqui

cathedral
cathédrale^F

Gothic cathedral
cathédrale^F gothique

vault
voûte^F

keystone
clé^F de voûte^F

traverse arch
arc^M-doubleau^M

lierne
lierne^F

tierceron
tierceron^M

formeret
arc^M-formeret^M

diagonal buttress
arc^M diagonal

tower
tour^F

abutment
culée^F

pinnacle
pinacle^M

transept spire
flèche^F de transept^M

flying buttress
arc^M-boutant

Lady chapel
chapelle^F axiale

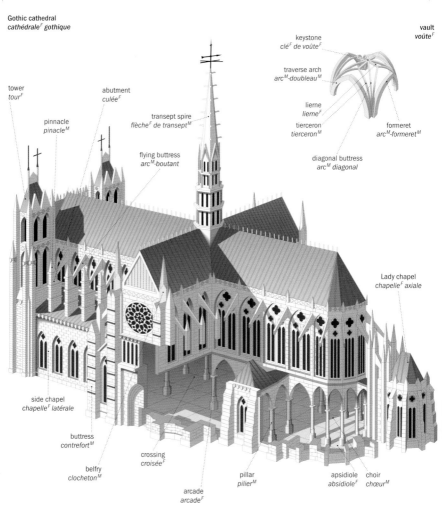

side chapel
chapelle^F latérale

buttress
contrefort^M

belfry
clocheton^M

crossing
croisée^F

arcade
arcade^F

pillar
pilier^M

apsidiole
absidiole^F

choir
chœur^M

façade
façade^F

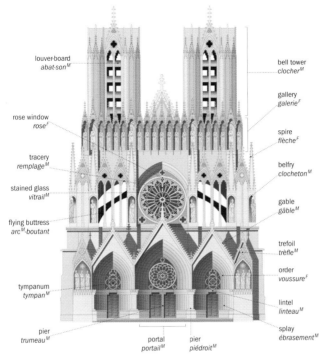

louver-board
abat-son^M

rose window
rose^F

tracery
remplage^M

stained glass
vitrail^M

flying buttress
arc^M-boutant

tympanum
tympan^M

pier
trumeau^M

portal
portail^M

pier
piédroit^M

bell tower
clocher^M

gallery
galerie^F

spire
flèche^F

belfry
clocheton^M

gable
gâble^M

trefoil
trèfle^M

order
voussure^F

lintel
linteau^M

splay
ébrasement^M

plan
plan^M

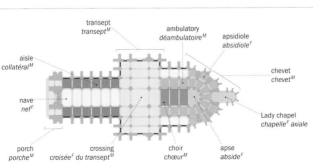

transept
transept^M

ambulatory
déambulatoire^M

apsidiole
absidiole^F

aisle
collatéral^M

chevet
chevet^M

nave
nef^F

Lady chapel
chapelle^F axiale

porch
porche^M

crossing
croisée^F du transept^M

choir
chœur^M

apse
abside^F

elements of architecture

éléments^M d'architecture^F

examples of doors
exemples^M de portes^F

manual revolving door
porte^F à tambour^M manuelle

canopy
couronne^F

wing
vantail^M

enclosure
sas^M

push bar
barre^F de poussée^F

compartment
compartiment^M

motion detector
détecteur^M de mouvement^M

automatic sliding door
porte^F coulissante automatique

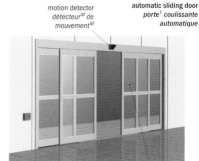

wing
vantail^M

strip
lanière^F

conventional door
porte^F classique

folding door
porte^F pliante

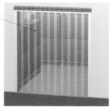

strip door
porte^F à lanières^F

fire door
porte^F coupe-feu

sliding folding door
porte^F accordéon^M

sliding door
porte^F coulissante

sectional garage door
porte^F de garage^M sectionnelle

up and over garage door
porte^F de garage^M basculante

examples of windows
exemples^M *de fenêtres*^{F}

sliding folding window
fenêtre^F *en accordéon*^{M}

French window
fenêtre^F *à la française*^{F}

casement window
fenêtre^F *à l'anglaise*^{F}

louvered window
fenêtre^F *à jalousies*^{F}

sliding window
fenêtre^F *coulissante*

sash window
fenêtre^F *à guillotine*^{F}

horizontal pivoting window
fenêtre^F *basculante*

vertical pivoting window
fenêtre^F *pivotante*

elevator
ascenseur^M

ARTS AND ARCHITECTURE

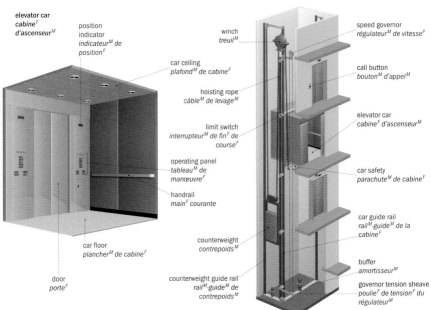

elevator car
cabine^F
d'ascenseur^M

position indicator
indicateur^M *de position*^{F}

winch
treuil^M

car ceiling
plafond^M *de cabine*^{F}

hoisting rope
câble^M *de levage*^{M}

limit switch
interrupteur^M *de fin*^{F} *de course*^{F}

operating panel
tableau^M *de manœuvre*^{F}

handrail
main^F *courante*

car floor
plancher^M *de cabine*^{F}

door
porte^F

counterweight
contrepoids^M

counterweight guide rail
rail^M*-guide*^{M} *de contrepoids*^{M}

speed governor
régulateur^M *de vitesse*^{F}

call button
bouton^M *d'appel*^{M}

elevator car
cabine^F *d'ascenseur*^{M}

car safety
parachute^M *de cabine*^{F}

car guide rail
rail^M*-guide*^{M} *de la cabine*^{F}

buffer
amortisseur^M

governor tension sheave
poulie^F *de tension*^{F} *du régulateur*^{M}

traditional houses
maisons^F traditionnelles

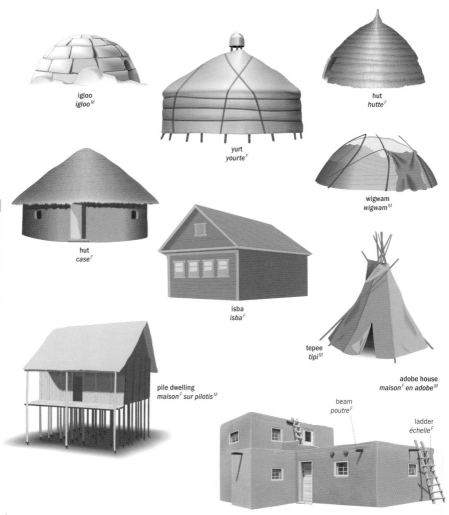

igloo
igloo^M

yurt
yourte^F

hut
hutte^F

hut
case^F

wigwam
wigwam^M

isba
isba^F

tepee
tipi^M

pile dwelling
maison^F sur pilotis^M

adobe house
maison^F en adobe^M

beam
poutre^F

ladder
échelle^F

city houses
maisons^F de ville^F

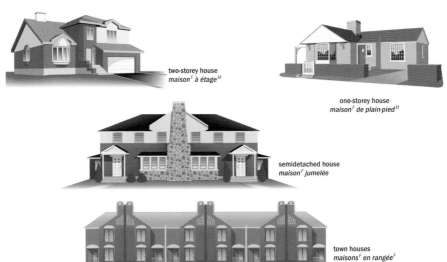

two-storey house
maison^F à étage^M

one-storey house
maison^F de plain-pied^M

semidetached house
maison^F jumelée

town houses
maisons^F en rangée^F

condominiums
*appartements^M en
copropriété^F*

high-rise apartment building
tour^F d'habitation^F

sound stage
plateau^M de tournage^M

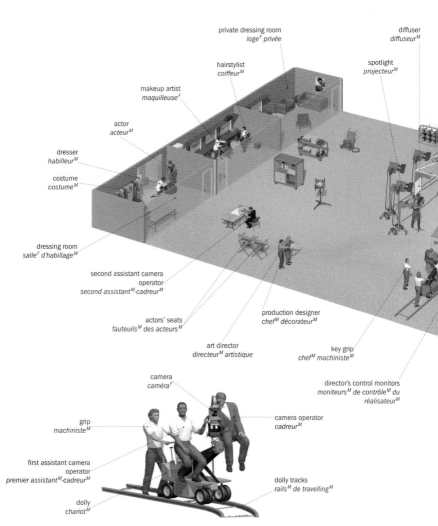

private dressing room
loge^F privée

diffuser
diffuseur^M

hairstylist
coiffeur^M

spotlight
projecteur^M

makeup artist
maquilleuse^F

actor
acteur^M

dresser
habilleur^M

costume
costume^M

dressing room
salle^F d'habillage^M

second assistant camera
operator
second assistant^M-cadreur^M

actors' seats
fauteuils^M des acteurs^M

production designer
chef^M décorateur^M

art director
directeur^M artistique

key grip
chef^M machiniste^M

director's control monitors
*moniteurs^M de contrôle^M du
réalisateur^M*

camera
caméra^F

grip
machiniste^M

camera operator
cadreur^M

first assistant camera
operator
premier assistant^M-cadreur^M

dolly tracks
rails^M de travelling^M

dolly
chariot^M

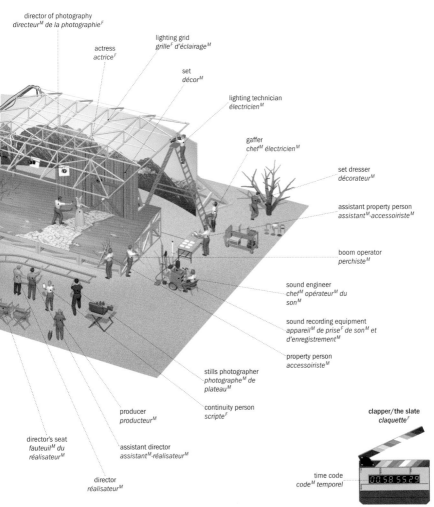

director of photography
directeur[M] *de la photographie*[F]

actress
actrice[F]

lighting grid
grille[F] *d'éclairage*[M]

set
décor[M]

lighting technician
électricien[M]

gaffer
chef[M] *électricien*[M]

set dresser
décorateur[M]

assistant property person
assistant[M]-*accessoiriste*[M]

boom operator
perchiste[M]

sound engineer
chef[M] *opérateur*[M] *du*
son[M]

sound recording equipment
appareil[M] *de prise*[F] *de son*[M] *et*
d'enregistrement[M]

property person
accessoiriste[M]

stills photographer
photographe[M] *de*
plateau[M]

continuity person
scripte[F]

producer
producteur[M]

assistant director
assistant[M]-*réalisateur*[M]

director's seat
fauteuil[M] *du*
réalisateur[M]

director
réalisateur[M]

clapper/the slate
claquette[F]

time code
code[M] *temporel*

00 58 55 29

theater
salle^F *de spectacle*^M

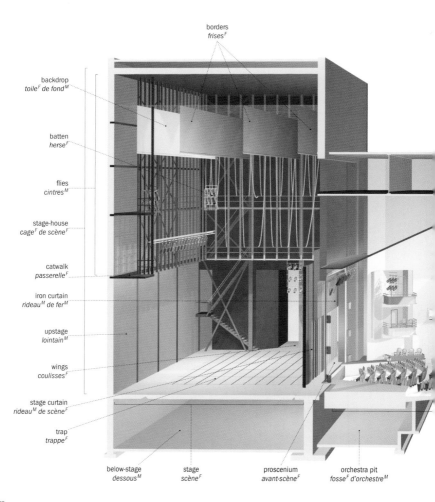

borders
frises^F

backdrop
toile^F *de fond*^M

batten
herse^F

flies
cintres^M

stage-house
cage^F *de scène*^F

catwalk
passerelle^F

iron curtain
rideau^M *de fer*^M

upstage
lointain^M

wings
coulisses^F

stage curtain
rideau^M *de scène*^F

trap
trappe^F

below-stage
dessous^M

stage
scène^F

proscenium
avant-scène^F

orchestra pit
fosse^F *d'orchestre*^M

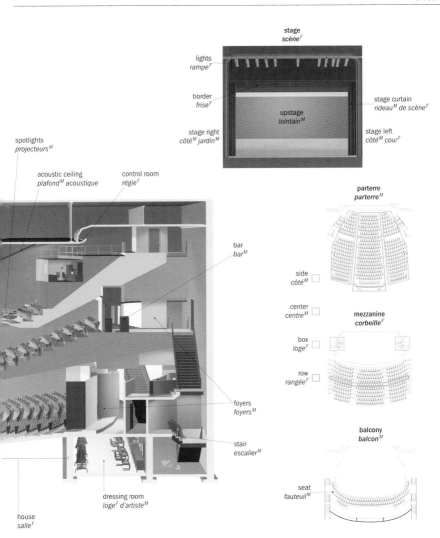

stage
scène^F

lights
rampe^F

border
frise^F

upstage
lointain^M

stage curtain
rideau^M de scène^F

stage right
côté^M jardin^M

stage left
côté^M cour^F

spotlights
projecteurs^M

acoustic ceiling
plafond^M acoustique

control room
régie^F

bar
bar^M

side
côté^M

center
centre^M

box
loge^F

row
rangée^F

parterre
parterre^M

mezzanine
corbeille^F

balcony
balcon^M

seat
fauteuil^M

foyers
foyers^M

stair
escalier^M

dressing room
loge^F d'artiste^M

house
salle^F

ARTS AND ARCHITECTURE

movie theater

cinéma[M]

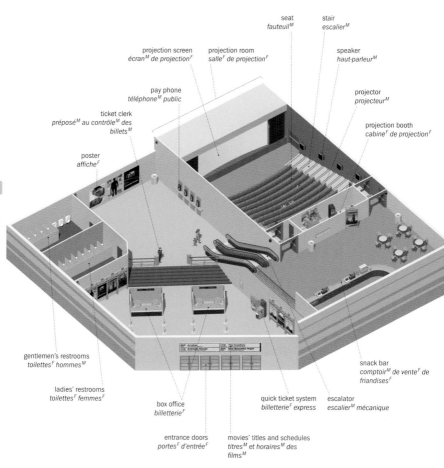

seat
fauteuil[M]

stair
escalier[M]

projection screen
écran[M] *de projection*[F]

projection room
salle[F] *de projection*[F]

speaker
haut-parleur[M]

pay phone
téléphone[M] *public*

projector
projecteur[M]

ticket clerk
préposé[M] *au contrôle*[M] *des billets*[M]

projection booth
cabine[F] *de projection*[F]

poster
affiche[F]

gentlemen's restrooms
toilettes[F] *hommes*[M]

snack bar
comptoir[M] *de vente*[F] *de friandises*[F]

ladies' restrooms
toilettes[F] *femmes*[F]

box office
billetterie[F]

quick ticket system
billetterie[F] *express*

escalator
escalier[M] *mécanique*

entrance doors
portes[F] *d'entrée*[F]

movies' titles and schedules
titres[M] *et horaires*[M] *des films*[M]

symphony orchestra
orchestre^M symphonique

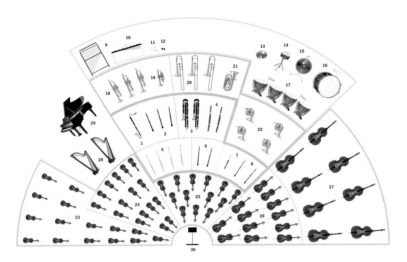

woodwind section
famille^F des bois^M

1 bass clarinet
clarinette^F basse

2 clarinets
clarinettes^F

3 contrabassoons
contrebassons^M

4 bassoons
bassons^M

5 flutes
flûtes^F

6 oboes
hautbois^M

7 piccolo
piccolo^M

8 English horns
cors^M anglais

percussion section
instruments^M à percussion^F

9 tubular bells
carillon^M tubulaire

10 xylophone
xylophone^M

11 triangle
triangle^M

12 castanets
castagnettes^F

13 cymbals
cymbales^F

14 snare drum
caisse^F claire

15 gong
gong^M

16 bass drum
grosse caisse^F

17 timpani
timbales^F

28 harps
harpes^F

brass section
famille^F des cuivres^M

18 trumpets
trompettes^F

19 cornet
cornet^M à pistons^M

20 trombones
trombones^M

21 tuba
tuba^M

22 French horns
cors^M d'harmonie^F

29 piano
piano^M

string section
famille^F du violon^M

23 first violins
premiers violons^M

24 second violins
seconds violons^M

25 violas
altos^M

26 cellos
violoncelles^M

27 double basses
contrebasses^F

30 conductor's podium
pupitre^M du chef^M d'orchestre^M

traditional musical instruments
instruments[M] *traditionnels*

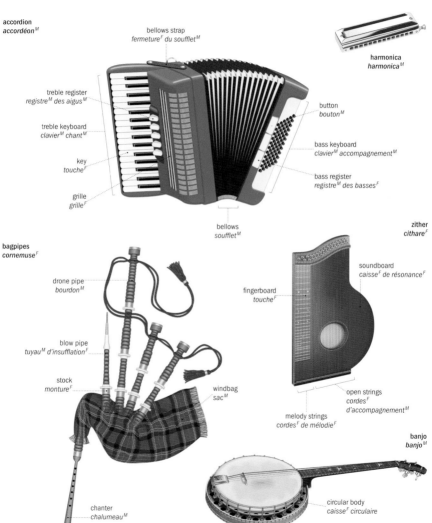

accordion
accordéon[M]

bellows strap
fermeture[F] *du soufflet*[M]

treble register
registre[M] *des aigus*[M]

treble keyboard
clavier[M] *chant*[M]

key
touche[F]

grille
grille[F]

bellows
soufflet[M]

harmonica
harmonica[M]

button
bouton[M]

bass keyboard
clavier[M] *accompagnement*[M]

bass register
registre[M] *des basses*[F]

zither
cithare[F]

bagpipes
cornemuse[F]

soundboard
caisse[F] *de résonance*[F]

drone pipe
bourdon[M]

fingerboard
touche[F]

blow pipe
tuyau[M] *d'insufflation*[F]

stock
monture[F]

windbag
sac[M]

open strings
cordes[F]
d'accompagnement[M]

melody strings
cordes[F] *de mélodie*[F]

banjo
banjo[M]

chanter
chalumeau[M]

circular body
caisse[F] *circulaire*

ARTS AND ARCHITECTURE

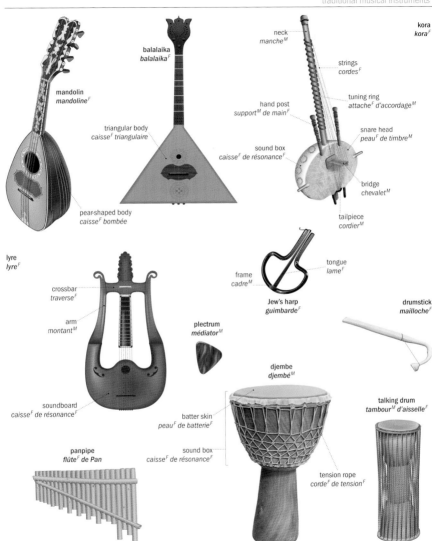

kora
kora^F

neck
manche^M

strings
cordes^F

tuning ring
attache^F *d'accordage*^M

hand post
support^M *de main*^F

snare head
peau^F *de timbre*^M

sound box
caisse^F *de résonance*^F

bridge
chevalet^M

tailpiece
cordier^M

balalaika
balalaïka^F

mandolin
mandoline^F

triangular body
caisse^F *triangulaire*

pear-shaped body
caisse^F *bombée*

lyre
lyre^F

crossbar
traverse^F

arm
montant^M

soundboard
caisse^F *de résonance*^F

frame
cadre^M

tongue
lame^F

Jew's harp
guimbarde^F

drumstick
mailloche^F

plectrum
médiator^M

djembe
djembé^M

batter skin
peau^F *de batterie*^F

talking drum
tambour^M *d'aisselle*^F

panpipe
flûte^F *de Pan*

sound box
caisse^F *de résonance*^F

tension rope
corde^F *de tension*^F

ARTS AND ARCHITECTURE

297

musical notation
notation^F musicale

staff
portée^F

space
interligne^M

line
ligne^F

ledger line
ligne^F supplémentaire

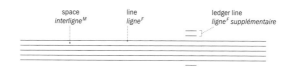

clefs
clés^F

treble clef
clé^F de sol^M

bass clef
clé^F de fa^M

C clef
clé^F d'ut^M

time signatures
mesures^F

two-two time
mesure^F à deux temps^M

four-four time
mesure^F à quatre temps^M

repeat mark
barre^F de reprise^F

three-four time
mesure^F à trois temps^M

bar line
barre^F de mesure^F

intervals
intervalles^M

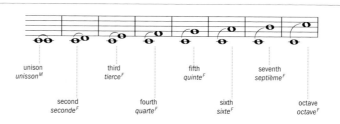

unison
unisson^M

third
tierce^F

fifth
quinte^F

seventh
septième^F

second
seconde^F

fourth
quarte^F

sixth
sixte^F

octave
octave^F

scale
gamme^F

C	D	E	F	G	A	B	C
do^M	*ré^M*	*mi^M*	*fa^M*	*sol^M*	*la^M*	*si^M*	*do^M*

ARTS AND ARCHITECTURE

rest symbols
valeur[F] des silences[M]

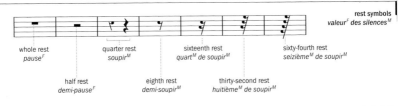

whole rest
pause[F]

quarter rest
soupir[M]

sixteenth rest
quart[M] de soupir[M]

sixty-fourth rest
seizième[M] de soupir[M]

half rest
demi-pause[F]

eighth rest
demi-soupir[M]

thirty-second rest
huitième[M] de soupir[M]

ornaments
ornements[M]

appoggiatura
appoggiature[F]

trill
trille[M]

turn
gruppetto[M]

mordent
mordant[M]

note symbols
valeur[F] des notes[F]

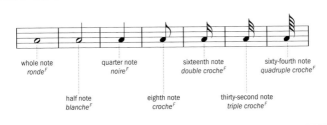

whole note
ronde[F]

quarter note
noire[F]

sixteenth note
double croche[F]

sixty-fourth note
quadruple croche[F]

half note
blanche[F]

eighth note
croche[F]

thirty-second note
triple croche[F]

accidentals
altérations[F]

flat
bémol[M]

double sharp
double dièse[M]

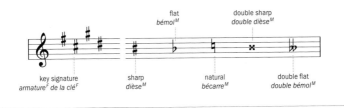

key signature
armature[F] de la clé[F]

sharp
dièse[M]

natural
bécarre[M]

double flat
double bémol[M]

other signs
autres signes[M]

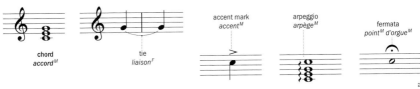

chord
accord[M]

tie
liaison[F]

accent mark
accent[M]

arpeggio
arpège[M]

fermata
point[M] d'orgue[M]

ARTS AND ARCHITECTURE

examples of instrumental groups

exemples^M de groupes^M instrumentaux

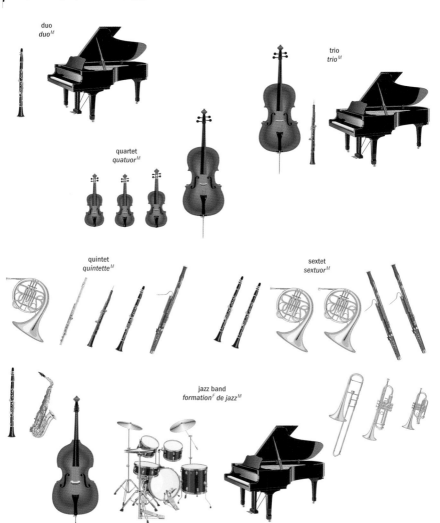

duo
duo^M

trio
trio^M

quartet
quatuor^M

quintet
quintette^M

sextet
sextuor^M

jazz band
formation^F de jazz^M

ARTS AND ARCHITECTURE

stringed instruments
instruments^M à cordes^F

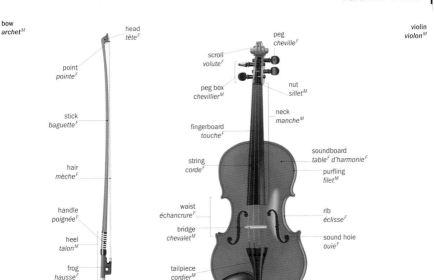

bow
archet^M

head
tête^F

point
pointe^F

stick
baguette^F

hair
mèche^F

handle
poignée^F

heel
talon^M

frog
hausse^F

screw
vis^F

violin
violon^M

peg
cheville^F

scroll
volute^F

peg box
chevillier^M

nut
sillet^M

neck
manche^M

fingerboard
touche^F

string
corde^F

soundboard
table^F d'harmonie^F

purfling
filet^M

waist
échancrure^F

rib
éclisse^F

bridge
chevalet^M

sound hole
ouïe^F

tailpiece
cordier^M

chin rest
mentonnière^F

end button
bouton^M

violin family
famille^F du violon^M

double bass
contrebasse^F

cello
violoncelle^M

viola
alto^M

violin
violon^M

ARTS AND ARCHITECTURE

harp
harpe[F]

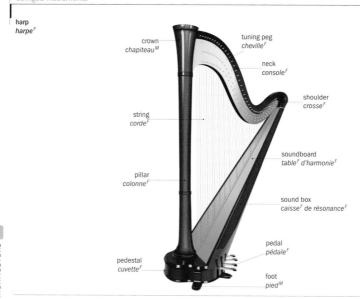

crown
chapiteau[M]

tuning peg
cheville[F]

neck
console[F]

shoulder
crosse[F]

string
corde[F]

soundboard
table[F] *d'harmonie*[F]

pillar
colonne[F]

sound box
caisse[F] *de résonance*[F]

pedal
pédale[F]

pedestal
cuvette[F]

foot
pied[M]

acoustic guitar
guitare[F] *acoustique*

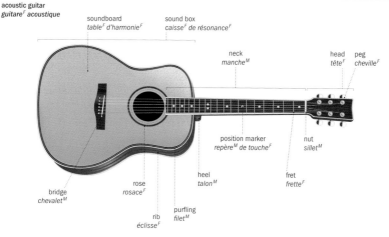

soundboard
table[F] *d'harmonie*[F]

sound box
caisse[F] *de résonance*[F]

neck
manche[M]

head
tête[F]

peg
cheville[F]

position marker
repère[M] *de touche*[F]

nut
sillet[M]

heel
talon[M]

fret
frette[F]

bridge
chevalet[M]

rose
rosace[F]

purfling
filet[M]

rib
éclisse[F]

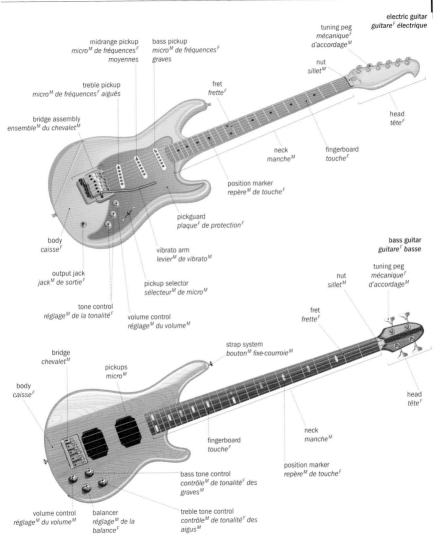

electric guitar
guitare^F électrique

tuning peg
*mécanique^F
d'accordage^M*

nut
sillet^M

midrange pickup
*micro^M de fréquences^F
moyennes*

bass pickup
*micro^M de fréquences^F
graves*

treble pickup
micro^M de fréquences^F aiguës

fret
frette^F

head
tête^F

bridge assembly
ensemble^M du chevalet^M

neck
manche^M

fingerboard
touche^F

position marker
repère^M de touche^F

body
caisse^F

pickguard
plaque^F de protection^F

output jack
jack^M de sortie^F

vibrato arm
levier^M de vibrato^M

tone control
réglage^M de la tonalité^F

pickup selector
sélecteur^M de micro^M

volume control
réglage^M du volume^M

bass guitar
guitare^F basse

tuning peg
*mécanique^F
d'accordage^M*

nut
sillet^M

fret
frette^F

head
tête^F

bridge
chevalet^M

pickups
micro^M

strap system
bouton^M fixe-courroie^M

body
caisse^F

fingerboard
touche^F

neck
manche^M

position marker
repère^M de touche^F

bass tone control
*contrôle^M de tonalité^F des
graves^M*

volume control
réglage^M du volume^M

balancer
*réglage^M de la
balance^F*

treble tone control
*contrôle^M de tonalité^F des
aigus^M*

ARTS AND ARCHITECTURE

keyboard instruments
instruments^M *à clavier*^M

upright piano
piano^M *droit*

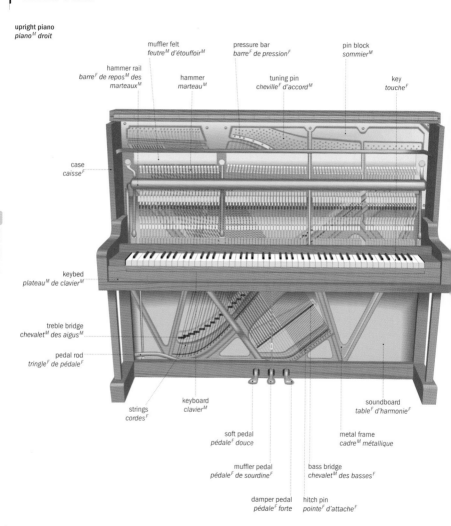

muffler felt
feutre^M *d'étouffoir*^M

pressure bar
barre^F *de pression*^F

pin block
sommier^M

hammer rail
barre^F *de repos*^M *des marteaux*^M

hammer
marteau^M

tuning pin
cheville^F *d'accord*^M

key
touche^F

case
caisse^F

keybed
plateau^M *de clavier*^M

treble bridge
chevalet^M *des aigus*^M

pedal rod
tringle^F *de pédale*^F

strings
cordes^F

keyboard
clavier^M

soundboard
table^F *d'harmonie*^F

soft pedal
pédale^F *douce*

metal frame
cadre^M *métallique*

muffler pedal
pédale^F *de sourdine*^F

bass bridge
chevalet^M *des basses*^F

damper pedal
pédale^F *forte*

hitch pin
pointe^F *d'attache*^F

organ
*orgue*M

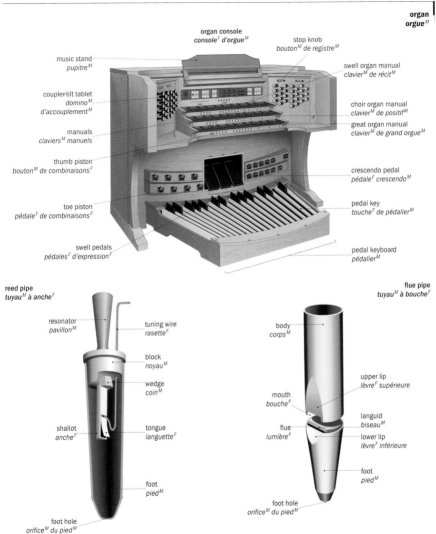

organ console
*console*F *d'orgue*M

music stand
*pupitre*M

coupler-tilt tablet
*domino*M
*d'accouplement*M

manuals
*claviers*M *manuels*

thumb piston
*bouton*M *de combinaisons*F

toe piston
*pédale*F *de combinaisons*F

swell pedals
*pédales*F *d'expression*F

stop knob
*bouton*M *de registre*M

swell organ manual
*clavier*M *de récit*M

choir organ manual
*clavier*M *de positif*M

great organ manual
*clavier*M *de grand orgue*M

crescendo pedal
*pédale*F *crescendo*M

pedal key
*touche*F *de pédalier*M

pedal keyboard
*pédalier*M

reed pipe
*tuyau*M *à anche*F

resonator
*pavillon*M

tuning wire
*rasette*F

block
*noyau*M

wedge
*coin*M

shallot
*anche*F

tongue
*languette*F

foot
*pied*M

foot hole
*orifice*M *du pied*M

flue pipe
*tuyau*M *à bouche*F

body
*corps*M

upper lip
*lèvre*F *supérieure*

mouth
*bouche*F

flue
*lumière*F

languid
*biseau*M

lower lip
*lèvre*F *inférieure*

foot
*pied*M

foot hole
*orifice*M *du pied*M

wind instruments
instruments^M *à vent*^M

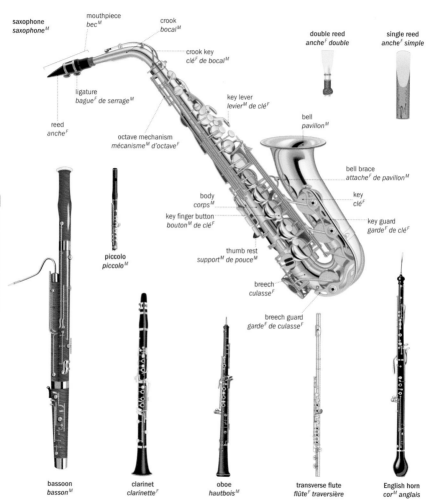

saxophone
saxophone^M

mouthpiece
bec^M

crook
bocal^M

crook key
clé^F *de bocal*^M

ligature
bague^F *de serrage*^M

reed
anche^F

octave mechanism
mécanisme^M *d'octave*^F

key lever
levier^M *de clé*^F

double reed
anche^F *double*

single reed
anche^F *simple*

bell
pavillon^M

bell brace
attache^F *de pavillon*^M

body
corps^M

key
clé^F

key finger button
bouton^M *de clé*^F

key guard
garde^F *de clé*^F

thumb rest
support^M *de pouce*^M

breech
culasse^F

breech guard
garde^F *de culasse*^F

piccolo
piccolo^M

bassoon
basson^M

clarinet
clarinette^F

oboe
hautbois^M

transverse flute
flûte^F *traversière*

English horn
cor^M *anglais*

ARTS AND ARCHITECTURE

wind instruments

trumpet
trompette^F

little finger hook
crochet^M *de petit doigt*^M

key
bouton^M *de piston*^M

bell
pavillon^M

mouthpipe
branche^F *d'embouchure*^F

ring
bague^F

mouthpiece receiver
boisseau^M *d'embouchure*^F

mouthpiece
embouchure^F

tuning slide
coulisse^F *d'accord*^M

first valve slide
coulisse^F *du premier piston*^M

spit valve
soupape^F *d'évacuation*^F

third valve slide
coulisse^F *du troisième piston*^M

thumb hook
crochet^M *de pouce*^M

valve
piston^M

mute
sourdine^F

valve casing
corps^M *de piston*^M

second valve slide
coulisse^F *du deuxième piston*^M

cornet
cornet^M *à pistons*^M

French horn
cor^M *d'harmonie*^F

bugle
clairon^M

saxhorn
saxhorn^M

tuba
tuba^M

trombone
trombone^M

ARTS AND ARCHITECTURE

percussion instruments

instruments^M à percussion^F

ARTS AND ARCHITECTURE

drums
batterie^F

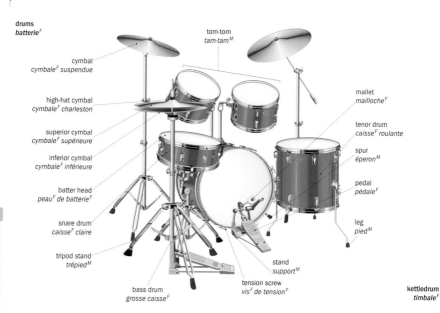

tom-tom
tam-tam^M

cymbal
cymbale^F suspendue

high-hat cymbal
cymbale^F charleston

superior cymbal
cymbale^F supérieure

inferior cymbal
cymbale^F inférieure

batter head
peau^F de batterie^F

snare drum
caisse^F claire

tripod stand
trépied^M

bass drum
grosse caisse^F

tension screw
vis^F de tension^F

stand
support^M

mallet
mailloche^F

tenor drum
caisse^F roulante

spur
éperon^M

pedal
pédale^F

leg
pied^M

kettledrum
timbale^F

snare drum
caisse^F claire

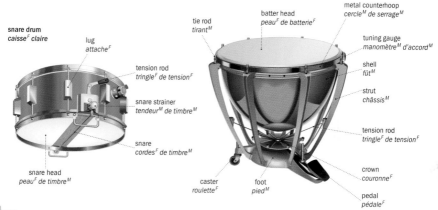

lug
attache^F

tension rod
tringle^F de tension^F

snare strainer
tendeur^M de timbre^M

snare
cordes^F de timbre^M

snare head
peau^F de timbre^M

tie rod
tirant^M

batter head
peau^F de batterie^F

metal counterhoop
cercle^M de serrage^M

tuning gauge
manomètre^M d'accord^M

shell
fût^M

strut
châssis^M

tension rod
tringle^F de tension^F

crown
couronne^F

caster
roulette^F

foot
pied^M

pedal
pédale^F

sleigh bells
grelots^M

set of bells
clochettes^F

sistrum
sistre^M

castanets
castagnettes^F

cymbals
cymbales^F

tambourine
tambour^M *de basque*^M

bongos
bongo^M

triangle
triangle^M

head
peau^F

jingle
cymbalette^F

metal rod
battant^M

wire brush
balai^M *métallique*

gong
gong^M

drum sticks
baguettes^F

xylophone
xylophone^M

resonator
tube^M *de résonance*^F

frame
châssis^M

bar
lame^F

tubular bells
carillon^M *tubulaire*

mallets
mailloches^F

ARTS AND ARCHITECTURE

309

electronic instruments
instruments^M électroniques

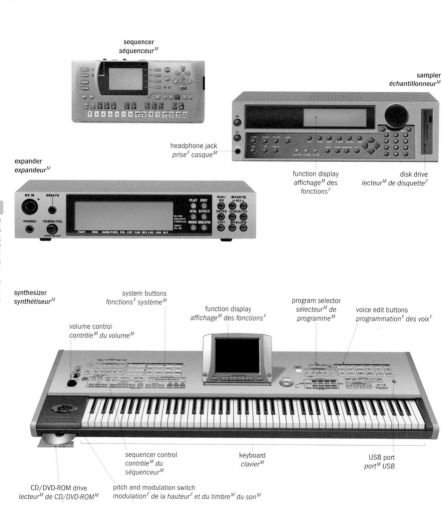

sequencer
séquenceur^M

sampler
échantillonneur^M

headphone jack
prise^F casque^M

expander
expandeur^M

function display
*affichage^M des
fonctions^F*

disk drive
lecteur^M de disquette^F

ARTS AND ARCHITECTURE

synthesizer
synthétiseur^M

system buttons
fonctions^F système^M

function display
affichage^M des fonctions^F

program selector
*sélecteur^M de
programme^M*

voice edit buttons
programmation^F des voix^F

volume control
contrôle^M du volume^M

sequencer control
*contrôle^M du
séquenceur^M*

keyboard
clavier^M

USB port
port^M USB

CD/DVD-ROM drive
lecteur^M de CD/DVD-ROM^M

pitch and modulation switch
modulation^F de la hauteur^F et du timbre^M du son^M

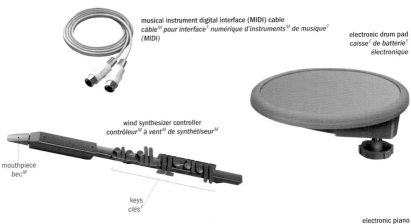

musical instrument digital interface (MIDI) cable
câble^M pour interface^F numérique d'instruments^M de musique^F
(MIDI)

electronic drum pad
caisse^F de batterie^F
électronique

wind synthesizer controller
contrôleur^M à vent^M de synthétiseur^M

mouthpiece
bec^M

keys
clés^F

electronic piano
piano^M électronique

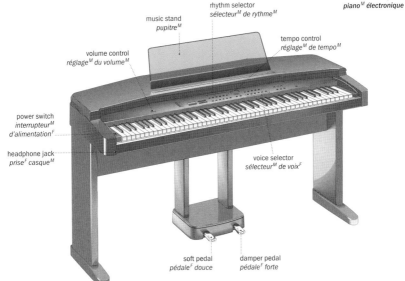

rhythm selector
sélecteur^M de rythme^M

music stand
pupitre^M

tempo control
réglage^M de tempo^M

volume control
réglage^M du volume^M

power switch
interrupteur^M
d'alimentation^F

headphone jack
prise^F casque^M

voice selector
sélecteur^M de voix^F

soft pedal
pédale^F douce

damper pedal
pédale^F forte

writing instruments
instruments^M d'écriture^F

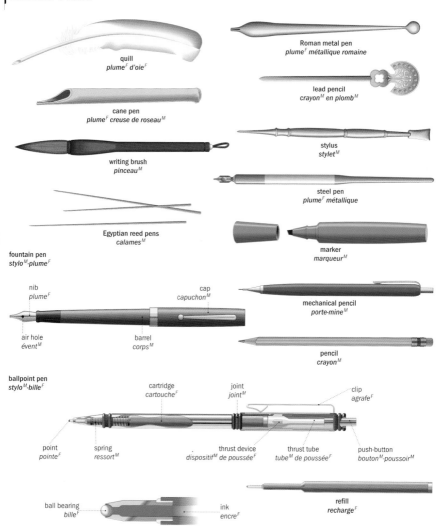

quill
plume^F d'oie^F

Roman metal pen
plume^F métallique romaine

cane pen
plume^F creuse de roseau^M

lead pencil
crayon^M en plomb^M

writing brush
pinceau^M

stylus
stylet^M

steel pen
plume^F métallique

Egyptian reed pens
calames^M

marker
marqueur^M

fountain pen
stylo^M-plume^F

nib
plume^F

cap
capuchon^M

mechanical pencil
porte-mine^M

air hole
évent^M

barrel
corps^M

pencil
crayon^M

ballpoint pen
stylo^M-bille^F

cartridge
cartouche^F

joint
joint^M

clip
agrafe^F

point
pointe^F

spring
ressort^M

thrust device
dispositif^M de poussée^F

thrust tube
tube^M de poussée^F

push-button
bouton^M-poussoir^M

ball bearing
bille^F

ink
encre^F

refill
recharge^F

newspaper
journal[M]

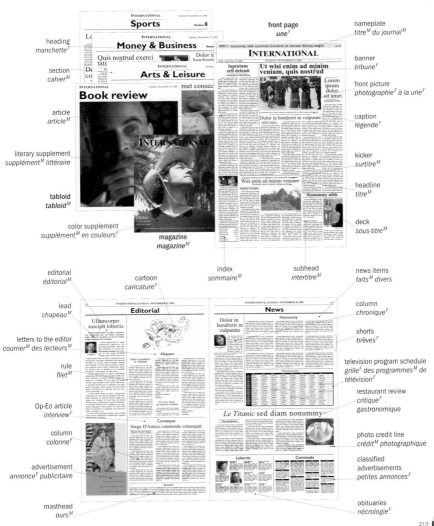

nameplate
titre[M] *du journal*[M]

front page
une[F]

heading
manchette[F]

banner
tribune[F]

section
cahier[M]

front picture
photographie[F] *à la une*[F]

article
article[M]

caption
légende[F]

literary supplement
supplément[M] *littéraire*

kicker
surtitre[M]

headline
titre[M]

tabloid
tabloid[M]

deck
sous-titre[M]

color supplement
supplément[M] *en couleurs*[F]

magazine
magazine[M]

index
sommaire[M]

subhead
intertitre[M]

news items
faits[M] *divers*

editorial
éditorial[M]

cartoon
caricature[F]

column
chronique[F]

lead
chapeau[M]

shorts
brèves[F]

letters to the editor
courrier[M] *des lecteurs*[M]

television program schedule
grille[F] *des programmes*[M] *de télévision*[F]

rule
filet[M]

restaurant review
critique[F] *gastronomique*

Op-Ed article
interview[F]

column
colonne[F]

photo credit line
crédit[M] *photographique*

advertisement
annonce[F] *publicitaire*

classified advertisements
petites annonces[F]

masthead
ours[M]

obituaries
nécrologie[F]

photography
photographie[F]

single-lens reflex (SLR) camera: front view
appareil[M] *à visée*[F] *reflex mono-objectif*[M] : vue avant

exposure adjustment knob
correction[F] *d'exposition*[F]

accessory shoe
griffe[F] *porte-accessoires*[M]

hot-shoe contact
contact[M] *électrique*

drive mode
mode[M] *d'acquisition*[F]

control panel
écran[M] *de contrôle*[M]

command control dial
sélecteur[M] *de fonctions*[F]

on-off switch
commutateur[M] *marche*[F]/*arrêt*[M]

shutter release button
déclencheur[M]

self-timer indicator
témoin[M] *du retardateur*[M]

camera body
boîtier[M]

lens release button
déverrouillage[M] *de l'objectif*[M]

objective lens
objectif[M]

exposure mode
mode[M] *d'exposition*[F]

multiple exposure mode
surimpression[F]

sensitivity
sensibilité[F]

remote control terminal
prise[F] *de télécommande*[F]

focus mode selector
mode[M] *de mise*[F] *au point*[M]

depth-of-field preview button
vérification[F] *de la profondeur*[F] *de champ*[M]

lenses
objectifs[M]

telephoto lens
téléobjectif[M]

zoom lens
objectif[M] *zoom*[M]

wide-angle lens
objectif[M] *grand-angulaire*

macro lens
objectif[M] *macro*

lens accessories
accessoires[M] **de l'objectif**[M]

lens cap
capuchon[M] *d'objectif*[M]

lens hood
parasoleil[M]

polarizing filter
filtre[M] *de polarisation*[F]

digital reflex camera: camera back
appareil^M à visée^F reflex numérique : dos^M

power switch
commutateur^M d'alimentation^F

menu button
touche^F de sélection^F des menus^M

settings display button
touche^F d'affichage^M des réglages^M

strap eyelet
œillet^M d'attache^F

multi-image jump button
touche^F de saut^M d'images^F

video and digital terminals
prises^F vidéo et numérique

image review button
touche^F de visualisation^F des images^F

remote control terminal
prise^F de télécommande^F

liquid crystal display
écran^M à cristaux^M liquides

viewfinder
viseur^M

compact memory card
carte^F de mémoire^F

cover
couvercle^M

index/enlarge button
touche^F d'index^M/agrandissement^M

erase button
touche^F d'effacement^M

four-way selector
sélecteur^M quadridirectionnel

eject button
bouton^M d'éjection^F

still cameras
appareils^M photographiques

Polaroid® camera
Polaroid^M

medium-format SLR (6 x 6)
appareil^M reflex 6 X 6 mono-objectif^M

ultracompact camera
appareil^M ultracompact

compact camera
appareil^M compact

disposable camera
appareil^M jetable

view camera
chambre^F photographique

broadcast satellite communication

télédiffusion^F par satellite^M

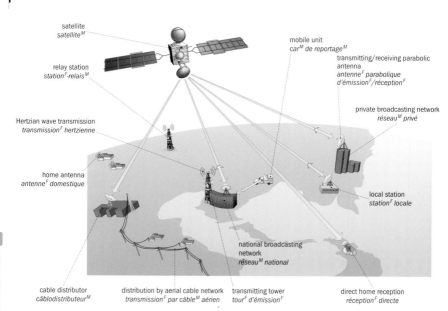

satellite
satellite^M

relay station
station^F-relais^M

mobile unit
car^M de reportage^M

transmitting/receiving parabolic antenna
antenne^F parabolique d'émission^F/réception^F

Hertzian wave transmission
transmission^F hertzienne

private broadcasting network
réseau^M privé

home antenna
antenne^F domestique

local station
station^F locale

national broadcasting network
réseau^M national

cable distributor
câblodistributeur^M

distribution by aerial cable network
transmission^F par câble^M aérien

transmitting tower
tour^F d'émission^F

direct home reception
réception^F directe

telecommunication satellites

satellites^M de télécommunications^F

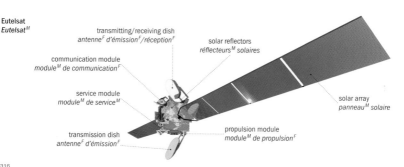

Eutelsat
Eutelsat^M

transmitting/receiving dish
antenne^F d'émission^F/réception^F

solar reflectors
réflecteurs^M solaires

communication module
module^M de communication^F

service module
module^M de service^M

solar array
panneau^M solaire

transmission dish
antenne^F d'émission^F

propulsion module
module^M de propulsion^F

telecommunications by satellite
télécommunications^F par satellite^M

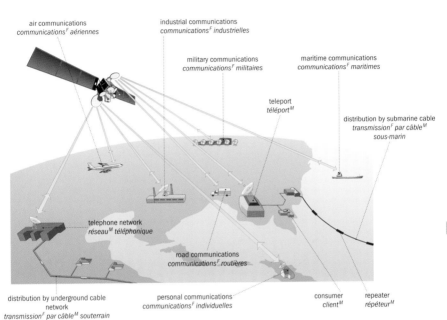

air communications
communications^F aériennes

industrial communications
communications^F industrielles

military communications
communications^F militaires

maritime communications
communications^F maritimes

teleport
téléport^M

distribution by submarine cable
*transmission^F par câble^M
sous-marin*

telephone network
réseau^M téléphonique

road communications
communications^F routières

distribution by underground cable
network
transmission^F par câble^M souterrain

personal communications
communications^F individuelles

consumer
client^M

repeater
répéteur^M

telecommunication satellites

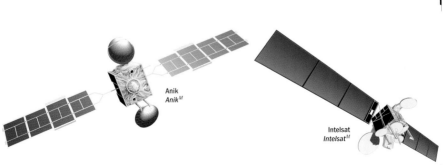

Anik
Anik^M

Intelsat
Intelsat^M

television
télévision[F]

liquid crystal display (LCD) television
téléviseur[M] *à cristaux*[M] *liquides*

plasma television
téléviseur[M] *à plasma*[M]

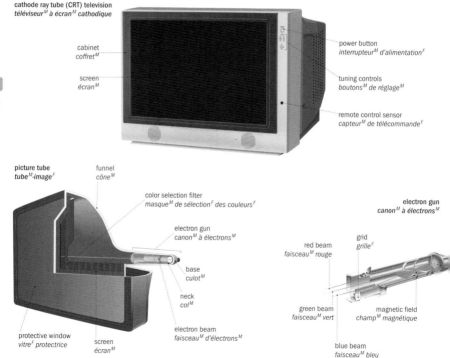

cathode ray tube (CRT) television
téléviseur[M] *à écran*[M] *cathodique*

cabinet
coffret[M]

screen
écran[M]

power button
interrupteur[M] *d'alimentation*[F]

tuning controls
boutons[M] *de réglage*[M]

remote control sensor
capteur[M] *de télécommande*[F]

picture tube
tube[M]*-image*[F]

funnel
cône[M]

color selection filter
masque[M] *de sélection*[F] *des couleurs*[F]

electron gun
canon[M] *à électrons*[M]

base
culot[M]

neck
col[M]

protective window
vitre[F] *protectrice*

screen
écran[M]

electron beam
faisceau[M] *d'électrons*[M]

electron gun
canon[M] *à électrons*[M]

red beam
faisceau[M] *rouge*

grid
grille[F]

green beam
faisceau[M] *vert*

magnetic field
champ[M] *magnétique*

blue beam
faisceau[M] *bleu*

COMMUNICATIONS AND OFFICE AUTOMATION

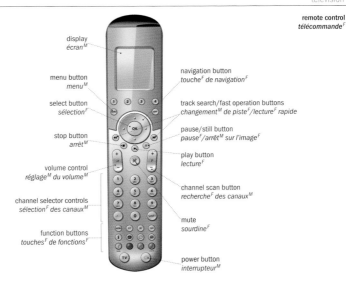

remote control
télécommande[F]

display
écran[M]

menu button
menu[M]

select button
sélection[F]

stop button
arrêt[M]

volume control
réglage[M] *du volume*[M]

channel selector controls
sélection[F] *des canaux*[M]

function buttons
touches[F] *de fonctions*[F]

navigation button
touche[F] *de navigation*[F]

track search/fast operation buttons
changement[M] *de piste*[F]/*lecture*[F] *rapide*

pause/still button
pause[F]/*arrêt*[M] *sur l'image*[F]

play button
lecture[F]

channel scan button
recherche[F] *des canaux*[M]

mute
sourdine[F]

power button
interrupteur[M]

DVD recorder
enregistreur[M] *de DVD*[M] *vidéo*

power button
interrupteur[M] *d'alimentation*[F]

channel selector
sélection[F] *des canaux*[M]

display
afficheur[M]

record button
touche[F] *d'enregistrement*[M]

play button
touche[F] *de lecture*[F]

stop button
touche[F] *d'arrêt*[M]

disc tray
plateau[M] *de chargement*[M]

disc compartment control
contrôle[M] *du plateau*[M]

pause/still button
pause[F]/*arrêt*[M] *sur l'image*[F]

track search/fast operation buttons
changement[M] *de piste*[F]/*lecture*[F] *rapide*

recording media
supports[M] *d'enregistrement*[M]

videocassette
cassette[F] *vidéo*

recording tape
bande[F] *magnétique*

reel
bobine[F]

digital versatile disc (DVD)
disque[M] *numérique polyvalent (DVD)*

mini-DV camcorder: front view
caméscope^M mini-DV : vue^F avant

electronic viewfinder
viseur^M électronique

photoshot button
touche^F photo^F

power/functions switch
commutateur^M
alimentation^F/fonctions^F

hand strap
dragonne^F

zoom button
commande^F du zoom^M

recording mode
mode^M d'enregistrement^M

zoom lens
objectif^M zoom^M

terminal cover
couvre-prises^M

lamp
lampe^F

microphone
microphone^M

mini-DV camcorder: rear view
caméscope^M mini-DV : vue^F arrière

focus button
touche^F de mise^F au
point^M

videotape operation controls
commandes^F de la bande^F vidéo

nightshot button
touche^F de prise^F de vues^F nocturne

liquid crystal display
écran^M à cristaux^M liquides

eyepiece
oculaire^M

recording start/stop button
touche^F d'enregistrement^M

rechargeable battery pack
pile^F rechargeable

card slot
logement^M de la carte^F mémoire^F

menu button
touche^F de menu^M

speaker
haut-parleur^M

backlighting button
touche^F de rétroéclairage^M

widescreen/data code button
touche^F écran^M large/code^M de données^F

dish antenna
antenne^F parabolique

receiver
terminal^M numérique

dish
réflecteur^M

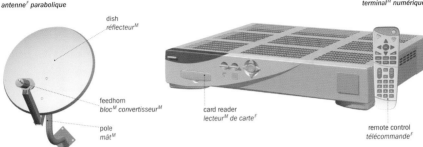

feedhorn
bloc^M convertisseur^M

pole
mât^M

card reader
lecteur^M de carte^F

remote control
télécommande^F

home theater
cinéma^M maison^F

surround loudspeaker
enceinte^F ambiophonique

center loudspeaker
enceinte^F centrale

large-screen television set
téléviseur^M grand écran^M

main loudspeaker
enceinte^F principale

subwoofers
enceintes^F d'extrêmes graves^M

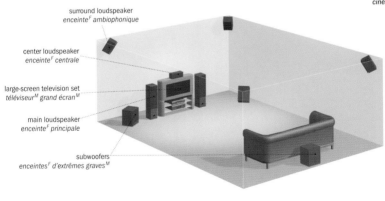

videocassette recorder
(VCR)
magnétoscope^M

cassette compartment
logement^M de la cassette^F

display
afficheur^M

power button
interrupteur^M
d'alimentation^F

sound reproducing system

chaîne^F stéréo

ampli-tuner: front view
ampli^M-syntoniseur^M : vue^F avant

sound mode lights
voyants^M d'indication^F du mode^M sonore

sound mode selector
sélecteur^M de mode^M sonore

input lights
voyants^M d'entrée^F

tape recorder select button
touche^F de sélection^F du magnétophone^M

power button
interrupteur^M d'alimentation^F

sound field control
contrôle^M du champ^M sonore

input select button
touche^F de sélection^F d'entrée^F

loudspeaker system select buttons
touches^F de sélection^F des enceintes^F

headphone jack
prise^F casque^M

tuning buttons
touches^F de sélection^F des stations^F

display
afficheur^M

volume control
réglage^M du volume^M

preset tuning button
touche^F de présélection^F

memory button
touche^F mémoire^F

input selector
sélecteur^M d'entrée^F

balance control
équilibrage^M des haut-parleurs^M

band select button
touche^F de modulation^F

FM mode select button
touche^F de sélection^F du mode^M FM

bass tone control
contrôle^M de tonalité^F des graves^M

treble tone control
contrôle^M de tonalité^F des aigus^M

ampli-tuner: back view
ampli^M-syntoniseur^M : vue^F arrière

ground terminal
borne^F de mise^F à la terre^F

cooling fan
ventilateur^M

power cord
cordon^M d'alimentation^F

antenna terminals
bornes^F de raccordement^M des antennes^F

input/output audio/video jacks
prises^F d'entrée^F/de sortie^F audio/vidéo

loudspeaker terminals
bornes^F de raccordement^M des enceintes^F

switched outlet
prise^F de courant^M commutée

sound reproducing system

cassette tape deck
platine^F cassette^F

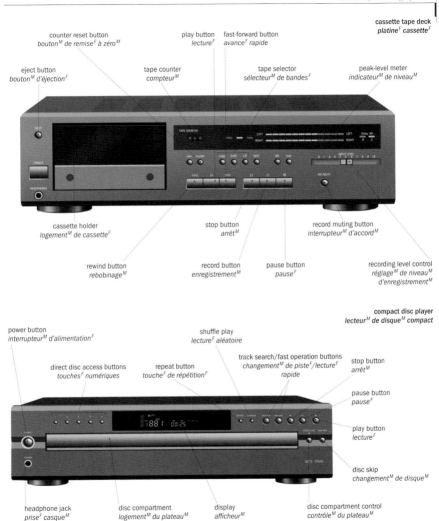

counter reset button
bouton^M de remise^F à zéro^M

play button
lecture^F

fast-forward button
avance^F rapide

eject button
bouton^M d'éjection^F

tape counter
compteur^M

tape selector
sélecteur^M de bandes^F

peak-level meter
indicateur^M de niveau^M

cassette holder
logement^M de cassette^F

stop button
arrêt^M

record muting button
interrupteur^M d'accord^M

rewind button
rebobinage^M

record button
enregistrement^M

pause button
pause^F

recording level control
réglage^M de niveau^M
d'enregistrement^M

compact disc player
lecteur^M de disque^M compact

power button
interrupteur^M d'alimentation^F

shuffle play
lecture^F aléatoire

direct disc access buttons
touches^F numériques

repeat button
touche^F de répétition^F

track search/fast operation buttons
changement^M de piste^F/lecture^F
rapide

stop button
arrêt^M

pause button
pause^F

play button
lecture^F

disc skip
changement^M de disque^M

headphone jack
prise^F casque^M

disc compartment
logement^M du plateau^M

display
afficheur^M

disc compartment control
contrôle^M du plateau^M

COMMUNICATIONS AND OFFICE AUTOMATION

sound reproducing system

headphones
casque^M *d'écoute*^F

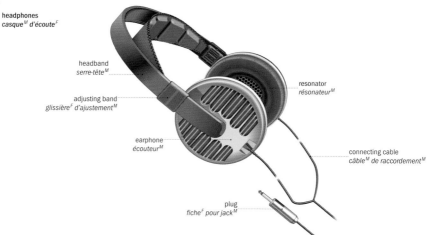

headband
serre-tête^M

adjusting band
glissière^F *d'ajustement*^M

earphone
écouteur^M

resonator
résonateur^M

connecting cable
câble^M *de raccordement*^M

plug
fiche^F *pour jack*^M

loudspeakers
enceinte^F *acoustique*

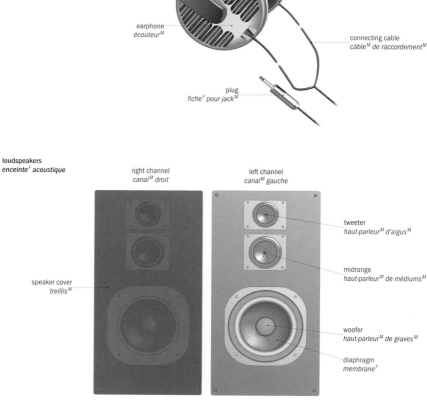

right channel
canal^M *droit*

left channel
canal^M *gauche*

tweeter
haut-parleur^M *d'aigus*^M

midrange
haut-parleur^M *de médiums*^M

speaker cover
treillis^M

woofer
haut-parleur^M *de graves*^M

diaphragm
membrane^F

mini stereo sound system

minichaîne^F stéréo

compact disc player
lecteur^M de disque^M compact

ampli-tuner
ampli^M-syntoniseur^M

loudspeaker
enceinte^F acoustique

compact disc recorder
graveur^M de disque^M compact

dual cassette deck
double platine^F cassette^F

portable sound systems

appareils^M de son^M portatifs

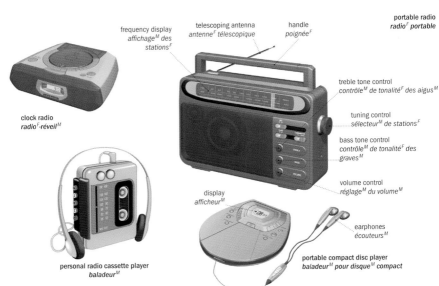

portable radio
radio^F portable

frequency display
affichage^M des stations^F

telescoping antenna
antenne^F télescopique

handle
poignée^F

treble tone control
contrôle^M de tonalité^F des aigus^M

tuning control
sélecteur^M de stations^F

bass tone control
contrôle^M de tonalité^F des graves^M

volume control
réglage^M du volume^M

clock radio
radio^F-réveil^M

display
afficheur^M

earphones
écouteurs^M

personal radio cassette player
baladeur^M

portable compact disc player
baladeur^M pour disque^M compact

portable digital audio player
baladeur^M numérique

cable
cordon^M

plug
fiche^F

display
écran^M

menu button
touche^F menu^M

previous/rewind button
touche^F précédent/retour^M rapide

select button
touche^F de sélection^F

next/fast-forward button
touche^F suivant/avance^F rapide

play/pause button
touche^F lecture^F/pause^F

earphones
écouteurs^M

satellite radio receiver
récepteur^M de radio^F par satellite^F

number buttons
touches^F numériques

liquid crystal display
écran^M à cristaux^M liquides

memory button
touche^F mémoire^F

preset button
touche^F de préréglage^M

menu button
touche^F de menu^M

category buttons
touches^F de catégories^F

display button
touche^F d'affichage^M

tuning control
sélecteur^M de stations^F

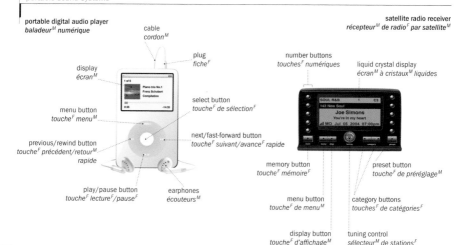

portable CD/radio/cassette recorder
radiocassette^F laser^M

mode selectors
sélecteur^M de mode^M

antenna
antenne^F

handle
poignée^F

on-off/volume
marche^F/arrêt^M/volume^M

compact disc player
lecteur^M de disque^M compact

stereo control
contrôle^M de la stéréophonie^F

compact disc
disque^M compact

headphone jack
prise^F casque^M

power plug
alimentation^F sur secteur^M

cassette player controls
contrôles^M du lecteur^M de cassette^F

cassette
cassette^F

cassette player
lecteur^M de cassette^F

tuner
radio^F

tuning control
sélecteur^M de stations^F

speaker
haut-parleur^M

compact disc player controls
contrôles^M du lecteur^M de disque^M compact

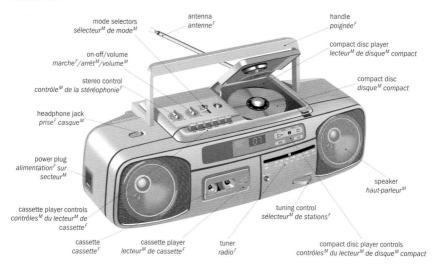

communication by telephone
communication^F par téléphone^M

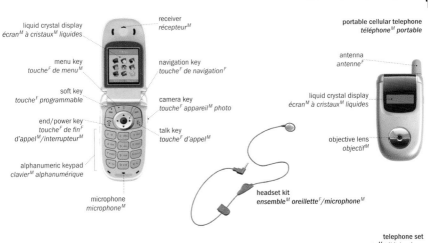

liquid crystal display
écran^M à cristaux^M liquides

receiver
récepteur^M

menu key
touche^F de menu^M

navigation key
touche^F de navigation^F

soft key
touche^F programmable

camera key
touche^F appareil^M photo

end/power key
*touche^F de fin^F
d'appel^M/interrupteur^M*

talk key
touche^F d'appel^M

alphanumeric keypad
clavier^M alphanumérique

microphone
microphone^M

headset kit
ensemble^M oreillette^F/microphone^M

portable cellular telephone
téléphone^M portable

antenna
antenne^F

liquid crystal display
écran^M à cristaux^M liquides

objective lens
objectif^M

telephone set
poste^M téléphonique

receiver
récepteur^M

display
afficheur^M

handset
combiné^M

on-off light
voyant^M de mise^F en circuit^M

receiver volume control
*commande^F de volume^M du
récepteur^M*

transmitter
microphone^M

display setting
réglage^M de l'afficheur^M

ringing volume control
*commande^F de volume^M de la
sonnerie^F*

handset cord
cordon^M de combiné^M

memory button
commande^F mémoire^F

function selectors
sélecteurs^M de fonctions^F

push buttons
clavier^M

telephone index
*répertoire^M
téléphonique*

automatic dialer index
index^M de composition^F automatique

COMMUNICATIONS AND OFFICE AUTOMATION

communication by telephone

digital answering machine
répondeur^M numérique

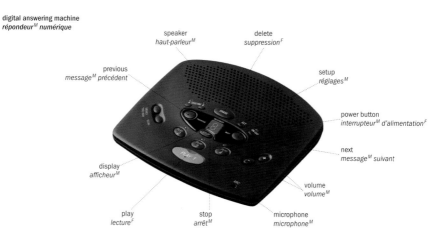

speaker
haut-parleur^M

delete
suppression^F

previous
message^M précédent

setup
réglages^M

power button
interrupteur^M d'alimentation^F

next
message^M suivant

display
afficheur^M

volume
volume^M

play
lecture^F

stop
arrêt^M

microphone
microphone^M

facsimile (fax) machine
télécopieur^M

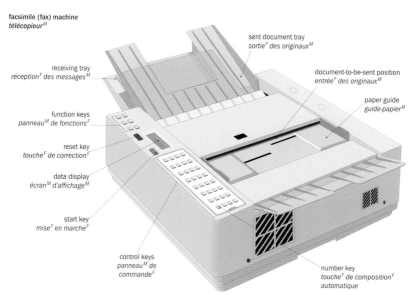

sent document tray
sortie^F des originaux^M

receiving tray
réception^F des messages^M

document-to-be-sent position
entrée^F des originaux^M

paper guide
guide-papier^M

function keys
panneau^M de fonctions^F

reset key
touche^F de correction^F

data display
écran^M d'affichage^M

start key
mise^F en marche^F

control keys
panneau^M de commande^F

number key
touche^F de composition^F automatique

personal computer
micro-ordinateur^M

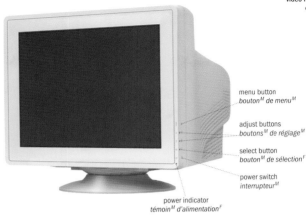

video monitor
écran^M

menu button
bouton^M *de menu*^M

adjust buttons
boutons^M *de réglage*^M

select button
bouton^M *de sélection*^F

power switch
interrupteur^M

power indicator
témoin^M *d'alimentation*^F

COMMUNICATIONS AND OFFICE AUTOMATION

tower case: back view
boitier^M *tour*^F : *vue*^F *arrière*

tower case: front view
boitier^M *tour*^F : *vue*^F *avant*

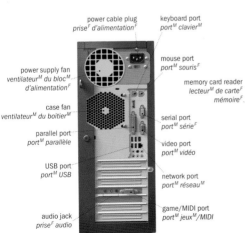

power cable plug
prise^F *d'alimentation*^F

keyboard port
port^M *clavier*^M

CD/DVD-ROM drive
lecteur^M *de CD/DVD-ROM*^M

CD/DVD-ROM eject button
bouton^M *d'éjection*^F *du CD/DVD-ROM*^M

power supply fan
ventilateur^M *du bloc*^M *d'alimentation*^F

mouse port
port^M *souris*^F

bay filler panel
obturateur^M *de baie*^F

memory card reader
lecteur^M *de carte*^F *mémoire*^F

case fan
ventilateur^M *du boitier*^M

reset button
bouton^M *de réinitialisation*^F

serial port
port^M *série*^F

parallel port
port^M *parallèle*

power button
bouton^M *de démarrage*^M

video port
port^M *vidéo*

USB port
port^M *USB*

USB port
port^M *USB*

network port
port^M *réseau*^M

audio jack
prise^F *audio*

game/MIDI port
port^M *jeux*^M/*MIDI*

input devices

périphériques^M d'entrée^F

keyboard and pictograms
clavier^M et pictogrammes^M

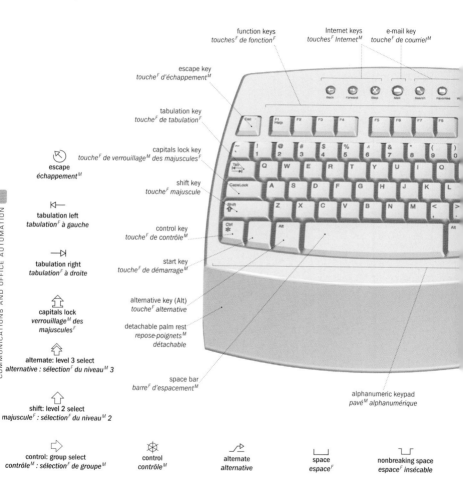

function keys
touches^F de fonction^F

Internet keys
touches^F Internet^M

e-mail key
touche^F de courriel^M

escape key
touche^F d'échappement^M

tabulation key
touche^F de tabulation^F

capitals lock key
touche^F de verrouillage^M des majuscules^F

escape
échappement^M

shift key
touche^F majuscule

tabulation left
tabulation^F à gauche

control key
touche^F de contrôle^M

tabulation right
tabulation^F à droite

start key
touche^F de démarrage^M

capitals lock
verrouillage^M des majuscules^F

alternative key (Alt)
touche^F alternative

detachable palm rest
repose-poignets^M détachable

alternate: level 3 select
alternative : sélection^F du niveau^M 3

space bar
barre^F d'espacement^M

alphanumeric keypad
pavé^M alphanumérique

shift: level 2 select
majuscule^F : sélection^F du niveau^M 2

control: group select
contrôle^M : sélection^F de groupe^M

control
contrôle^M

alternate
alternative

space
espace^F

nonbreaking space
espace^F insécable

COMMUNICATIONS AND OFFICE AUTOMATION

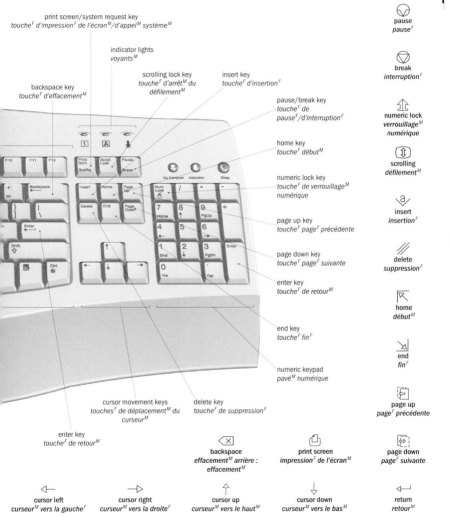

print screen/system request key
touche^F d'impression^F de l'écran^M/d'appel^M système^M

indicator lights
voyants^M

scrolling lock key
touche^F d'arrêt^M du défilement^M

insert key
touche^F d'insertion^F

backspace key
touche^F d'effacement^M

pause/break key
touche^F de pause^F/d'interruption^F

home key
touche^F début^M

numeric lock key
touche^F de verrouillage^M numérique

page up key
touche^F page^F précédente

page down key
touche^F page^F suivante

enter key
touche^F de retour^M

end key
touche^F fin^F

numeric keypad
pavé^M numérique

cursor movement keys
touches^F de déplacement^M du curseur^M

delete key
touche^F de suppression^F

enter key
touche^F de retour^M

pause
pause^F

break
interruption^F

numeric lock
verrouillage^M numérique

scrolling
défilement^M

insert
insertion^F

delete
suppression^F

home
début^M

end
fin^F

page up
page^F précédente

backspace
effacement^M arrière : effacement^M

print screen
impression^F de l'écran^M

page down
page^F suivante

cursor left
curseur^M vers la gauche^F

cursor right
curseur^M vers la droite^F

cursor up
curseur^M vers le haut^M

cursor down
curseur^M vers le bas^M

return
retour^M

COMMUNICATIONS AND OFFICE AUTOMATION

input devices

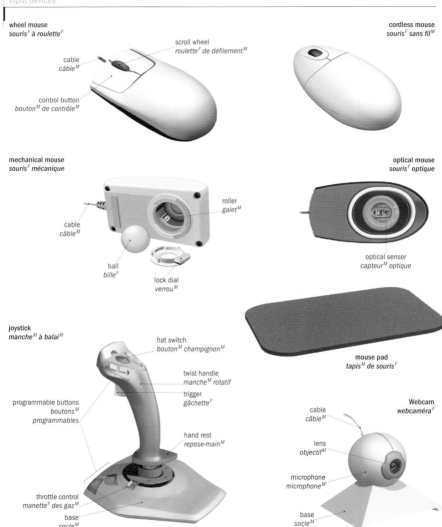

wheel mouse
souris[F] *à roulette*[F]

scroll wheel
roulette[F] *de défilement*[M]

cable
câble[M]

control button
bouton[M] *de contrôle*[M]

cordless mouse
souris[F] *sans fil*[M]

mechanical mouse
souris[F] *mécanique*

roller
galet[M]

cable
câble[M]

ball
bille[F]

lock dial
verrou[M]

optical mouse
souris[F] *optique*

optical sensor
capteur[M] *optique*

mouse pad
tapis[M] *de souris*[F]

joystick
manche[M] *à balai*[M]

hat switch
bouton[M] *champignon*[M]

twist handle
manche[M] *rotatif*

trigger
gâchette[F]

programmable buttons
boutons[M]
programmables

hand rest
repose-main[M]

throttle control
manette[F] *des gaz*[M]

base
socle[M]

Webcam
webcaméra[F]

cable
câble[M]

lens
objectif[M]

microphone
microphone[M]

base
socle[M]

COMMUNICATIONS AND OFFICE AUTOMATION

output devices
périphériques^M de sortie^F

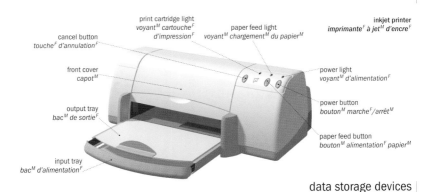

print cartridge light
voyant^M cartouche^F d'impression^F

cancel button
touche^F d'annulation^F

paper feed light
voyant^M chargement^M du papier^M

inkjet printer
imprimante^F à jet^M d'encre^F

front cover
capot^M

power light
voyant^M d'alimentation^F

output tray
bac^M de sortie^F

power button
bouton^M marche^F/arrêt^M

paper feed button
bouton^M alimentation^F papier^M

input tray
bac^M d'alimentation^F

data storage devices
périphériques^M de stockage^M

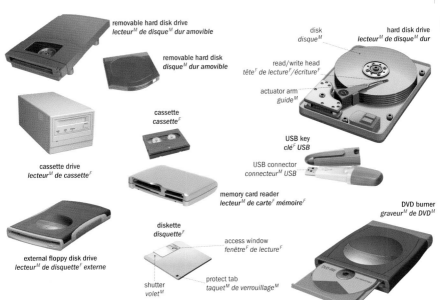

removable hard disk drive
lecteur^M de disque^M dur amovible

disk
disque^M

hard disk drive
lecteur^M de disque^M dur

removable hard disk
disque^M dur amovible

read/write head
tête^F de lecture^F/écriture^F

actuator arm
guide^M

cassette
cassette^F

USB key
clé^F USB

USB connector
connecteur^M USB

cassette drive
lecteur^M de cassette^F

memory card reader
lecteur^M de carte^F mémoire^F

DVD burner
graveur^M de DVD^M

diskette
disquette^F

access window
fenêtre^F de lecture^F

external floppy disk drive
lecteur^M de disquette^F externe

protect tab
taquet^M de verrouillage^M

shutter
volet^M

COMMUNICATIONS AND OFFICE AUTOMATION

333

Internet

Internet^M

uniform resource locator (URL)
adresse^F URL^F (localisateur^M universel de ressources^F)

communication protocol
protocole^M de communication^F

domain name
nom^M de domaine^M

file format
format^M du fichier^M

http://www.un.org/aboutun/index.html

double virgule
double barre^F oblique

second-level domain
domaine^M de second niveau^M

file
fichier^M

server
serveur^M

top-level domain
domaine^M de premier niveau^M

directory
répertoire^M

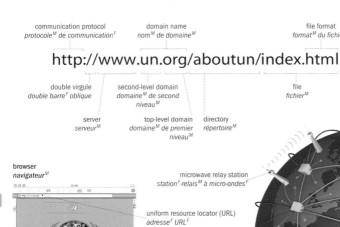

browser
navigateur^M

microwave relay station
station^F-relais^M à micro-ondes^F

uniform resource locator (URL)
adresse^F URL^F

submarine line
ligne^F sous-marine

hyperlinks
hyperliens^M

e-mail software
logiciel^M de courrier^M électronique

browser
navigateur^M

router
routeur^M

telephone line
ligne^F téléphonique

Internet user
internaute^F

dedicated line
ligne^F dédiée

modem
modem^M

desktop computer
ordinateur^M de bureau^M

Internet uses
utilisations^F d'Internet^M

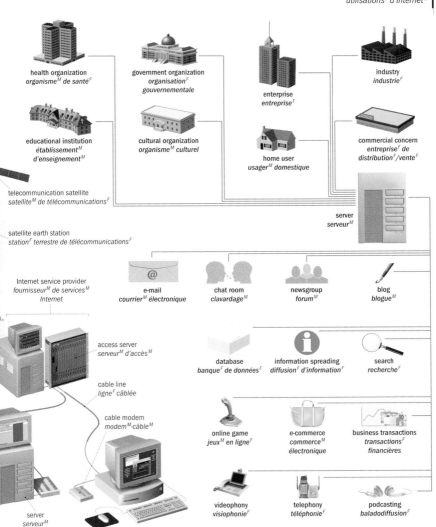

health organization
organisme^M de santé^F

government organization
*organisation^F
gouvernementale*

enterprise
entreprise^F

industry
industrie^F

educational institution
*établissement^M
d'enseignement^M*

cultural organization
organisme^M culturel

home user
usager^M domestique

commercial concern
*entreprise^F de
distribution^F/vente^F*

telecommunication satellite
satellite^M de télécommunications^F

satellite earth station
station^F terrestre de télécommunications^F

server
serveur^M

Internet service provider
*fournisseur^M de services^M
Internet*

e-mail
courrier^M électronique

chat room
clavardage^M

newsgroup
forum^M

blog
blogue^M

access server
serveur^M d'accès^M

database
banque^F de données^F

information spreading
diffusion^F d'information^F

search
recherche^F

cable line
ligne^F câblée

cable modem
modem^M-câble^M

online game
jeux^M en ligne^F

e-commerce
*commerce^M
électronique*

business transactions
*transactions^F
financières*

videophony
visiophonie^F

telephony
téléphonie^F

podcasting
baladodiffusion^F

server
serveur^M

laptop computer
ordinateur^M portable

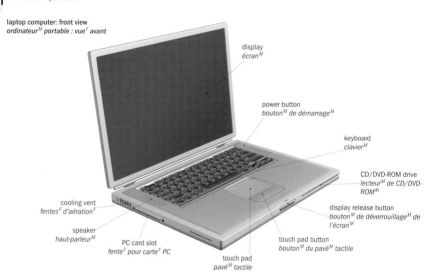

laptop computer: front view
ordinateur^M portable : vue^F avant

display
écran^M

power button
bouton^M de démarrage^M

keyboard
clavier^M

CD/DVD-ROM drive
lecteur^M de CD/DVD-ROM^M

display release button
bouton^M de déverrouillage^M de l'écran^M

cooling vent
fentes^F d'aération^F

speaker
haut-parleur^M

PC card slot
fente^F pour carte^F PC

touch pad button
bouton^M du pavé^M tactile

touch pad
pavé^M tactile

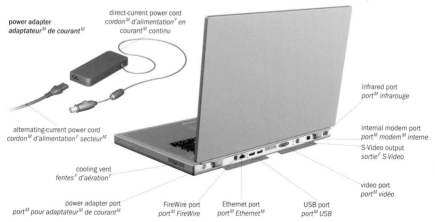

laptop computer: rear view
ordinateur^M portable : vue^F arrière

power adapter
adaptateur^M de courant^M

direct-current power cord
cordon^M d'alimentation^F en courant^M continu

infrared port
port^M infrarouge

internal modem port
port^M modem^M interne

S-Video output
sortie^F S-Video

alternating-current power cord
cordon^M d'alimentation^F secteur^M

cooling vent
fentes^F d'aération^F

power adapter port
port^M pour adaptateur^M de courant^M

FireWire port
port^M FireWire

Ethernet port
port^M Ethernet^M

USB port
port^M USB

video port
port^M vidéo

handheld computer/personal digital assistant (PDA)

ordinateur^M de poche^F

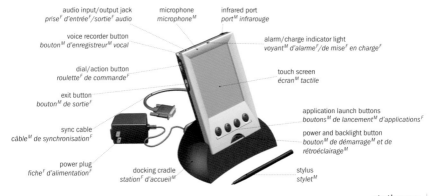

audio input/output jack
prise^F d'entrée^F/sortie^F audio

microphone
microphone^M

infrared port
port^M infrarouge

voice recorder button
bouton^M d'enregistreur^M vocal

alarm/charge indicator light
voyant^M d'alarme^F/de mise^F en charge^F

dial/action button
roulette^F de commande^F

touch screen
écran^M tactile

exit button
bouton^M de sortie^F

application launch buttons
boutons^M de lancement^M d'applications^F

sync cable
câble^M de synchronisation^F

power and backlight button
bouton^M de démarrage^M et de rétroéclairage^M

power plug
fiche^F d'alimentation^F

docking cradle
station^F d'accueil^M

stylus
stylet^M

stationery

articles^M de bureau^M

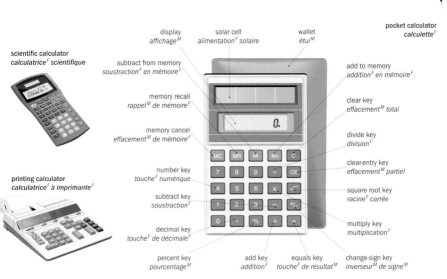

scientific calculator
calculatrice^F scientifique

display
affichage^M

solar cell
alimentation^F solaire

wallet
étui^M

pocket calculator
calculette^F

subtract from memory
soustraction^F en mémoire^F

add to memory
addition^F en mémoire^F

memory recall
rappel^M de mémoire^F

clear key
effacement^M total

memory cancel
effacement^M de mémoire^F

divide key
division^F

printing calculator
calculatrice^F à imprimante^F

number key
touche^F numérique

clear-entry key
effacement^M partiel

subtract key
soustraction^F

square root key
racine^F carrée

decimal key
touche^F de décimale^F

multiply key
multiplication^F

percent key
pourcentage^M

add key
addition^F

equals key
touche^F de résultat^M

change-sign key
inverseur^M de signe^M

COMMUNICATIONS AND OFFICE AUTOMATION

stationery

for time management
pour l'emploi[M] du temps[M]

calendar pad
bloc[M]-éphéméride[F]

electronic organizer
organiseur[M]

tear-off calendar
calendrier[M]-mémorandum[M]

display
écran[M]

alphabetical keypad
pavé[M] alphabétique

numeric keypad
pavé[M] numérique

appointment book
agenda[M]

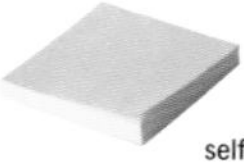

self-stick note
feuillet[M] adhésif

memo pad
bloc[M]-notes[F]

for correspondence
pour la correspondance[F]

rubber stamp
timbre[M] caoutchouc[M]

numbering machine
numéroteur[M]

dater
timbre[M] dateur

stamp pad
tampon[M] encreur

desk tray
boîte[F] à courrier[M]

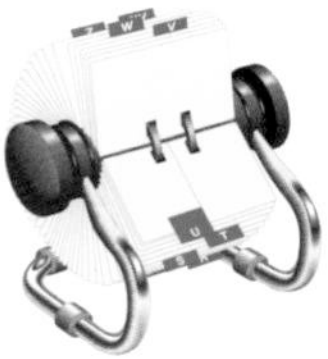

rotary file
fichier[M] rotatif

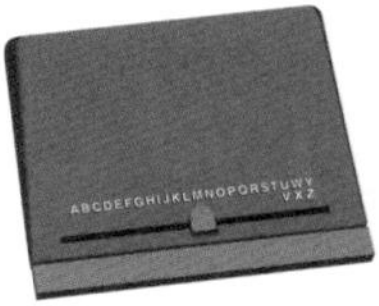

telephone index
répertoire[M] téléphonique

padded envelope
enveloppe^F *matelassée*

self-sealing flap
patte^F *autocollante*

air bubbles
bulles^F *d'air*^M

letter scale
pèse-lettres^M

finger tip
doigtier^M

moistener
mouilleur^M

letter opener
coupe-papier^M

for filing
pour le classement^M

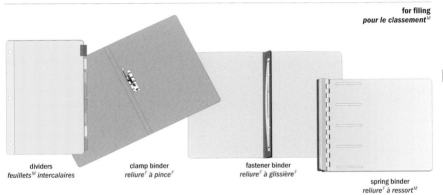

dividers
feuillets^M *intercalaires*

clamp binder
reliure^F *à pince*^F

fastener binder
reliure^F *à glissière*^F

spring binder
reliure^F *à ressort*^M

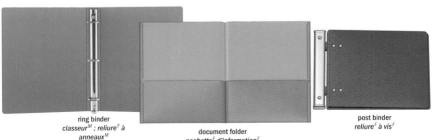

ring binder
classeur^M ; *reliure*^F *à anneaux*^M

document folder
pochette^F *d'information*^F

post binder
reliure^F *à vis*^F

COMMUNICATIONS AND OFFICE AUTOMATION

stationery

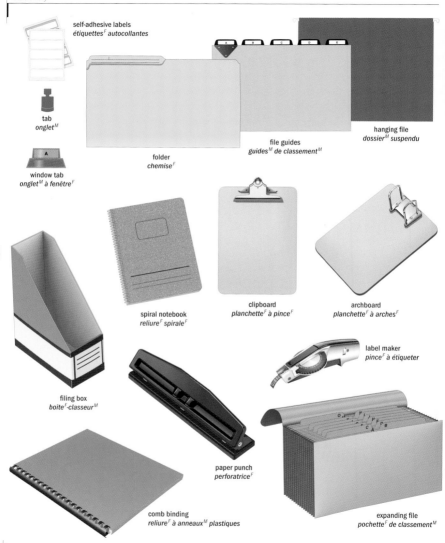

self-adhesive labels
étiquettes^F autocollantes

tab
onglet^M

window tab
onglet^M à fenêtre^F

folder
chemise^F

file guides
guides^M de classement^M

hanging file
dossier^M suspendu

spiral notebook
reliure^F spirale^F

clipboard
planchette^F à pince^F

archboard
planchette^F à arches^F

filing box
boîte^F-classeur^M

label maker
pince^F à étiqueter

comb binding
reliure^F à anneaux^M plastiques

paper punch
perforatrice^F

expanding file
pochette^F de classement^M

miscellaneous articles
articles *divers*

paper clips
trombones

thumb tacks
punaises

paper fasteners
attaches parisiennes

packing tape dispenser
dévidoir pistolet

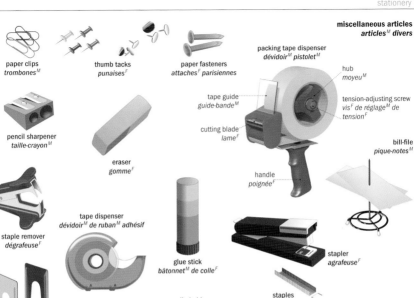

hub
moyeu

tape guide
guide-bande

tension-adjusting screw
vis de réglage de tension

cutting blade
lame

pencil sharpener
taille-crayon

eraser
gomme

bill-file
pique-notes

handle
poignée

staple remover
dégrafeuse

tape dispenser
dévidoir de ruban adhésif

glue stick
bâtonnet de colle

stapler
agrafeuse

staples
agrafes

book ends
serre-livres

paper clip holder
distributeur de trombones

pencil sharpener
taille-crayon

magnet
aimant

bulletin board
*tableau d'affichage ;
babillard*

cutting head
tête de coupe

waste basket
corbeille à papier

waste basket
corbeille à papier

posting surface
surface d'affichage

paper shredder
*destructeur de documents ;
déchiqueteuse*

road system
système^M routier

cross section of a road
coupe^F d'une route^F

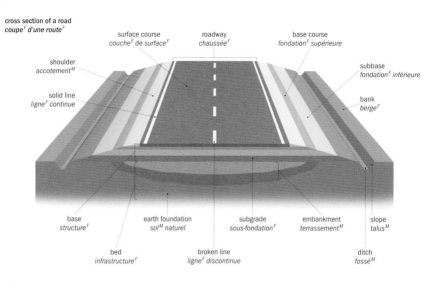

surface course
couche^F de surface^F

roadway
chaussée^F

base course
fondation^F supérieure

shoulder
accotement^M

subbase
fondation^F inférieure

solid line
ligne^F continue

bank
berge^F

base
structure^F

earth foundation
sol^M naturel

subgrade
sous-fondation^F

embankment
terrassement^M

slope
talus^M

bed
infrastructure^F

broken line
ligne^F discontinue

ditch
fossé^M

examples of interchanges
exemples^M d'échangeurs^M

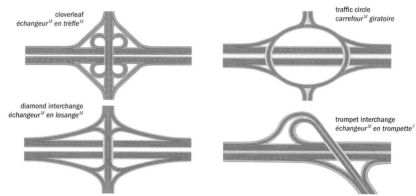

cloverleaf
échangeur^M en trèfle^M

traffic circle
carrefour^M giratoire

diamond interchange
échangeur^M en losange^M

trumpet interchange
échangeur^M en trompette^F

cloverleaf
échangeur^M *en trèfle*^M

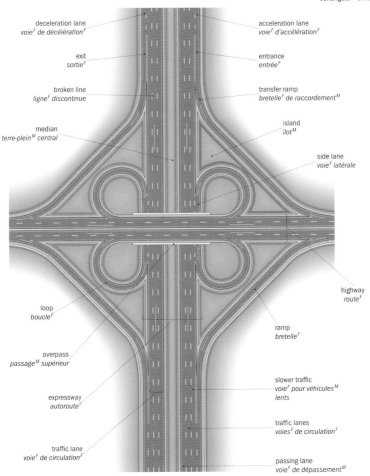

deceleration lane
voie^F *de décélération*^F

acceleration lane
voie^F *d'accélération*^F

exit
sortie^F

entrance
entrée^F

broken line
ligne^F *discontinue*

transfer ramp
bretelle^F *de raccordement*^M

median
terre-plein^M *central*

island
îlot^M

side lane
voie^F *latérale*

loop
boucle^F

highway
route^F

overpass
passage^M *supérieur*

ramp
bretelle^F

expressway
autoroute^F

slower traffic
voie^F *pour véhicules*^M
lents

traffic lanes
voies^F *de circulation*^F

traffic lane
voie^F *de circulation*^F

passing lane
voie^F *de dépassement*^M

TRANSPORT AND MACHINERY

fixed bridges
ponts^M fixes

beam bridge
pont^M à poutre^F

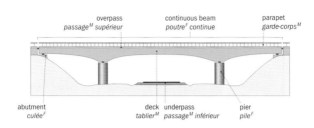

overpass
passage^M supérieur

continuous beam
poutre^F continue

parapet
garde-corps^M

abutment
culée^F

deck
tablier^M

underpass
passage^M inférieur

pier
pile^F

suspension bridge
pont^M suspendu à câble^M
porteur

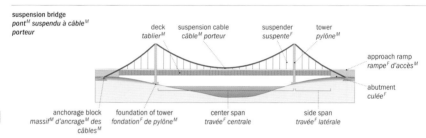

deck
tablier^M

suspension cable
câble^M porteur

suspender
suspente^F

tower
pylône^M

approach ramp
rampe^F d'accès^M

abutment
culée^F

anchorage block
massif^M d'ancrage^M des
câbles^M

foundation of tower
fondation^F de pylône^M

center span
travée^F centrale

side span
travée^F latérale

cantilever bridge
pont^M cantilever

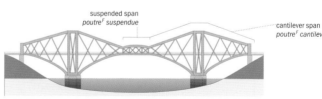

suspended span
poutre^F suspendue

cantilever span
poutre^F cantilever

movable bridges
ponts^M mobiles

swing bridge
pont^M tournant

turntable
plaque^F tournante

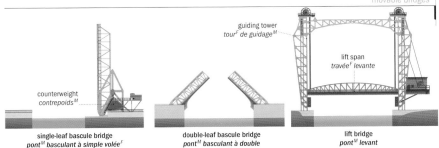

counterweight
contrepoids^M

guiding tower
tour^F *de guidage*^M

lift span
travée^F *levante*

single-leaf bascule bridge
pont^M *basculant à simple volée*^F

double-leaf bascule bridge
pont^M *basculant à double
volée*^F

lift bridge
pont^M *levant*

road tunnel
tunnel^M *routier*

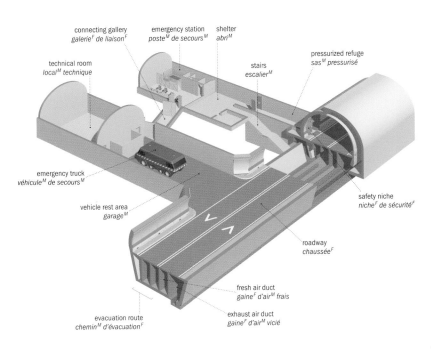

connecting gallery
galerie^F *de liaison*^F

emergency station
poste^M *de secours*^M

shelter
abri^M

technical room
local^M *technique*

stairs
escalier^M

pressurized refuge
sas^M *pressurisé*

emergency truck
véhicule^M *de secours*^M

vehicle rest area
garage^M

safety niche
niche^F *de sécurité*^F

roadway
chaussée^F

fresh air duct
gaine^F *d'air*^M *frais*

evacuation route
chemin^M *d'évacuation*^F

exhaust air duct
gaine^F *d'air*^M *vicié*

TRANSPORT AND MACHINERY

345

service station
station^F-service^M

gasoline pump
distributeur^M
d'essence^F

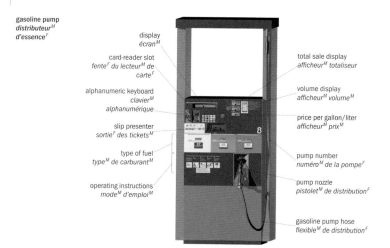

display
écran^M

card-reader slot
fente^F du lecteur^M de carte^F

alphanumeric keyboard
clavier^M alphanumérique

slip presenter
sortie^F des tickets^M

type of fuel
type^M de carburant^M

operating instructions
mode^M d'emploi^M

total sale display
afficheur^M totaliseur

volume display
afficheur^M volume^M

price per gallon/liter
afficheur^M prix^M

pump number
numéro^M de la pompe^F

pump nozzle
pistolet^M de distribution^F

gasoline pump hose
flexible^M de distribution^F

service station
station^F-service^M

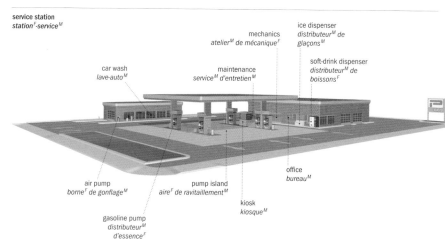

ice dispenser
distributeur^M de glaçons^M

mechanics
atelier^M de mécanique^F

soft-drink dispenser
distributeur^M de boissons^F

car wash
lave-auto^M

maintenance
service^M d'entretien^M

air pump
borne^F de gonflage^M

pump island
aire^F de ravitaillement^M

office
bureau^M

kiosk
kiosque^M

gasoline pump
distributeur^M d'essence^F

automobile
automobile^F

examples of bodies
exemples^M *de carrosseries*^F

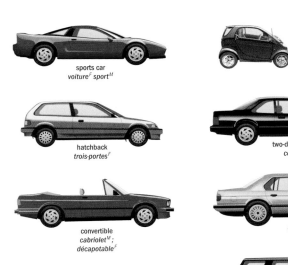

sports car
voiture^F *sport*^M

hatchback
trois-portes^F

convertible
cabriolet^M ;
décapotable^F

station wagon
break^M ; *familiale*^F

sport-utility vehicle
véhicule^M *tout-terrain*^M

micro compact car
voiture^F *micro-compacte*

two-door sedan
coupé^M

four-door sedan
berline^F

minivan
fourgonnette^F

pickup truck
camionnette^F

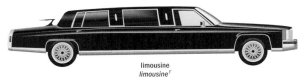

limousine
limousine^F

TRANSPORT AND MACHINERY

body
carrosserie^F

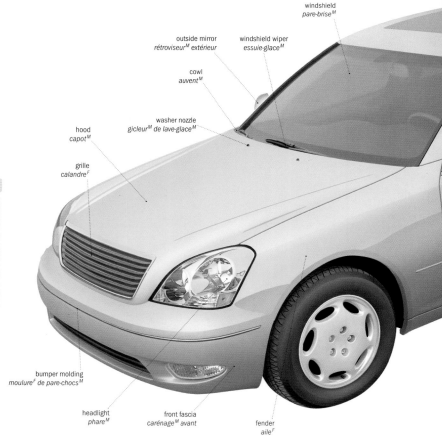

windshield
pare-brise^M

outside mirror
rétroviseur^M *extérieur*

windshield wiper
essuie-glace^M

cowl
auvent^M

washer nozzle
gicleur^M *de lave-glace*^M

hood
capot^M

grille
calandre^F

bumper molding
moulure^F *de pare-chocs*^M

headlight
phare^M

front fascia
carénage^M *avant*

fender
aile^F

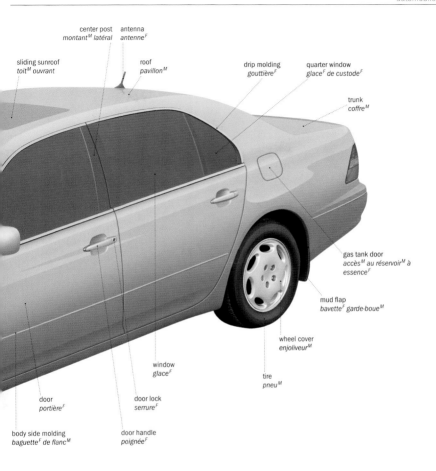

center post
montant^M latéral

antenna
antenne^F

sliding sunroof
toit^M ouvrant

roof
pavillon^M

drip molding
gouttière^F

quarter window
glace^F de custode^F

trunk
coffre^M

gas tank door
accès^M au réservoir^M à
essence^F

mud flap
bavette^F garde-boue^M

wheel cover
enjoliveur^M

window
glace^F

tire
pneu^M

door
portière^F

door lock
serrure^F

body side molding
baguette^F de flanc^M

door handle
poignée^F

automobile systems: main parts
principaux organes^M *des systèmes*^M *automobiles*

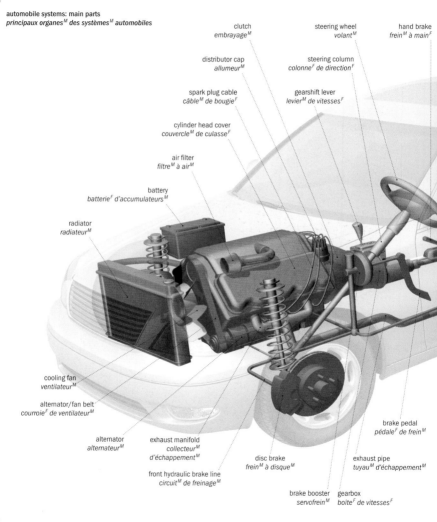

clutch
embrayage^M

steering wheel
volant^M

hand brake
frein^M *à main*^F

distributor cap
allumeur^M

steering column
colonne^F *de direction*^F

spark plug cable
câble^M *de bougie*^F

gearshift lever
levier^M *de vitesses*^F

cylinder head cover
couvercle^M *de culasse*^F

air filter
filtre^M *à air*^M

battery
batterie^F *d'accumulateurs*^M

radiator
radiateur^M

cooling fan
ventilateur^M

alternator/fan belt
courroie^F *de ventilateur*^M

alternator
alternateur^M

exhaust manifold
collecteur^M
d'échappement^M

front hydraulic brake line
circuit^M *de freinage*^M

disc brake
frein^M *à disque*^M

brake booster
servofrein^M

gearbox
boite^F *de vitesses*^F

exhaust pipe
tuyau^M *d'échappement*^M

brake pedal
pédale^F *de frein*^M

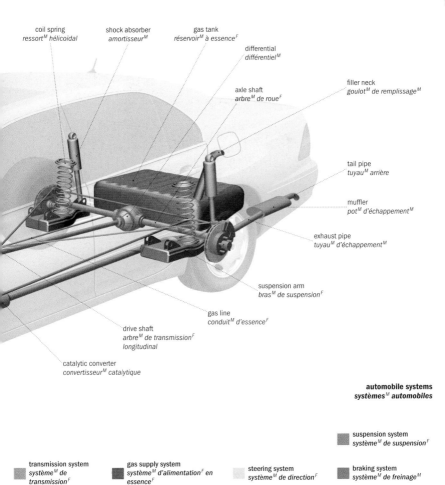

coil spring
ressort^M hélicoïdal

shock absorber
amortisseur^M

gas tank
réservoir^M à essence^F

differential
différentiel^M

axle shaft
arbre^M de roue^F

filler neck
goulot^M de remplissage^M

tail pipe
tuyau^M arrière

muffler
pot^M d'échappement^M

exhaust pipe
tuyau^M d'échappement^M

suspension arm
bras^M de suspension^F

gas line
conduit^M d'essence^F

drive shaft
arbre^M de transmission^F
longitudinal

catalytic converter
convertisseur^M catalytique

**automobile systems
systèmes^M automobiles**

suspension system
système^M de suspension^F

transmission system
système^M de
transmission^F

gas supply system
système^M d'alimentation^F en
essence^F

steering system
système^M de direction^F

braking system
système^M de freinage^M

electrical system
système^M électrique

exhaust system
système^M d'échappement^M

gasoline engine
moteur^M à essence^F

cooling system
système^M de refroidissement^M

automobile

headlights
feux^M avant

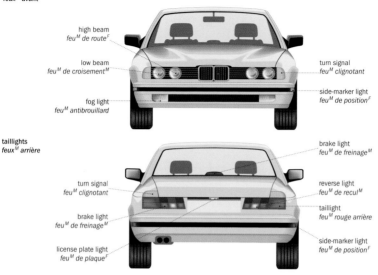

high beam
feu^M de route^F

low beam
feu^M de croisement^M

fog light
feu^M antibrouillard

turn signal
feu^M clignotant

side-marker light
feu^M de position^F

taillights
feux^M arrière

brake light
feu^M de freinage^M

turn signal
feu^M clignotant

reverse light
feu^M de recul^M

brake light
feu^M de freinage^M

taillight
feu^M rouge arrière

license plate light
feu^M de plaque^F

side-marker light
feu^M de position^F

door
portière^F

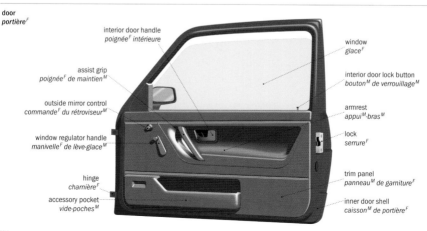

interior door handle
poignée^F intérieure

window
glace^F

assist grip
poignée^F de maintien^M

interior door lock button
bouton^M de verrouillage^M

outside mirror control
commande^F du rétroviseur^M

armrest
appui^M-bras^M

window regulator handle
manivelle^F de lève-glace^M

lock
serrure^F

hinge
charnière^F

trim panel
panneau^M de garniture^F

accessory pocket
vide-poches^M

inner door shell
caisson^M de portière^F

bucket seat: front view
siège^M-baquet^M : vue^F de face^F

bucket seat: side view
siège^M-baquet^M : vue^F de profil^M

shoulder belt
baudrier^M

sliding rail
rail^M de glissement^M

sliding lever
manette^F de glissement^M

headrest
appui^M-tête^F

backrest
dossier^M

seat
siège^M

adjustment knob
commande^F de dossier^M

seat belt
ceinture^F de sécurité^F

rear seat
banquette^F arrière

armrest
appui^M-bras^M

webbing
sangle^F

buckle
boucle^F

bench seat
banquette^F

automobile

dashboard
tableau^M *de bord*^M

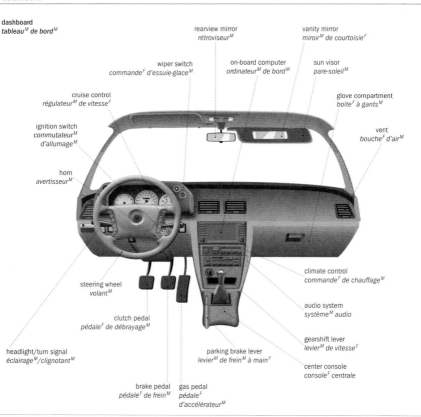

rearview mirror
rétroviseur^M

vanity mirror
miroir^M *de courtoisie*^F

wiper switch
commande^F *d'essuie-glace*^M

on-board computer
ordinateur^M *de bord*^M

sun visor
pare-soleil^M

cruise control
régulateur^M *de vitesse*^F

glove compartment
boîte^F *à gants*^M

ignition switch
commutateur^M
d'allumage^M

vent
bouche^F *d'air*^M

horn
avertisseur^M

steering wheel
volant^M

climate control
commande^F *de chauffage*^M

clutch pedal
pédale^F *de débrayage*^M

audio system
système^M *audio*

gearshift lever
levier^M *de vitesse*^F

headlight/turn signal
éclairage^M/*clignotant*^M

parking brake lever
levier^M *de frein*^M *à main*^F

center console
console^F *centrale*

brake pedal
pédale^F *de frein*^M

gas pedal
pédale^F
d'accélérateur^M

air bag restraint system
système^M *de retenue*^F *à sacs*^M
gonflables

safing sensor
détecteur^M *de sécurité*^F

air bag
sac^M *gonflable*

primary crash sensor
détecteur^M *d'impact*^M *primaire*

electrical cable
câble^M *électrique*

instrument panel
instruments^M *de bord*^M

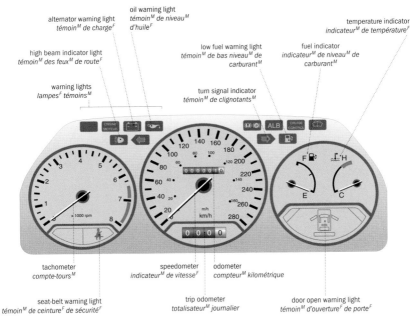

alternator warning light
témoin^M *de charge*^F

oil warning light
témoin^M *de niveau*^M
d'huile^F

temperature indicator
indicateur^M *de température*^F

high beam indicator light
témoin^M *des feux*^M *de route*^F

low fuel warning light
témoin^M *de bas niveau*^M *de*
carburant^M

fuel indicator
indicateur^M *de niveau*^M *de*
carburant^M

warning lights
lampes^F *témoins*^M

turn signal indicator
témoin^M *de clignotants*^M

tachometer
compte-tours^M

speedometer
indicateur^M *de vitesse*^F

odometer
compteur^M *kilométrique*

seat-belt warning light
témoin^M *de ceinture*^F *de sécurité*^F

trip odometer
totalisateur^M *journalier*

door open warning light
témoin^M *d'ouverture*^F *de porte*^F

windshield wiper
essuie-glace^M

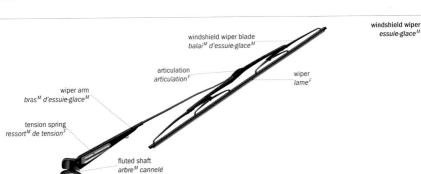

windshield wiper blade
balai^M *d'essuie-glace*^M

articulation
articulation^F

wiper
lame^F

wiper arm
bras^M *d'essuie-glace*^M

tension spring
ressort^M *de tension*^F

fluted shaft
arbre^M *cannelé*

TRANSPORT AND MACHINERY

automobile

accessories
accessoires^M

jumper cables
câbles^M *de démarrage*^M

black clamp
pince^F *noire*

floor mat
tapis^M *de plancher*^M

roller shade
store^M *à enroulement*^M *automatique*

red clamp
pince^F *rouge*

cable
câble^M

snow brush with scraper
balai^M *à neige*^F *à grattoir*^M

ball mount
ferrure^F *d'attelage*^M

hitch ball
boule^F *d'attelage*^M

four-way lug wrench
clé^F *en croix*^F

bike carrier
porte-vélos^M

ski rack
porte-skis^M

vehicle jack
cric^M

sun visor
pare-soleil^M

handle
manivelle^F

car cover
housse^F *pour automobile*^F

child safety seat
siège^M *de sécurité*^F *pour enfant*^M

TRANSPORT AND MACHINERY

356

brakes
freins[M]

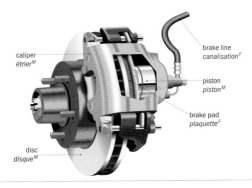

disc brake
frein[M] *à disque*[M]

caliper
étrier[M]

brake line
canalisation[F]

piston
piston[M]

brake pad
plaquette[F]

disc
disque[M]

---

drum brake
frein[M] *à tambour*[M]

brake shoe
segment[M]

anchor pin
point[M] *fixe*

return spring
ressort[M] *de rappel*[M]

strut
piston[M]

wheel stud
goujon[M]

wheel cylinder
cylindre[M] *de roue*[F]

backing plate
plateau[M] *de frein*[M]

brake lining
garniture[F] *de frein*[M]

drum
tambour[M]

---

antilock braking system (ABS)
système[M] *de freinage*[M]
antiblocage

brake fluid reservoir
réservoir[M] *de liquide*[M]
de frein[M]

brake booster
servofrein[M]

electronic control unit
module[M] *de commande*[F]
électronique

master cylinder
maître[M]-*cylindre*[M]

brake pedal
pédale[F] *de frein*[M]

wheel speed sensor
capteur[M] *de vitesse*[F] *de*
roue[F]

pump and motor
assembly
groupe[M] *électropompe*[F]

disc brake
frein[M] *à disque*[M]

braking circuit
circuit[M] *de freinage*[M]

brake pressure modulator
modulateur[M] *de pression*[F] *de*
freinage[M]

sensor wiring circuit
circuit[M] *capteurs*[M]

accumulator
accumulateur[M]

TRANSPORT AND MACHINERY

tire
pneu^M

technical specifications
spécifications^F *techniques*

tread design
sculptures^F

rubbing strip
bourrelet^M

rubber wall
flanc^M

bead
talon^M

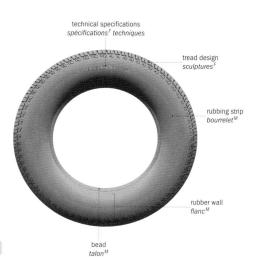

examples of tires
exemples^M *de pneus*^M

performance tire
pneu^M *de performance*^F

all-season tire
pneu^M *toutes saisons*^F

studded tire
pneu^M *à crampons*^M

winter tire
pneu^M *d'hiver*^M

touring tire
pneu^M *autoroutier*

radiator
radiateur^M

filler cap
bouchon^M *de*
remplissage^M

cooling fan
ventilateur^M

temperature sensor
thermocontact^M

lower radiator hose
durite^F *de radiateur*^M

grille
grille^F

electric fan motor
moteur^M *électrique*

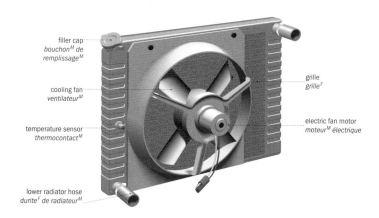

spark plug
bougie^F d'allumage^M

spline
cannelure^F

hex nut
écrou^M hexagonal

spark plug body
culot^M

spark plug gap
écartement^M des électrodes^F

spark plug terminal
borne^F

center electrode
électrode^F centrale

insulator
isolateur^M

spark plug seat
joint^M de bougie^F

ground electrode
électrode^F de masse^F

battery
batterie^F d'accumulateurs^M

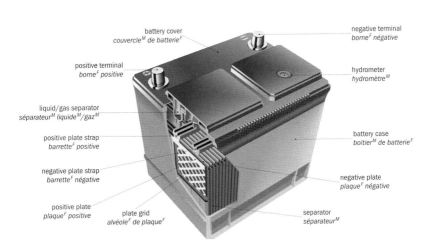

battery cover
couvercle^M de batterie^F

positive terminal
borne^F positive

liquid/gas separator
séparateur^M liquide^M/gaz^M

positive plate strap
barrette^F positive

negative plate strap
barrette^F négative

positive plate
plaque^F positive

plate grid
alvéole^F de plaque^F

negative terminal
borne^F négative

hydrometer
hydromètre^M

battery case
boîtier^M de batterie^F

negative plate
plaque^F négative

separator
séparateur^M

gasoline engine
moteur^M à essence^F

fuel injector
injecteur^M

rocker arm
culbuteur^M

camshaft
arbre^M à cames^F

inlet valve
soupape^F d'admission^F

intake manifold
tubulure^F d'admission^F

distributor cap
allumeur^M

timing belt
*courroie^F de
distribution^F*

valve spring
ressort^M de soupape^F

valve cover
couvercle^M de culasse^F

piston skirt
jupe^F de piston^M

vacuum diaphragm
capsule^F à membrane^F

combustion chamber
*chambre^F de
combustion^F*

piston ring
segment^M

spark plug cable
câble^M de bougie^F

connecting rod
bielle^F

spark plug
bougie^F d'allumage^M

alternator
alternateur^M

exhaust manifold
*collecteur^M
d'échappement^M*

cooling fan
ventilateur^M

flywheel
volant^M

pulley
poulie^F

exhaust valve
soupape^F d'échappement^M

alternator fan belt
*courroie^F de
ventilateur^M*

engine block
bloc^M-cylindres^M

crankshaft
vilebrequin^M

oil pan
carter^M

air conditioner compressor
compresseur^M du climatiseur^M

oil pan gasket
joint^M de carter^M

oil drain plug
*bouchon^M de vidange^F
d'huile^F*

piston head
piston^M

camping trailers
caravane^F

trailer
caravane^F tractée

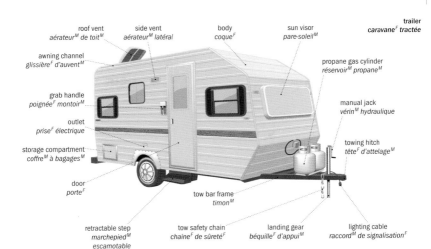

roof vent
aérateur^M de toit^M

side vent
aérateur^M latéral

body
coque^F

sun visor
pare-soleil^M

awning channel
glissière^F d'auvent^M

propane gas cylinder
réservoir^M propane^M

grab handle
poignée^F montoir^M

manual jack
vérin^M hydraulique

outlet
prise^F électrique

towing hitch
tête^F d'attelage^M

storage compartment
coffre^M à bagages^M

door
porte^F

tow bar frame
timon^M

retractable step
*marchepied^M
escamotable*

tow safety chain
chaîne^F de sûreté^F

landing gear
béquille^F d'appui^M

lighting cable
raccord^M de signalisation^F

tent trailer
tente^F-caravane^F

roof
toit^M

canopy
auvent^M

window
fenêtre^F

bunk
lit^M

body
coque^F

spare tire
roue^F de secours^M

stabilizer jack
béquille^F d'appoint^M

screen door
porte^F moustiquaire^F

motor home
auto^F-caravane^F

air conditioner
climatiseur^M

luggage rack
porte-bagages^M

ladder
échelle^F

TRANSPORT AND MACHINERY

buses
autobus^M

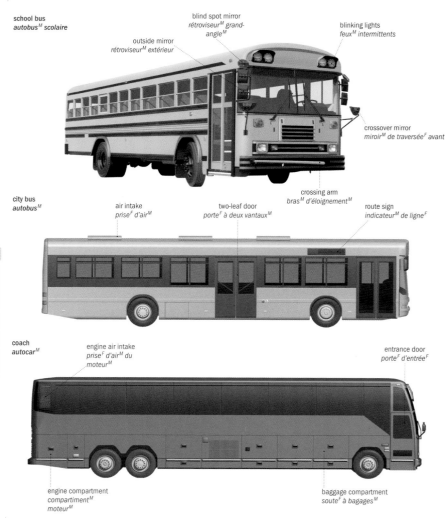

school bus
autobus^M *scolaire*

blind spot mirror
rétroviseur^M *grand-angle*^M

blinking lights
feux^M *intermittents*

outside mirror
rétroviseur^M *extérieur*

crossover mirror
miroir^M *de traversée*^F *avant*

crossing arm
bras^M *d'éloignement*^M

city bus
autobus^M

air intake
prise^F *d'air*^M

two-leaf door
porte^F *à deux vantaux*^M

route sign
indicateur^M *de ligne*^F

coach
autocar^M

engine air intake
prise^F *d'air*^M *du moteur*^M

entrance door
porte^F *d'entrée*^F

engine compartment
compartiment^M *moteur*^M

baggage compartment
soute^F *à bagages*^M

TRANSPORT AND MACHINERY

double-decker bus
autobus[M] *à impériale*[F]

route sign
indicateur[M] *de ligne*[F]

upper deck
impériale[F]

minibus
minibus[M]

blind spot mirror
rétroviseur[M] *grand-angle*[M]

lift door
porte[F] *de l'élévateur*[M]

West Coast mirror
rétroviseur[M]

handrail
barre[F] *de maintien*[M]

wheelchair lift
élévateur[M] *pour fauteuils*[M] *roulants*

entrance door
porte[F] *d'entrée*[F]

platform
plate-forme[F]

articulated bus
autobus[M] *articulé*

articulated joint
section[F] *articulée*

rear rigid section
tronçon[M] *rigide arrière*

front rigid section
tronçon[M] *rigide avant*

trucking
camionnage M

truck tractor
tracteur M *routier*

exhaust stack
cheminée F
d'échappement M

windshield
pare-brise M

wind deflector
déflecteur M

West Coast mirror
rétroviseur M

air horn
avertisseur M
pneumatique

sleeper-cab
compartiment M-
couchette F

marker light
feu M *de gabarit* M

grab handle
poignée F *montoir* M

hood
capot M

storage compartment
coffre M *de rangement* M

headlight
phare M

fifth wheel
sellette F *d'attelage* M

mud flap
bavette F *garde-boue* M

tire
pneu M

fog light
feu M *antibrouillard*

filler cap
bouchon M *du réservoir* M

bumper
pare-chocs M

step
marchepied M

radiator grille
calandre F

fender
aile F

wheel
roue F

fuel tank
réservoir M *à carburant* M

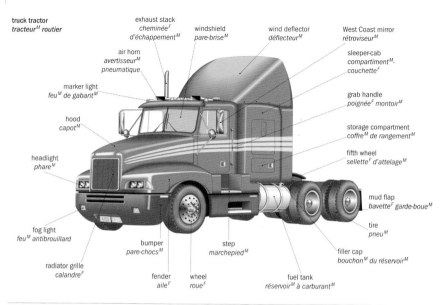

examples of trucks
exemples M *de camions* M

tank body
citerne F

tank truck
camion M-*citerne* F

garbage collection truck
benne F *à ordures* F *; camion* M *à
ordures* F

boom
poutre F *de levage* M

tow truck
dépanneuse F

cable
câble M

hook
crochet M

towing device
dispositif M *de
remorquage* M

loading hopper
trémie F *de
chargement* M

packer body
benne F *tasseuse*

winch controls
commandes F *du treuil* M

elevating cylinder
vérin M

winch
treuil M

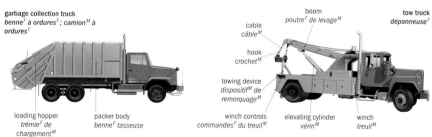

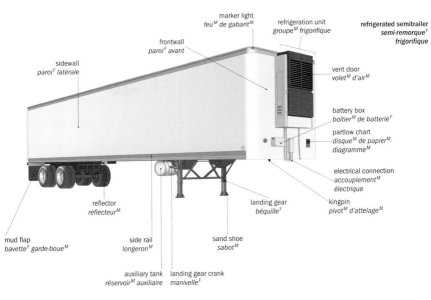

marker light
feu^M de gabarit^M

refrigeration unit
groupe^M frigorifique

refrigerated semitrailer
semi-remorque^F
frigorifique

frontwall
paroi^F avant

sidewall
paroi^F latérale

vent door
volet^M d'air^M

battery box
boîtier^M de batterie^F

partlow chart
disque^M de papier^M-
diagramme^M

electrical connection
accouplement^M
électrique

reflector
réflecteur^M

landing gear
béquille^F

kingpin
pivot^M d'attelage^M

mud flap
bavette^F garde-boue^M

side rail
longeron^M

sand shoe
sabot^M

auxiliary tank
réservoir^M auxiliaire

landing gear crank
manivelle^F

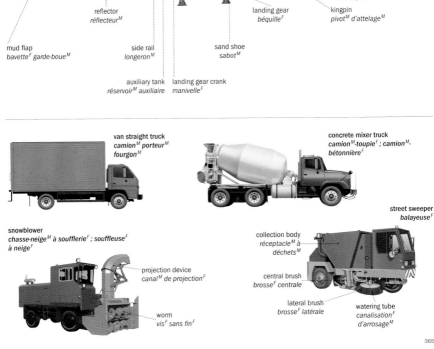

van straight truck
camion^M porteur^M
fourgon^M

concrete mixer truck
camion^M-toupie^F ; camion^M-
bétonnière^F

street sweeper
balayeuse^F

snowblower
chasse-neige^M à soufflerie^F ; souffleuse^F
à neige^F

collection body
réceptacle^M à
déchets^M

projection device
canal^M de projection^F

central brush
brosse^F centrale

lateral brush
brosse^F latérale

watering tube
canalisation^F
d'arrosage^M

worm
vis^F sans fin^F

motorcycle
moto^F

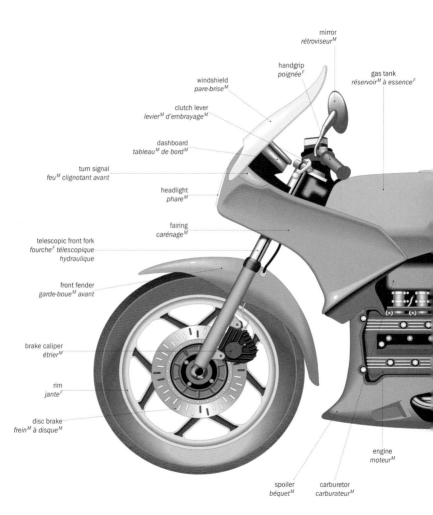

mirror
rétroviseur^M

handgrip
poignée^F

gas tank
réservoir^M *à essence*^F

windshield
pare-brise^M

clutch lever
levier^M *d'embrayage*^M

dashboard
tableau^M *de bord*^M

turn signal
feu^M *clignotant avant*

headlight
phare^M

fairing
carénage^M

telescopic front fork
fourche^F *télescopique
hydraulique*

front fender
garde-boue^M *avant*

brake caliper
étrier^M

rim
jante^F

disc brake
frein^M *à disque*^M

spoiler
béquet^M

carburetor
carburateur^M

engine
moteur^M

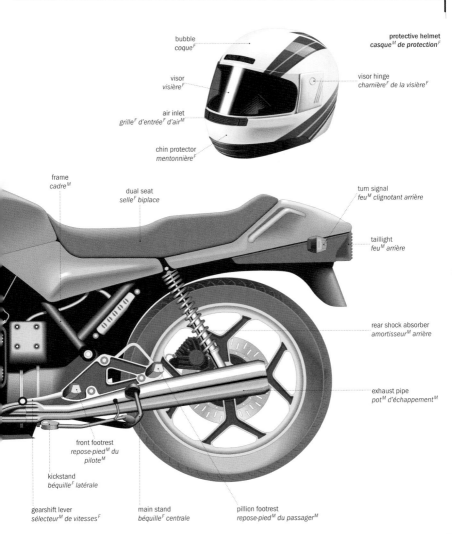

bubble
coque^F

protective helmet
casque^M *de protection*^{F}

visor
visière^F

visor hinge
charnière^F *de la visière*^{F}

air inlet
grille^F *d'entrée*^{F} *d'air*^{M}

chin protector
mentonnière^F

frame
cadre^M

dual seat
selle^F *biplace*

turn signal
feu^M *clignotant arrière*

taillight
feu^M *arrière*

rear shock absorber
amortisseur^M *arrière*

exhaust pipe
pot^M *d'échappement*^{M}

front footrest
repose-pied^M *du pilote*^{M}

kickstand
béquille^F *latérale*

gearshift lever
sélecteur^M *de vitesses*^{F}

main stand
béquille^F *centrale*

pillion footrest
repose-pied^M *du passager*^{M}

motorcycle

motorcycle dashboard
tableau^M de bord^M

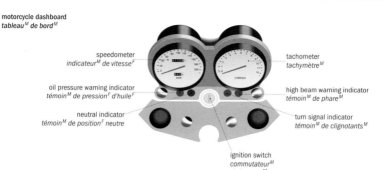

speedometer
indicateur^F de vitesse^F

tachometer
tachymètre^M

oil pressure warning indicator
témoin^M de pression^F d'huile^F

high beam warning indicator
témoin^M de phare^M

neutral indicator
témoin^M de position^F neutre

turn signal indicator
témoin^M de clignotants^M

ignition switch
commutateur^M
d'allumage^M

motorcycle: view from above
moto^F : vue^F en plongée^F

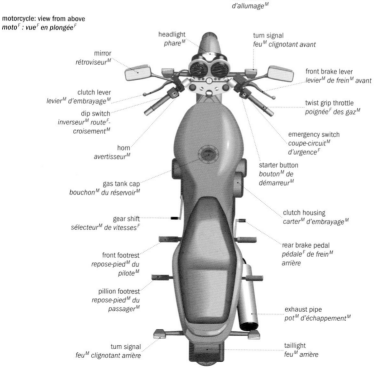

headlight
phare^M

turn signal
feu^M clignotant avant

mirror
rétroviseur^M

front brake lever
levier^M de frein^M avant

clutch lever
levier^M d'embrayage^M

twist grip throttle
poignée^F des gaz^M

dip switch
inverseur^M route^F-
croisement^M

emergency switch
coupe-circuit^M
d'urgence^F

horn
avertisseur^M

starter button
bouton^M de
démarreur^M

gas tank cap
bouchon^M du réservoir^M

clutch housing
carter^M d'embrayage^M

gear shift
sélecteur^M de vitesses^F

rear brake pedal
pédale^F de frein^M
arrière

front footrest
repose-pied^M du
pilote^M

pillion footrest
repose-pied^M du
passager^M

exhaust pipe
pot^M d'échappement^M

turn signal
feu^M clignotant arrière

taillight
feu^M arrière

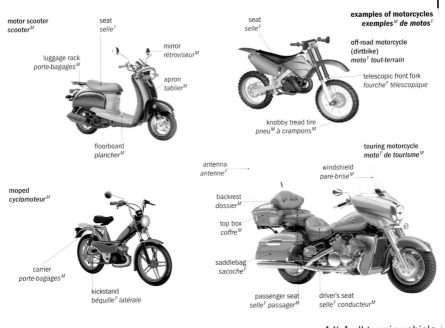

motor scooter
scooter^M

luggage rack
porte-bagages^M

seat
selle^F

mirror
rétroviseur^M

apron
tablier^M

floorboard
plancher^M

moped
cyclomoteur^M

carrier
porte-bagages^M

kickstand
béquille^F latérale

seat
selle^F

off-road motorcycle
(dirtbike)
moto^F tout-terrain

telescopic front fork
fourche^F télescopique

knobby tread tire
pneu^M à crampons^M

**examples of motorcycles
exemples^M de motos^F**

touring motorcycle
moto^F de tourisme^M

antenna
antenne^F

backrest
dossier^M

top box
coffre^M

saddlebag
sacoche^F

windshield
pare-brise^M

passenger seat
selle^F passager^M

driver's seat
selle^F conducteur^M

4 X 4 all-terrain vehicle
quad^M

rear cargo rack
porte-bagages^M arrière

rear fender
garde-boue^M arrière

muffler
pot^M d'échappement^M

seat
selle^F

gas tank
réservoir^M à essence^F

handgrip
poignée^F

bumper
pare-chocs^M

front shock absorber
amortisseur^M avant

gearshift lever
sélecteur^M de vitesses^F

TRANSPORT AND MACHINERY

bicycle
bicyclette^F

parts of a bicycle
parties^F *d'une*
bicyclette^F

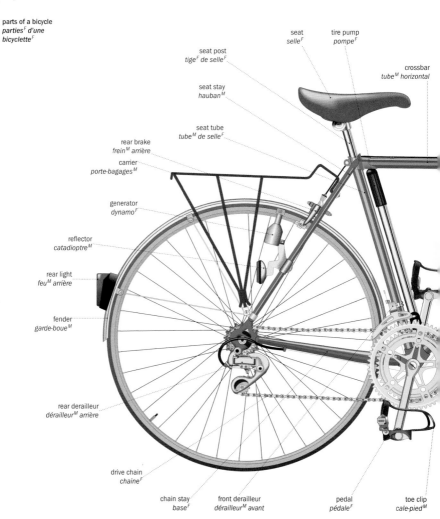

seat
selle^F

tire pump
pompe^F

crossbar
tube^M *horizontal*

seat post
tige^F *de selle*^F

seat stay
hauban^M

seat tube
tube^M *de selle*^F

rear brake
frein^M *arrière*

carrier
porte-bagages^M

generator
dynamo^F

reflector
catadioptre^M

rear light
feu^M *arrière*

fender
garde-boue^M

rear derailleur
dérailleur^M *arrière*

drive chain
chaîne^F

chain stay
base^F

front derailleur
dérailleur^M *avant*

pedal
pédale^F

toe clip
cale-pied^M

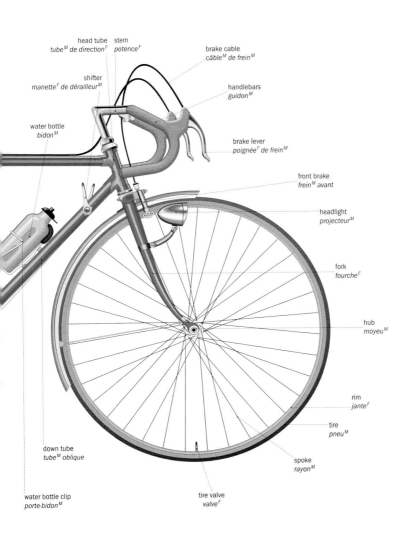

head tube
tube^M de direction^F

stem
potence^F

brake cable
câble^M de frein^M

shifter
manette^F de dérailleur^M

handlebars
guidon^M

water bottle
bidon^M

brake lever
poignée^F de frein^M

front brake
frein^M avant

headlight
projecteur^M

fork
fourche^F

hub
moyeu^M

rim
jante^F

tire
pneu^M

down tube
tube^M oblique

spoke
rayon^M

water bottle clip
porte-bidon^M

tire valve
valve^F

bicycle

power train
mécanisme^M de propulsion^F

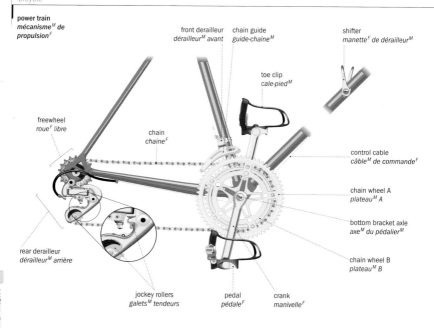

front derailleur
dérailleur^M avant

chain guide
guide-chaine^M

shifter
manette^F de dérailleur^M

toe clip
cale-pied^M

freewheel
roue^F libre

chain
chaine^F

control cable
câble^M de commande^F

chain wheel A
plateau^M A

bottom bracket axle
axe^M du pédalier^M

rear derailleur
dérailleur^M arrière

chain wheel B
plateau^M B

jockey rollers
galets^M tendeurs

pedal
pédale^F

crank
manivelle^F

accessories
accessoires^M

lock
cadenas^M

protective helmet
casque^M de protection^F

tool kit
trousse^F de dépannage^M

bicycle bag (pannier)
sacoche^F

child carrier
siège^M de vélo^M pour enfant^M

bicycle

examples of bicycles
exemples^M de bicyclettes^F

BMX bike
vélo^M cross^M

child's tricycle
tricycle^M d'enfant^M

mountain bike
bicyclette^F tout-terrain

Dutch bicycle
bicyclette^F hollandaise

road bicycle
bicyclette^F de course^F

city bicycle
bicyclette^F de ville^F

touring bicycle
bicyclette^F de tourisme^M

tandem bicycle
tandem^M

passenger station
gare^F de voyageurs^M

office
locaux^M administratifs

indicator board
panneau^M indicateur

baggage cart
chariot^M à bagages^M

baggage lockers
consigne^F automatique

glassed roof
verrière^F

metal structure
structure^F métallique

platform number
numéro^M de quai^M

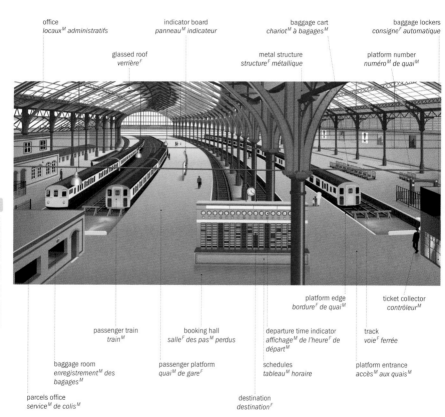

platform edge
bordure^F de quai^M

ticket collector
contrôleur^M

passenger train
train^M

booking hall
salle^F des pas^M perdus

departure time indicator
affichage^M de l'heure^F de départ^M

track
voie^F ferrée

baggage room
enregistrement^M des bagages^M

passenger platform
quai^M de gare^F

schedules
tableau^M horaire

platform entrance
accès^M aux quais^M

parcels office
service^M de colis^M

destination
destination^F

railroad station
gare^F

passenger station
gare^F *de voyageurs*^M

station platform
quai^M

commuter train
train^M *de banlieue*^F

main line
grandes lignes^F

suburban commuter railroad
voie^F *de banlieue*^F

subsidiary track
voie^F *de service*^M

bumper
butoir^M

level crossing
passage^M *à niveau*^M

parking
parking^M ;
stationnement^M

platform shelter
abri^M

footbridge
passerelle^F

signal
signal^M *de voie*^F

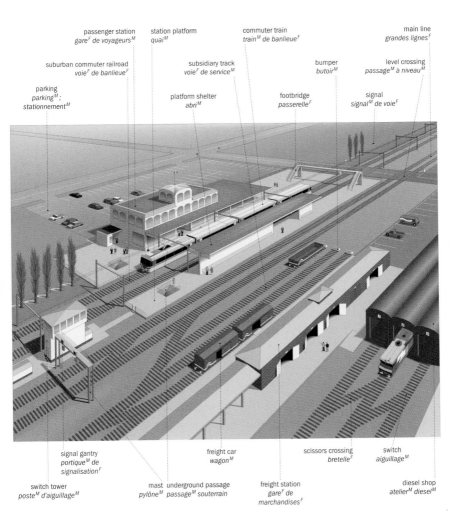

signal gantry
portique^M *de*
signalisation^F

freight car
wagon^M

scissors crossing
bretelle^F

switch
aiguillage^M

switch tower
poste^M *d'aiguillage*^M

mast
pylône^M

underground passage
passage^M *souterrain*

freight station
gare^F *de*
marchandises^F

diesel shop
atelier^M *diesel*^M

high-speed train
train^M à grande vitesse^F (T.G.V.)

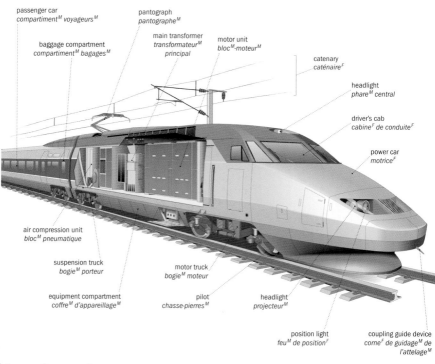

passenger car
compartiment^M voyageurs^M

pantograph
pantographe^M

baggage compartment
compartiment^M bagages^M

main transformer
*transformateur^M
principal*

motor unit
bloc^M-moteur^M

catenary
caténaire^F

headlight
phare^M central

driver's cab
cabine^F de conduite^F

power car
motrice^F

air compression unit
bloc^M pneumatique

suspension truck
bogie^M porteur

motor truck
bogie^M moteur

equipment compartment
coffre^M d'appareillage^M

pilot
chasse-pierres^M

headlight
projecteur^M

position light
feu^M de position^F

coupling guide device
*corne^F de guidage^M de
l'attelage^M*

types of passenger cars
types^M de voitures^F

sleeping car
voiture^F-lit^M

dining car
voiture^F restaurant^M

coach car
voiture^F classique

diesel-electric locomotive
locomotive^F diesel-électrique

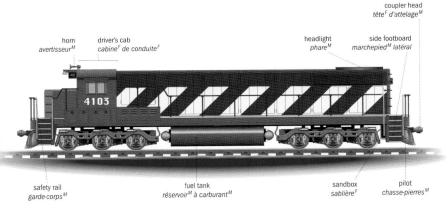

coupler head
tête^F d'attelage^M

horn
avertisseur^M

driver's cab
cabine^F de conduite^F

headlight
phare^M

side footboard
marchepied^M latéral

4103

safety rail
garde-corps^M

fuel tank
réservoir^M à carburant^M

sandbox
sablière^F

pilot
chasse-pierres^M

examples of freight cars
exemples^M de wagons^M

refrigerator car
wagon^M réfrigérant

intermodal car
wagon^M intermodal

caboose
wagon^M de queue^F

flat car
wagon^M plat

tank car
wagon^M-citerne^F

livestock car
wagon^M à bestiaux^M

container car
wagon^M porte-conteneurs^M

automobile car
wagon^M porte-automobiles^M

TRANSPORT AND MACHINERY

subway
chemin^M de fer^M métropolitain

subway station
station^F de métro^M

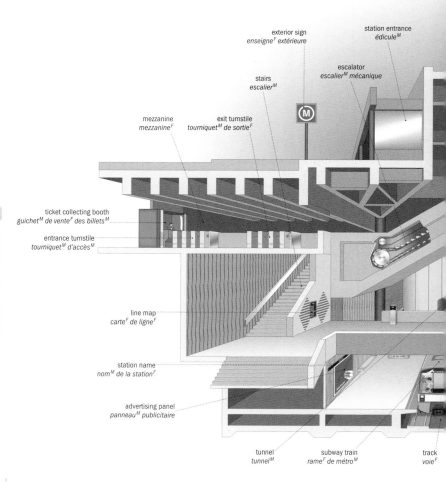

exterior sign
enseigne^F extérieure

station entrance
édicule^M

escalator
escalier^M mécanique

stairs
escalier^M

mezzanine
mezzanine^F

exit turnstile
tourniquet^M de sortie^F

ticket collecting booth
guichet^M de vente^F des billets^M

entrance turnstile
tourniquet^M d'accès^M

line map
carte^F de ligne^F

station name
nom^M de la station^F

advertising panel
panneau^M publicitaire

tunnel
tunnel^M

subway train
rame^F de métro^M

track
voie^F

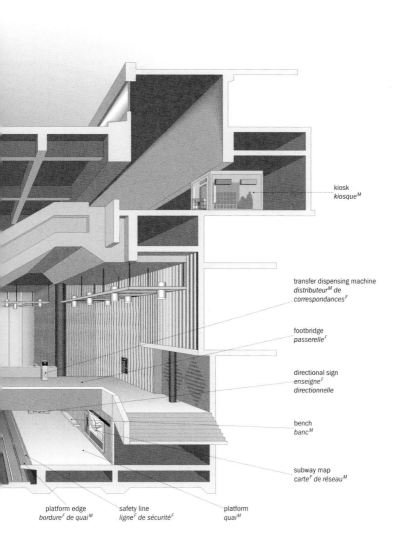

kiosk
kiosque^M

transfer dispensing machine
distributeur^M *de*
correspondances^F

footbridge
passerelle^F

directional sign
enseigne^F
directionnelle

bench
banc^M

subway map
carte^F *de réseau*^M

platform edge
bordure^F *de quai*^M

safety line
ligne^F *de sécurité*^F

platform
quai^M

TRANSPORT AND MACHINERY

subway

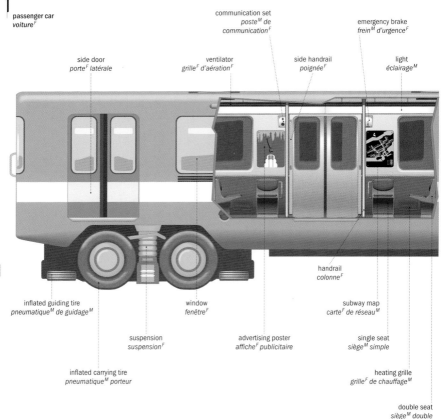

passenger car
voiture^F

communication set
poste^M de
communication^F

emergency brake
frein^M d'urgence^F

side door
porte^F latérale

ventilator
grille^F d'aération^F

side handrail
poignée^F

light
éclairage^M

handrail
colonne^F

inflated guiding tire
pneumatique^M de guidage^M

window
fenêtre^F

subway map
carte^F de réseau^M

suspension
suspension^F

advertising poster
affiche^F publicitaire

single seat
siège^M simple

inflated carrying tire
pneumatique^M porteur

heating grille
grille^F de chauffage^M

double seat
siège^M double

subway train
rame^F de métro^M

motor car
motrice^F

trailer car
remorque^F

motor car
motrice^F

harbor
port^M maritime

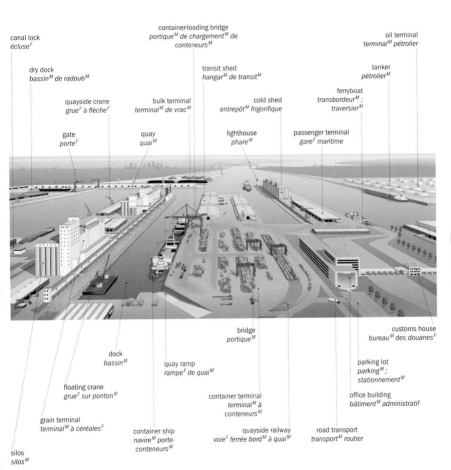

canal lock
écluse^F

container-loading bridge
*portique^M de chargement^M de
conteneurs^M*

oil terminal
terminal^M pétrolier

dry dock
bassin^M de radoub^M

transit shed
hangar^M de transit^M

tanker
pétrolier^M

ferryboat
*transbordeur^M ;
traversier^M*

quayside crane
grue^F à flèche^F

bulk terminal
terminal^M de vrac^M

cold shed
entrepôt^M frigorifique

gate
porte^F

quay
quai^M

lighthouse
phare^M

passenger terminal
gare^F maritime

bridge
portique^M

customs house
bureau^M des douanes^F

dock
bassin^M

quay ramp
rampe^F de quai^M

parking lot
*parking^M ;
stationnement^M*

floating crane
grue^F sur ponton^M

container terminal
*terminal^M à
conteneurs^M*

office building
bâtiment^M administratif

grain terminal
terminal^M à céréales^F

container ship
*navire^M porte-
conteneurs^M*

quayside railway
voie^F ferrée bord^M à quai^M

road transport
transport^M routier

silos
silos^M

examples of boats and ships
exemples^M de bateaux^M et d'embarcations^F

drill ship
navire^M de forage^M

derrick
tour^F de forage^M

bulk carrier
vraquier^M

container ship
*navire^M porte-
conteneurs^M*

radar
radar^M

stack
cheminée^F

chart room
salle^F des cartes^F

radio antenna
antenne^F radio^F

compass bridge
*passerelle^F de
navigation^F*

crew quarters
locaux^M de l'équipage^M

lifeboat
*chaloupe^F de
sauvetage^M*

examples of boats and ships

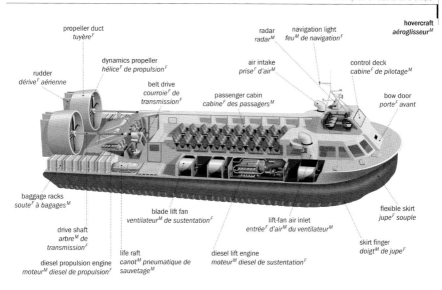

hovercraft
aéroglisseur^M

propeller duct
tuyère^F

radar
radar^M

navigation light
feu^M *de navigation*^{F}

dynamics propeller
hélice^F *de propulsion*^{F}

air intake
prise^F *d'air*^{M}

control deck
cabine^F *de pilotage*^{M}

rudder
dérive^F *aérienne*

belt drive
courroie^F *de transmission*^{F}

passenger cabin
cabine^F *des passagers*^{M}

bow door
porte^F *avant*

baggage racks
soute^F *à bagages*^{M}

blade lift fan
ventilateur^M *de sustentation*^{F}

lift-fan air inlet
entrée^F *d'air*^{M} *du ventilateur*^{M}

flexible skirt
jupe^F *souple*

drive shaft
arbre^M *de transmission*^{F}

life raft
canot^M *pneumatique de sauvetage*^{M}

diesel lift engine
moteur^M *diesel de sustentation*^{F}

skirt finger
doigt^M *de jupe*^{F}

diesel propulsion engine
moteur^M *diesel de propulsion*^{F}

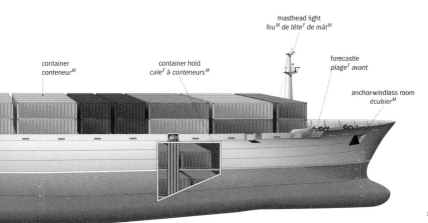

masthead light
feu^M *de tête*^{F} *de mât*^{M}

container
conteneur^M

container hold
cale^F *à conteneurs*^{M}

forecastle
plage^F *avant*

anchor-windlass room
écubier^M

examples of boats and ships

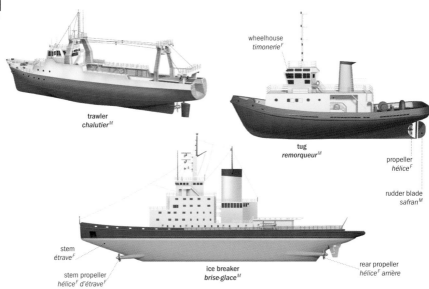

trawler
chalutier^M

wheelhouse
timonerie^F

tug
remorqueur^M

propeller
hélice^F

rudder blade
safran^M

stem
étrave^F

stem propeller
hélice^F *d'étrave*^F

ice breaker
brise-glace^M

rear propeller
hélice^F *arrière*

tanker
pétrolier^M

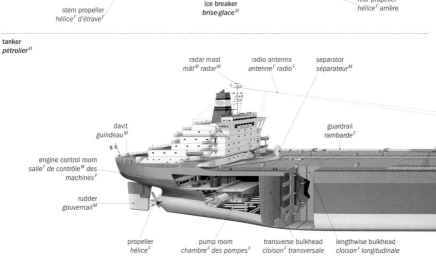

radar mast
mât^M *radar*^M

radio antenna
antenne^F *radio*^F

separator
séparateur^M

davit
guindeau^M

guardrail
rambarde^F

engine control room
salle^F *de contrôle*^M *des machines*^F

rudder
gouvernail^M

propeller
hélice^F

pump room
chambre^F *des pompes*^F

transverse bulkhead
cloison^F *transversale*

lengthwise bulkhead
cloison^F *longitudinale*

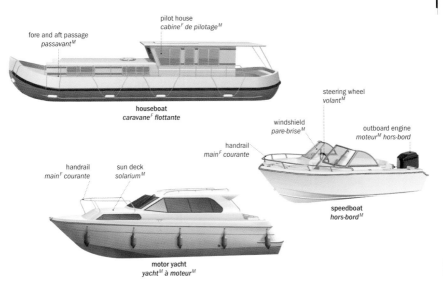

fore and aft passage
passavant[M]

pilot house
cabine[F] *de pilotage*[M]

houseboat
caravane[F] *flottante*

steering wheel
volant[M]

windshield
pare-brise[M]

outboard engine
moteur[M] *hors-bord*

handrail
main[F] *courante*

handrail
main[F] *courante*

sun deck
solarium[M]

speedboat
hors-bord[M]

motor yacht
yacht[M] *à moteur*[M]

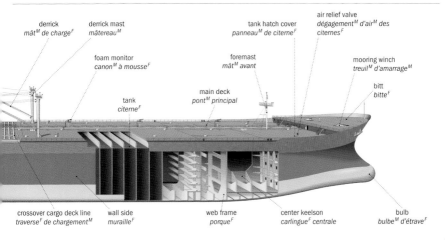

derrick
mât[M] *de charge*[F]

derrick mast
mâtereau[M]

foam monitor
canon[M] *à mousse*[F]

tank hatch cover
panneau[M] *de citerne*[F]

air relief valve
dégagement[M] *d'air*[M] *des citernes*[F]

foremast
mât[M] *avant*

mooring winch
treuil[M] *d'amarrage*[M]

tank
citerne[F]

main deck
pont[M] *principal*

bitt
bitte[F]

crossover cargo deck line
traverse[F] *de chargement*[M]

wall side
muraille[F]

web frame
porque[F]

center keelson
carlingue[F] *centrale*

bulb
bulbe[M] *d'étrave*[F]

examples of boats and ships

catamaran ferryboat
transbordeur^M ;
traversier^M

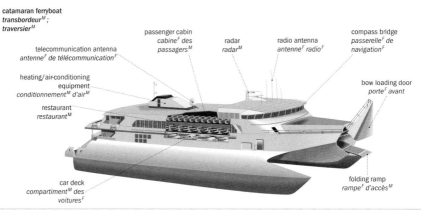

passenger cabin
cabine^F *des passagers*^M

radar
radar^M

radio antenna
antenne^F *radio*^F

compass bridge
passerelle^F *de navigation*^F

telecommunication antenna
antenne^F *de télécommunication*^F

heating/air-conditioning equipment
conditionnement^M *d'air*^M

bow loading door
porte^F *avant*

restaurant
restaurant^M

car deck
compartiment^M *des voitures*^F

folding ramp
rampe^F *d'accès*^M

passenger liner
paquebot^M

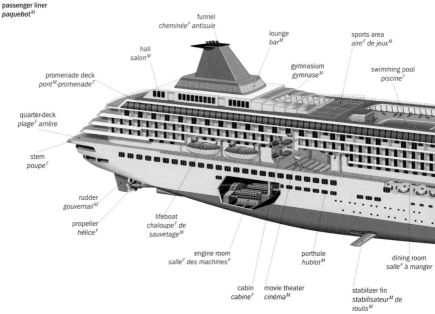

funnel
cheminée^F *antisuie*

lounge
bar^M

sports area
aire^F *de jeux*^M

hall
salon^M

gymnasium
gymnase^M

swimming pool
piscine^F

promenade deck
pont^M-*promenade*^F

quarter-deck
plage^F *arrière*

stem
poupe^F

rudder
gouvernail^M

propeller
hélice^F

lifeboat
chaloupe^F *de sauvetage*^M

engine room
salle^F *des machines*^F

cabin
cabine^F

movie theater
cinéma^M

porthole
hublot^M

stabilizer fin
stabilisateur^M *de roulis*^M

dining room
salle^F *à manger*

TRANSPORT AND MACHINERY

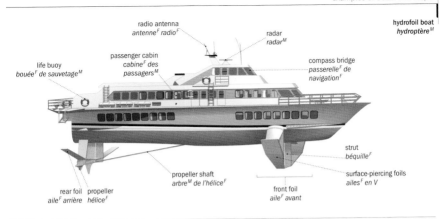

hydrofoil boat
hydroptère^M

radio antenna
antenne^F *radio*^F

radar
radar^M

passenger cabin
cabine^F *des
passagers*^M

life buoy
bouée^F *de sauvetage*^M

compass bridge
passerelle^F *de
navigation*^F

strut
béquille^F

surface-piercing foils
ailes^F *en V*

propeller shaft
arbre^M *de l'hélice*^F

front foil
aile^F *avant*

rear foil
aile^F *arrière*

propeller
hélice^F

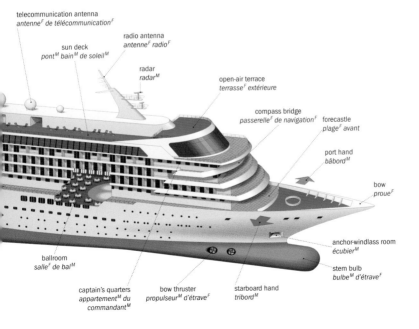

telecommunication antenna
antenne^F *de télécommunication*^F

radio antenna
antenne^F *radio*^F

sun deck
pont^M *bain*^M *de soleil*^M

radar
radar^M

open-air terrace
terrasse^F *extérieure*

compass bridge
passerelle^F *de navigation*^F

forecastle
plage^F *avant*

port hand
bâbord^M

bow
proue^F

anchor-windlass room
écubier^M

stem bulb
bulbe^M *d'étrave*^F

ballroom
salle^F *de bal*^M

captain's quarters
appartement^M *du
commandant*^M

bow thruster
propulseur^M *d'étrave*^F

starboard hand
tribord^M

TRANSPORT AND MACHINERY

airport
aéroport^M

high-speed exit taxiway
sortie^F *de piste*^F *à grande vitesse*^F

control tower cab
vigie^F

control tower
tour^F *de contrôle*^M

access road
route^F *d'accès*^M

taxiway
voie^F *de circulation*^F

by-pass taxiway
bretelle^F

taxiway
voie^F *de circulation*^F

apron
aire^F *de trafic*^M

service road
voie^F *de service*^M

maneuvering area
aire^F *de manœuvre*^F

passenger terminal
*aérogare^F de
passagers^M*

maintenance hangar
hangar^M

parking area
*aire^F de
stationnement^M*

telescopic corridor
*passerelle^F
télescopique*

service area
aire^F de service^M

boarding walkway
quai^M d'embarquement^M

taxiway line
*marques^F de
circulation^F*

radial passenger-loading area
aérogare^F satellite^M

airport

TRANSPORT AND MACHINERY

passenger terminal
aérogare^F

information counter
comptoir^M *de
renseignements*^M

baggage claim area
zone^F *de retrait*^M *des
bagages*^M

hotel reservation desk
bureau^M *de réservation*^F *de
chambres*^F *d'hôtel*^M

ticket counter
billetterie^F

automatically controlled
door
porte^F *automatique*

lobby
hall^M *public*

baggage check-in counter
comptoir^M
d'enregistrement^M

parking lot
parc^M *de
stationnement*^M

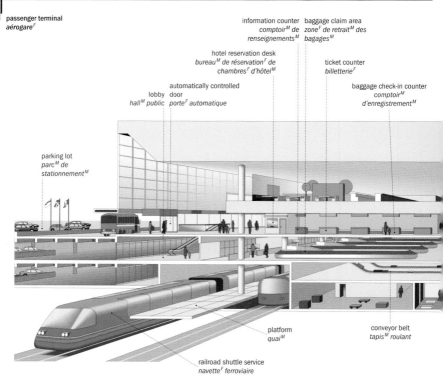

platform
quai^M

conveyor belt
tapis^M *roulant*

railroad shuttle service
navette^F *ferroviaire*

runway
piste^F

holding area marking
marque^F *de point*^M
d'attente^F

runway designation marking
marques^F *d'identification*^F

runway center line markings
marque^F *d'axe*^M *de piste*^F

runway side stripe markings
marques^F *latérales de piste*^F

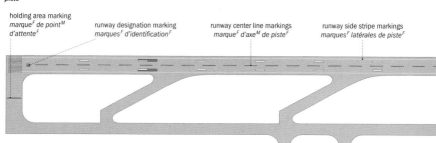

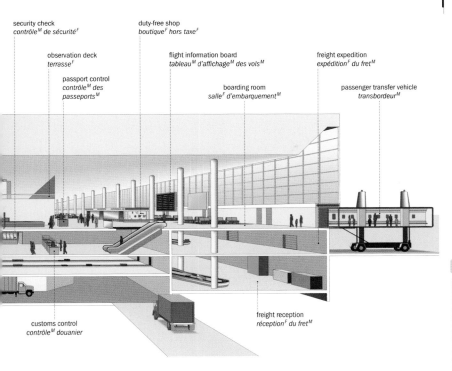

security check
contrôle^M de sécurité^F

observation deck
terrasse^F

passport control
contrôle^M des
passeports^M

duty-free shop
boutique^F hors taxe^F

flight information board
tableau^M d'affichage^M des vols^M

boarding room
salle^F d'embarquement^M

freight expedition
expédition^F du fret^M

passenger transfer vehicle
transbordeur^M

customs control
contrôle^M douanier

freight reception
réception^F du fret^M

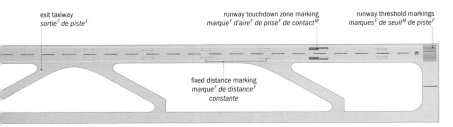

exit taxiway
sortie^F de piste^F

runway touchdown zone marking
marque^F d'aire^F de prise^F de contact^M

runway threshold markings
marques^F de seuil^M de piste^F

fixed distance marking
marque^F de distance^F
constante

TRANSPORT AND MACHINERY

long-range jet
avion^M long-courrier^M

TRANSPORT AND MACHINERY

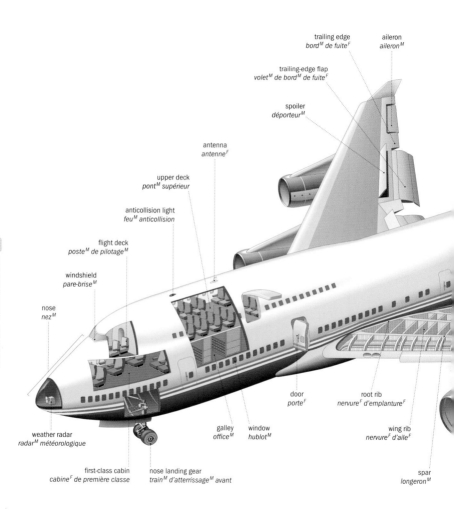

trailing edge
bord^M de fuite^F

aileron
aileron^M

trailing-edge flap
volet^M de bord^M de fuite^F

spoiler
déporteur^M

antenna
antenne^F

upper deck
pont^M supérieur

anticollision light
feu^M anticollision

flight deck
poste^M de pilotage^M

windshield
pare-brise^M

nose
nez^M

weather radar
radar^M météorologique

first-class cabin
cabine^F de première classe

nose landing gear
train^M d'atterrissage^M avant

galley
office^M

window
hublot^M

door
porte^F

root rib
nervure^F d'emplanture^F

wing rib
nervure^F d'aile^F

spar
longeron^M

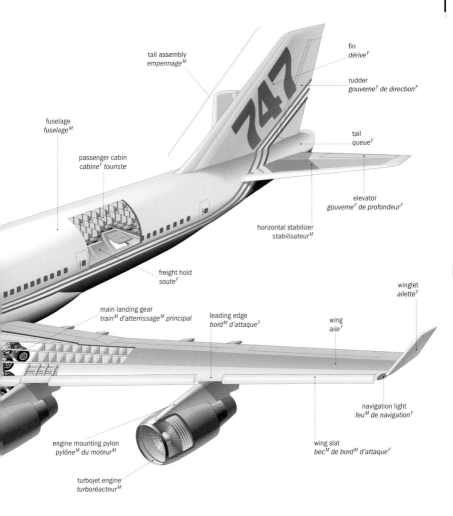

tail assembly
empennage^M

fin
dérive^F

rudder
gouverne^F de direction^F

fuselage
fuselage^M

tail
queue^F

passenger cabin
cabine^F touriste

elevator
gouverne^F de profondeur^F

horizontal stabilizer
stabilisateur^M

freight hold
soute^F

winglet
ailette^F

main landing gear
train^M d'atterrissage^M principal

leading edge
bord^M d'attaque^F

wing
aile^F

navigation light
feu^M de navigation^F

engine mounting pylon
pylône^M du moteur^M

wing slat
bec^M de bord^M d'attaque^F

turbojet engine
turboréacteur^M

examples of airplanes
exemples^M d'avions^M

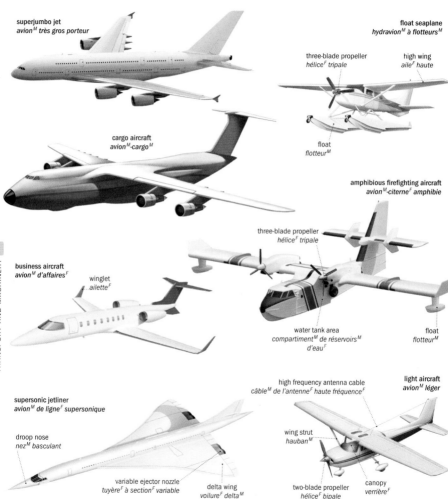

superjumbo jet
avion^M très gros porteur

float seaplane
hydravion^M à flotteurs^M

three-blade propeller
hélice^F tripale

high wing
aile^F haute

cargo aircraft
avion^M-cargo^M

float
flotteur^M

amphibious firefighting aircraft
avion^M-citerne^F amphibie

three-blade propeller
hélice^F tripale

business aircraft
avion^M d'affaires^F

winglet
ailette^F

water tank area
compartiment^M de réservoirs^M d'eau^F

float
flotteur^M

light aircraft
avion^M léger

high frequency antenna cable
câble^M de l'antenne^F haute fréquence^F

supersonic jetliner
avion^M de ligne^F supersonique

wing strut
hauban^M

droop nose
nez^M basculant

variable ejector nozzle
tuyère^F à section^F variable

delta wing
voilure^F delta^M

two-blade propeller
hélice^F bipale

canopy
verrière^F

movements of an airplane
mouvements^M de l'avion^M

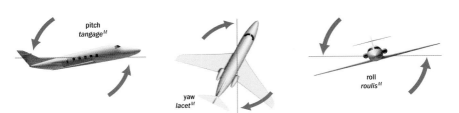

pitch
tangage^M

yaw
lacet^M

roll
roulis^M

helicopter
hélicoptère^M

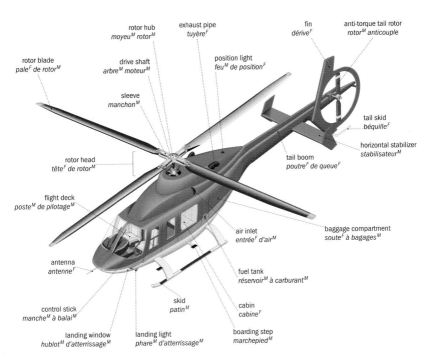

rotor hub
moyeu^M rotor^M

exhaust pipe
tuyère^F

fin
dérive^F

anti-torque tail rotor
rotor^M anticouple

rotor blade
pale^F de rotor^M

drive shaft
arbre^M moteur^M

position light
feu^M de position^F

sleeve
manchon^M

tail skid
béquille^F

rotor head
tête^F de rotor^M

tail boom
poutre^F de queue^F

horizontal stabilizer
stabilisateur^M

flight deck
poste^M de pilotage^M

air inlet
entrée^F d'air^M

baggage compartment
soute^F à bagages^M

antenna
antenne^F

fuel tank
réservoir^M à carburant^M

control stick
manche^M à balai^M

skid
patin^M

cabin
cabine^F

landing window
hublot^M d'atterrissage^M

landing light
phare^M d'atterrissage^M

boarding step
marchepied^M

TRANSPORT AND MACHINERY

material handling
manutention^F

forklift truck
chariot^M *élévateur*

mast
mât^M

crosshead
tête^F *du vérin*^M *de levage*^M

lifting chain
chaîne^F *de levage*^M

hydraulic hoses
système^M *hydraulique*

carriage
tablier^M

fork arm
bras^M *de fourche*^F

fork
fourches^F

overhead guard
toit^M *de protection*^F

mast-operating lever
levier^M *de manœuvre*^F *du mât*^M

engine compartment
moteur^M

frame
châssis^M

hand truck
diable^M

pallet truck
transpalette^F *manuelle*

wing pallet
palette^F *à ailes*^F

top deckboard
plancher^M *supérieur*

stringer
entretoise^F

entry
entrée^F

bottom deckboard
plancher^M *inférieur*

TRANSPORT AND MACHINERY

cranes
grues^F et portique^M

tower crane
grue^F à tour^F

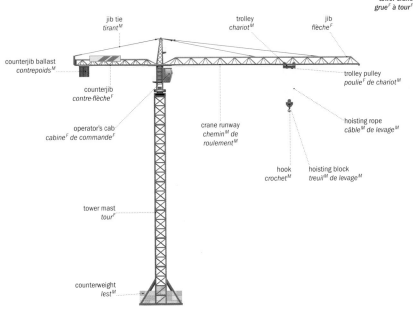

jib tie
tirant^M

trolley
chariot^M

jib
flèche^F

counterjib ballast
contrepoids^M

trolley pulley
poulie^F de chariot^M

counterjib
contre-flèche^F

operator's cab
cabine^F de commande^F

crane runway
chemin^M de roulement^M

hoisting rope
câble^M de levage^M

hook
crochet^M

hoisting block
treuil^M de levage^M

tower mast
tour^F

counterweight
lest^M

truck crane
grue^F sur porteur^M

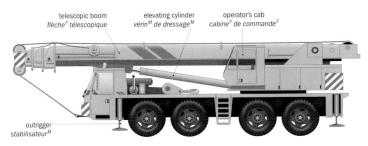

telescopic boom
flèche^F télescopique

elevating cylinder
vérin^M de dressage^M

operator's cab
cabine^F de commande^F

outrigger
stabilisateur^M

bulldozer

bouteur^M

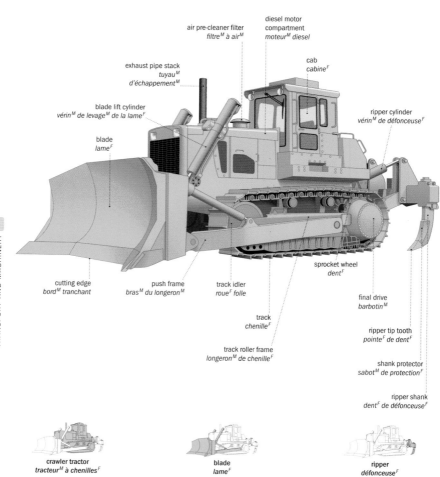

air pre-cleaner filter
filtre^M *à air*^M

diesel motor
compartment
moteur^M *diesel*

cab
cabine^F

exhaust pipe stack
tuyau^M
d'échappement^M

ripper cylinder
vérin^M *de défonceuse*^F

blade lift cylinder
vérin^M *de levage*^M *de la lame*^F

blade
lame^F

cutting edge
bord^M *tranchant*

push frame
bras^M *du longeron*^M

track idler
roue^F *folle*

sprocket wheel
dent^F

final drive
barbotin^M

track
chenille^F

ripper tip tooth
pointe^F *de dent*^F

track roller frame
longeron^M *de chenille*^F

shank protector
sabot^M *de protection*^F

ripper shank
dent^F *de défonceuse*^F

crawler tractor
tracteur^M *à chenilles*^F

blade
lame^F

ripper
défonceuse^F

wheel loader
chargeuse^F*-pelleteuse*^F

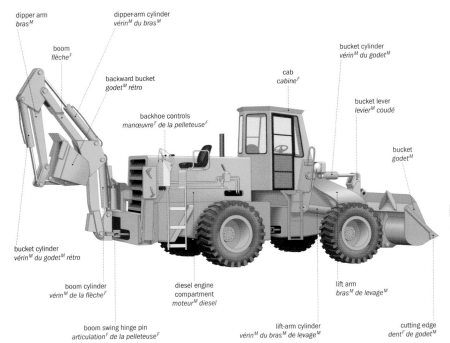

dipper arm
bras^M

dipper-arm cylinder
vérin^M *du bras*^M

boom
flèche^F

bucket cylinder
vérin^M *du godet*^M

backward bucket
godet^M *rétro*

cab
cabine^F

bucket lever
levier^M *coudé*

backhoe controls
manœuvre^F *de la pelleteuse*^F

bucket
godet^M

bucket cylinder
vérin^M *du godet*^M *rétro*

boom cylinder
vérin^M *de la flèche*^F

diesel engine
compartment
moteur^M *diesel*

lift arm
bras^M *de levage*^M

boom swing hinge pin
articulation^F *de la pelleteuse*^F

lift-arm cylinder
vérin^M *du bras*^M *de levage*^M

cutting edge
dent^F *de godet*^M

TRANSPORT AND MACHINERY

front-end loader
chargeuse^F *frontale*

wheel tractor
tracteur^M

backhoe
pelleteuse^F

scraper

décapeuse^F

tractor engine compartment
tracteur^M*-remorqueur*^M

gooseneck
col^M*-de-cygne*^M

steering cylinder
vérin^M *de direction*^F

elevator
élévateur^M

draft tube
palonnier^M

bowl
benne^F

cutting edge
lame^F *racleuse*

draft arm
brancard^M

hydraulic shovel

pelle^F *hydraulique*

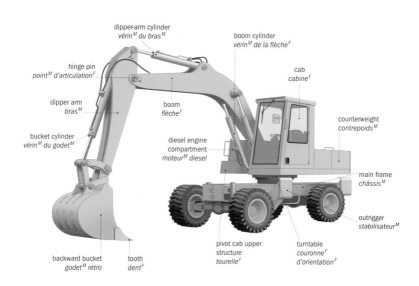

dipper-arm cylinder
vérin^M *du bras*^M

boom cylinder
vérin^M *de la flèche*^F

hinge pin
point^M *d'articulation*^F

cab
cabine^F

dipper arm
bras^M

boom
flèche^F

counterweight
contrepoids^M

bucket cylinder
vérin^M *du godet*^M

diesel engine compartment
moteur^M *diesel*

main frame
châssis^M

outrigger
stabilisateur^M

backward bucket
godet^M *rétro*

tooth
dent^F

pivot cab upper structure
tourelle^F

turntable
couronne^F
d'orientation^F

grader
niveleuse^F

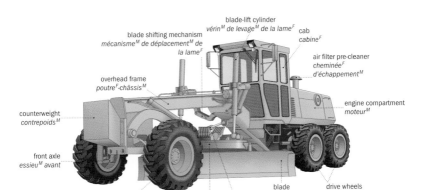

blade-lift cylinder
vérin^M de levage^M de la lame^F

cab
cabine^F

blade shifting mechanism
mécanisme^M de déplacement^M de la lame^F

air filter pre-cleaner
cheminée^F d'échappement^M

overhead frame
poutre^F-châssis^M

engine compartment
moteur^M

counterweight
contrepoids^M

front axle
essieu^M avant

front wheel
roue^F avant

turntable
cercle^M porte-lame^M

blade
lame^F

drive wheels
roues^F motrices

blade rotation cylinder
vérin^M d'orientation^F de la lame^F

dump truck
camion^M-benne^F

canopy
auvent^M

rib
nervure^F

cab
cabine^F

dump body
benne^F basculante

diesel engine compartment
moteur^M diesel

ladder
échelle^F

frame
châssis^M

TRANSPORT AND MACHINERY

production of electricity from geothermal energy

production[F] d'électricité[F] par énergie[F] géothermique

turbine
turbine[F]

generator
alternateur[M]

condenser
condenseur[M]

high-tension electricity transmission tower
transport[M] de l'électricité[F] à haute tension[F]

steam
vapeur[F]

separator
séparateur[M]

transformer (voltage increase)
élévation[F] de la tension[F]

water-steam mix
mélange[M] eau[F]-vapeur[F]

cooling tower
tour[F] de refroidissement[M]

upper confining bed
toit[M] imperméable

water
eau[F]

geothermal field
champ[M] géothermique

lower confining bed
substratum[M] imperméable

production well
puits[M] de production[F]

confined aquifer
aquifère[M] captif

injection well
puits[M] d'injection[F]

magma chamber
réservoir[M] magmatique

thermal energy

énergie[F] thermique

geothermal energy
énergie[F] géothermique

crusher
broyeur[M]

stack
cheminée[F]

cooling tower
tour[F] de refroidissement[M]

coal storage yard
parc[M] à charbon[M]

high-tension electricity transmission tower
transport[M] de l'électricité[F] à haute tension[F]

transformer (voltage decrease)
abaissement[M] de la tension[F]

conveyor
convoyeur[M]

belt loader
sauterelle[F]

pulverizer
pulvérisateur[M]

steam generator
générateur[M] de vapeur[F]

transmission to consumers
transport[M] vers les usagers[M]

coal-fired thermal power plant
centrale[F] thermique au charbon[M]

condenser
condenseur[M]

turbo-alternator unit
groupe[M] turbo-alternateur[M]

transformer (voltage increase)
élévation[F] de la tension[F]

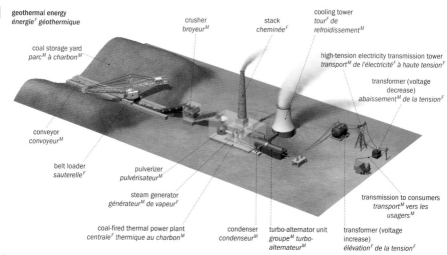

ENERGY

oil
pétrole^M

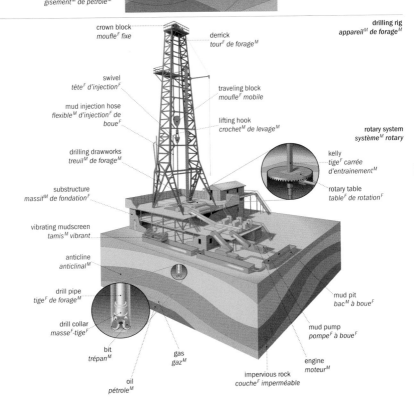

surface prospecting
prospection^F *terrestre*

seismographic recording
enregistrement^M
sismographique

shock wave
onde^F *de choc*^{M}

petroleum trap
gisement^M *de pétrole*^{M}

drilling rig
appareil^M *de forage*^{M}

crown block
moufle^F *fixe*

derrick
tour^F *de forage*^{M}

swivel
tête^F *d'injection*^{F}

traveling block
moufle^F *mobile*

mud injection hose
flexible^M *d'injection*^{F} *de*
boue^F

lifting hook
crochet^M *de levage*^{M}

rotary system
système^M *rotary*

drilling drawworks
treuil^M *de forage*^{M}

kelly
tige^F *carrée*
d'entraînement^M

rotary table
table^F *de rotation*^{F}

substructure
massif^M *de fondation*^{F}

vibrating mudscreen
tamis^M *vibrant*

anticline
anticlinal^M

drill pipe
tige^F *de forage*^{M}

mud pit
bac^M *à boue*^{F}

drill collar
masse^F-*tige*^{F}

mud pump
pompe^F *à boue*^{F}

bit
trépan^M

gas
gaz^M

engine
moteur^M

oil
pétrole^M

impervious rock
couche^F *imperméable*

ENERGY

floating-roof tank
réservoir^M à toit^M flottant

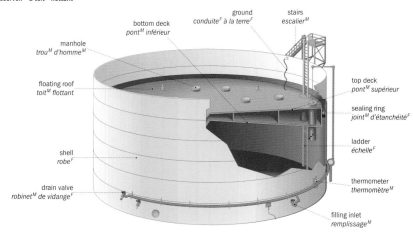

ground
conduite^F à la terre^F

stairs
escalier^M

bottom deck
pont^M inférieur

manhole
trou^M d'homme^M

floating roof
toit^M flottant

top deck
pont^M supérieur

sealing ring
joint^M d'étanchéité^F

ladder
échelle^F

shell
robe^F

thermometer
thermomètre^M

drain valve
robinet^M de vidange^F

filling inlet
remplissage^M

crude-oil pipeline
réseau^M d'oléoducs^M

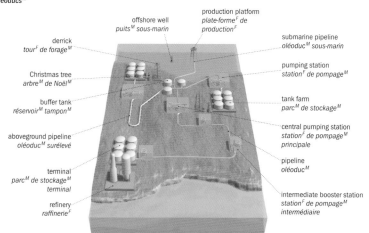

offshore well
puits^M sous-marin

production platform
plate-forme^F de production^F

derrick
tour^F de forage^M

submarine pipeline
oléoduc^M sous-marin

Christmas tree
arbre^M de Noël^M

pumping station
station^F de pompage^M

buffer tank
réservoir^M tampon^M

tank farm
parc^M de stockage^M

aboveground pipeline
oléoduc^M surélevé

central pumping station
station^F de pompage^M principale

terminal
parc^M de stockage^M terminal

pipeline
oléoduc^M

refinery
raffinerie^F

intermediate booster station
station^F de pompage^M intermédiaire

ENERGY

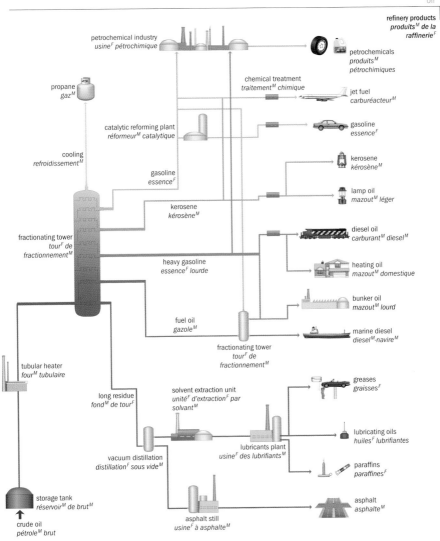

refinery products
*produits^M de la
raffinerie^F*

petrochemical industry
usine^F pétrochimique

petrochemicals
*produits^M
pétrochimiques*

chemical treatment
traitement^M chimique

jet fuel
carburéacteur^M

propane
gaz^M

catalytic reforming plant
réformeur^M catalytique

gasoline
essence^F

cooling
refroidissement^M

kerosene
kérosène^M

gasoline
essence^F

lamp oil
mazout^M léger

kerosene
kérosène^M

fractionating tower
*tour^F de
fractionnement^M*

diesel oil
carburant^M diesel^M

heavy gasoline
essence^F lourde

heating oil
mazout^M domestique

bunker oil
mazout^M lourd

fuel oil
gazole^M

marine diesel
diesel^M-navire^M

fractionating tower
*tour^F de
fractionnement^M*

tubular heater
four^M tubulaire

greases
graisses^F

long residue
fond^M de tour^F

solvent extraction unit
*unité^F d'extraction^F par
solvant^M*

lubricating oils
huiles^F lubrifiantes

vacuum distillation
distillation^F sous vide^M

lubricants plant
usine^F des lubrifiants^M

paraffins
paraffines^F

storage tank
réservoir^M de brut^M

asphalt
asphalte^M

crude oil
pétrole^M brut

asphalt still
usine^F à asphalte^M

ENERGY

hydroelectric complex
complexe^M hydroélectrique

crest of spillway
seuil^M de l'évacuateur^M

spillway gate
vanne^F

top of dam
crête^F

reservoir
réservoir^M

headbay
bief^M d'amont^M

spillway
évacuateur^M

penstock
conduite^F forcée

gantry crane
portique^M

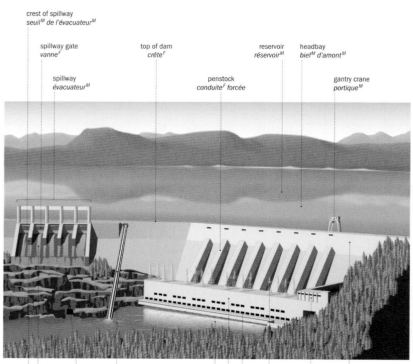

ENERGY

diversion tunnel
galerie^F de dérivation^F

afterbay
bief^M d'aval^M

control room
salle^F de commande^F

spillway chute
*coursier^M
d'évacuateur^M*

power plant
centrale^F

bushing
*traversée^F de
transformateur^M*

training wall
mur^M bajoyer^M

log chute
passe^F à billes^F

machine hall
salle^F des machines^F

dam
barrage^M

cross section of a hydroelectric power plant
coupe^F d'une centrale^F hydroélectrique

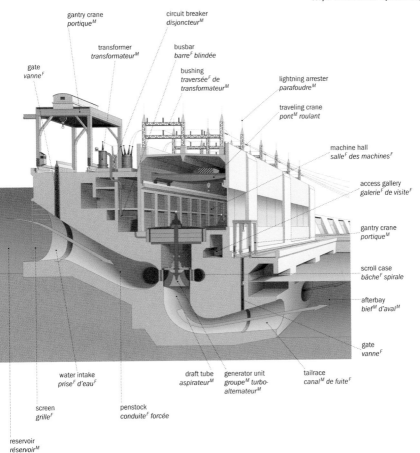

gantry crane
portique^M

circuit breaker
disjoncteur^M

transformer
transformateur^M

busbar
barre^F blindée

gate
vanne^F

bushing
*traversée^F de
transformateur^M*

lightning arrester
parafoudre^M

traveling crane
pont^M roulant

machine hall
salle^F des machines^F

access gallery
galerie^F de visite^F

gantry crane
portique^M

scroll case
bâche^F spirale

afterbay
bief^M d'aval^M

gate
vanne^F

water intake
prise^F d'eau^F

draft tube
aspirateur^M

generator unit
*groupe^M turbo-
alternateur^M*

tailrace
canal^M de fuite^F

screen
grille^F

penstock
conduite^F forcée

reservoir
réservoir^M

production of electricity from nuclear energy
production^F d'électricité^F par énergie^F nucléaire

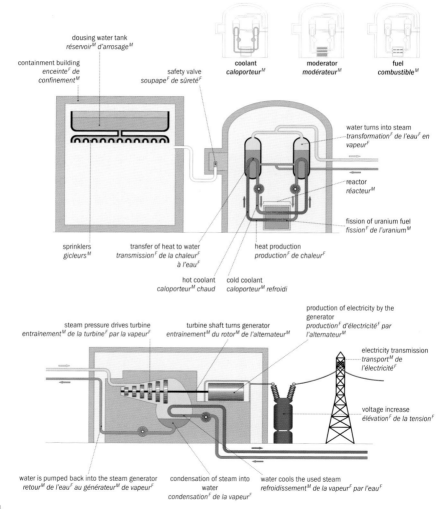

coolant
caloporteur^M

moderator
modérateur^M

fuel
combustible^M

dousing water tank
réservoir^M d'arrosage^M

containment building
*enceinte^F de
confinement^M*

safety valve
soupape^F de sûreté^F

water turns into steam
*transformation^F de l'eau^F en
vapeur^F*

reactor
réacteur^M

fission of uranium fuel
fission^F de l'uranium^M

sprinklers
gicleurs^M

transfer of heat to water
*transmission^F de la chaleur^F
à l'eau^F*

heat production
production^F de chaleur^F

hot coolant
caloporteur^M chaud

cold coolant
caloporteur^M refroidi

production of electricity by the
generator
*production^F d'électricité^F par
l'alternateur^M*

steam pressure drives turbine
entrainement^M de la turbine^F par la vapeur^F

turbine shaft turns generator
entrainement^M du rotor^M de l'alternateur^M

electricity transmission
*transport^M de
l'électricité^F*

voltage increase
élévation^F de la tension^F

water is pumped back into the steam generator
retour^M de l'eau^F au générateur^M de vapeur^F

condensation of steam into
water
condensation^F de la vapeur^F

water cools the used steam
refroidissement^M de la vapeur^F par l'eau^F

ENERGY

fuel bundle
grappe^F de combustible^M

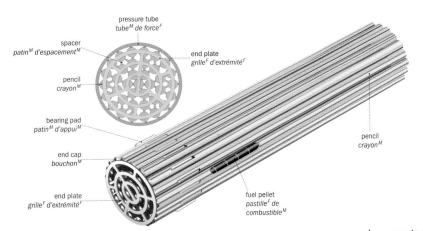

pressure tube
tube^M de force^F

spacer
patin^M d'espacement^M

end plate
grille^F d'extrémité^F

pencil
crayon^M

bearing pad
patin^M d'appui^M

end cap
bouchon^M

end plate
grille^F d'extrémité^F

pencil
crayon^M

fuel pellet
pastille^F de combustible^M

nuclear reactor
réacteur^M nucléaire

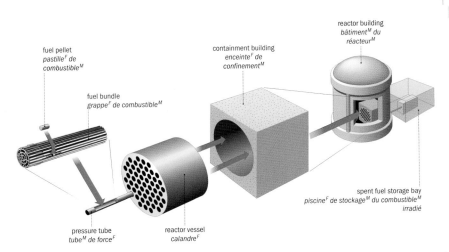

fuel pellet
pastille^F de combustible^M

fuel bundle
grappe^F de combustible^M

containment building
enceinte^F de confinement^M

reactor building
bâtiment^M du réacteur^M

spent fuel storage bay
piscine^F de stockage^M du combustible^M irradié

pressure tube
tube^M de force^F

reactor vessel
calandre^F

ENERGY

solar cell

photopile[F]

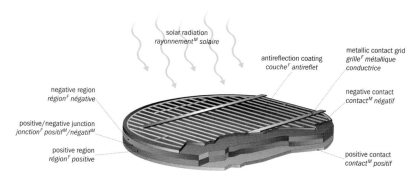

solar radiation
rayonnement[M] *solaire*

antireflection coating
couche[F] *antireflet*

metallic contact grid
grille[F] *métallique*
conductrice

negative region
région[F] *négative*

negative contact
contact[M] *négatif*

positive/negative junction
jonction[F] *positif*[M]/*négatif*[M]

positive region
région[F] *positive*

positive contact
contact[M] *positif*

flat-plate solar collector

capteur[M] *solaire plan*

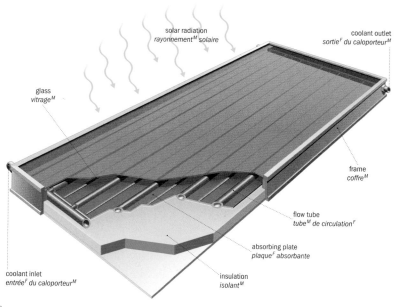

solar radiation
rayonnement[M] *solaire*

coolant outlet
sortie[F] *du caloporteur*[M]

glass
vitrage[M]

frame
coffre[M]

flow tube
tube[M] *de circulation*[F]

absorbing plate
plaque[F] *absorbante*

coolant inlet
entrée[F] *du caloporteur*[M]

insulation
isolant[M]

ENERGY

solar-cell system
circuit^M de photopiles^F

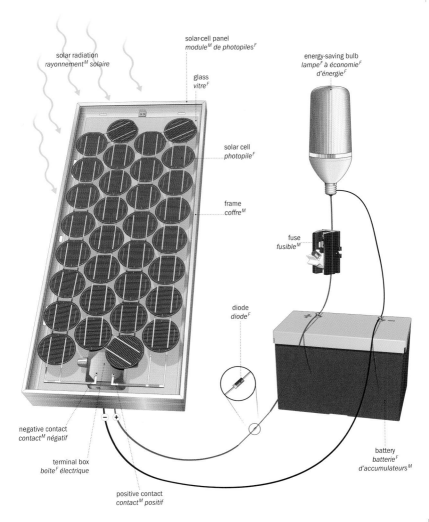

solar radiation
rayonnement^M solaire

solar-cell panel
module^M de photopiles^F

glass
vitre^F

energy-saving bulb
*lampe^F à économie^F
d'énergie^F*

solar cell
photopile^F

frame
coffre^M

fuse
fusible^M

diode
diode^F

negative contact
contact^M négatif

terminal box
boîte^F électrique

positive contact
contact^M positif

battery
*batterie^F
d'accumulateurs^M*

windmill
moulin^M à vent^M

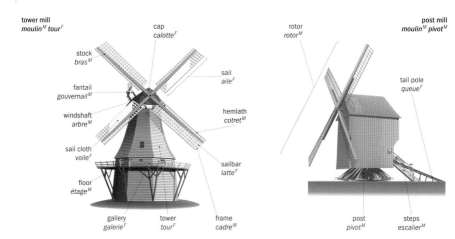

tower mill
moulin^M tour^F

stock
bras^M

fantail
gouvernail^M

windshaft
arbre^M

sail cloth
voile^F

floor
étage^M

gallery
galerie^F

tower
tour^F

frame
cadre^M

cap
calotte^F

sail
aile^F

hemlath
cotret^M

sailbar
latte^F

rotor
rotor^M

post mill
moulin^M pivot^M

tail pole
queue^F

post
pivot^M

steps
escalier^M

wind turbines and electricity production
éoliennes^F et production^F d'électricité^F

vertical-axis wind turbine
éolienne^F à axe^M vertical

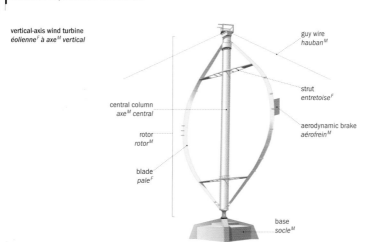

guy wire
hauban^M

central column
axe^M central

strut
entretoise^F

rotor
rotor^M

aerodynamic brake
aérofrein^M

blade
pale^F

base
socle^M

horizontal-axis wind turbine
éolienne^F à axe^M horizontal

nacelle cross-section
coupe^F de la nacelle^F

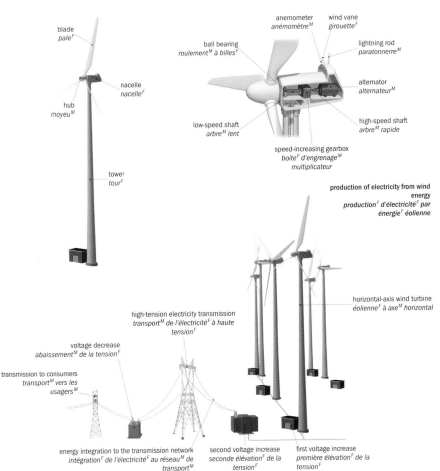

blade
pale^F

nacelle
nacelle^F

hub
moyeu^M

tower
tour^F

anemometer
anémomètre^M

wind vane
girouette^F

ball bearing
roulement^M à billes^F

lightning rod
paratonnerre^M

alternator
alternateur^M

low-speed shaft
arbre^M lent

high-speed shaft
arbre^M rapide

speed-increasing gearbox
boîte^F d'engrenage^M
multiplicateur

production of electricity from wind
energy
production^F d'électricité^F par
énergie^F éolienne

horizontal-axis wind turbine
éolienne^F à axe^M horizontal

high-tension electricity transmission
transport^M de l'électricité^F à haute
tension^F

voltage decrease
abaissement^M de la tension^F

transmission to consumers
transport^M vers les
usagers^M

energy integration to the transmission network
intégration^F de l'électricité^F au réseau^M de
transport^M

second voltage increase
seconde élévation^F de la
tension^F

first voltage increase
première élévation^F de la
tension^F

matter

matière^F

atom
atome^M

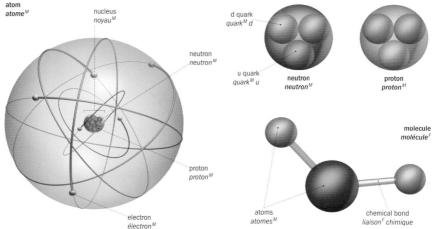

nucleus
noyau^M

neutron
neutron^M

proton
proton^M

electron
électron^M

d quark
quark^M d

u quark
quark^M u

neutron
neutron^M

proton
proton^M

molecule
molécule^F

atoms
atomes^M

chemical bond
liaison^F chimique

states of matter
états^M de la matière^F

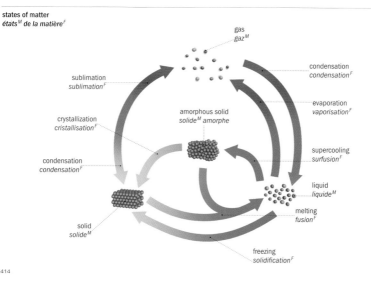

gas
gaz^M

sublimation
sublimation^F

crystallization
cristallisation^F

amorphous solid
solide^M amorphe

condensation
condensation^F

condensation
condensation^F

evaporation
vaporisation^F

supercooling
surfusion^F

liquid
liquide^M

melting
fusion^F

solid
solide^M

freezing
solidification^F

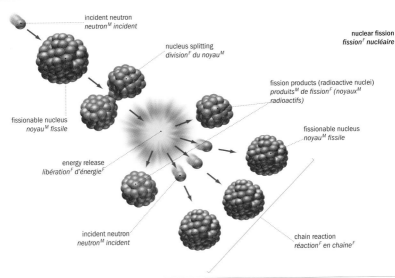

nuclear fission
fission^F nucléaire

incident neutron
neutron^M incident

nucleus splitting
division^F du noyau^M

fission products (radioactive nuclei)
produits^M de fission^F (noyaux^M radioactifs)

fissionable nucleus
noyau^M fissile

fissionable nucleus
noyau^M fissile

energy release
libération^F d'énergie^F

incident neutron
neutron^M incident

chain reaction
réaction^F en chaîne^F

heat transfer
transfert^M de la chaleur^F

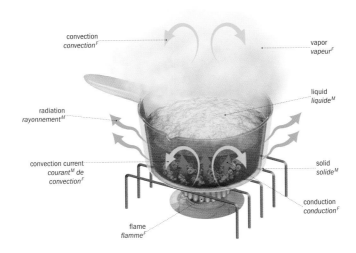

convection
convection^F

vapor
vapeur^F

liquid
liquide^M

radiation
rayonnement^M

convection current
courant^M de convection^F

solid
solide^M

conduction
conduction^F

flame
flamme^F

magnetism
*magnétisme*M

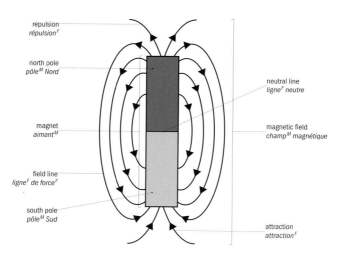

repulsion
*répulsion*F

north pole
*pôle*M *Nord*

neutral line
*ligne*F *neutre*

magnet
*aimant*M

magnetic field
*champ*M *magnétique*

field line
*ligne*F *de force*F

south pole
*pôle*M *Sud*

attraction
*attraction*F

parallel electrical circuit
*circuit*M *électrique en parallèle*F

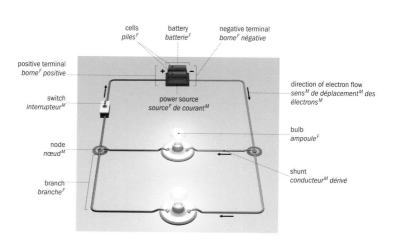

cells
*piles*F

battery
*batterie*F

negative terminal
*borne*F *négative*

positive terminal
*borne*F *positive*

direction of electron flow
*sens*M *de déplacement*M *des*
*électrons*M

switch
*interrupteur*M

power source
*source*F *de courant*M

node
*nœud*M

bulb
*ampoule*F

shunt
*conducteur*M *dérivé*

branch
*branche*F

dry cells
piles[F] sèches

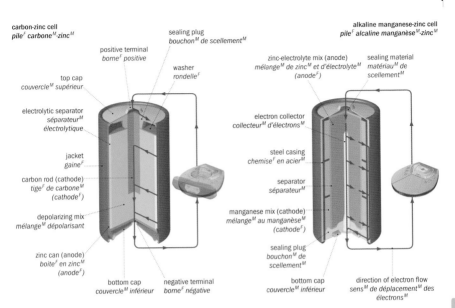

carbon-zinc cell
pile[F] carbone[M]-zinc[M]

sealing plug
bouchon[M] de scellement[M]

positive terminal
borne[F] positive

washer
rondelle[F]

top cap
couvercle[M] supérieur

electrolytic separator
séparateur[M] électrolytique

jacket
gaine[F]

carbon rod (cathode)
tige[F] de carbone[M] (cathode[F])

depolarizing mix
mélange[M] dépolarisant

zinc can (anode)
boîte[F] en zinc[M] (anode[F])

bottom cap
couvercle[M] inférieur

negative terminal
borne[F] négative

alkaline manganese-zinc cell
pile[F] alcaline manganèse[M]-zinc[M]

zinc-electrolyte mix (anode)
mélange[M] de zinc[M] et d'électrolyte[M] (anode[F])

sealing material
matériau[M] de scellement[M]

electron collector
collecteur[M] d'électrons[M]

steel casing
chemise[F] en acier[M]

separator
séparateur[M]

manganese mix (cathode)
mélange[M] au manganèse[M] (cathode[F])

sealing plug
bouchon[M] de scellement[M]

bottom cap
couvercle[M] inférieur

direction of electron flow
sens[M] de déplacement[M] des électrons[M]

electronics
électronique[F]

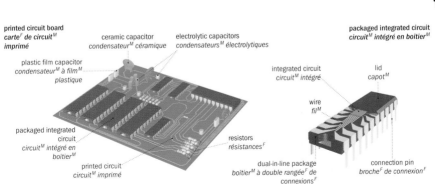

printed circuit board
carte[F] de circuit[M] imprimé

ceramic capacitor
condensateur[M] céramique

electrolytic capacitors
condensateurs[M] électrolytiques

plastic film capacitor
condensateur[M] à film[M] plastique

packaged integrated circuit
circuit[M] intégré en boîtier[M]

printed circuit
circuit[M] imprimé

resistors
résistances[F]

packaged integrated circuit
circuit[M] intégré en boîtier[M]

integrated circuit
circuit[M] intégré

lid
capot[M]

wire
fil[M]

dual-in-line package
boîtier[M] à double rangée[F] de connexions[F]

connection pin
broche[F] de connexion[F]

electromagnetic spectrum

spectre[M] électromagnétique

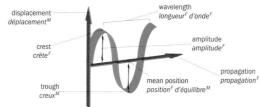

microwaves
micro-ondes[F]

ultraviolet radiation
rayonnement[M] ultraviolet

infrared radiation
rayonnement[M]
infrarouge

radio waves
ondes[F] radio

X-rays
rayons[M] X

gamma rays
rayons[M] gamma

visible light
lumière[F] visible

wave

onde[F]

displacement
déplacement[M]

wavelength
longueur[F] d'onde[F]

amplitude
amplitude[F]

crest
crête[F]

propagation
propagation[F]

trough
creux[M]

mean position
position[F] d'équilibre[M]

color synthesis

synthèse[F] des couleurs[F]

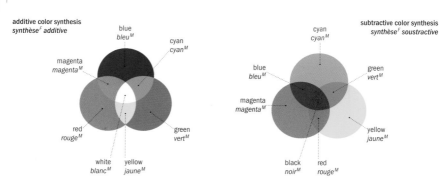

additive color synthesis
synthèse[F] additive

blue
bleu[M]

cyan
cyan[M]

magenta
magenta[M]

red
rouge[M]

green
vert[M]

white
blanc[M]

yellow
jaune[M]

subtractive color synthesis
synthèse[F] soustractive

cyan
cyan[M]

blue
bleu[M]

green
vert[M]

magenta
magenta[M]

yellow
jaune[M]

black
noir[M]

red
rouge[M]

SCIENCE

vision
vision[F]

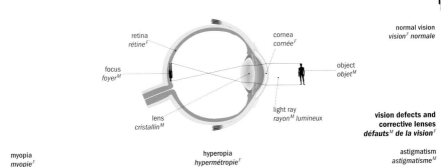

retina
rétine[F]

cornea
cornée[F]

focus
foyer[M]

object
objet[M]

lens
cristallin[M]

light ray
rayon[M] *lumineux*

normal vision
vision[F] *normale*

**vision defects and
corrective lenses
défauts[M] *de la vision*[F]**

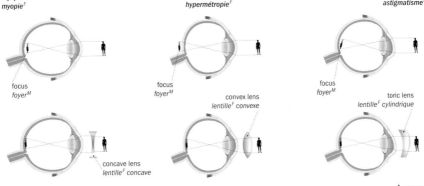

myopia
myopie[F]

hyperopia
hypermétropie[F]

astigmatism
astigmatisme[M]

focus
foyer[M]

focus
foyer[M]

focus
foyer[M]

convex lens
lentille[F] *convexe*

toric lens
lentille[F] *cylindrique*

concave lens
lentille[F] *concave*

convex lens
lentille[F] *convexe*

lenses
lentilles[F]

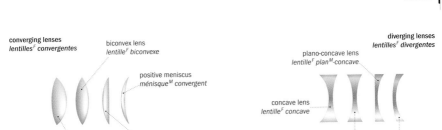

converging lenses
lentilles[F] *convergentes*

biconvex lens
lentille[F] *biconvexe*

positive meniscus
ménisque[M] *convergent*

convex lens
lentille[F] *convexe*

plano-convex lens
lentille[F] *plan*[M]*-convexe*

diverging lenses
lentilles[F] *divergentes*

plano-concave lens
lentille[F] *plan*[M]*-concave*

concave lens
lentille[F] *concave*

biconcave lens
lentille[F] *biconcave*

negative meniscus
ménisque[M] *divergent*

SCIENCE

pulsed ruby laser
laser^M à rubis^M pulsé

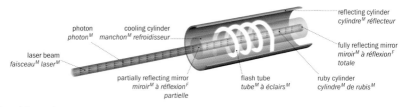

reflecting cylinder
cylindre^M réflecteur

photon
photon^M

cooling cylinder
manchon^M refroidisseur

fully reflecting mirror
miroir^M à réflexion^F totale

laser beam
faisceau^M laser^M

partially reflecting mirror
miroir^M à réflexion^F partielle

flash tube
tube^M à éclairs^M

ruby cylinder
cylindre^M de rubis^M

prism binoculars
jumelles^F à prismes^M

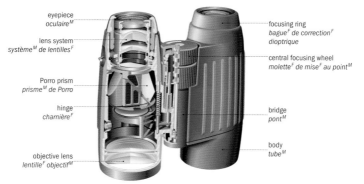

eyepiece
oculaire^M

focusing ring
bague^F de correction^F dioptrique

lens system
système^M de lentilles^F

central focusing wheel
molette^F de mise^F au point^M

Porro prism
prisme^M de Porro

hinge
charnière^F

bridge
pont^M

body
tube^M

objective lens
lentille^F objectif^M

telescopic sight
lunette^F de visée^F

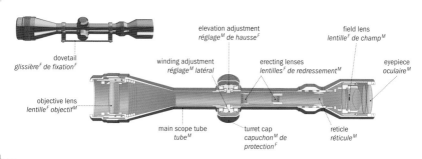

elevation adjustment
réglage^M de hausse^F

field lens
lentille^F de champ^M

dovetail
glissière^F de fixation^F

winding adjustment
réglage^M latéral

erecting lenses
lentilles^F de redressement^M

eyepiece
oculaire^M

objective lens
lentille^F objectif^M

main scope tube
tube^M

turret cap
capuchon^M de protection^F

reticle
réticule^M

SCIENCE

magnifying glass and microscopes
loupe^F et microscopes^M

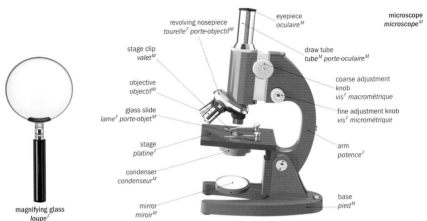

microscope
microscope^M

revolving nosepiece
tourelle^F porte-objectif^M

eyepiece
oculaire^M

stage clip
valet^M

draw tube
tube^M porte-oculaire^M

objective
objectif^M

coarse adjustment knob
vis^F macrométrique

glass slide
lame^F porte-objet^M

fine adjustment knob
vis^F micrométrique

stage
platine^F

arm
potence^F

condenser
condenseur^M

base
pied^M

mirror
miroir^M

magnifying glass
loupe^F

binocular microscope
*microscope^M
binoculaire*

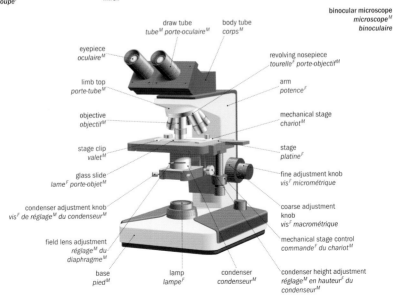

draw tube
tube^M porte-oculaire^M

body tube
corps^M

eyepiece
oculaire^M

revolving nosepiece
tourelle^F porte-objectif^M

limb top
porte-tube^M

arm
potence^F

objective
objectif^M

mechanical stage
chariot^M

stage clip
valet^M

stage
platine^F

glass slide
lame^F porte-objet^M

fine adjustment knob
vis^F micrométrique

condenser adjustment knob
vis^F de réglage^M du condenseur^M

coarse adjustment knob
vis^F macrométrique

field lens adjustment
réglage^M du diaphragme^M

mechanical stage control
commande^F du chariot^M

base
pied^M

lamp
lampe^F

condenser
condenseur^M

condenser height adjustment
réglage^M en hauteur^F du condenseur^M

SCIENCE

measurement of weight
mesure^F de la masse^F

beam balance
balance^F à fléau^M

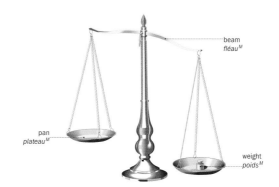

beam
fléau^M

pan
plateau^M

weight
poids^M

steelyard
balance^F romaine

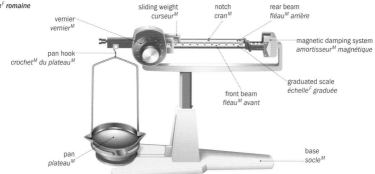

sliding weight
curseur^M

notch
cran^M

rear beam
fléau^M arrière

vernier
vernier^M

pan hook
crochet^M du plateau^M

magnetic damping system
amortisseur^M magnétique

graduated scale
échelle^F graduée

front beam
fléau^M avant

pan
plateau^M

base
socle^M

Roberval's balance
balance^F de Roberval

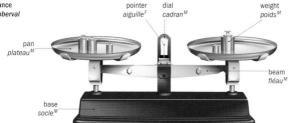

pointer
aiguille^F

dial
cadran^M

weight
poids^M

pan
plateau^M

beam
fléau^M

base
socle^M

SCIENCE

spring balance
peson^M

electronic scale
balance^F *électronique*

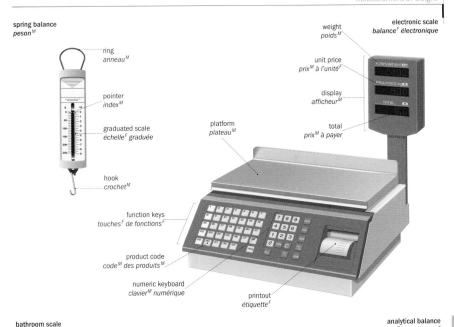

ring
anneau^M

pointer
index^M

graduated scale
échelle^F *graduée*

hook
crochet^M

weight
poids^M

unit price
prix^M *à l'unité*^F

display
afficheur^M

total
prix^M *à payer*

platform
plateau^M

function keys
touches^F *de fonctions*^F

product code
code^M *des produits*^M

numeric keyboard
clavier^M *numérique*

printout
étiquette^F

bathroom scale
pèse-personne^M

analytical balance
balance^F *de précision*^F

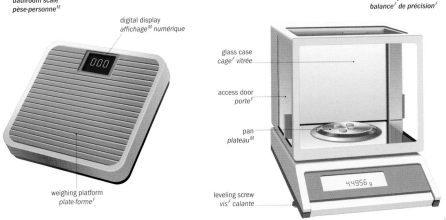

digital display
affichage^M *numérique*

weighing platform
plate-forme^F

glass case
cage^F *vitrée*

access door
porte^F

pan
plateau^M

leveling screw
vis^F *calante*

SCIENCE

measurement of temperature
mesure^F de la température^F

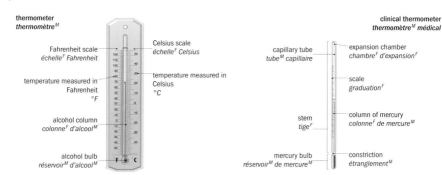

thermometer
thermomètre^M

Fahrenheit scale
échelle^F Fahrenheit

Celsius scale
échelle^F Celsius

temperature measured in
Fahrenheit
°F

temperature measured in
Celsius
°C

alcohol column
colonne^F d'alcool^M

alcohol bulb
réservoir^F d'alcool^M

clinical thermometer
thermomètre^M médical

capillary tube
tube^M capillaire

expansion chamber
chambre^F d'expansion^F

scale
graduation^F

stem
tige^F

column of mercury
colonne^F de mercure^M

mercury bulb
réservoir^M de mercure^M

constriction
étranglement^M

measurement of time
mesure^F du temps^M

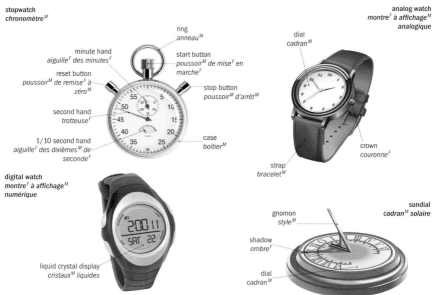

stopwatch
chronomètre^M

ring
anneau^M

minute hand
aiguille^F des minutes^F

start button
poussoir^M de mise^F en marche^F

reset button
poussoir^M de remise^F à zéro^M

stop button
poussoir^M d'arrêt^M

second hand
trotteuse^F

1/10 second hand
aiguille^F des dixièmes^M de seconde^F

case
boitier^M

analog watch
montre^F à affichage^M analogique

dial
cadran^M

crown
couronne^F

strap
bracelet^M

digital watch
montre^F à affichage^M numérique

liquid crystal display
cristaux^M liquides

sundial
cadran^M solaire

gnomon
style^M

shadow
ombre^F

dial
cadran^M

SCIENCE

measurement of length
mesure^F de la longueur^F

ruler
règle^F graduée

scales
graduation^F

measurement of thickness
mesure^F de l'épaisseur^F

vernier caliper
pied^M à coulisse^F à vernier^M

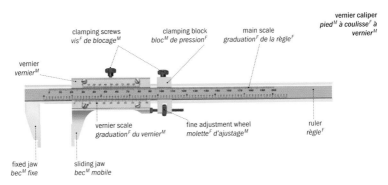

clamping screws
vis^F de blocage^M

clamping block
bloc^M de pression^F

main scale
graduation^F de la règle^F

vernier
vernier^M

vernier scale
graduation^F du vernier^M

fine adjustment wheel
molette^F d'ajustage^M

ruler
règle^F

fixed jaw
bec^M fixe

sliding jaw
bec^M mobile

micrometer caliper
micromètre^M palmer^M

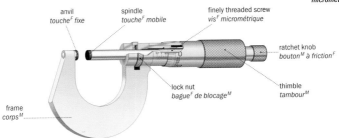

anvil
touche^F fixe

spindle
touche^F mobile

finely threaded screw
vis^F micrométrique

ratchet knob
bouton^M à friction^F

lock nut
bague^F de blocage^M

thimble
tambour^M

frame
corps^M

SCIENCE

international system of units

système[M] international d'unités[F]

unit of frequency
mesure[F] de la fréquence[F]

Hz

hertz
hertz[M]

unit of electric potential difference
mesure[F] de la différence[F] de potentiel[M] électrique

V

volt
volt[M]

unit of electric charge
mesure[F] de la charge[F] électrique

C

coulomb
coulomb[M]

unit of energy
mesure[F] de l'énergie[F]

J

joule
joule[M]

unit of power
mesure[F] de la puissance[F]

W

watt
watt[M]

unit of force
mesure[F] de la force[F]

N

newton
newton[M]

unit of electric resistance
mesure[F] de la résistance[F] électrique

Ω

ohm
ohm[M]

unit of electric current
mesure[F] du courant[M] électrique

A

ampere
ampère[M]

unit of length
mesure[F] de la longueur[F]

m

meter
mètre[M]

unit of mass
mesure[F] de la masse[F]

kg

kilogram
kilogramme[M]

unit of temperature
mesure[F] de la température[F]

°C

degree Celsius
degré[M] Celsius

unit of thermodynamic temperature
mesure[F] de la température[F] thermodynamique

K

kelvin
kelvin[M]

unit of amount of substance
mesure[F] de la quantité[F] de matière[F]

mol

mole
mole[F]

unit of radioactivity
mesure[F] de la radioactivité[F]

Bq

becquerel
becquerel[M]

unit of pressure
mesure[F] de la pression[F]

Pa

pascal
pascal[M]

unit of luminous intensity
mesure[F] de l'intensité[F] lumineuse

cd

candela
candela[F]

biology

biologie[F]

female
femelle[F]

Rh-

blood factor RH negative
facteur[M] rhésus négatif

★

birth
naissance[F]

male
mâle[M]

Rh+

blood factor RH positive
facteur[M] rhésus positif

†

death
mort[F]

SCIENCE

mathematics
mathématiques[F]

—
minus/negative
soustraction[F]

+
plus/positive
addition[F]

X
multiplied by
multiplication[F]

÷
divided by
division[F]

=
equals
égale

≠
is not equal to
n'égale pas

⇌
is approximately equal
to
égale à peu près

⌣
is equivalent to
équivaut à

≡
is identical to
est identique à

≢
is not identical to
n'est pas identique à

±
plus or minus
plus ou moins

≤
is less than or equal to
égal ou plus petit que

>
is greater than
plus grand que

≥
is greater than or equal
to
égal ou plus grand que

<
is less than
plus petit que

∅
empty set
ensemble[M] *vide*

∪
union of two sets
réunion[F]

∩
intersection of two sets
intersection[F]

⊂
is included in/is a
subset of
inclusion[F]

%
percent
pourcentage[M]

∈
is an element of
appartenance[F]

∉
is not an element of
non-appartenance[F]

Σ
sum
sommation[F]

√
square root of
racine[F] *carrée de*

½
fraction
fraction[F]

∞
infinity
infini[M]

∫
integral
intégrale[F]

!
factorial
factorielle[F]

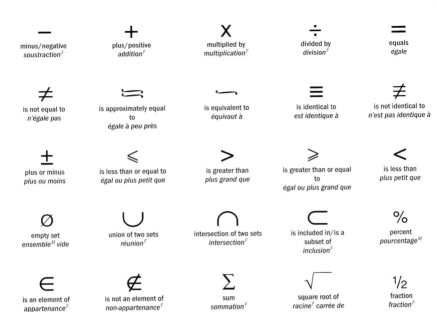

Roman numerals
chiffres[M] ***romains***

I
one
un[M]

V
five
cinq[M]

X
ten
dix[M]

L
fifty
cinquante[M]

C
one hundred
cent[M]

D
five hundred
cinq cents[M]

M
one thousand
mille[M]

SCIENCE

geometry

géométrie[F]

○	'	"	π	⊥
degree	minute	second	pi	perpendicular
degré[M]	*minute*[F]	*seconde*[F]	*pi*[M]	*perpendiculaire*[F]

‖	⧧	⌐	⟍	∠
is parallel to	is not parallel to	right angle	obtuse angle	acute angle
parallèle	*non-parallèle*	*angle*[M] *droit*	*angle*[M] *obtus*	*angle*[M] *aigu*

geometrical shapes

formes[F] *géométriques*

examples of angles
exemples[M] *d'angles*[M]

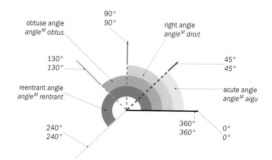

obtuse angle
angle[M] *obtus*

90°
90°

right angle
angle[M] *droit*

130°
130°

45°
45°

reentrant angle
angle[M] *rentrant*

acute angle
angle[M] *aigu*

240°
240°

360°
360°

0°
0°

plane surfaces
surfaces[F]

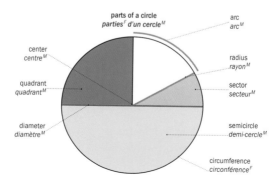

parts of a circle
parties[F] *d'un cercle*[M]

arc
arc[M]

center
centre[M]

radius
rayon[M]

quadrant
quadrant[M]

sector
secteur[M]

diameter
diamètre[M]

semicircle
demi-cercle[M]

circumference
circonférence[F]

polygons
polygones^M

triangle
triangle^M

square
carré^M

rectangle
rectangle^M

rhombus
losange^M

trapezoid
trapèze^M

parallelogram
parallélogramme^M

quadrilateral
quadrilatère^M

regular pentagon
pentagone^M *régulier*

regular hexagon
hexagone^M *régulier*

regular heptagon
heptagone^M *régulier*

regular octagon
octogone^M *régulier*

regular nonagon
ennéagone^M *régulier*

regular decagon
décagone^M *régulier*

regular hendecagon
hendécagone^M *régulier*

regular dodecagon
dodécagone^M *régulier*

solids
volumes^M

SCIENCE

helix
hélice^F

torus
tore^M

hemisphere
hémisphère^M

sphere
sphère^F

cube
cube^M

cone
cône^M

pyramid
pyramide^F

cylinder
cylindre^M

parallelepiped
parallélépipède^M

regular octahedron
octaèdre^M *régulier*

agglomeration

agglomération^F

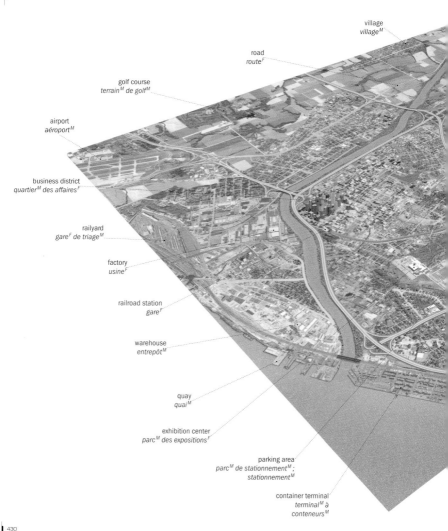

village
village^M

road
route^F

golf course
terrain^M *de golf*^M

airport
aéroport^M

business district
quartier^M *des affaires*^F

railyard
gare^F *de triage*^M

factory
usine^F

railroad station
gare^F

warehouse
entrepôt^M

quay
quai^M

exhibition center
parc^M *des expositions*^F

parking area
parc^M *de stationnement*^M *;*
stationnement^M

container terminal
terminal^M *à*
conteneurs^M

SOCIETY

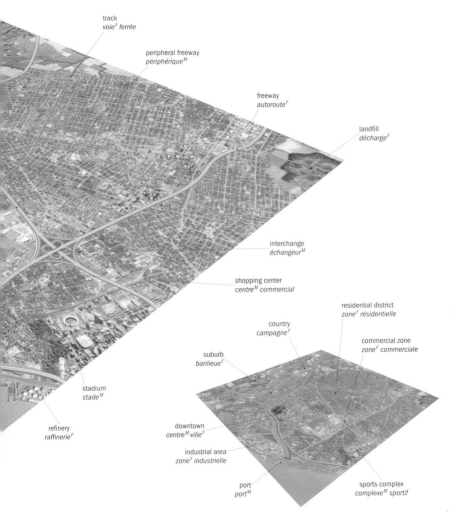

track
voie^F ferrée

peripheral freeway
périphérique^M

freeway
autoroute^F

landfill
décharge^F

interchange
échangeur^M

shopping center
centre^M commercial

residential district
zone^F résidentielle

country
campagne^F

commercial zone
zone^F commerciale

suburb
banlieue^F

stadium
stade^M

refinery
raffinerie^F

downtown
centre^M-ville^F

industrial area
zone^F industrielle

port
port^M

sports complex
complexe^M sportif

downtown

centre^M-ville^F

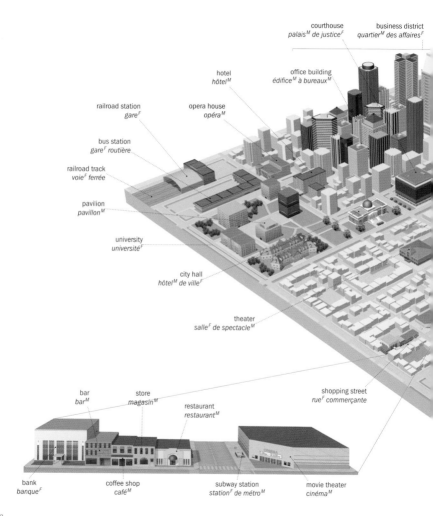

courthouse
palais^M de justice^F

business district
quartier^M des affaires^F

hotel
hôtel^M

office building
édifice^M à bureaux^M

railroad station
gare^F

opera house
opéra^M

bus station
gare^F routière

railroad track
voie^F ferrée

pavilion
pavillon^M

university
université^F

city hall
hôtel^M de ville^F

theater
salle^F de spectacle^M

shopping street
rue^F commerçante

bar
bar^M

store
magasin^M

restaurant
restaurant^M

bank
banque^F

coffee shop
café^M

subway station
station^F de métro^M

movie theater
cinéma^M

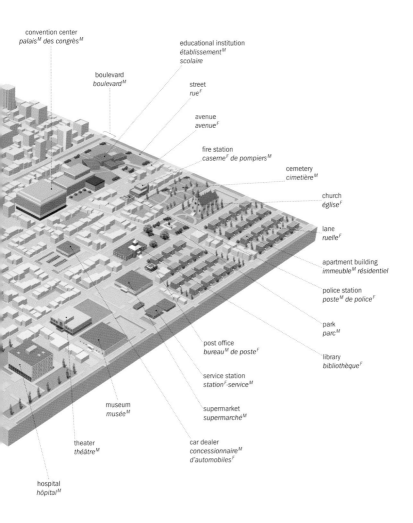

convention center
palais^M des congrès^M

educational institution
établissement^M
scolaire

boulevard
boulevard^M

street
rue^F

avenue
avenue^F

fire station
caserne^F de pompiers^M

cemetery
cimetière^M

church
église^F

lane
ruelle^F

apartment building
immeuble^M résidentiel

police station
poste^M de police^F

park
parc^M

post office
bureau^M de poste^F

library
bibliothèque^F

service station
station^F-service^M

supermarket
supermarché^M

museum
musée^M

theater
théâtre^M

car dealer
concessionnaire^M
d'automobiles^F

hospital
hôpital^M

SOCIETY

cross section of a street
coupe^F d'une rue^F

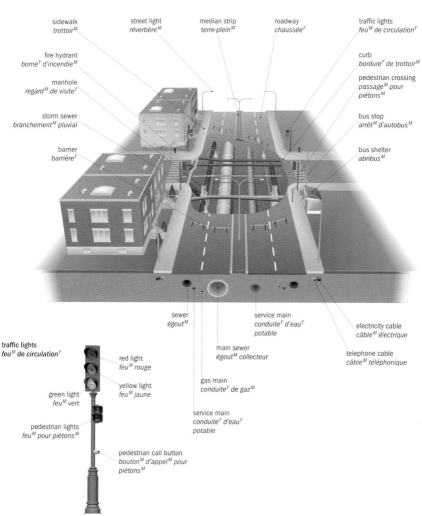

sidewalk
trottoir^M

street light
réverbère^M

median strip
terre-plein^M

roadway
chaussée^F

traffic lights
feu^M *de circulation*^F

fire hydrant
borne^F *d'incendie*^M

curb
bordure^F *de trottoir*^M

manhole
regard^M *de visite*^F

pedestrian crossing
passage^M *pour piétons*^M

storm sewer
branchement^M *pluvial*

bus stop
arrêt^M *d'autobus*^M

barrier
barrière^F

bus shelter
abribus^M

sewer
égout^M

service main
conduite^F *d'eau*^F *potable*

electricity cable
câble^M *électrique*

main sewer
égout^M *collecteur*

telephone cable
câble^M *téléphonique*

traffic lights
feu^M *de circulation*^F

red light
feu^M *rouge*

gas main
conduite^F *de gaz*^M

yellow light
feu^M *jaune*

green light
feu^M *vert*

service main
conduite^F *d'eau*^F *potable*

pedestrian lights
feu^M *pour piétons*^M

pedestrian call button
bouton^M *d'appel*^M *pour piétons*^M

office building
édifice^M à bureaux^M

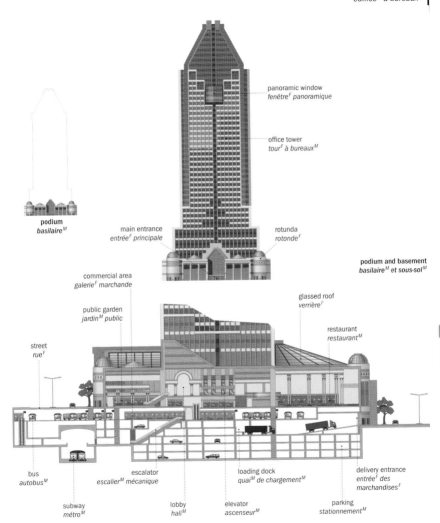

panoramic window
fenêtre^F panoramique

office tower
tour^F à bureaux^M

podium
basilaire^M

main entrance
entrée^F principale

rotunda
rotonde^F

podium and basement
basilaire^M et sous-sol^M

commercial area
galerie^F marchande

glassed roof
verrière^F

public garden
jardin^M public

restaurant
restaurant^M

street
rue^F

bus
autobus^M

escalator
escalier^M mécanique

loading dock
quai^M de chargement^M

delivery entrance
entrée^F des marchandises^F

subway
métro^M

lobby
hall^M

elevator
ascenseur^M

parking
stationnement^M

SOCIETY

shopping center
centre^M commercial

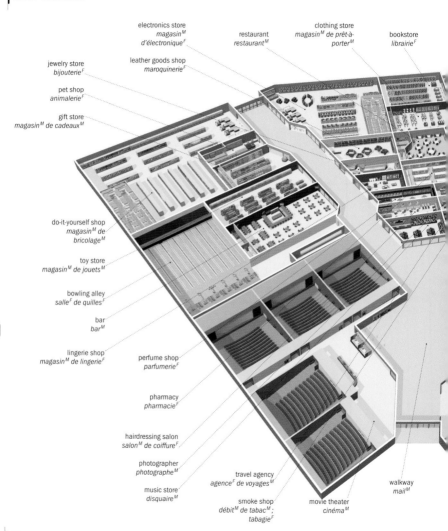

electronics store
*magasin^M
d'électronique^F*

restaurant
restaurant^M

clothing store
*magasin^M de prêt-à-
porter^M*

bookstore
librairie^F

jewelry store
bijouterie^F

leather goods shop
maroquinerie^F

pet shop
animalerie^F

gift store
magasin^M de cadeaux^M

do-it-yourself shop
*magasin^M de
bricolage^M*

toy store
magasin^M de jouets^M

bowling alley
salle^F de quilles^F

bar
bar^M

lingerie shop
magasin^M de lingerie^F

perfume shop
parfumerie^F

pharmacy
pharmacie^F

hairdressing salon
salon^M de coiffure^F

photographer
photographe^M

music store
disquaire^M

travel agency
agence^F de voyages^M

smoke shop
*débit^M de tabac^M ;
tabagie^F*

movie theater
cinéma^M

walkway
mail^M

SOCIETY

shopping center

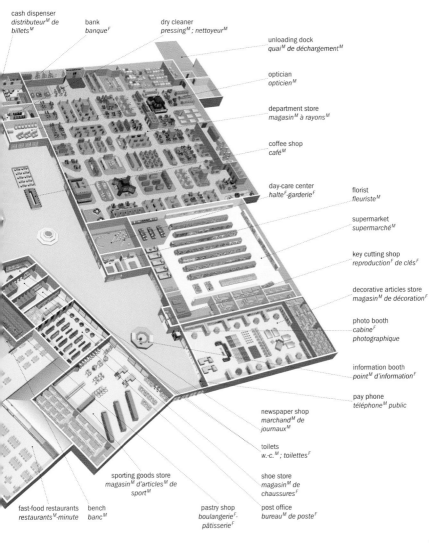

cash dispenser
distributeur^M *de billets*^M

bank
banque^F

dry cleaner
pressing^M ; *nettoyeur*^M

unloading dock
quai^M *de déchargement*^M

optician
opticien^M

department store
magasin^M *à rayons*^M

coffee shop
café^M

day-care center
halte^F*-garderie*^F

florist
fleuriste^M

supermarket
supermarché^M

key cutting shop
reproduction^F *de clés*^F

decorative articles store
magasin^M *de décoration*^F

photo booth
cabine^F *photographique*

information booth
point^M *d'information*^F

pay phone
téléphone^M *public*

newspaper shop
marchand^M *de journaux*^M

toilets
w.-c.^M ; *toilettes*^F

shoe store
magasin^M *de chaussures*^F

sporting goods store
magasin^M *d'articles*^M *de sport*^M

fast-food restaurants
restaurants^M*-minute*

bench
banc^M

pastry shop
boulangerie^F*- pâtisserie*^F

post office
bureau^M *de poste*^F

SOCIETY

restaurant

restaurant^M

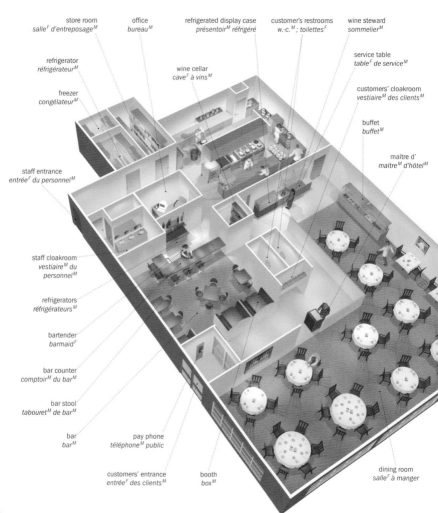

store room
salle^F d'entreposage^M

office
bureau^M

refrigerated display case
présentoir^M réfrigéré

customer's restrooms
w.-c.^M; toilettes^F

wine steward
sommelier^M

refrigerator
réfrigérateur^M

wine cellar
cave^F à vins^M

service table
table^F de service^M

freezer
congélateur^M

customers' cloakroom
vestiaire^M des clients^M

buffet
buffet^M

staff entrance
entrée^F du personnel^M

maître d'
maître^M d'hôtel^M

staff cloakroom
*vestiaire^M du
personnel^M*

refrigerators
réfrigérateurs^M

bartender
barmaid^F

bar counter
comptoir^M du bar^M

bar stool
tabouret^M de bar^M

bar
bar^M

pay phone
téléphone^M public

customers' entrance
entrée^F des clients^M

booth
box^M

dining room
salle^F à manger

SOCIETY

hotel
hôtel^M

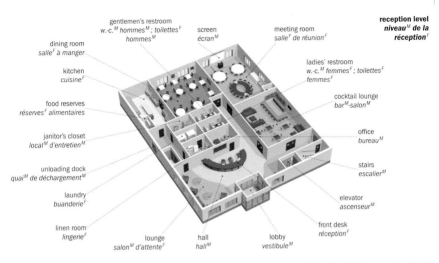

reception level
niveau^M de la réception^F

gentlemen's restroom
w.-c.^M hommes^M; toilettes^F hommes^M

screen
écran^M

meeting room
salle^F de réunion^F

dining room
salle^F à manger

kitchen
cuisine^F

food reserves
réserves^F alimentaires

janitor's closet
local^M d'entretien^M

unloading dock
quai^M de déchargement^M

laundry
buanderie^F

linen room
lingerie^F

lounge
salon^M d'attente^F

hall
hall^M

lobby
vestibule^M

front desk
réception^F

ladies' restroom
w.-c.^M femmes^F; toilettes^F femmes^F

cocktail lounge
bar^M-salon^M

office
bureau^M

stairs
escalier^M

elevator
ascenseur^M

hotel rooms
chambres^F d'hôtel^M

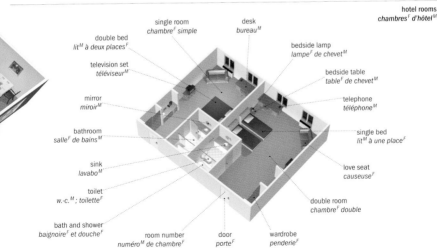

single room
chambre^F simple

desk
bureau^M

double bed
lit^M à deux places^F

bedside lamp
lampe^F de chevet^M

television set
téléviseur^M

bedside table
table^F de chevet^M

mirror
miroir^M

telephone
téléphone^M

bathroom
salle^F de bains^M

single bed
lit^M à une place^F

sink
lavabo^M

love seat
causeuse^F

toilet
w.-c.^M; toilette^F

double room
chambre^F double

bath and shower
baignoire^F et douche^F

room number
numéro^M de chambre^F

door
porte^F

wardrobe
penderie^F

SOCIETY

court
tribunal^M

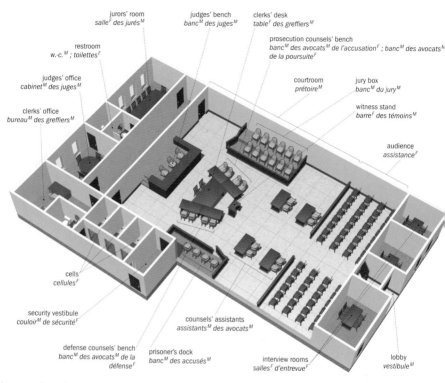

jurors' room
salle^F *des jurés*^M

judges' bench
banc^M *des juges*^M

clerks' desk
table^F *des greffiers*^M

restroom
w.-c.^M ; *toilettes*^F

prosecution counsels' bench
banc^M *des avocats*^M *de l'accusation*^F ; *banc*^M *des avocats*^M *de la poursuite*^F

judges' office
cabinet^M *des juges*^M

courtroom
prétoire^M

jury box
banc^M *du jury*^M

clerks' office
bureau^M *des greffiers*^M

witness stand
barre^F *des témoins*^M

audience
assistance^F

cells
cellules^F

security vestibule
couloir^M *de sécurité*^F

counsels' assistants
assistants^M *des avocats*^M

defense counsels' bench
banc^M *des avocats*^M *de la défense*^F

prisoner's dock
banc^M *des accusés*^M

interview rooms
salles^F *d'entrevue*^F

lobby
vestibule^M

examples of currency abbreviations
exemples^M *d'unités*^F *monétaires*

dollar
dollar^M

cent
cent^M

rupee
roupie^F

euro
euro^M

new shekel
nouveau shekel^M

peso
peso^M

yen
yen^M

pound
livre^F

money and modes of payment
monnaie^F et modes^M de paiement^M

coin: obverse
pièce^F : avers^M

initials of the issuing bank
initiales^F de la banque^F émettrice

banknote: front
billet^M de banque^F : recto^M

security thread
fil^M de sécurité^F

hologram foil strip
bande^F métallisée holographique

date
millésime^M

official signature
signature^F officielle

watermark
filigrane^M

color shifting ink
encre^F à couleur^F changeante

edge
tranche^F

portrait
effigie^F

serial number
numéro^M de série^F

coin: reverse
pièce^F : revers^M

banknote: back
billet^M de banque^F : verso^M

flag of the European Union
drapeau^M de l'Union^F européenne

serial number
numéro^M de série^F

outer ring
couronne^F

motto
devise^F

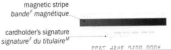

denomination
valeur^F

denomination
valeur^F

name of the currency
nom^M de la monnaie^F

magnetic stripe
bande^F magnétique

cardholder's signature
signature^F du titulaire^M

credit card
carte^F de crédit^M

card number
numéro^M de carte^F

checks
chèques^M

cardholder's name
nom^M du titulaire^M

expiration date
date^F d'expiration^F

traveler's check
chèque^M de voyage^M

bank
banque^F

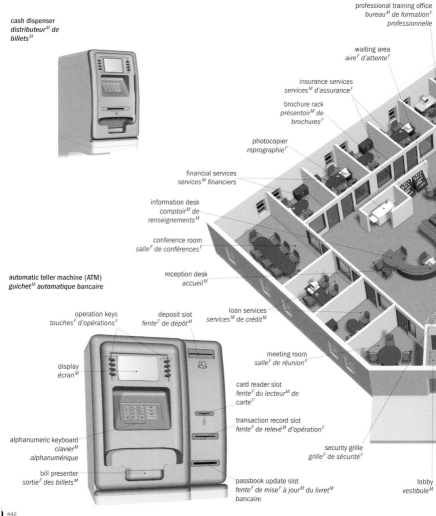

cash dispenser
distributeur^M *de*
billets^M

professional training office
bureau^M *de formation*^F
professionnelle

waiting area
aire^F *d'attente*^F

insurance services
services^M *d'assurance*^F

brochure rack
présentoir^M *de*
brochures^F

photocopier
reprographie^F

financial services
services^M *financiers*

information desk
comptoir^M *de*
renseignements^M

conference room
salle^F *de conférences*^F

reception desk
accueil^M

automatic teller machine (ATM)
guichet^M *automatique bancaire*

loan services
services^M *de crédit*^M

operation keys
touches^F *d'opérations*^F

deposit slot
fente^F *de dépôt*^M

meeting room
salle^F *de réunion*^F

display
écran^M

card reader slot
fente^F *du lecteur*^M *de*
carte^F

transaction record slot
fente^F *de relevé*^M *d'opération*^F

alphanumeric keyboard
clavier^M
alphanumérique

security grille
grille^F *de sécurité*^F

bill presenter
sortie^F *des billets*^M

passbook update slot
fente^F *de mise*^F *à jour*^M *du livret*^M
bancaire

lobby
vestibule^M

SOCIETY

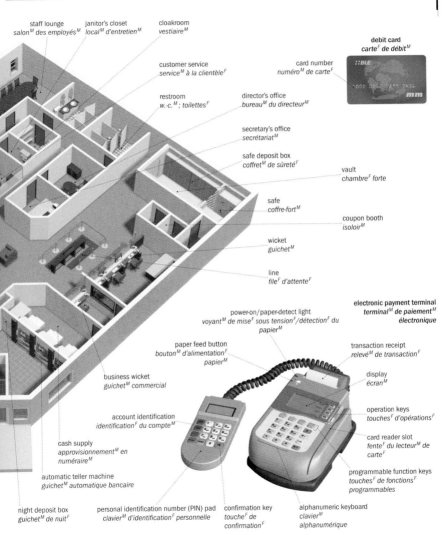

staff lounge
salon^M des employés^M

janitor's closet
local^M d'entretien^M

cloakroom
vestiaire^M

debit card
carte^F de débit^M

card number
numéro^M de carte^F

customer service
service^M à la clientèle^F

restroom
w.-c.^{M}; toilettes^F

director's office
bureau^M du directeur^M

secretary's office
secrétariat^M

safe deposit box
coffret^M de sûreté^F

vault
chambre^F forte

safe
coffre-fort^M

coupon booth
isoloir^M

wicket
guichet^M

line
file^F d'attente^F

electronic payment terminal
terminal^M de paiement^M
électronique

power-on/paper-detect light
voyant^M de mise^F sous tension^F/détection^F du
papier^M

paper feed button
bouton^M d'alimentation^F
papier^M

transaction receipt
relevé^M de transaction^F

display
écran^M

business wicket
guichet^M commercial

account identification
identification^F du compte^M

operation keys
touches^F d'opérations^F

card reader slot
fente^F du lecteur^M de
carte^F

cash supply
approvisionnement^M en
numéraire^M

automatic teller machine
guichet^M automatique bancaire

programmable function keys
touches^F de fonctions^F
programmables

night deposit box
guichet^M de nuit^F

personal identification number (PIN) pad
clavier^M d'identification^F personnelle

confirmation key
touche^F de
confirmation^F

alphanumeric keyboard
clavier^M
alphanumérique

SOCIETY

443

school
école[F]

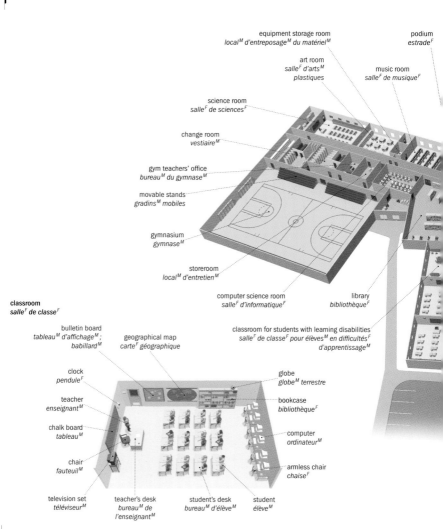

equipment storage room
local[M] *d'entreposage*[M] *du matériel*[M]

podium
estrade[F]

art room
salle[F] *d'arts*[M]
plastiques

music room
salle[F] *de musique*[F]

science room
salle[F] *de sciences*[F]

change room
vestiaire[M]

gym teachers' office
bureau[M] *du gymnase*[M]

movable stands
gradins[M] *mobiles*

gymnasium
gymnase[M]

storeroom
local[M] *d'entretien*[M]

computer science room
salle[F] *d'informatique*[F]

library
bibliothèque[F]

classroom for students with learning disabilities
salle[F] *de classe*[F] *pour élèves*[M] *en difficultés*[F]
d'apprentissage[M]

classroom
salle[F] *de classe*[F]

bulletin board
tableau[M] *d'affichage*[M] ;
babillard[M]

geographical map
carte[F] *géographique*

clock
pendule[F]

globe
globe[M] *terrestre*

teacher
enseignant[M]

bookcase
bibliothèque[F]

chalk board
tableau[M]

computer
ordinateur[M]

chair
fauteuil[M]

armless chair
chaise[F]

television set
téléviseur[M]

teacher's desk
bureau[M] *de*
l'enseignant[M]

student's desk
bureau[M] *d'élève*[M]

student
élève[M]

SOCIETY

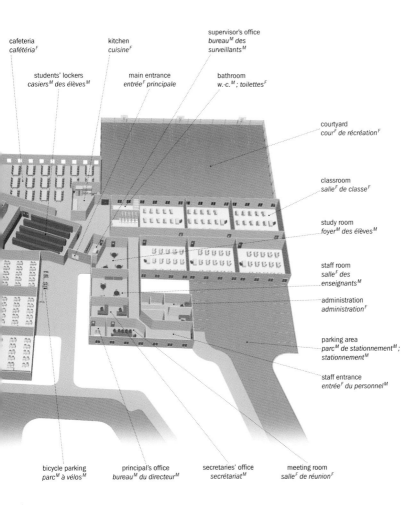

cafeteria
cafétéria^F

kitchen
cuisine^F

supervisor's office
bureau^M *des*
surveillants^M

students' lockers
casiers^M *des élèves*^M

main entrance
entrée^F *principale*

bathroom
w.-c.^M ; *toilettes*^F

courtyard
cour^F *de récréation*^F

classroom
salle^F *de classe*^F

study room
foyer^M *des élèves*^M

staff room
salle^F *des*
enseignants^M

administration
administration^F

parking area
parc^M *de stationnement*^M ;
stationnement^M

staff entrance
entrée^F *du personnel*^M

bicycle parking
parc^M *à vélos*^M

principal's office
bureau^M *du directeur*^M

secretaries' office
secrétariat^M

meeting room
salle^F *de réunion*^F

SOCIETY

Catholic church

église^F

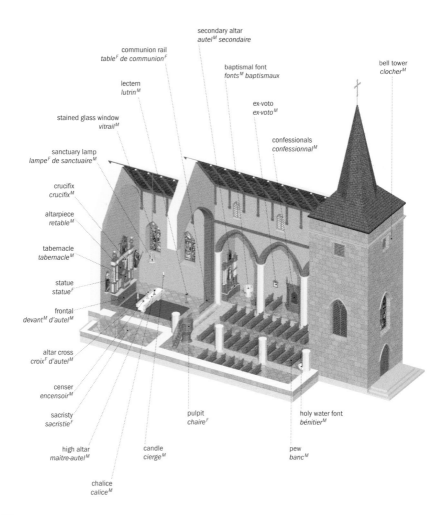

secondary altar
autel^M *secondaire*

communion rail
table^F *de communion*^F

baptismal font
fonts^M *baptismaux*

bell tower
clocher^M

lectern
lutrin^M

ex-voto
ex-voto^M

stained glass window
vitrail^M

confessionals
confessionnal^M

sanctuary lamp
lampe^F *de sanctuaire*^M

crucifix
crucifix^M

altarpiece
retable^M

tabernacle
tabernacle^M

statue
statue^F

frontal
devant^M *d'autel*^M

altar cross
croix^F *d'autel*^M

censer
encensoir^M

sacristy
sacristie^F

high altar
maître-autel^M

chalice
calice^M

candle
cierge^M

pulpit
chaire^F

holy water font
bénitier^M

pew
banc^M

synagogue
synagogue^F

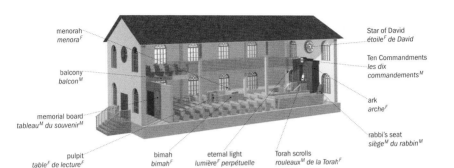

menorah
menora^F

Star of David
étoile^F de David

balcony
balcon^M

Ten Commandments
les dix commandements^M

memorial board
tableau^M du souvenir^M

ark
arche^F

pulpit
table^F de lecture^F

rabbi's seat
siège^M du rabbin^M

bimah
bimah^F

eternal light
lumière^F perpétuelle

Torah scrolls
rouleaux^M de la Torah^F

mosque
mosquée^F

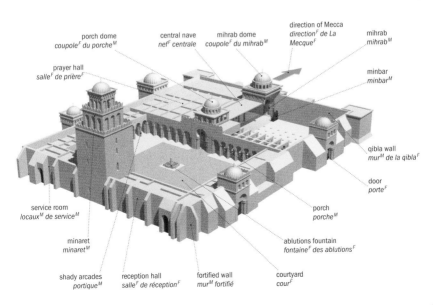

porch dome
coupole^F du porche^M

central nave
nef^F centrale

mihrab dome
coupole^F du mihrab^M

direction of Mecca
direction^F de La Mecque^F

mihrab
mihrab^M

prayer hall
salle^F de prière^F

minbar
minbar^M

qibla wall
mur^M de la qibla^F

door
porte^F

service room
locaux^M de service^M

porch
porche^M

minaret
minaret^M

ablutions fountain
fontaine^F des ablutions^F

shady arcades
portique^M

reception hall
salle^F de réception^F

fortified wall
mur^M fortifié

courtyard
cour^F

SOCIETY

447

flags
drapeaux^M

Americas
Amériques^F

1 Canada
Canada^M

2 United States of America
États-Unis^M *d'Amérique*^F

3 Mexico
Mexique^M

4 Honduras
Honduras^M

5 Guatemala
Guatemala^M

6 Belize
Belize^M

7 El Salvador
El Salvador^M

8 Nicaragua
Nicaragua^M

9 Costa Rica
Costa Rica^M

10 Panama
Panama^M

11 Colombia
Colombie^F

12 Venezuela
Venezuela^M

13 Guyana
Guyana^F

14 Suriname
Suriname^M

15 Ecuador
Équateur^M

16 Peru
Pérou^M

17 Brazil
Brésil^M

18 Bolivia
Bolivie^F

19 Paraguay
Paraguay^M

20 Chile
Chili^M

21 Argentina
Argentine^F

22 Uruguay
Uruguay^M

Caribbean Islands
Antilles^F

23 The Bahamas
Bahamas^F

24 Cuba
Cuba^F

25 Jamaica
Jamaïque^F

26 Haiti
Haïti^M

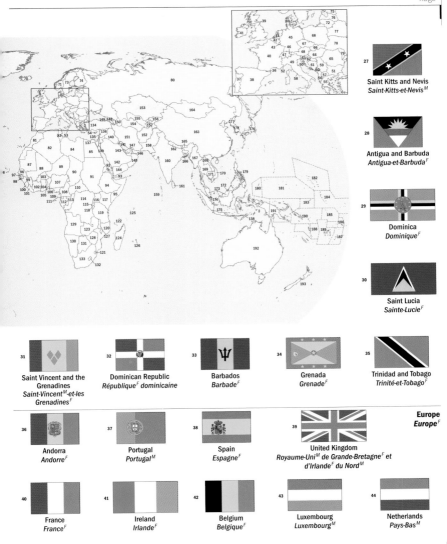

27 Saint Kitts and Nevis
Saint-Kitts-et-Nevis[M]

28 Antigua and Barbuda
Antigua-et-Barbuda[F]

29 Dominica
Dominique[F]

30 Saint Lucia
Sainte-Lucie[F]

31 Saint Vincent and the Grenadines
Saint-Vincent[M]*-et-les Grenadines*[F]

32 Dominican Republic
République[F] *dominicaine*

33 Barbados
Barbade[F]

34 Grenada
Grenade[F]

35 Trinidad and Tobago
Trinité-et-Tobago[F]

Europe
Europe[F]

36 Andorra
Andorre[F]

37 Portugal
Portugal[M]

38 Spain
Espagne[F]

39 United Kingdom
Royaume-Uni[M] *de Grande-Bretagne*[F] *et d'Irlande*[F] *du Nord*[M]

40 France
France[F]

41 Ireland
Irlande[F]

42 Belgium
Belgique[F]

43 Luxembourg
Luxembourg[M]

44 Netherlands
Pays-Bas[M]

flags

45 Germany
Allemagne^F

46 Liechtenstein
Liechtenstein^M

47 Switzerland
Suisse^F

48 Austria
Autriche^F

49 Italy
Italie^F

50 San Marino
Saint-Marin^M

51 Bulgaria
Bulgarie^F

52 Monaco
Monaco^M

53 Malta
Malte^F

54 Cyprus
Chypre^F

55 Greece
Grèce^F

56 Albania
Albanie^F

57 The Former Yugoslav Republic of Macedonia
Ex-République^F *yougoslave de Macédoine*^F

58 Holy See (Vatican City)
État^M *de la cité*^F *du Vatican*^M

59 Serbia
Serbie^F

60 Montenegro
Monténégro^M

61 Bosnia and Herzegovina
Bosnie-Herzégovine^F

62 Croatia
Croatie^F

63 Slovenia
Slovénie^F

64 Hungary
Hongrie^F

65 Romania
Roumanie^F

66 Slovakia
Slovaquie^F

67 Czech Republic
République^F *tchèque*

68 Poland
Pologne^F

69 Denmark
Danemark^M

70 Iceland
Islande^F

71 Norway
Norvège^F

72 Lithuania
Lituanie^F

73 Sweden
Suède^F

74 Finland
Finlande^F

75 Estonia
Estonie^F

76 Latvia
Lettonie^F

77 Belarus
Bélarus^M

78 Ukraine
Ukraine^F

79 Moldova
République^F *de Moldova*^F

80 Russia
Fédération^F *de Russie*^F

SOCIETY

flags

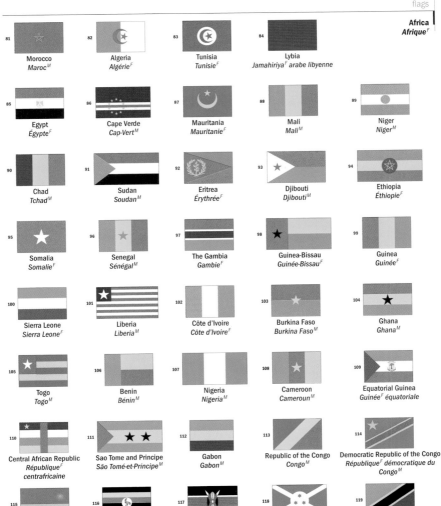

81 Morocco
Maroc^M

82 Algeria
Algérie^F

83 Tunisia
Tunisie^F

84 Lybia
Jamahiriya^F arabe libyenne

85 Egypt
Égypte^F

86 Cape Verde
Cap-Vert^M

87 Mauritania
Mauritanie^F

88 Mali
Mali^M

89 Niger
Niger^M

90 Chad
Tchad^M

91 Sudan
Soudan^M

92 Eritrea
Érythrée^F

93 Djibouti
Djibouti^M

94 Ethiopia
Éthiopie^F

95 Somalia
Somalie^F

96 Senegal
Sénégal^M

97 The Gambia
Gambie^F

98 Guinea-Bissau
Guinée-Bissau^F

99 Guinea
Guinée^F

100 Sierra Leone
Sierra Leone^F

101 Liberia
Liberia^M

102 Côte d'Ivoire
Côte d'Ivoire^F

103 Burkina Faso
Burkina Faso^M

104 Ghana
Ghana^M

105 Togo
Togo^M

106 Benin
Bénin^M

107 Nigeria
Nigeria^M

108 Cameroon
Cameroun^M

109 Equatorial Guinea
Guinée^F équatoriale

110 Central African Republic
*République^F
centrafricaine*

111 Sao Tome and Principe
São Tomé-et-Principe^M

112 Gabon
Gabon^M

113 Republic of the Congo
Congo^M

114 Democratic Republic of the Congo
*République^F démocratique du
Congo^M*

115 Rwanda
Rwanda^M

116 Uganda
Ouganda^M

117 Kenya
Kenya^M

118 Burundi
Burundi^M

119 Tanzania
*République^F-Unie de
Tanzanie^F*

SOCIETY

flags

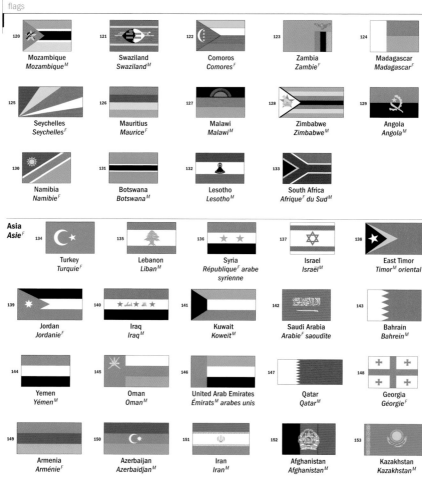

120 Mozambique
Mozambique^M

121 Swaziland
Swaziland^M

122 Comoros
Comores^F

123 Zambia
Zambie^F

124 Madagascar
Madagascar^F

125 Seychelles
Seychelles^F

126 Mauritius
Maurice^F

127 Malawi
Malawi^M

128 Zimbabwe
Zimbabwe^M

129 Angola
Angola^M

130 Namibia
Namibie^F

131 Botswana
Botswana^M

132 Lesotho
Lesotho^M

133 South Africa
Afrique^F *du Sud*^{M}

Asia
Asie^F

134 Turkey
Turquie^F

135 Lebanon
Liban^M

136 Syria
République^F *arabe syrienne*

137 Israel
Israël^M

138 East Timor
Timor^M *oriental*

139 Jordan
Jordanie^F

140 Iraq
Iraq^M

141 Kuwait
Koweït^M

142 Saudi Arabia
Arabie^F *saoudite*

143 Bahrain
Bahrein^M

144 Yemen
Yémen^M

145 Oman
Oman^M

146 United Arab Emirates
Émirats^M *arabes unis*

147 Qatar
Qatar^M

148 Georgia
Géorgie^F

149 Armenia
Arménie^F

150 Azerbaijan
Azerbaïdjan^M

151 Iran
Iran^M

152 Afghanistan
Afghanistan^M

153 Kazakhstan
Kazakhstan^M

154 Turkmenistan
Turkménistan^M

155 Uzbekistan
Ouzbékistan^M

156 Kyrgyzstan
Kirghizistan^M

157 Tajikistan
Tadjikistan^M

158 Pakistan
Pakistan^M

SOCIETY

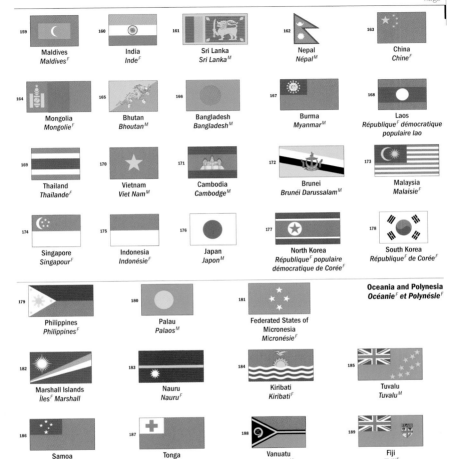

159 Maldives
Maldives^F

160 India
Inde^F

161 Sri Lanka
Sri Lanka^M

162 Nepal
Népal^M

163 China
Chine^F

164 Mongolia
Mongolie^F

165 Bhutan
Bhoutan^M

166 Bangladesh
Bangladesh^M

167 Burma
Myanmar^M

168 Laos
République^F *démocratique populaire lao*

169 Thailand
Thaïlande^F

170 Vietnam
Viet Nam^M

171 Cambodia
Cambodge^M

172 Brunei
Brunéi Darussalam^M

173 Malaysia
Malaisie^F

174 Singapore
Singapour^F

175 Indonesia
Indonésie^F

176 Japan
Japon^M

177 North Korea
République^F *populaire démocratique de Corée*^F

178 South Korea
République^F *de Corée*^F

Oceania and Polynesia
Océanie^F *et Polynésie*^F

179 Philippines
Philippines^F

180 Palau
Palaos^M

181 Federated States of Micronesia
Micronésie^F

182 Marshall Islands
Îles^F *Marshall*

183 Nauru
Nauru^F

184 Kiribati
Kiribati^F

185 Tuvalu
Tuvalu^M

186 Samoa
Samoa^F

187 Tonga
Tonga^F

188 Vanuatu
Vanuatu^M

189 Fiji
Fidji^F

190 Solomon Islands
Îles^F *Salomon*

191 Papua New Guinea
Papouasie-Nouvelle-Guinée^F

192 Australia
Australie^F

193 New Zealand
Nouvelle-Zélande^F

SOCIETY

fire prevention

prévention^F *des incendies*^M

fire-fighting materials
matériel^M **de lutte**^F **contre les**
incendies^M

firefighter
pompier^M

helmet
casque^M

compressed-air cylinder
bouteille^F *d'air*^M
comprimé

smoke detector
détecteur^M *de fumée*^F

base
base^F

full face mask
masque^M *complet*

cover
couvercle^M

self-contained breathing
apparatus
appareil^M *de protection*^F
respiratoire

test button
bouton^M *d'essai*^M

indicator light
témoin^M *lumineux*

air-supply tube
tube^M *d'alimentation*^F *en air*^M

portable fire extinguisher
extincteur^M

trigger
gâchette^F

pressure demand regulator
robinet^M *de réglage*^M *de débit*^M

pin
goupille^F

hose
tuyau^M

mandown alarm
avertisseur^M *de détresse*^F

turnouts
tenue^F *d'intervention*^F

tank
réservoir^M

pike pole
gaffe^F

hatchet
hache^F

fire hose
tuyau^M *de*
refoulement^M

fire hydrant
borne^F *d'incendie*^M

rubber boot
botte^F *de caoutchouc*^M

SOCIETY

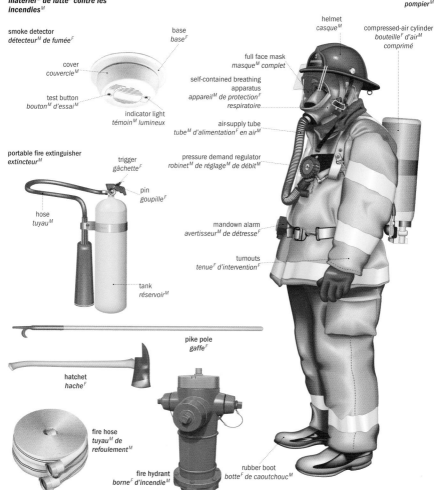

fire trucks
camions^M
d'incendie^M

pumper
fourgon^M*-pompe*^F

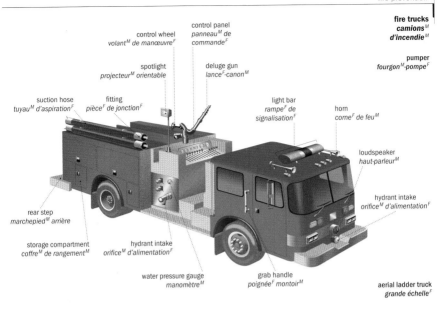

control panel
panneau^M *de*
commande^F

control wheel
volant^M *de manœuvre*^F

deluge gun
lance^F*-canon*^M

spotlight
projecteur^M *orientable*

suction hose
tuyau^M *d'aspiration*^F

fitting
pièce^F *de jonction*^F

light bar
rampe^F *de*
signalisation^F

horn
corne^F *de feu*^M

loudspeaker
haut-parleur^M

hydrant intake
orifice^M *d'alimentation*^F

rear step
marchepied^M *arrière*

storage compartment
coffre^M *de rangement*^M

hydrant intake
orifice^M *d'alimentation*^F

water pressure gauge
manomètre^M

grab handle
poignée^F *montoir*^M

aerial ladder truck
grande échelle^F

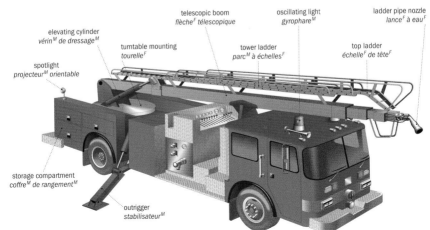

elevating cylinder
vérin^M *de dressage*^M

telescopic boom
flèche^F *télescopique*

oscillating light
gyrophare^M

ladder pipe nozzle
lance^F *à eau*^F

turntable mounting
tourelle^F

tower ladder
parc^M *à échelles*^F

top ladder
échelle^F *de tête*^F

spotlight
projecteur^M *orientable*

storage compartment
coffre^M *de rangement*^M

outrigger
stabilisateur^M

SOCIETY

crime prevention
prévention^F de la criminalité^F

police officer
agent^M de police^F

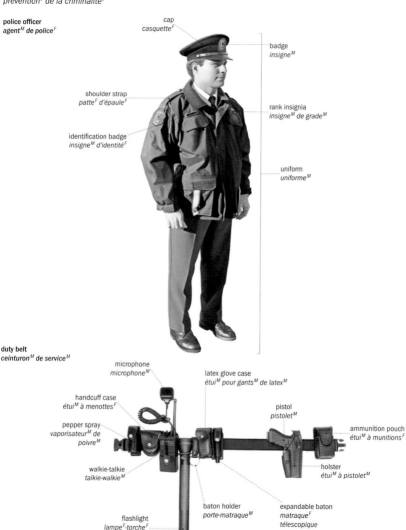

cap
casquette^F

badge
insigne^M

shoulder strap
patte^F d'épaule^F

rank insignia
insigne^M de grade^M

identification badge
insigne^M d'identité^F

uniform
uniforme^M

duty belt
ceinturon^M de service^M

microphone
microphone^M

latex glove case
étui^M pour gants^M de latex^M

handcuff case
étui^M à menottes^F

pistol
pistolet^M

pepper spray
vaporisateur^M de poivre^M

ammunition pouch
étui^M à munitions^F

walkie-talkie
talkie-walkie^M

holster
étui^M à pistolet^M

baton holder
porte-matraque^M

expandable baton
matraque^F télescopique

flashlight
lampe^F-torche^F

SOCIETY

crime prevention

dashboard equipment
équipement^M du tableau^M de bord^M

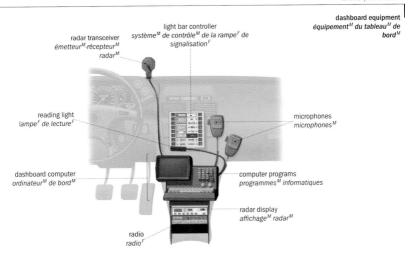

radar transceiver
émetteur^M-récepteur^M radar^M

light bar controller
système^M de contrôle^M de la rampe^F de signalisation^F

reading light
lampe^F de lecture^F

microphones
microphones^M

dashboard computer
ordinateur^M de bord^M

computer programs
programmes^M informatiques

radar display
affichage^M radar^M

radio
radio^F

police car
voiture^F de police^F

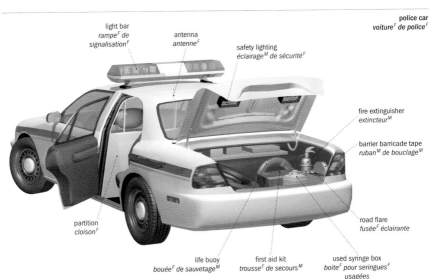

light bar
rampe^F de signalisation^F

antenna
antenne^F

safety lighting
éclairage^M de sécurité^F

fire extinguisher
extincteur^M

barrier barricade tape
ruban^M de bouclage^M

partition
cloison^F

road flare
fusée^F éclairante

life buoy
bouée^F de sauvetage^M

first aid kit
trousse^F de secours^M

used syringe box
boîte^F pour seringues^F usagées

SOCIETY

457

ear protection
protection^F de l'ouïe^F

safety earmuffs
serre-tête^M antibruit

headband
serre-tête^M

foam cushion
coussinet^M en mousse^F

earplugs
protège-tympan^M

eye protection
protection^F des yeux^M

safety glasses
lunettes^F de sécurité^F

safety goggles
lunettes^F de protection^F

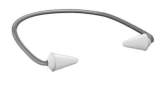

head protection
protection^F de la tête^F

hard hat
casque^M de sécurité^F

rib
nervure^F

peak
visière^F

suspension band
sangle^F d'amortissement^M

headband
tour^M de tête^F

neck strap
sangle^F de nuque^F

respiratory system protection
protection^F des voies^F respiratoires

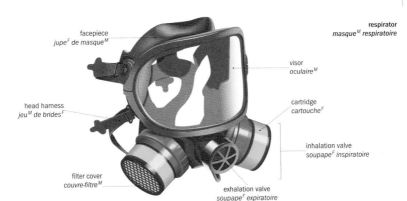

respirator
masque^M respiratoire

facepiece
jupe^F de masque^M

visor
oculaire^M

head harness
jeu^M de brides^F

cartridge
cartouche^F

inhalation valve
soupape^F inspiratoire

filter cover
couvre-filtre^M

exhalation valve
soupape^F expiratoire

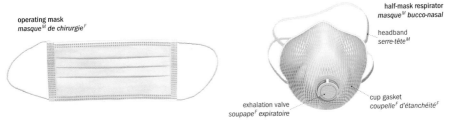

operating mask
masque^M de chirurgie^F

half-mask respirator
masque^M bucco-nasal

headband
serre-tête^M

exhalation valve
soupape^F expiratoire

cup gasket
coupelle^F d'étanchéité^F

foot protection
protection^F des pieds^M

safety boot
brodequin^M de sécurité^F

toe guard
protège-orteils^M

reinforced toe
embout^M de protection^F

first aid equipment
matériel^M de secours^M

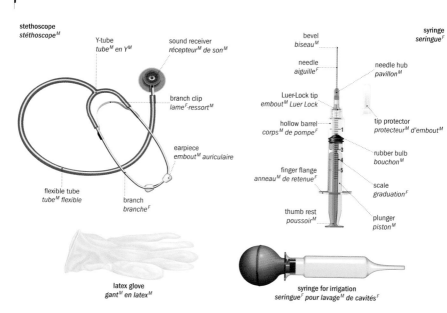

stethoscope
stéthoscope^M

Y-tube
tube^M en Y^M

sound receiver
récepteur^M de son^M

branch clip
lame^F-ressort^M

earpiece
embout^M auriculaire

flexible tube
tube^M flexible

branch
branche^F

latex glove
gant^M en latex^M

bevel
biseau^M

needle
aiguille^F

needle hub
pavillon^M

Luer-Lock tip
embout^M Luer Lock

tip protector
protecteur^M d'embout^M

hollow barrel
corps^M de pompe^F

rubber bulb
bouchon^M

finger flange
anneau^M de retenue^F

scale
graduation^F

thumb rest
poussoir^M

plunger
piston^M

syringe
seringue^F

syringe for irrigation
seringue^F pour lavage^M de cavités^F

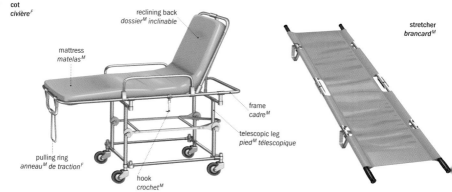

cot
civière^F

reclining back
dossier^M inclinable

mattress
matelas^M

frame
cadre^M

telescopic leg
pied^M télescopique

pulling ring
anneau^M de traction^F

hook
crochet^M

stretcher
brancard^M

first aid kit
trousse^F de secours^M

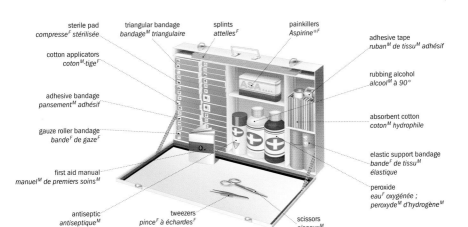

sterile pad
compresse^F stérilisée

triangular bandage
bandage^M triangulaire

splints
attelles^F

painkillers
Aspirine^®^F

adhesive tape
ruban^M de tissu^M adhésif

cotton applicators
coton^M-tige^F

rubbing alcohol
alcool^M à 90°

adhesive bandage
pansement^M adhésif

absorbent cotton
coton^M hydrophile

gauze roller bandage
bande^F de gaze^F

elastic support bandage
bande^F de tissu^M élastique

first aid manual
manuel^M de premiers soins^M

peroxide
eau^F oxygénée ; peroxyde^M d'hydrogène^M

antiseptic
antiseptique^M

tweezers
pince^F à échardes^F

scissors
ciseaux^M

clinical thermometers
thermomètres^M médicaux

digital thermometer
thermomètre^M numérique

mercury thermometer
thermomètre^M à mercure^M

blood pressure monitor
tensiomètre^M

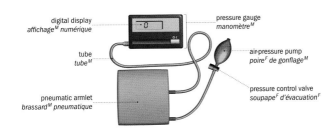

digital display
affichage^M numérique

pressure gauge
manomètre^M

tube
tube^M

air-pressure pump
poire^F de gonflage^M

pneumatic armlet
brassard^M pneumatique

pressure control valve
soupape^F d'évacuation^F

SOCIETY

hospital
hôpital^M

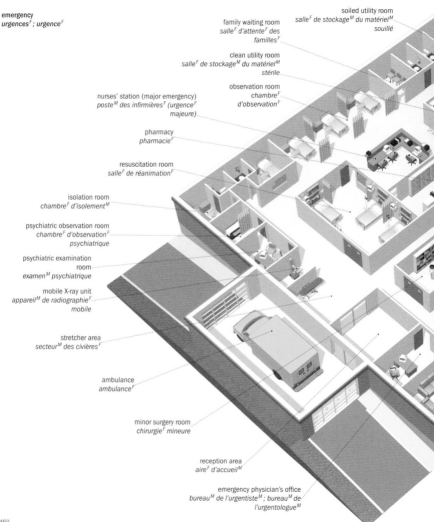

emergency
urgences^F ; urgence^F

family waiting room
salle^F d'attente^F des familles^F

soiled utility room
salle^F de stockage^M du matériel^M souillé

clean utility room
salle^F de stockage^M du matériel^M stérile

observation room
chambre^F d'observation^F

nurses' station (major emergency)
poste^M des infirmières^F (urgence^F majeure)

pharmacy
pharmacie^F

resuscitation room
salle^F de réanimation^F

isolation room
chambre^F d'isolement^M

psychiatric observation room
chambre^F d'observation^F psychiatrique

psychiatric examination room
examen^M psychiatrique

mobile X-ray unit
appareil^M de radiographie^F mobile

stretcher area
secteur^M des civières^F

ambulance
ambulance^F

minor surgery room
chirurgie^F mineure

reception area
aire^F d'accueil^M

emergency physician's office
bureau^M de l'urgentiste^M ; bureau^M de l'urgentologue^M

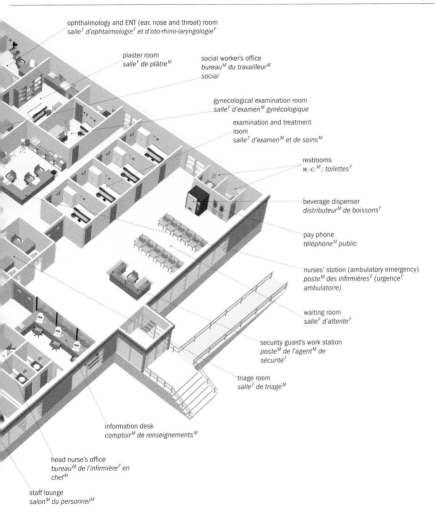

ophthalmology and ENT (ear, nose and throat) room
salle^F d'ophtalmologie^F et d'oto-rhino-laryngologie^F

plaster room
salle^F de plâtre^M

social worker's office
bureau^M du travailleur^M social

gynecological examination room
salle^F d'examen^M gynécologique

examination and treatment room
salle^F d'examen^M et de soins^M

restrooms
w.-c.^M; toilettes^F

beverage dispenser
distributeur^M de boissons^F

pay phone
téléphone^M public

nurses' station (ambulatory emergency)
poste^M des infirmières^F (urgence^F ambulatoire)

waiting room
salle^F d'attente^F

security guard's work station
poste^M de l'agent^M de sécurité^F

triage room
salle^F de triage^M

information desk
comptoir^M de renseignements^M

head nurse's office
bureau^M de l'infirmière^F en chef^M

staff lounge
salon^M du personnel^M

SOCIETY

hospital

patient room
chambre[F] d'hôpital[M]

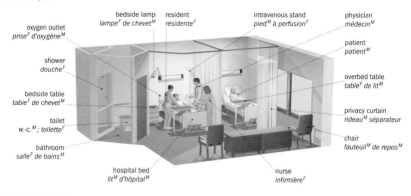

oxygen outlet
prise[F] d'oxygène[M]

bedside lamp
lampe[F] de chevet[M]

resident
résidente[F]

intravenous stand
pied[M] à perfusion[F]

physician
médecin[M]

patient
patient[M]

shower
douche[F]

overbed table
table[F] de lit[M]

bedside table
table[F] de chevet[M]

privacy curtain
rideau[M] séparateur

toilet
w.-c.[M] ; toilette[F]

chair
fauteuil de repos[M]

bathroom
salle[F] de bains[M]

hospital bed
lit[M] d'hôpital[M]

nurse
infirmière[F]

operating suite
bloc[M] opératoire

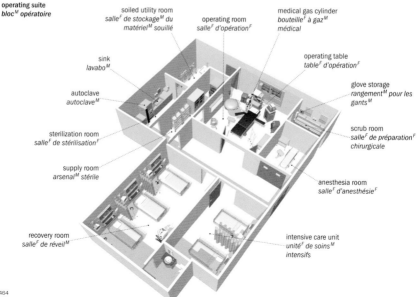

soiled utility room
*salle[F] de stockage[M] du
matériel[M] souillé*

operating room
salle[F] d'opération[F]

medical gas cylinder
*bouteille[F] à gaz[M]
médical*

sink
lavabo[M]

operating table
table[F] d'opération[F]

autoclave
autoclave[M]

glove storage
*rangement[M] pour les
gants[M]*

sterilization room
salle[F] de stérilisation[F]

scrub room
*salle[F] de préparation[F]
chirurgicale*

supply room
arsenal[M] stérile

anesthesia room
salle[F] d'anesthésie[F]

recovery room
salle[F] de réveil[M]

intensive care unit
*unité[F] de soins[M]
intensifs*

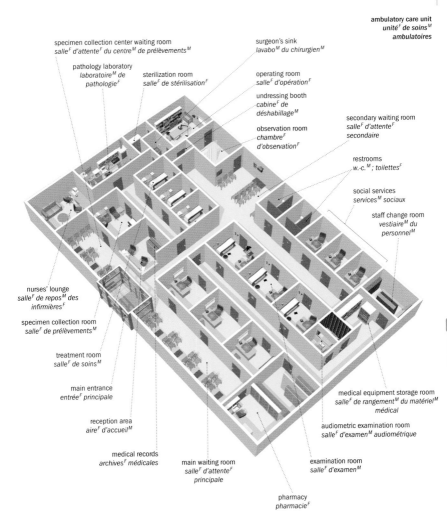

ambulatory care unit
unité^F de soins^M
ambulatoires

specimen collection center waiting room
salle^F d'attente^F du centre^M de prélèvements^M

surgeon's sink
lavabo^M du chirurgien^M

pathology laboratory
laboratoire^M de
pathologie^F

sterilization room
salle^F de stérilisation^F

operating room
salle^F d'opération^F

undressing booth
cabine^F de
déshabillage^M

observation room
chambre^F
d'observation^F

secondary waiting room
salle^F d'attente^F
secondaire

restrooms
w.-c.^M ; toilettes^F

social services
services^M sociaux

staff change room
vestiaire^M du
personnel^M

nurses' lounge
salle^F de repos^M des
infirmières^F

specimen collection room
salle^F de prélèvements^M

treatment room
salle^F de soins^M

main entrance
entrée^F principale

reception area
aire^F d'accueil^M

medical records
archives^F médicales

main waiting room
salle^F d'attente^F
principale

medical equipment storage room
salle^F de rangement^M du matériel^M
médical

audiometric examination room
salle^F d'examen^M audiométrique

examination room
salle^F d'examen^M

pharmacy
pharmacie^F

walking aids
aides[F] *à la marche*[F]

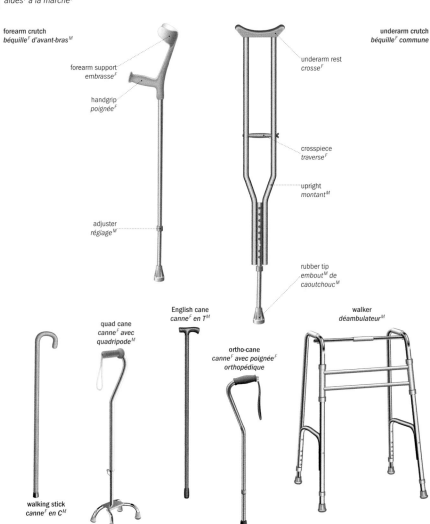

forearm crutch
béquille[F] *d'avant-bras*[M]

forearm support
embrasse[F]

handgrip
poignée[F]

adjuster
réglage[M]

underarm crutch
béquille[F] *commune*

underarm rest
crosse[F]

crosspiece
traverse[F]

upright
montant[M]

rubber tip
embout[M] *de caoutchouc*[M]

quad cane
canne[F] *avec quadripode*[M]

English cane
canne[F] *en T*[M]

ortho-cane
canne[F] *avec poignée*[F] *orthopédique*

walker
déambulateur[M]

walking stick
canne[F] *en C*[M]

wheelchair
fauteuil^M roulant

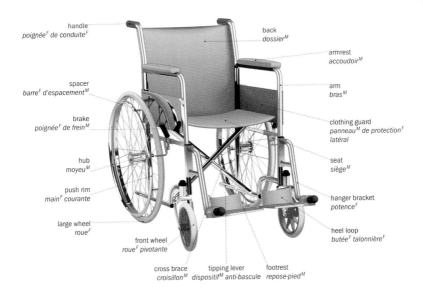

handle
poignée^F de conduite^F

back
dossier^M

armrest
accoudoir^M

spacer
barre^F d'espacement^M

arm
bras^M

brake
poignée^F de frein^M

clothing guard
*panneau^M de protection^F
latéral*

hub
moyeu^M

seat
siège^M

push rim
main^F courante

hanger bracket
potence^F

large wheel
roue^F

heel loop
butée^F talonnière^F

front wheel
roue^F pivotante

cross brace
croisillon^M

tipping lever
dispositif^M anti-bascule

footrest
repose-pied^M

forms of medications
formes^F pharmaceutiques des médicaments^M

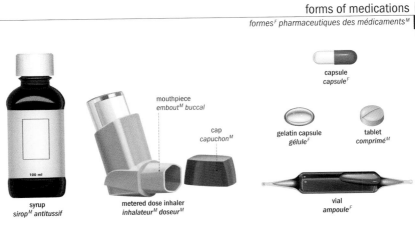

SOCIETY

capsule
capsule^F

mouthpiece
embout^M buccal

cap
capuchon^M

gelatin capsule
gélule^F

tablet
comprimé^M

100 ml

syrup
sirop^M antitussif

metered dose inhaler
inhalateur^M doseur^M

vial
ampoule^F

dice and dominoes
dés[M] et dominos[M]

ordinary die
dé[M] régulier

poker die
dé[M] à poker[M]

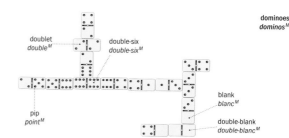

dominoes
dominos[M]

doublet
double[M]

double-six
double-six[M]

blank
blanc[M]

double-blank
double-blanc[M]

pip
point[M]

cards
cartes[F]

symbols
symboles[M]

heart
cœur[M]

diamond
carreau[M]

club
trèfle[M]

spade
pique[M]

joker
Joker[M]

ace
As[M]

king
Roi[M]

queen
Dame[F]

jack
Valet[M]

standard poker hands
combinaisons[F] au poker[M]

high card
carte[F] isolée

one pair
paire[F]

two pairs
double paire[F]

three-of-a-kind
brelan[M]

straight
séquence[F]

flush
couleur[F]

full house
main[F] pleine

four-of-a-kind
carré[M]

straight flush
quinte[F]

royal flush
quinte[F] royale

board games
jeux^M *de plateau*^M

backgammon
jacquet^M

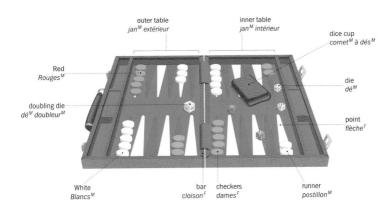

outer table
jan^M *extérieur*

inner table
jan^M *intérieur*

dice cup
cornet^M *à dés*^M

Red
Rouges^M

die
dé^M

doubling die
dé^M *doubleur*^M

point
flèche^F

White
Blancs^M

bar
cloison^F

checkers
dames^F

runner
postillon^M

snakes and ladders
serpents^M *et échelles*^F

token
pion^M

die
dé^M

snake
serpent^M

ladder
échelle^F

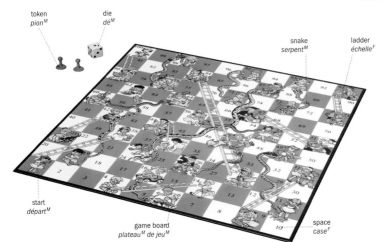

start
départ^M

game board
plateau^M *de jeu*^M

space
case^F

SPORTS AND GAMES

board games

chess
échecs^M

queen's side
aile^F *Dame*^F

king's side
aile^F *Roi*^M

chessboard
échiquier^M

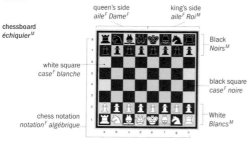

Black
Noirs^M

white square
case^F *blanche*

black square
case^F *noire*

chess notation
notation^F *algébrique*

White
Blancs^M

chess pieces
pièces^F

pawn
Pion^M

rook
Tour^F

bishop
Fou^M

knight
Cavalier^M

king
Roi^M

queen
Dame^F

types of movements
types^M **de déplacements**^M

diagonal movement
déplacement^M *diagonal*

vertical movement
déplacement^M *vertical*

square movement
déplacement^M *en équerre*^F

horizontal movement
déplacement^M *horizontal*

go
go^M

board
plateau^M

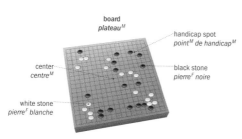

handicap spot
point^M *de handicap*^M

center
centre^M

black stone
pierre^F *noire*

white stone
pierre^F *blanche*

major motions
principaux mouvements^M

connection
connexion^F

capture
capture^F

contact
contact^M

checkers
jeu^M *de dames*^F

checker
Dame^F

checkerboard
damier^M

video entertainment system
système^M de jeux^M vidéo

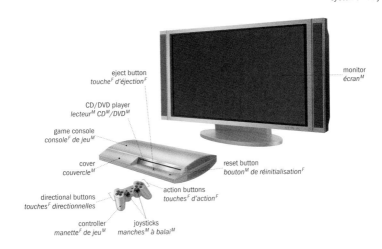

eject button
touche^F d'éjection^F

CD/DVD player
lecteur^M CD^M/DVD^M

game console
console^F de jeu^M

cover
couvercle^M

monitor
écran^M

reset button
bouton^M de réinitialisation^F

directional buttons
touches^F directionnelles

action buttons
touches^F d'action^F

controller
manette^F de jeu^M

joysticks
manches^M à balai^M

darts
jeu^M de fléchettes^F

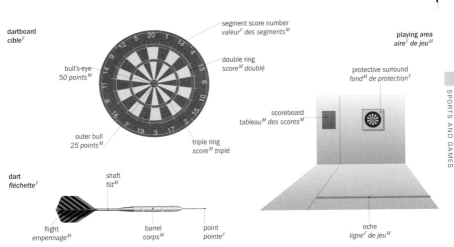

dartboard
cible^F

segment score number
valeur^F des segments^M

bull's-eye
50 points^M

double ring
score^M doublé

outer bull
25 points^M

triple ring
score^M triplé

playing area
aire^F de jeu^M

protective surround
fond^M de protection^F

scoreboard
tableau^M des scores^M

dart
fléchette^F

shaft
fût^M

flight
empennage^M

barrel
corps^M

point
pointe^F

oche
ligne^F de jeu^M

SPORTS AND GAMES

arena
stade^M

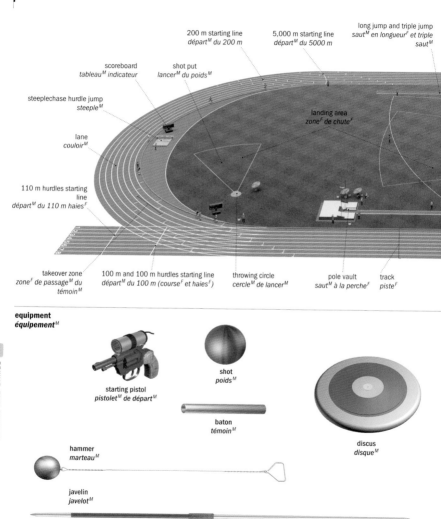

200 m starting line
départ^M *du 200 m*

5,000 m starting line
départ^M *du 5000 m*

long jump and triple jump
saut^M *en longueur*^F *et triple*
saut^M

scoreboard
tableau^M *indicateur*

shot put
lancer^M *du poids*^M

steeplechase hurdle jump
steeple^M

landing area
zone^F *de chute*^F

lane
couloir^M

110 m hurdles starting
line
départ^M *du 110 m haies*^F

takeover zone
zone^F *de passage*^M *du*
témoin^M

100 m and 100 m hurdles starting line
départ^M *du 100 m (course*^F *et haies*^F*)*

throwing circle
cercle^M *de lancer*^M

pole vault
saut^M *à la perche*^F

track
piste^F

equipment
équipement^M

starting pistol
pistolet^M *de départ*^M

shot
poids^M

baton
témoin^M

discus
disque^M

hammer
marteau^M

javelin
javelot^M

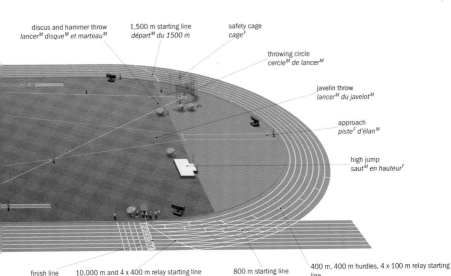

discus and hammer throw
lancer^M disque^M et marteau^M

1,500 m starting line
départ^M du 1500 m

safety cage
cage^F

throwing circle
cercle^M de lancer^M

javelin throw
lancer^M du javelot^M

approach
piste^F d'élan^M

high jump
saut^M en hauteur^F

finish line
ligne^F d'arrivée^F

10,000 m and 4 x 400 m relay starting line
départ^M du 10 000 m et du relais^M 4 x 400 m

800 m starting line
départ^M du 800 m

400 m, 400 m hurdles, 4 x 100 m relay starting
line
départ^M des 400 (course^F, haies^F, relais^M)

athlete: starting block
athlète^F : bloc^M de
départ^M

singlet
maillot^M

number
dossard^M

shorts
short^M

pedal
sabot^M

track shoe
chaussure^F de piste^F

notch
cran^M

starting line
ligne^F de départ^M

anchor
fixation^F

lane line
ligne^F de couloir^M

rack
crémaillère^F

spike
pointe^F

block
bloc^M

base
embase^F

SPORTS AND GAMES

473

baseball
baseball^M

player positions
position^F *des joueurs*^M

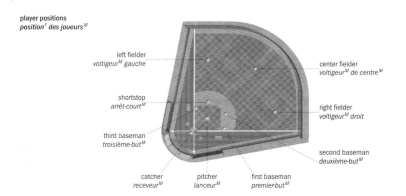

left fielder
voltigeur^M *gauche*

center fielder
voltigeur^M *de centre*^M

shortstop
arrêt-court^M

right fielder
voltigeur^M *droit*

third baseman
troisième-but^M

second baseman
deuxième-but^M

catcher
receveur^M

pitcher
lanceur^M

first baseman
premier-but^M

field
terrain^M

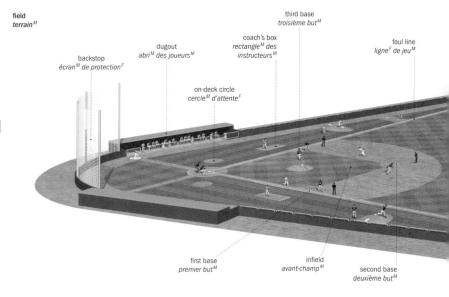

third base
troisième but^M

coach's box
rectangle^M *des
instructeurs*^M

foul line
ligne^F *de jeu*^M

dugout
abri^M *des joueurs*^M

backstop
écran^M *de protection*^F

on-deck circle
cercle^M *d'attente*^F

first base
premier but^M

infield
avant-champ^M

second base
deuxième but^M

pitch
lancer^M

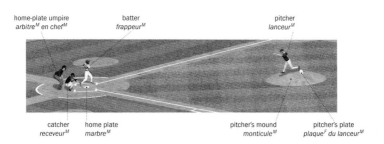

home-plate umpire
arbitre^M *en chef*^M

batter
frappeur^M

pitcher
lanceur^M

catcher
receveur^M

home plate
marbre^M

pitcher's mound
monticule^M

pitcher's plate
plaque^F *du lanceur*^M

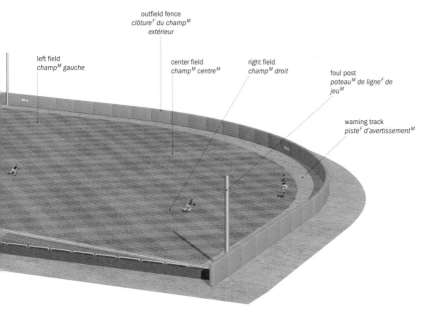

outfield fence
clôture^F *du champ*^M
extérieur

left field
champ^M *gauche*

center field
champ^M *centre*^M

right field
champ^M *droit*

foul post
poteau^M *de ligne*^F *de
jeu*^M

warning track
piste^F *d'avertissement*^M

baseball

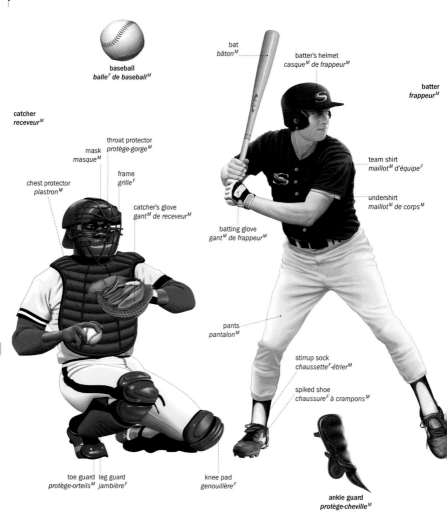

baseball
balle^F de baseball^M

bat
bâton^M

batter's helmet
casque^M de frappeur^M

batter
frappeur^M

catcher
receveur^M

throat protector
protège-gorge^M

mask
masque^M

frame
grille^F

chest protector
plastron^M

catcher's glove
gant^M de receveur^M

team shirt
maillot^M d'équipe^F

undershirt
maillot^M de corps^M

batting glove
gant^M de frappeur^M

pants
pantalon^M

stirrup sock
chaussette^F-étrier^M

spiked shoe
chaussure^F à crampons^M

toe guard
protège-orteils^M

leg guard
jambière^F

knee pad
genouillère^F

ankle guard
protège-cheville^M

baseball

bat
bâton^M

knob
pommeau^M

handle
manche^M

crest
écusson^M

hitting area
surface^F *de frappe*^F

fielder's glove
gant^M

web
panier^M

cross section of a baseball
coupe^F *de la balle*^F

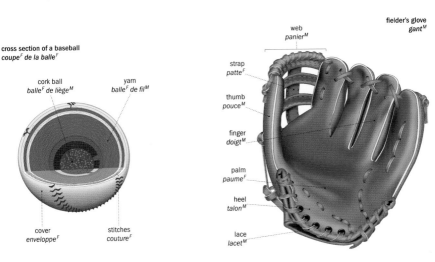

cork ball
balle^F *de liège*^M

yarn
balle^F *de fil*^M

strap
patte^F

thumb
pouce^M

finger
doigt^M

palm
paume^F

heel
talon^M

cover
enveloppe^F

stitches
couture^F

lace
lacet^M

softball
softball^M

softball glove
gant^M *de softball*^M

softball
balle^F *de softball*^M

softball bat
bâton^M *de softball*^M

cricket

cricket[M]

cricket player: batsman
joueur[M] *de cricket*[M] :
batteur[M]

cricket ball
balle[F] *de cricket*[M]

leather skin
enveloppe[F]

seam
couture[F]

helmet
casque[M]

face mask
masque[M]

bat
batte[F]

glove
gant[M]

bat
batte[F]

handle
manche[M]

willow
plat[M]

pad
jambière[F]

cricket shoe
chaussure[F]

stud
crampon[M]

front view
vue[F] *de face*[F]

side view
vue[F] *de profil*[M]

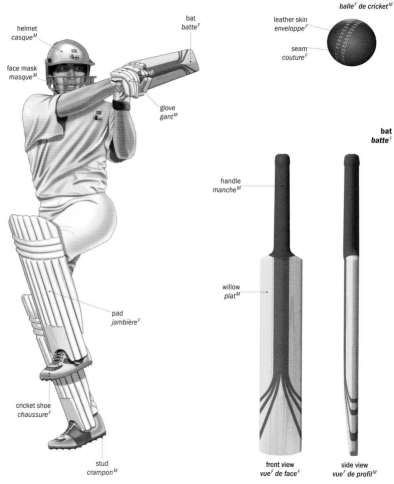

cricket

field
terrain^M

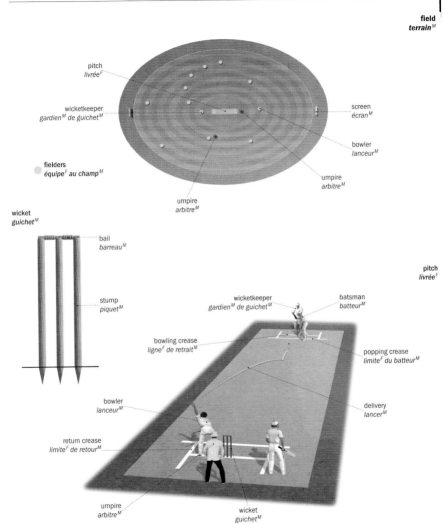

pitch
livrée^F

wicketkeeper
gardien^M *de guichet*^M

fielders
équipe^F *au champ*^M

screen
écran^M

bowler
lanceur^M

umpire
arbitre^M

umpire
arbitre^M

wicket
guichet^M

bail
barreau^M

stump
piquet^M

pitch
livrée^F

wicketkeeper
gardien^M *de guichet*^M

batsman
batteur^M

bowling crease
ligne^F *de retrait*^M

popping crease
limite^F *du batteur*^M

bowler
lanceur^M

delivery
lancer^M

return crease
limite^F *de retour*^M

umpire
arbitre^M

wicket
guichet^M

SPORTS AND GAMES

soccer
football^M

soccer player
footballeur^M

team shirt
maillot^M *d'équipe*^F

goalkeeper's gloves
gants^M *de gardien*^M *de*
but^M

shorts
short^M

interchangeable studs
crampons^M
interchangeables

soccer shoe
chaussure^F *de*
football^M

shin guard
protège-tibia^M

sock
chaussette^F

soccer ball
ballon^M *de football*^M

playing field
terrain^M

penalty spot
point^M *de réparation*^F

center flag
drapeau^M *de centre*^M

goal area
surface^F *de but*^M

goal
but^M

penalty area
surface^F *de réparation*^F

penalty marker
ligne^F *de surface*^F *de*
réparation^F

penalty arc
arc^M *de cercle*^M

player positions
position^F des joueurs^M

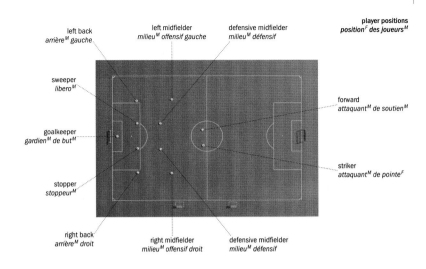

left back
arrière^M gauche

left midfielder
milieu^M offensif gauche

defensive midfielder
milieu^M défensif

sweeper
libero^M

forward
attaquant^M de soutien^M

goalkeeper
gardien^M de but^M

striker
attaquant^M de pointe^F

stopper
stoppeur^M

right back
arrière^M droit

right midfielder
milieu^M offensif droit

defensive midfielder
milieu^M défensif

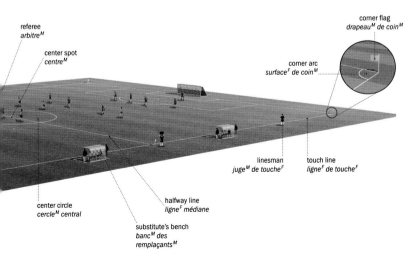

referee
arbitre^M

center spot
centre^M

corner flag
drapeau^M de coin^M

corner arc
surface^F de coin^M

linesman
juge^M de touche^F

touch line
ligne^F de touche^F

halfway line
ligne^F médiane

center circle
cercle^M central

substitute's bench
*banc^M des
remplaçants^M*

SPORTS AND GAMES

rugby
rugby^M

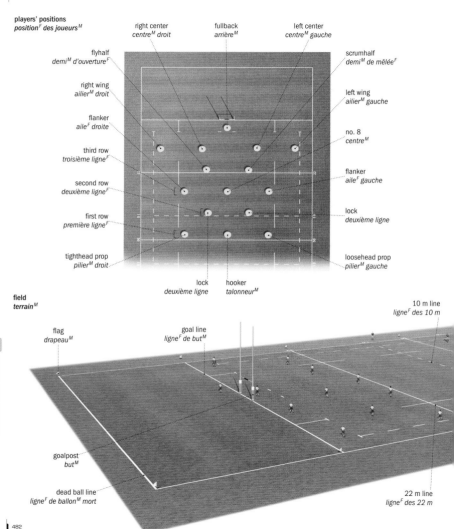

players' positions
position^F des joueurs^M

right center
centre^M droit

fullback
arrière^M

left center
centre^M gauche

flyhalf
demi^M d'ouverture^F

scrumhalf
demi^M de mêlée^F

right wing
ailier^M droit

left wing
ailier^M gauche

flanker
aile^F droite

no. 8
centre^M

third row
troisième ligne^F

flanker
aile^F gauche

second row
deuxième ligne^F

lock
deuxième ligne

first row
première ligne^F

tighthead prop
pilier^M droit

loosehead prop
pilier^M gauche

lock
deuxième ligne

hooker
talonneur^M

field
terrain^M

10 m line
ligne^F des 10 m

flag
drapeau^M

goal line
ligne^F de but^M

goalpost
but^M

dead ball line
ligne^F de ballon^M mort

22 m line
ligne^F des 22 m

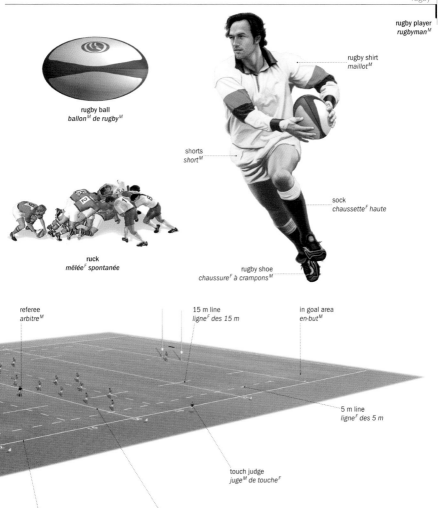

rugby player
rugbyman^M

rugby shirt
maillot^M

rugby ball
ballon^M *de rugby*^{M}

shorts
short^M

sock
chaussette^F *haute*

ruck
mêlée^F *spontanée*

rugby shoe
chaussure^F *à crampons*^{M}

referee
arbitre^M

15 m line
ligne^F *des 15 m*

in goal area
en-but^M

5 m line
ligne^F *des 5 m*

touch judge
juge^M *de touche*^{F}

touchline
ligne^F *de touche*^{F}

halfway dash line
ligne^F *médiane*

American football

football^M américain

scrimmage: defense
mêlée^F : défense^F

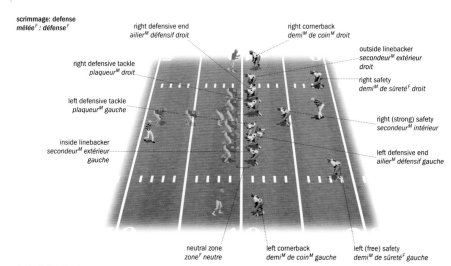

right defensive end
ailier^M défensif droit

right cornerback
demi^M de coin^M droit

outside linebacker
secondeur^M extérieur droit

right defensive tackle
plaqueur^M droit

right safety
demi^M de sûreté^F droit

left defensive tackle
plaqueur^M gauche

right (strong) safety
secondeur^M intérieur

inside linebacker
secondeur^M extérieur gauche

left defensive end
ailier^M défensif gauche

neutral zone
zone^F neutre

left cornerback
demi^M de coin^M gauche

left (free) safety
demi^M de sûreté^F gauche

playing field for American football
terrain^M de football^M américain

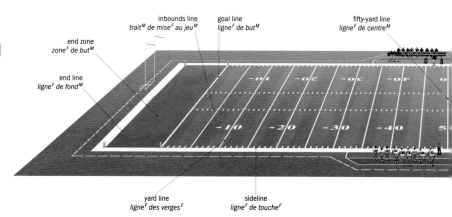

inbounds line
trait^M de mise^F au jeu^M

goal line
ligne^F de but^M

fifty-yard line
ligne^F de centre^M

end zone
zone^F de but^M

end line
ligne^F de fond^M

yard line
ligne^F des verges^F

sideline
ligne^F de touche^F

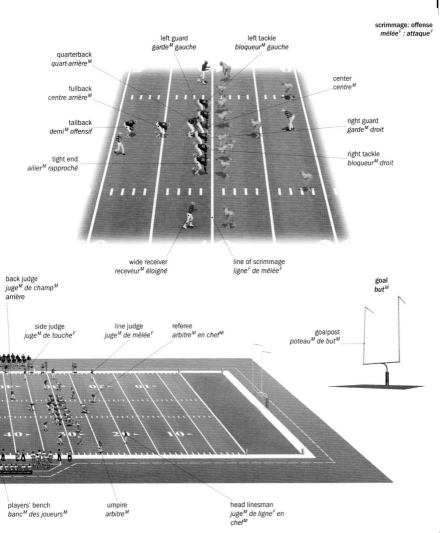

scrimmage: offense
mêlée^F : attaque^F

quarterback
quart-arrière^M

fullback
centre arrière^M

tailback
demi^M offensif

tight end
ailier^M rapproché

left guard
garde^M gauche

left tackle
bloqueur^M gauche

center
centre^M

right guard
garde^M droit

right tackle
bloqueur^M droit

wide receiver
receveur^M éloigné

line of scrimmage
ligne^F de mêlée^F

back judge
juge^M de champ^M arrière

side judge
juge^M de touche^F

line judge
juge^M de mêlée^F

referee
arbitre^M en chef^M

goal
but^M

goalpost
poteau^M de but^M

players' bench
banc^M des joueurs^M

umpire
arbitre^M

head linesman
juge^M de ligne^F en chef^M

American football

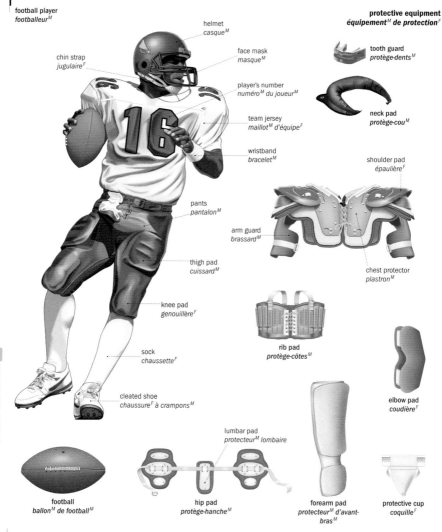

football player
footballeur^M

helmet
casque^M

face mask
masque^M

chin strap
jugulaire^F

player's number
numéro^M du joueur^M

team jersey
maillot^M d'équipe^F

wristband
bracelet^M

pants
pantalon^M

arm guard
brassard^M

thigh pad
cuissard^M

knee pad
genouillère^F

sock
chaussette^F

cleated shoe
chaussure^F à crampons^M

protective equipment
équipement^M de protection^F

tooth guard
protège-dents^M

neck pad
protège-cou^M

shoulder pad
épaulière^F

chest protector
plastron^M

rib pad
protège-côtes^M

elbow pad
coudière^F

lumbar pad
protecteur^M lombaire

football
ballon^M de football^M

hip pad
protège-hanche^M

forearm pad
protecteur^M d'avant-bras^M

protective cup
coquille^F

SPORTS AND GAMES

volleyball
volleyball^M

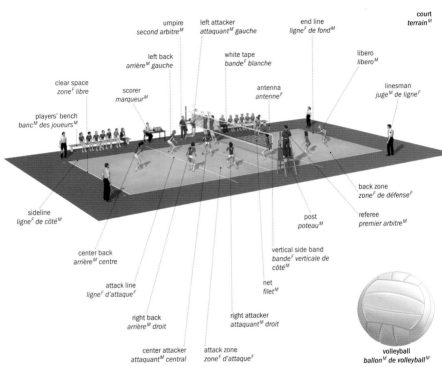

court
terrain^M

umpire
second arbitre^M

left attacker
attaquant^M *gauche*

end line
ligne^F *de fond*^M

left back
arrière^M *gauche*

white tape
bande^F *blanche*

libero
libero^M

clear space
zone^F *libre*

scorer
marqueur^M

antenna
antenne^F

linesman
juge^M *de ligne*^F

players' bench
banc^M *des joueurs*^M

back zone
zone^F *de défense*^F

sideline
ligne^F *de côté*^M

post
poteau^M

referee
premier arbitre^M

center back
arrière^M *centre*

vertical side band
bande^F *verticale de côté*^M

attack line
ligne^F *d'attaque*^F

net
filet^M

right back
arrière^M *droit*

right attacker
attaquant^M *droit*

center attacker
attaquant^M *central*

attack zone
zone^F *d'attaque*^F

volleyball
ballon^M *de volleyball*^M

techniques
techniques^F

tip
touche^F

bump
manchette^F

serve
service^M

basketball
basketball^M

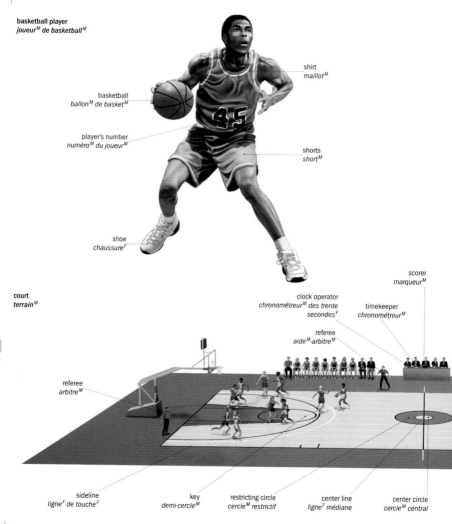

basketball player
joueur^M *de basketball*^M

shirt
maillot^M

basketball
ballon^M *de basket*^M

player's number
numéro^M *du joueur*^M

shorts
short^M

shoe
chaussure^F

court
terrain^M

scorer
marqueur^M

clock operator
chronométreur^M *des trente
secondes*^F

timekeeper
chronométreur^M

referee
aide^M-*arbitre*^M

referee
arbitre^M

sideline
ligne^F *de touche*^F

key
demi-cercle^M

restricting circle
cercle^M *restrictif*

center line
ligne^F *médiane*

center circle
cercle^M *central*

player positions
position^F des joueurs^M

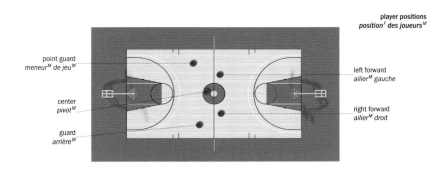

point guard
meneur^M de jeu^M

center
pivot^M

guard
arrière^M

left forward
ailier^M gauche

right forward
ailier^M droit

backstop
but^M

backboard
panneau^M

rim
anneau^M

net
filet^M

basket
panier^M

backboard support
support^M de panneau^M

padded upright
montant^M rembourré

padded base
socle^M rembourré

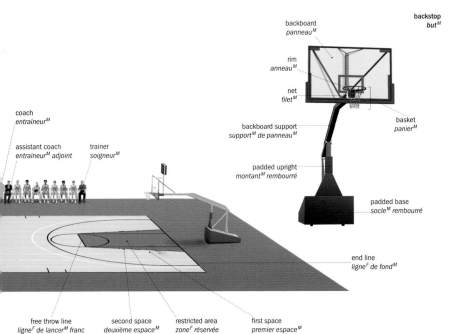

coach
entraîneur^M

assistant coach
entraîneur^M adjoint

trainer
soigneur^M

end line
ligne^F de fond^M

free throw line
ligne^F de lancer^M franc

second space
deuxième espace^M

restricted area
zone^F réservée

first space
premier espace^M

tennis
tennis[M]

court
court[M]

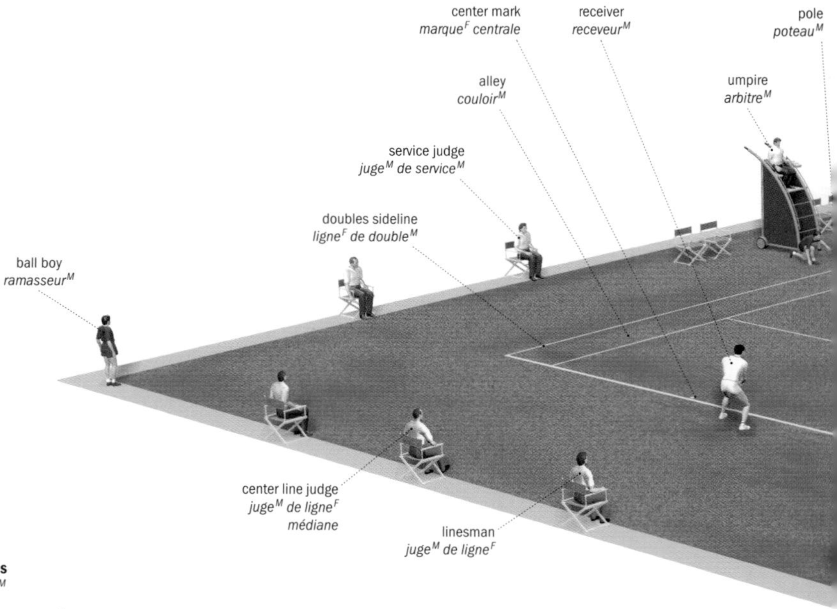

center mark
marque[F] *centrale*

receiver
receveur[M]

pole
poteau[M]

alley
couloir[M]

umpire
arbitre[M]

service judge
juge[M] *de service*[M]

doubles sideline
ligne[F] *de double*[M]

ball boy
ramasseur[M]

center line judge
juge[M] *de ligne*[F]
médiane

linesman
juge[M] *de ligne*[F]

strokes
coups[M]

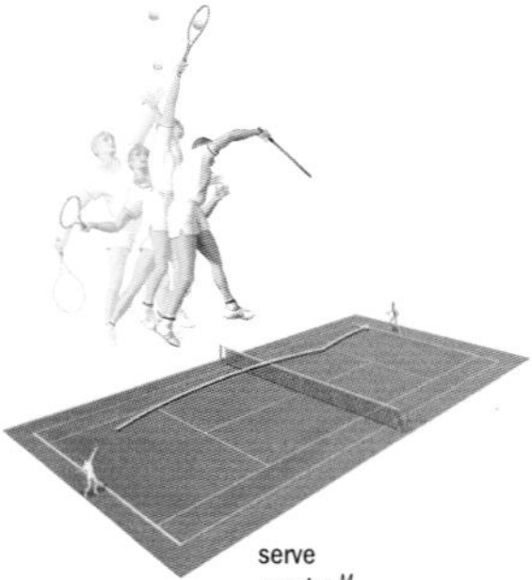

serve
service[M]

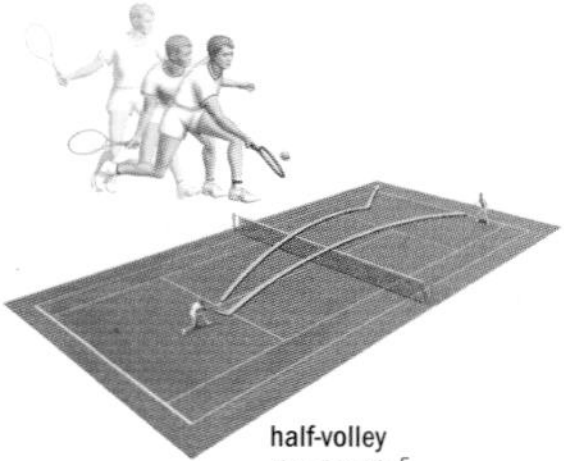

half-volley
demi-volée[F]

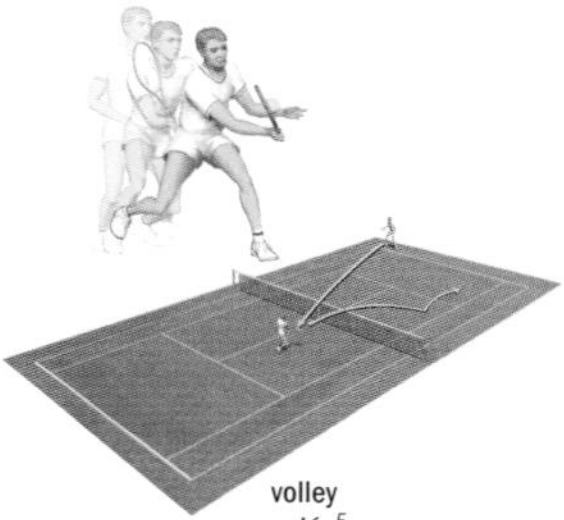

volley
volée[F]

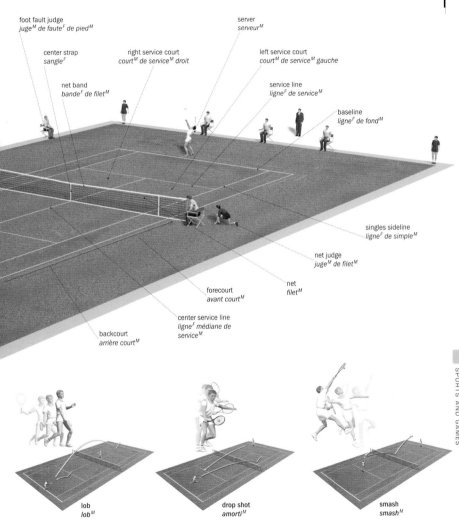

foot fault judge
juge^M de faute^F de pied^M

server
serveur^M

center strap
sangle^F

right service court
court^M de service^M droit

left service court
court^M de service^M gauche

net band
bande^F de filet^M

service line
ligne^F de service^M

baseline
ligne^F de fond^M

singles sideline
ligne^F de simple^M

net judge
juge^M de filet^M

net
filet^M

forecourt
avant court^M

center service line
ligne^F médiane de service^M

backcourt
arrière court^M

lob
lob^M

drop shot
amorti^M

smash
smash^M

tennis

tennis racket
raquette[F] *de tennis*[M]

frame
cadre[M]

stringing
tamis[M]

head
tête[F]

shoulder
épaule[F]

throat
cœur[M]

shaft
manche[M]

handle
poignée[F]

butt
talon[M]

polo shirt
polo[M]

tennis player
joueuse[F] *de tennis*[M]

wristband
serre-poignet[M]

tennis skirt
jupette[F]

sock
chaussette[F]

tennis ball
balle[F] *de tennis*[M]

tennis shoe
chaussure[F] *de tennis*[M]

scoreboard
tableau[M] *d'affichage*[M]

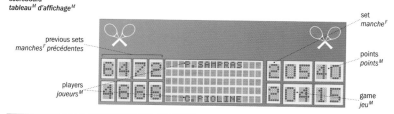

previous sets
manches[F] *précédentes*

players
joueurs[M]

set
manche[F]

points
points[M]

game
jeu[M]

playing surfaces
surfaces[F] *de jeu*[M]

grass
gazon[M]

clay
terre[F] *battue*

hard surface (cement)
surface[F] *dure*
(ciment[M]*)*

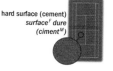

synthetic surface
revêtement[M]
synthétique

table tennis
tennis^M de table^F

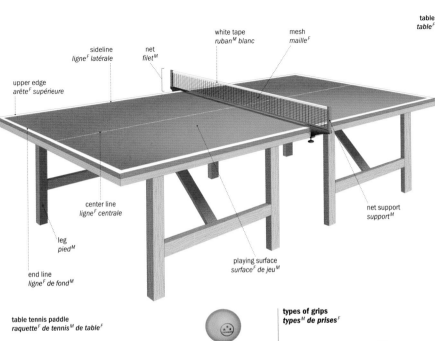

table
table^F

white tape
ruban^M blanc

mesh
maille^F

sideline
ligne^F latérale

net
filet^M

upper edge
arête^F supérieure

center line
ligne^F centrale

net support
support^M

leg
pied^M

playing surface
surface^F de jeu^M

end line
ligne^F de fond^M

table tennis paddle
raquette^F de tennis^M de table^F

handle
manche^M

table tennis ball
balle^F de tennis^M de table^F

face
face^F

blade
palette^F

covering
revêtement^M

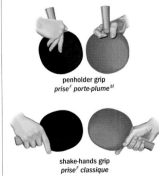

types of grips
types^M de prises^F

penholder grip
prise^F porte-plume^M

shake-hands grip
prise^F classique

SPORTS AND GAMES

badminton
badminton^M

court
terrain^M

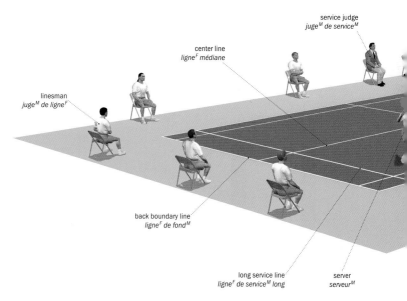

service judge
juge^M *de service*^M

center line
ligne^F *médiane*

linesman
juge^M *de ligne*^F

back boundary line
ligne^F *de fond*^M

long service line
ligne^F *de service*^M *long*

server
serveur^M

badminton racket
raquette^F *de badminton*^M

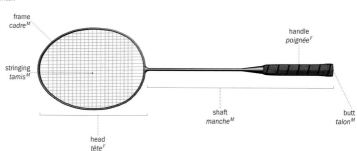

frame
cadre^M

handle
poignée^F

stringing
tamis^M

shaft
manche^M

butt
talon^M

head
tête^F

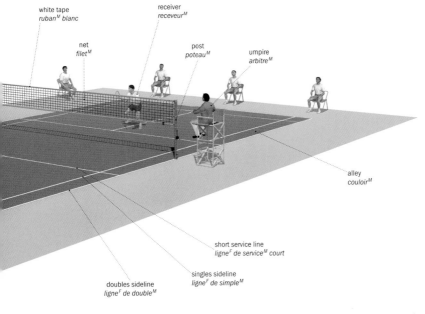

white tape
ruban^M blanc

receiver
receveur^M

net
filet^M

post
poteau^M

umpire
arbitre^M

alley
couloir^M

short service line
ligne^F de service^M court

singles sideline
ligne^F de simple^M

doubles sideline
ligne^F de double^M

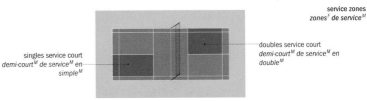

service zones
zones^F de service^M

singles service court
demi-court^M de service^M en simple^M

doubles service court
demi-court^M de service^M en double^M

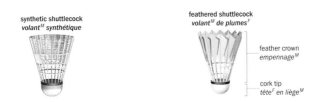

synthetic shuttlecock
volant^M synthétique

feathered shuttlecock
volant^M de plumes^F

feather crown
empennage^M

cork tip
tête^F en liège^M

gymnastics
gymnastique^F

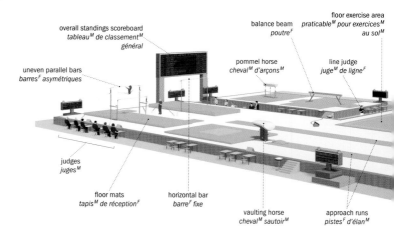

event platform
*podium^M des
épreuves^F*

overall standings scoreboard
*tableau^M de classement^M
général*

uneven parallel bars
barres^F asymétriques

balance beam
poutre^F

floor exercise area
*praticable^M pour exercices^M
au sol^M*

pommel horse
cheval^M d'arçons^M

line judge
juge^M de ligne^F

judges
juges^M

floor mats
tapis^M de réception^F

horizontal bar
barre^F fixe

vaulting horse
cheval^M sautoir^M

approach runs
pistes^F d'élan^M

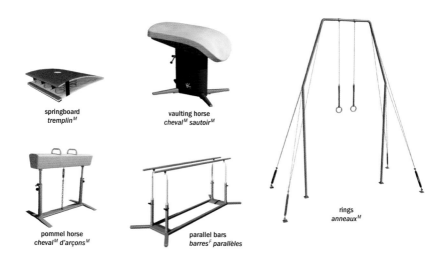

springboard
tremplin^M

vaulting horse
cheval^M sautoir^M

pommel horse
cheval^M d'arçons^M

parallel bars
barres^F parallèles

rings
anneaux^M

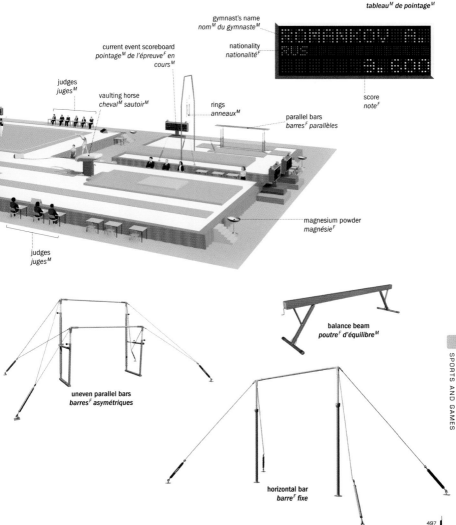

scoreboard
tableau^M de pointage^M

gymnast's name
nom^M du gymnaste^M

nationality
nationalité^F

score
note^F

current event scoreboard
pointage^M de l'épreuve^F en cours^M

rings
anneaux^M

parallel bars
barres^F parallèles

judges
juges^M

vaulting horse
cheval^M sautoir^M

magnesium powder
magnésie^F

judges
juges^M

uneven parallel bars
barres^F asymétriques

balance beam
poutre^F d'équilibre^M

horizontal bar
barre^F fixe

boxing
boxe^F

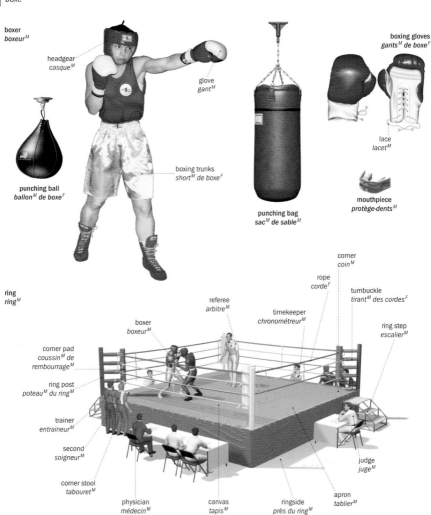

boxer
boxeur^M

headgear
casque^M

glove
gant^M

boxing trunks
short^M *de boxe*^F

punching ball
ballon^M *de boxe*^F

punching bag
sac^M *de sable*^M

boxing gloves
gants^M *de boxe*^F

lace
lacet^M

mouthpiece
protège-dents^M

ring
ring^M

corner
coin^M

rope
corde^F

turnbuckle
tirant^M *des cordes*^F

referee
arbitre^M

timekeeper
chronométreur^M

ring step
escalier^M

boxer
boxeur^M

corner pad
coussin^M *de*
rembourrage^M

ring post
poteau^M *du ring*^M

trainer
entraîneur^M

second
soigneur^M

judge
juge^M

corner stool
tabouret^M

physician
médecin^M

canvas
tapis^M

ringside
près du ring^M

apron
tablier^M

judo
judo[M]

scorers and timekeepers
marqueurs[M] *et chronométreurs*[M]

medical team
équipe[F] *médicale*

mat
tapis[M]

safety area
surface[F] *de sécurité*[F]

contestant
combattant[M]

danger area
zone[F] *de danger*[M]

scoreboard
tableau[M] *d'affichage*[M]

contest area
surface[F] *de combat*[M]

referee
arbitre[M]

judge
juge[M]

examples of holds and throws
exemples[M] **de prises**[F]

judogi
judogi[M]

jacket
veste[F]

holding
immobilisation[F]

stomach throw
projection[F] *en cercle*[M]

sweeping hip throw
hanche[F] *ailée*

major outer reaping throw
grand fauchage[M] *extérieur*

major inner reaping throw
grand fauchage[M] *intérieur*

naked strangle
étranglement[M]

trousers
pantalon[M]

belt
ceinture[F]

arm lock
clé[F] *de bras*[M]

one-arm shoulder throw
projection[F] *d'épaule*[F] *par un côté*[M]

SPORTS AND GAMES

499

weightlifting
haltérophilie^F

barbell
haltère^M long

wristband
poignet^M de force^F

weightlifting belt
ceinture^F d'haltérophilie^F

sleeveless jersey
maillot^M de corps^M

trunks
culotte^F

knee wrap
genouillère^F

strap
lanière^F

weightlifting shoe
chaussure^F d'haltérophilie^F

clean and jerk
épaulé^M-jeté^M

snatch
arraché^M

fitness equipment
appareils^M de conditionnement^M physique

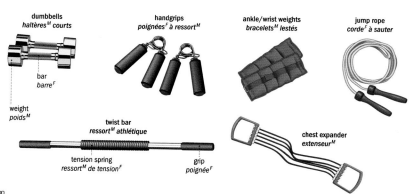

dumbbells
haltères^M courts

handgrips
poignées^F à ressort^M

ankle/wrist weights
bracelets^M lestés

jump rope
corde^F à sauter

bar
barre^F

weight
poids^M

twist bar
ressort^M athlétique

chest expander
extenseur^M

tension spring
ressort^M de tension^F

grip
poignée^F

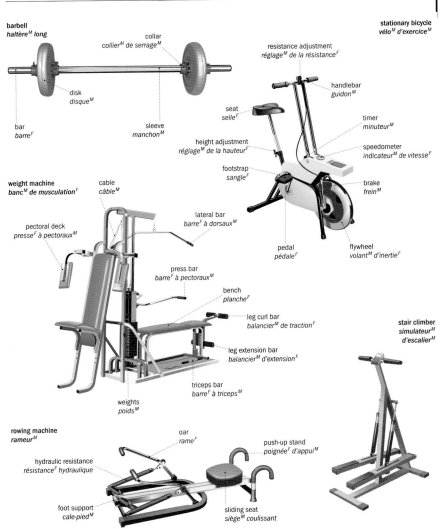

barbell
haltère^M long

collar
collier^M de serrage^M

disk
disque^M

bar
barre^F

sleeve
manchon^M

stationary bicycle
vélo^M d'exercice^M

resistance adjustment
réglage^M de la résistance^F

handlebar
guidon^M

seat
selle^F

timer
minuteur^M

height adjustment
réglage^M de la hauteur^F

speedometer
indicateur^M de vitesse^F

footstrap
sangle^F

brake
frein^M

pedal
pédale^F

flywheel
volant^M d'inertie^F

weight machine
banc^M de musculation^F

cable
câble^M

lateral bar
barre^F à dorsaux^M

pectoral deck
presse^F à pectoraux^M

press bar
barre^F à pectoraux^M

bench
planche^F

leg curl bar
balancier^M de traction^F

leg extension bar
balancier^M d'extension^F

triceps bar
barre^F à triceps^M

weights
poids^M

stair climber
*simulateur^M
d'escalier^M*

rowing machine
rameur^M

oar
rame^F

push-up stand
poignée^F d'appui^M

hydraulic resistance
résistance^F hydraulique

foot support
cale-pied^M

sliding seat
siège^M coulissant

billiards

billard^M

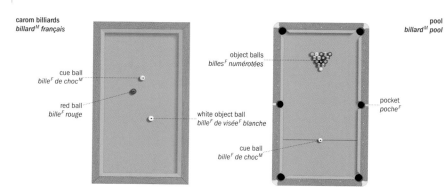

carom billiards
billard^M français

pool
billard^M pool

cue ball
bille^F de choc^M

red ball
bille^F rouge

object balls
billes^F numérotées

white object ball
bille^F de visée^F blanche

pocket
poche^F

cue ball
bille^F de choc^M

table
table^F

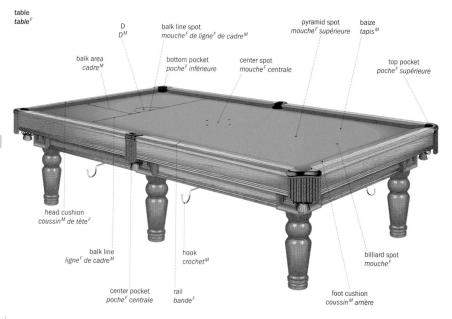

D
D^M

balk line spot
mouche^F de ligne^F de cadre^M

balk area
cadre^M

bottom pocket
poche^F inférieure

center spot
mouche^F centrale

pyramid spot
mouche^F supérieure

baize
tapis^M

top pocket
poche^F supérieure

head cushion
coussin^M de tête^F

balk line
ligne^F de cadre^M

center pocket
poche^F centrale

hook
crochet^M

rail
bande^F

billiard spot
mouche^F

foot cushion
coussin^M arrière

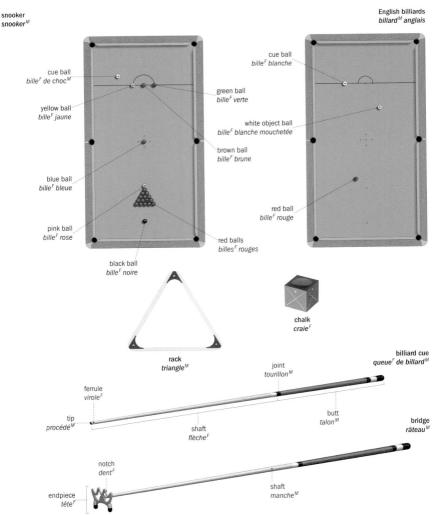

snooker
snooker^M

English billiards
billard^M *anglais*

cue ball
bille^F *de choc*^M

yellow ball
bille^F *jaune*

green ball
bille^F *verte*

brown ball
bille^F *brune*

blue ball
bille^F *bleue*

pink ball
bille^F *rose*

red balls
billes^F *rouges*

black ball
bille^F *noire*

cue ball
bille^F *blanche*

white object ball
bille^F *blanche mouchetée*

red ball
bille^F *rouge*

rack
triangle^M

chalk
craie^F

billiard cue
queue^F *de billard*^M

ferrule
virole^F

joint
tourillon^M

tip
procédé^M

shaft
flèche^F

butt
talon^M

bridge
râteau^M

notch
dent^F

endpiece
tête^F

shaft
manche^M

SPORTS AND GAMES

503

golf
golf^M

course
parcours^M

hole
trou^M

clubhouse
pavillon^M

practice green
vert^M *d'entraînement*^M

parking
stationnement^M

sand bunker
fosse^F *de sable*^M

green
vert^M

cart path
chemin^M

fairway
allée^F

pond
étang^M

trees
arbres^M

rough
herbe^F *longue*

teeing ground
tertre^M *de départ*^M

water hazard
obstacle^M *d'eau*^F

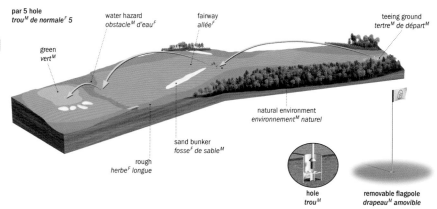

par 5 hole
trou^M *de normale*^F 5

water hazard
obstacle^M *d'eau*^F

fairway
allée^F

teeing ground
tertre^M *de départ*^M

green
vert^M

natural environment
environnement^M *naturel*

rough
herbe^F *longue*

sand bunker
fosse^F *de sable*^M

hole
trou^M

removable flagpole
drapeau^M *amovible*

SPORTS AND GAMES

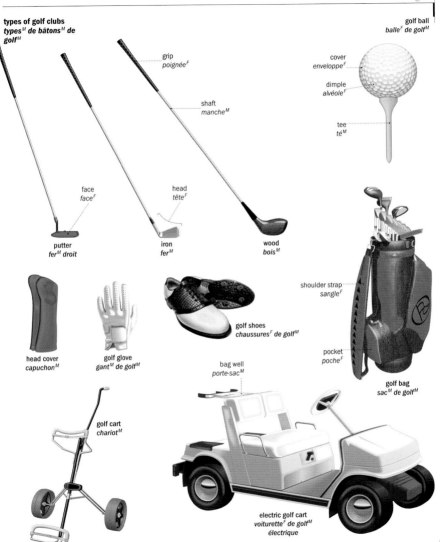

types of golf clubs
types^M de bâtons^M de golf^M

golf ball
balle^F de golf^M

grip
poignée^F

cover
enveloppe^F

dimple
alvéole^F

shaft
manche^M

tee
té^M

face
face^F

head
tête^F

putter
fer^M droit

iron
fer^M

wood
bois^M

shoulder strap
sangle^F

head cover
capuchon^M

golf glove
gant^M de golf^M

golf shoes
chaussures^F de golf^M

pocket
poche^F

golf bag
sac^M de golf^M

bag well
porte-sac^M

golf cart
chariot^M

electric golf cart
voiturette^F de golf^M électrique

ice hockey
hockey^M sur glace^F

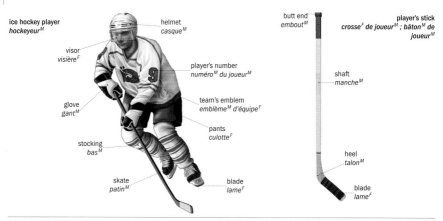

ice hockey player
hockeyeur^M

helmet
casque^M

visor
visière^F

player's number
numéro^M du joueur^M

glove
gant^M

team's emblem
emblème^M d'équipe^F

pants
culotte^F

stocking
bas^M

skate
patin^M

blade
lame^F

butt end
embout^M

player's stick
crosse^F de joueur^M ; bâton^M de joueur^M

shaft
manche^M

heel
talon^M

blade
lame^F

rink
patinoire^F

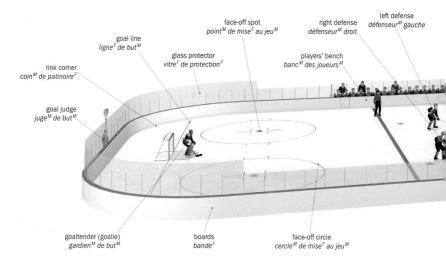

rink corner
coin^M de patinoire^F

goal line
ligne^F de but^M

glass protector
vitre^F de protection^F

face-off spot
point^M de mise^F au jeu^M

right defense
défenseur^M droit

left defense
défenseur^M gauche

players' bench
banc^M des joueurs^M

goal judge
juge^M de but^M

goaltender (goalie)
gardien^M de but^M

boards
bande^F

face-off circle
cercle^M de mise^F au jeu^M

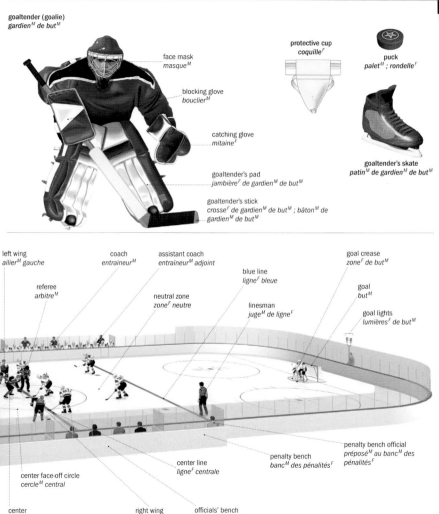

goaltender (goalie)
gardien^M de but^M

face mask
masque^M

blocking glove
bouclier^M

catching glove
mitaine^F

goaltender's pad
jambière^F de gardien^M de but^M

goaltender's stick
crosse^F de gardien^M de but^M ; bâton^M de gardien^M de but^M

protective cup
coquille^F

puck
palet^M ; rondelle^F

goaltender's skate
patin^M de gardien^M de but^M

left wing
ailier^M gauche

coach
entraineur^M

assistant coach
entraineur^M adjoint

referee
arbitre^M

neutral zone
zone^F neutre

blue line
ligne^F bleue

linesman
juge^M de ligne^F

goal crease
zone^F de but^M

goal
but^M

goal lights
lumières^F de but^M

penalty bench official
préposé^M au banc^M des pénalités^F

penalty bench
banc^M des pénalités^F

center line
ligne^F centrale

officials' bench
banc^M des officiels^M

center face-off circle
cercle^M central

right wing
ailier^M droit

center
centre^M

speed skating
patinage^M *de vitesse*^{F}

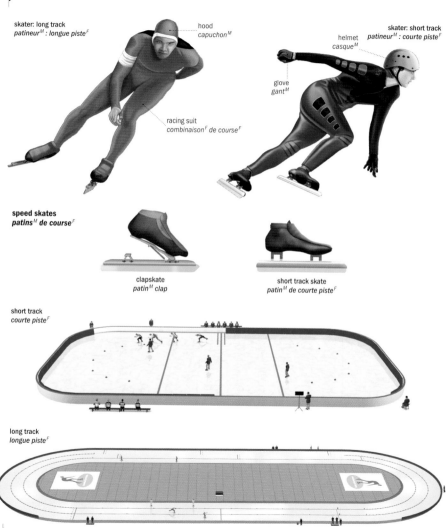

skater: long track
patineur^M *: longue piste*^{F}

hood
capuchon^M

racing suit
combinaison^F *de course*^{F}

skater: short track
patineur^M *: courte piste*^{F}

helmet
casque^M

glove
gant^M

speed skates
patins^M ***de course***^{F}

clapskate
patin^M *clap*

short track skate
patin^M *de courte piste*^{F}

short track
courte piste^F

long track
longue piste^F

figure skating
patinage^M artistique

figure skate
patin^M de figure^F

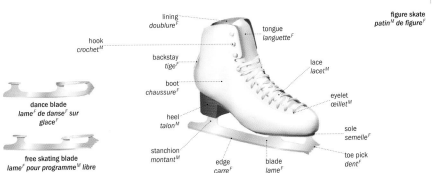

lining
doublure^F

hook
crochet^M

tongue
languette^F

backstay
tige^F

lace
lacet^M

boot
chaussure^F

dance blade
lame^F de danse^F sur glace^F

free skating blade
lame^F pour programme^M libre

heel
talon^M

eyelet
œillet^M

sole
semelle^F

stanchion
montant^M

edge
carre^F

blade
lame^F

toe pick
dent^F

examples of jumps
exemples^M de sauts^M

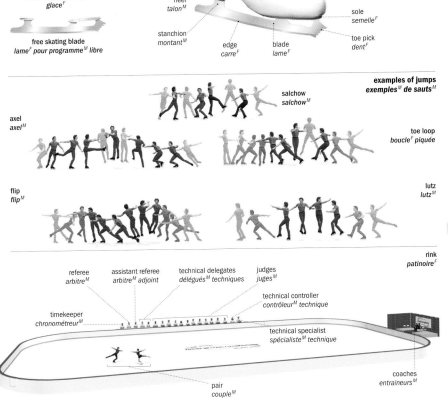

salchow
salchow^M

axel
axel^M

toe loop
boucle^F piquée

flip
flip^M

lutz
lutz^M

rink
patinoire^F

referee
arbitre^M

assistant referee
arbitre^M adjoint

technical delegates
délégués^M techniques

judges
juges^M

technical controller
contrôleur^M technique

timekeeper
chronométreur^M

technical specialist
spécialiste^M technique

pair
couple^M

coaches
entraineurs^M

SPORTS AND GAMES

alpine skiing
ski^M alpin

alpine skier
skieur^M alpin

ski goggles
lunettes^F de ski^M

helmet
casque^M

ski suit
combinaison^F de ski^M

basket
rondelle^F

ski pole
bâton^M de ski^M

ski glove
gant^M de ski^M

ski boot
chaussure^F de ski^M

wrist strap
dragonne^F

handle
poignée^F

groove
rainure^F

bottom
semelle^F

ski
ski^M

ski
ski^M

tip
pointe^F

tail
talon^M

edge
carre^F

safety binding
fixation^F de sécurité^F

shovel
spatule^F

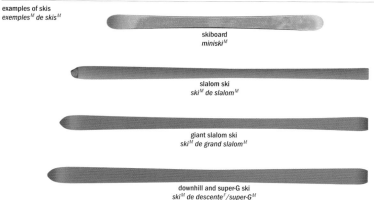

examples of skis
exemples^M de skis^M

skiboard
miniski^M

slalom ski
ski^M de slalom^M

giant slalom ski
ski^M de grand slalom^M

downhill and super-G ski
ski^M de descente^F/super-G^M

alpine skiing

technical events
épreuves^F

downhill
descente^F

super giant (super-G)
slalom
super-géant^M

giant slalom
slalom^M *géant*

special slalom
slalom^M *spécial*

ski boot
chaussure^F *de ski*^M

inner boot
chausson^M *intérieur*

upper cuff
collier^M

upper
tige^F

tongue
languette^F

upper shell
coque^F *supérieure*

upper strap
courroie^F *de tige*^F

buckle
boucle^F

adjusting catch
cran^M *de réglage*^M

hinge
charnière^F

sole
semelle^F

lower shell
coque^F *inférieure*

safety binding
fixation^F *de sécurité*^F

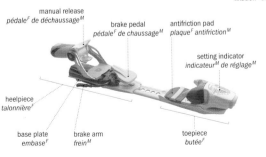

manual release
pédale^F *de déchaussage*^M

brake pedal
pédale^F *de chaussage*^M

antifriction pad
plaque^F *antifriction*^M

setting indicator
indicateur^M *de réglage*^M

heelpiece
talonnière^F

base plate
embase^F

brake arm
frein^M

toepiece
butée^F

ski resort
station^F de ski^M

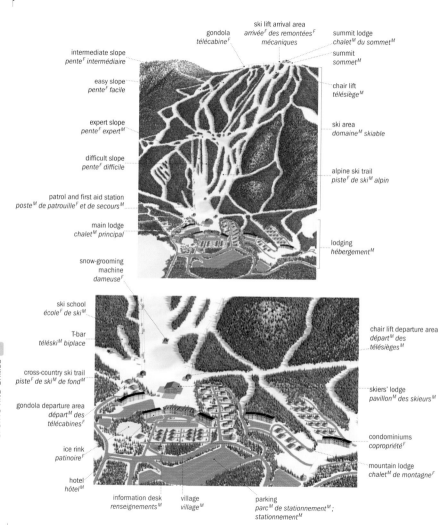

ski lift arrival area
arrivée^F des remontées^F mécaniques

gondola
télécabine^F

summit lodge
chalet^M du sommet^M

summit
sommet^M

intermediate slope
pente^F intermédiaire

easy slope
pente^F facile

chair lift
télésiège^M

expert slope
pente^F expert^M

ski area
domaine^M skiable

difficult slope
pente^F difficile

alpine ski trail
piste^F de ski^M alpin

patrol and first aid station
poste^M de patrouille^F et de secours^M

main lodge
chalet^M principal

lodging
hébergement^M

snow-grooming machine
dameuse^F

ski school
école^F de ski^M

T-bar
téléski^M biplace

chair lift departure area
départ^M des télésièges^M

cross-country ski trail
piste^F de ski^M de fond^M

skiers' lodge
pavillon^M des skieurs^M

gondola departure area
départ^M des télécabines^F

ice rink
patinoire^F

condominiums
copropriété^F

mountain lodge
chalet^M de montagne^F

hotel
hôtel^M

information desk
renseignements^M

village
village^M

parking
parc^M de stationnement^M ; stationnement^M

snowboarding
surf^M des neiges^F

snowboarder
surfeur^M

helmet
casque^M

coveralls
combinaison^F

goggles
lunettes^F

shin guard
protège-tibia^M

snowboard
surf^M des neiges^F

glove
gant^M

hard boot
botte^F rigide

flexible boot
botte^F souple

freestyle snowboard
surf^M acrobatique

alpine snowboard
surf^M alpin

ski jumping
saut^M à ski^M

ski jumper
sauteur^M

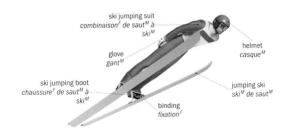

ski jumping suit
combinaison^F de saut^M à ski^M

glove
gant^M

helmet
casque^M

ski jumping boot
chaussure^F de saut^M à ski^M

jumping ski
ski^M de saut^M

binding
fixation^F

cross-country skiing
ski^M de fond^M

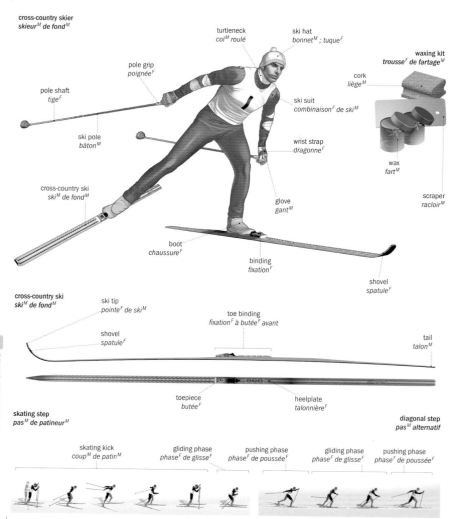

cross-country skier
skieur^M de fond^M

turtleneck
col^M roulé

ski hat ;
bonnet^M ; tuque^F

waxing kit
trousse^F de fartage^M

cork
liège^M

pole grip
poignée^F

pole shaft
tige^F

ski suit
combinaison^F de ski^M

ski pole
bâton^M

wrist strap
dragonne^F

wax
fart^M

cross-country ski
ski^M de fond^M

glove
gant^M

scraper
racloir^M

boot
chaussure^F

binding
fixation^F

shovel
spatule^F

cross-country ski
ski^M de fond^M

ski tip
pointe^F de ski^M

toe binding
fixation^F à butée^F avant

tail
talon^M

shovel
spatule^F

toepiece
butée^F

heelplate
talonnière^F

skating step
pas^M de patineur^M

diagonal step
pas^M alternatif

skating kick
coup^M de patin^M

gliding phase
phase^F de glisse^F

pushing phase
phase^F de poussée^F

gliding phase
phase^F de glisse^F

pushing phase
phase^F de poussée^F

curling
curling^M

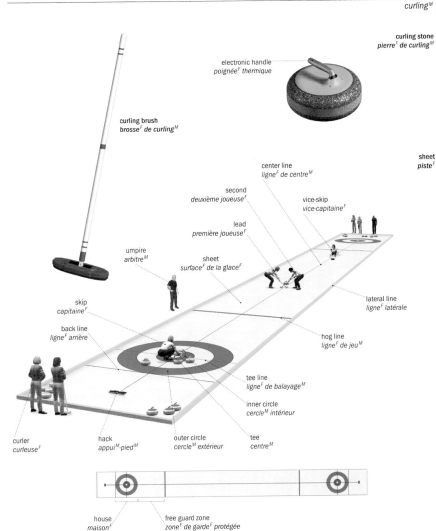

curling stone
pierre^F de curling^M

electronic handle
poignée^F thermique

curling brush
brosse^F de curling^M

sheet
piste^F

center line
ligne^F de centre^M

second
deuxième joueuse^F

vice-skip
vice-capitaine^F

lead
première joueuse^F

umpire
arbitre^M

sheet
surface^F de la glace^F

skip
capitaine^F

lateral line
ligne^F latérale

back line
ligne^F arrière

hog line
ligne^F de jeu^M

tee line
ligne^F de balayage^M

inner circle
cercle^M intérieur

curler
curleuse^F

hack
appui^M-pied^M

outer circle
cercle^M extérieur

tee
centre^M

house
maison^F

free guard zone
zone^F de garde^F protégée

swimming
natation^F

starting block
plot^M de départ^M

swimsuit
maillot^M de bain^M

cap
bonnet^M

platform
plate-forme^F

swimming goggles
lunettes^F de nage^F

starting grip (backstroke)
poignée^F de départ^M (dos^M)

stroke judge
juge^M de nage^F

false start rope
corde^F de faux départ^M

referee
juge^M arbitre^M

starter
juge^M de départ^M

finish wall
mur^M d'arrivée^F

lane timekeeper
chronométreur^M de couloir^M

lane
couloir^M

starting block
plot^M de départ^M

chief timekeeper
chronométreur^M en chef^M

placing judge
juge^M de classement^M

types of strokes
types^M de nages^F

front crawl
crawl^M

butterfly stroke
papillon^M

breaststroke
brasse^F

backstroke
nage^F sur le dos^M

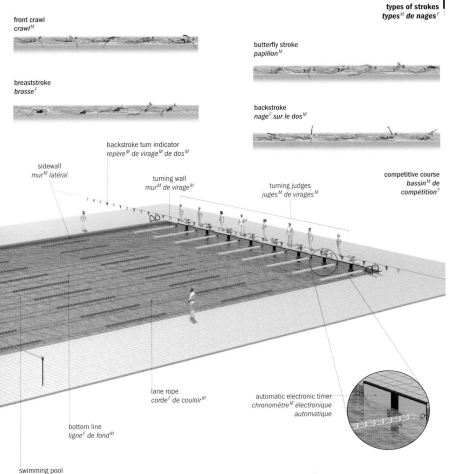

backstroke turn indicator
repère^M de virage^M de dos^M

sidewall
mur^M latéral

turning wall
mur^M de virage^M

turning judges
juges^M de virages^M

competitive course
*bassin^M de
compétition^F*

lane rope
corde^F de couloir^M

bottom line
ligne^F de fond^M

automatic electronic timer
*chronomètre^M électronique
automatique*

swimming pool
bassin^M

diving
plongeon^M

starting positions
positions^F *de départ*^M

flights
vols^M

reverse
renversé

inward
retourné

backward
arrière

forward
avant

armstand
en équilibre^M

tuck position
position^F *groupée*

straight position
position^F *droite*

pike position
position^F *carpée*

diving installations
plongeoir^M

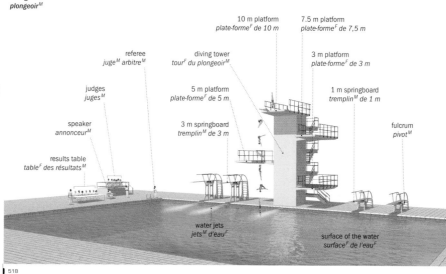

10 m platform
plate-forme^F *de 10 m*

7.5 m platform
plate-forme^F *de 7,5 m*

referee
juge^M *arbitre*^M

diving tower
tour^F *du plongeoir*^M

3 m platform
plate-forme^F *de 3 m*

judges
juges^M

5 m platform
plate-forme^F *de 5 m*

1 m springboard
tremplin^M *de 1 m*

speaker
annonceur^M

3 m springboard
tremplin^M *de 3 m*

fulcrum
pivot^M

results table
table^F *des résultats*^M

water jets
jets^M *d'eau*^F

surface of the water
surface^F *de l'eau*^F

sailboard
planche^F à voile^F

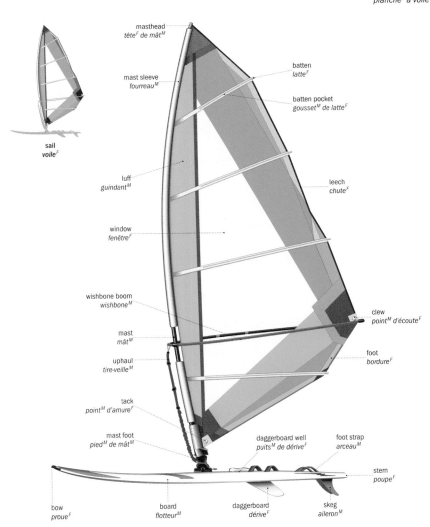

sail
voile^F

masthead
tête^F de mât^M

mast sleeve
fourreau^M

batten
latte^F

batten pocket
gousset^M de latte^F

luff
guindant^M

leech
chute^F

window
fenêtre^F

wishbone boom
wishbone^M

clew
point^M d'écoute^F

mast
mât^M

uphaul
tire-veille^M

foot
bordure^F

tack
point^M d'amure^F

mast foot
pied^M de mât^M

daggerboard well
puits^M de dérive^F

foot strap
arceau^M

stern
poupe^F

bow
proue^F

board
flotteur^M

daggerboard
dérive^F

skeg
aileron^M

SPORTS AND GAMES

519

sailing
voile^F

sailboat
dériveur^M

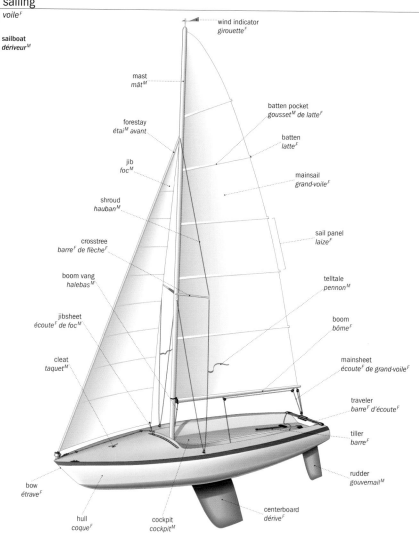

wind indicator
girouette^F

mast
mât^M

batten pocket
gousset^M *de latte*^F

forestay
étai^M *avant*

batten
latte^F

jib
foc^M

mainsail
grand-voile^F

shroud
hauban^M

sail panel
laize^F

crosstree
barre^F *de flèche*^F

boom vang
halebas^M

telltale
pennon^M

jibsheet
écoute^F *de foc*^M

boom
bôme^F

cleat
taquet^M

mainsheet
écoute^F *de grand-voile*^F

traveler
barre^F *d'écoute*^F

tiller
barre^F

rudder
gouvernail^M

bow
étrave^F

centerboard
dérive^F

hull
coque^F

cockpit
cockpit^M

multihulls
multicoques^M

monohulls
monocoques^M

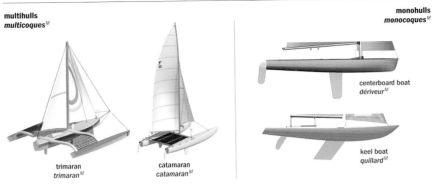

centerboard boat
dériveur^M

keel boat
quillard^M

trimaran
trimaran^M

catamaran
catamaran^M

upperworks
accastillage^M

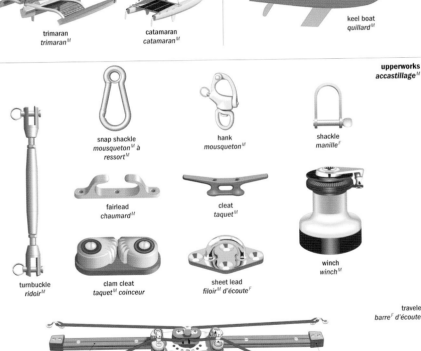

snap shackle
mousqueton^M à
ressort^M

hank
mousqueton^M

shackle
manille^F

fairlead
chaumard^M

cleat
taquet^M

turnbuckle
ridoir^M

clam cleat
taquet^M *coinceur*

sheet lead
filoir^M *d'écoute*^F

winch
winch^M

traveler
barre^F *d'écoute*^F

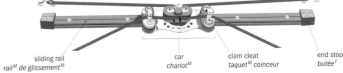

sliding rail
rail^M *de glissement*^M

car
chariot^M

clam cleat
taquet^M *coinceur*

end stop
butée^F

road racing
cyclisme^M sur route^F

road-racing bicycle and cyclist
vélo^M de course^F et cycliste^M

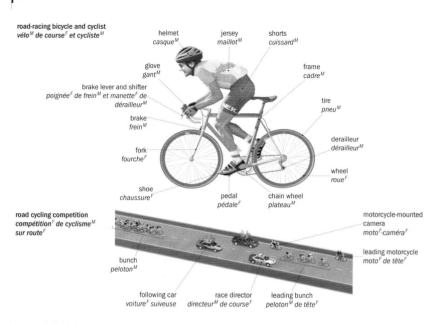

helmet
casque^M

jersey
maillot^M

shorts
cuissard^M

glove
gant^M

frame
cadre^M

brake lever and shifter
poignée^F de frein^M et manette^F de dérailleur^M

tire
pneu^M

brake
frein^M

derailleur
dérailleur^M

fork
fourche^F

wheel
roue^F

shoe
chaussure^F

pedal
pédale^F

chain wheel
plateau^M

road cycling competition
compétition^F de cyclisme^M sur route^F

motorcycle-mounted camera
moto^F-caméra^F

leading motorcycle
moto^F de tête^F

bunch
peloton^M

following car
voiture^F suiveuse

race director
directeur^M de course^F

leading bunch
peloton^M de tête^F

mountain biking
vélo^M de montagne^F

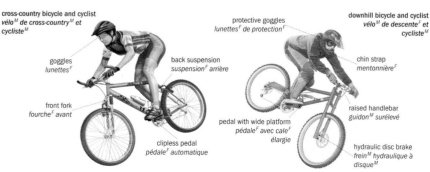

cross-country bicycle and cyclist
vélo^M de cross-country^M et cycliste^M

protective goggles
lunettes^F de protection^F

downhill bicycle and cyclist
vélo^M de descente^F et cycliste^M

goggles
lunettes^F

back suspension
suspension^F arrière

chin strap
mentonnière^F

front fork
fourche^F avant

raised handlebar
guidon^M surélevé

pedal with wide platform
pédale^F avec cale^F élargie

clipless pedal
pédale^F automatique

hydraulic disc brake
frein^M hydraulique à disque^M

personal watercraft
scooter^M de mer^F; motomarine^F

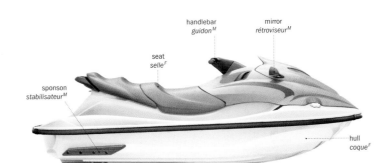

handlebar
guidon^M

mirror
rétroviseur^M

seat
selle^F

sponson
stabilisateur^M

hull
coque^F

snowmobile
motoneige^F

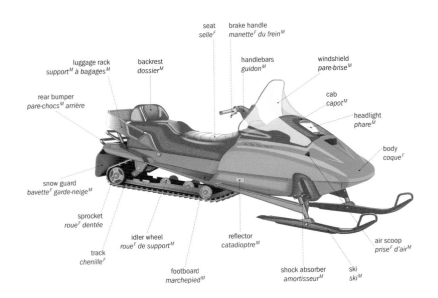

seat
selle^F

brake handle
manette^F du frein^M

luggage rack
support^M à bagages^M

backrest
dossier^M

handlebars
guidon^M

windshield
pare-brise^M

rear bumper
pare-chocs^M arrière

cab
capot^M

headlight
phare^M

body
coque^F

snow guard
bavette^F garde-neige^M

sprocket
roue^F dentée

idler wheel
roue^F de support^M

reflector
catadioptre^M

air scoop
prise^F d'air^M

track
chenille^F

footboard
marchepied^M

shock absorber
amortisseur^M

ski
ski^M

car racing
course^F automobile

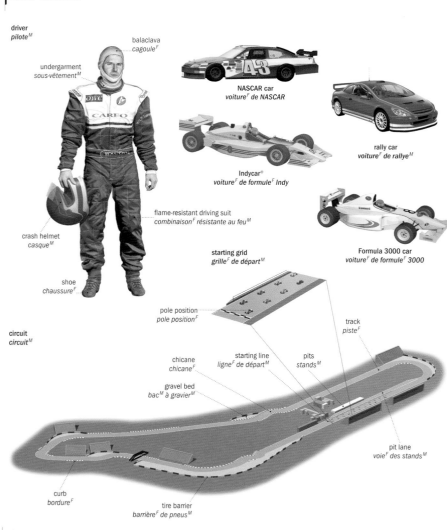

driver
pilote^M

balaclava
cagoule^F

undergarment
sous-vêtement^M

NASCAR car
voiture^F de NASCAR

rally car
voiture^F de rallye^M

Indycar®
voiture^F de formule^F Indy

flame-resistant driving suit
combinaison^F résistante au feu^M

crash helmet
casque^M

starting grid
grille^F de départ^M

Formula 3000 car
voiture^F de formule^F 3000

shoe
chaussure^F

pole position
pole position^F

track
piste^F

circuit
circuit^M

chicane
chicane^F

starting line
ligne^F de départ^M

pits
stands^M

gravel bed
bac^M à gravier^M

pit lane
voie^F des stands^M

curb
bordure^F

tire barrier
barrière^F de pneus^M

Formula 1® car
voiture^F de Formule^F 1

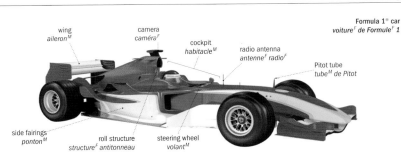

wing
aileron^M

camera
caméra^F

cockpit
habitacle^M

radio antenna
antenne^F radio^F

Pitot tube
tube^M de Pitot

side fairings
ponton^M

roll structure
structure^F antitonneau

steering wheel
volant^M

motorcycling
motocyclisme^M

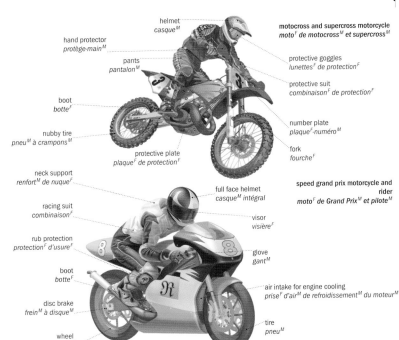

helmet
casque^M

motocross and supercross motorcycle
moto^F de motocross^M et supercross^M

hand protector
protège-main^M

pants
pantalon^M

protective goggles
lunettes^F de protection^F

protective suit
combinaison^F de protection^F

boot
botte^F

nubby tire
pneu^M à crampons^M

number plate
plaque^F-numéro^M

protective plate
plaque^F de protection^F

fork
fourche^F

neck support
renfort^M de nuque^F

full face helmet
casque^M intégral

speed grand prix motorcycle and
rider
moto^F de Grand Prix^M et pilote^M

racing suit
combinaison^F

visor
visière^F

rub protection
protection^F d'usure^F

glove
gant^M

boot
botte^F

air intake for engine cooling
prise^F d'air^M de refroidissement^M du moteur^M

disc brake
frein^M à disque^M

tire
pneu^M

wheel
roue^F

skateboarding
planche^F à roulettes^F

skateboard
planche^F à roulettes^F

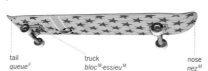

tail
queue^F

truck
bloc^M-essieu^M

nose
nez^M

grip tape
bande^F antidérapante

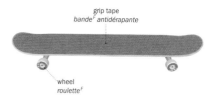

wheel
roulette^F

skateboarder
planchiste^M

knee pad
genouillère^F

elbow pad
protège-coude^M

helmet
casque^M

coping
arête^F

ramp
rampe^F

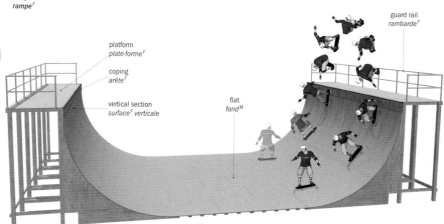

platform
plate-forme^F

coping
arête^F

vertical section
surface^F verticale

guard rail
rambarde^F

flat
fond^M

in-line skating
patin^M à roues^F alignées

acrobatic skate
patin^M acrobatique

inner boot
chausson^M intérieur

upper shell
coque^F supérieure

frame
platine^F

wheel
roue^F

skater
patineuse^F

helmet
casque^M

elbow pad
coudière^F

knee pad
genouillère^F

wrist guard
protège-poignet^M

in-line speed skate
patin^M de vitesse^F

in-line skate
patin^M à roues^F alignées

upper shell
coque^F supérieure

inner boot
chausson^M intérieur

adjusting buckle
boucle^F de réglage^M

boot
chaussure^F

axle
essieu^M

in-line hockey skate
patin^M de hockey^M

heel stop
frein^M de talon^M

wheel
roue^F

truck
bloc^M-essieu^M

SPORTS AND GAMES

527

camping
camping^M

examples of tents
exemples^M de tentes^F

rainfly
double toit^M

two-person tent
tente^F deux places^F

door
porte^F

canopy
auvent^M

guy line
hauban^M

stake
piquet^M

strainer
tendeur^M

zipper
fermeture^F à glissière^F

inner tent
tente^F intérieure

elastic strainer
Sandow®^M

family tent
tente^F familiale

window canopy
auvent^M de fenêtre^F

living room
séjour^M

guy line
hauban^M

elastic strainer
Sandow®^M

bedroom
chambre^F

sewn-in floor
tapis^M de sol^M cousu

wall
mur^M

stake loop
boucle^F de piquet^M

canvas divider
cloison^F

frame
armature^F

screen window
fenêtre^F moustiquaire^F

wagon tent
tente^F grange^F

wall tent
tente^F rectangulaire

pup tent
tente^F canadienne

rainfly
double toit^M

roof pole
mât^M de toit^M

inner tent
tente^F intérieure

elastic strainer
Sandow®^{M}

door
porte^F

stake loop
boucle^F de piquet^M

sewn-in floor
tapis^M de sol^M cousu

stake
piquet^M

one-person tent
tente^F individuelle

dome tent
tente^F dôme^M

pop-up tent
tente^F igloo^M

lantern
lanterne^F

propane or butane accessories
accessoires^M au propane^M ou au butane^M

globe
globe^M

burner frame
bâti^M du brûleur^M

pressure regulator
régulateur^M de pression^F

heater
chaufferette^F

pump
pompe^F

leakproof cap
bouchon^M antifuite

tank
réservoir^M

double-burner camp stove
réchaud^M à deux feux^M

burner
brûleur^M

tank
réservoir^M

wire support
grille^F stabilisatrice

single-burner camp stove
réchaud^M à un feu^M

control valve
robinet^M relais^M

SPORTS AND GAMES

examples of sleeping bags
exemples^M de sacs^M de couchage^M

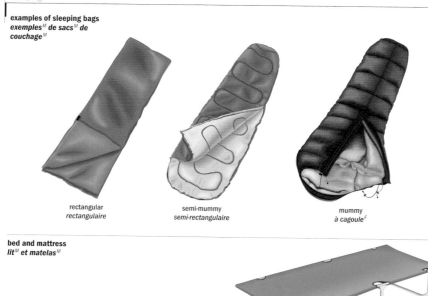

rectangular
rectangulaire

semi-mummy
semi-rectangulaire

mummy
à cagoule^F

bed and mattress
lit^M et matelas^M

folding cot
lit^M de camp^M pliant

inflator-deflator
gonfleur^M-dégonfleur^M

inflator
gonfleur^M

air mattress
matelas^M pneumatique

self-inflating mattress
matelas^M autogonflant

foam pad
matelas^M mousse^F

cutlery set
ustensiles^M de
campeur^M

cooking set
popote^F

belt loop
ganse^F

spoon
cuiller^F

fork
fourchette^F

sheath
étui^M

knife
couteau^M

plate
assiette^F plate

saucepan
faitout^M

handle
queue^F

frying pan
poêle^F à frire

coffee pot
cafetière^F

cup
tasse^F

camping equipment
matériel^M de camping^M

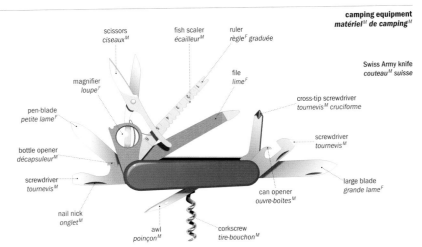

scissors
ciseaux^M

fish scaler
écailleur^M

ruler
règle^F graduée

file
lime^F

Swiss Army knife
couteau^M suisse

magnifier
loupe^F

cross-tip screwdriver
tournevis^M cruciforme

pen-blade
petite lame^F

screwdriver
tournevis^M

bottle opener
décapsuleur^M

screwdriver
tournevis^M

large blade
grande lame^F

can opener
ouvre-boites^M

nail nick
onglet^M

awl
poinçon^M

corkscrew
tire-bouchon^M

camping

backpack
sac^M à dos^M

top flap
rabat^M

shoulder strap
bretelle^F

tightening buckle
boucle^F de réglage^M

side compression strap
sangle^F de
compression^F

front compression strap
sangle^F de fermeture^F

strap loop
passe-sangle^M

hip belt
ceinture^F

folding shovel
pelle^F-pioche^F pliante

hurricane lamp
lampe^F-tempête^F

vacuum bottle
bouteille^F isolante

bottle
bouteille^F

stopper
bouchon^M

cup
tasse^F

canteen
gourde^F

cooler
glacière^F

water carrier
cruche^F

SPORTS AND GAMES

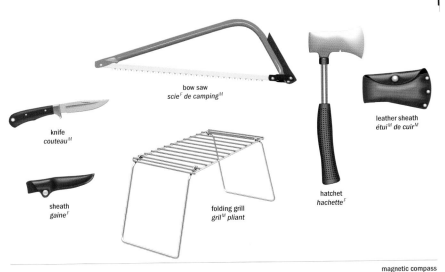

bow saw
scie^F de camping^M

leather sheath
étui^M de cuir^M

knife
couteau^M

hatchet
hachette^F

sheath
gaine^F

folding grill
gril^M pliant

magnetic compass
boussole^F magnétique

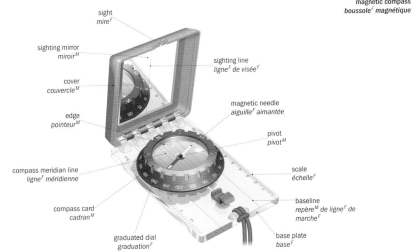

sight
mire^F

sighting mirror
miroir^M

sighting line
ligne^F de visée^F

cover
couvercle^M

magnetic needle
aiguille^F aimantée

edge
pointeur^M

pivot
pivot^M

compass meridian line
ligne^F méridienne

scale
échelle^F

compass card
cadran^M

baseline
repère^M de ligne^F de marche^F

graduated dial
graduation^F

base plate
base^F

hunting
chasse^F

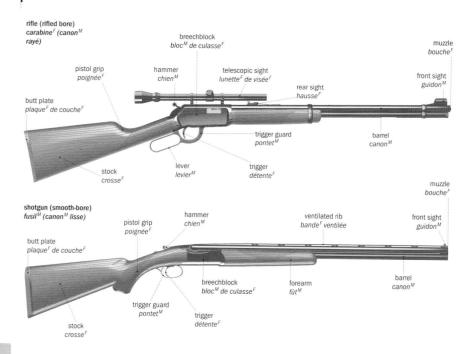

rifle (rifled bore)
carabine^F (canon^M rayé)

breechblock
bloc^M de culasse^F

muzzle
bouche^F

pistol grip
poignée^F

hammer
chien^M

telescopic sight
lunette^F de visée^F

rear sight
hausse^F

front sight
guidon^M

butt plate
plaque^F de couche^F

trigger guard
pontet^M

barrel
canon^M

stock
crosse^F

lever
levier^M

trigger
détente^F

shotgun (smooth-bore)
fusil^M (canon^M lisse)

hammer
chien^M

ventilated rib
bande^F ventilée

front sight
guidon^M

pistol grip
poignée^F

butt plate
plaque^F de couche^F

breechblock
bloc^M de culasse^F

forearm
fût^M

barrel
canon^M

trigger guard
pontet^M

trigger
détente^F

stock
crosse^F

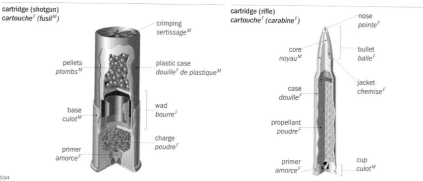

cartridge (shotgun)
cartouche^F (fusil^M)

crimping
sertissage^M

pellets
plombs^M

plastic case
douille^F de plastique^M

base
culot^M

wad
bourre^F

primer
amorce^F

charge
poudre^F

cartridge (rifle)
cartouche^F (carabine^F)

nose
pointe^F

core
noyau^M

bullet
balle^F

case
douille^F

jacket
chemise^F

propellant
poudre^F

primer
amorce^F

cup
culot^M

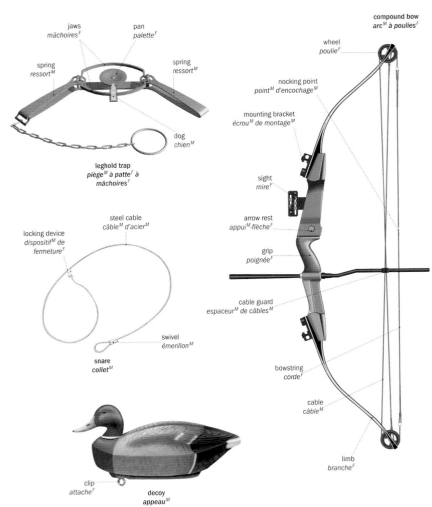

jaws
mâchoires^F

pan
palette^F

spring
ressort^M

spring
ressort^M

dog
chien^M

leghold trap
piège^M *à patte*^F *à
mâchoires*^F

compound bow
arc^M *à poulies*^F

wheel
poulie^F

nocking point
point^M *d'encochage*^M

mounting bracket
écrou^M *de montage*^M

sight
mire^F

arrow rest
appui^M-*flèche*^F

grip
poignée^F

cable guard
espaceur^M *de câbles*^M

bowstring
corde^F

cable
câble^M

limb
branche^F

steel cable
câble^M *d'acier*^M

locking device
dispositif^M *de
fermeture*^F

swivel
émerillon^M

snare
collet^M

clip
attache^F

decoy
appeau^M

fishing
pêche^F

flyfishing
pêche^F *à la mouche*^F

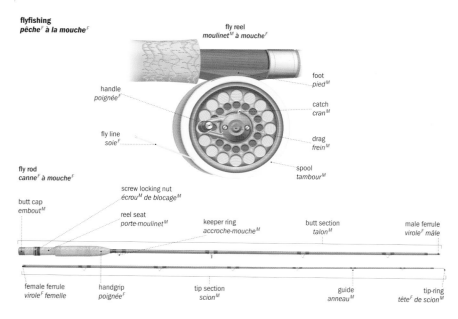

fly reel
moulinet^M *à mouche*^F

foot
pied^M

handle
poignée^F

catch
cran^M

fly line
soie^F

drag
frein^M

spool
tambour^M

fly rod
canne^F *à mouche*^F

screw locking nut
écrou^M *de blocage*^M

butt cap
embout^M

reel seat
porte-moulinet^M

keeper ring
accroche-mouche^M

butt section
talon^M

male ferrule
virole^F *mâle*

female ferrule
virole^F *femelle*

handgrip
poignée^F

tip section
scion^M

guide
anneau^M

tip-ring
tête^F *de scion*^M

artificial fly
mouche^F *artificielle*

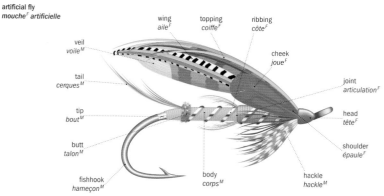

wing
aile^F

topping
coiffe^F

ribbing
côte^F

veil
voile^M

cheek
joue^F

tail
cerques^M

joint
articulation^F

tip
bout^M

head
tête^F

butt
talon^M

shoulder
épaule^F

fishhook
hameçon^M

body
corps^M

hackle
hackle^M

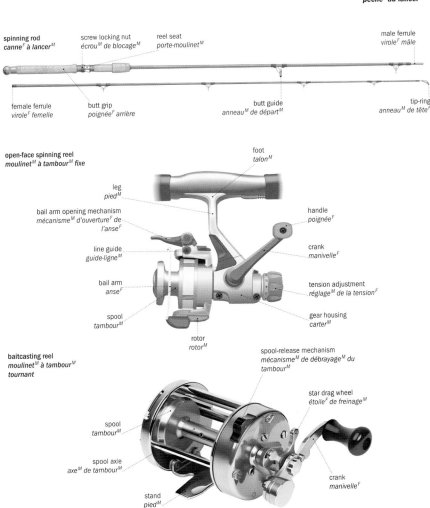

casting
pêche^F au lancer^M

spinning rod
canne^F à lancer^M

screw locking nut
écrou^M de blocage^M

reel seat
porte-moulinet^M

male ferrule
virole^F mâle

female ferrule
virole^F femelle

butt grip
poignée^F arrière

butt guide
anneau^M de départ^M

tip-ring
anneau^M de tête^F

open-face spinning reel
moulinet^M à tambour^M fixe

foot
talon^M

leg
pied^M

bail arm opening mechanism
*mécanisme^M d'ouverture^F de
l'anse^F*

handle
poignée^F

line guide
guide-ligne^M

crank
manivelle^F

bail arm
anse^F

tension adjustment
réglage^M de la tension^F

spool
tambour^M

gear housing
carter^M

rotor
rotor^M

baitcasting reel
*moulinet^M à tambour^M
tournant*

spool-release mechanism
*mécanisme^M de débrayage^M du
tambour^M*

star drag wheel
étoile^F de freinage^M

spool
tambour^M

spool axle
axe^M de tambour^M

crank
manivelle^F

stand
pied^M

SPORTS AND GAMES

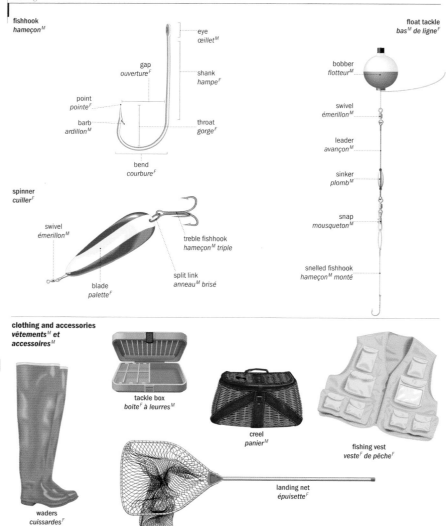

fishhook
hameçon^M

eye
œillet^M

gap
ouverture^F

shank
hampe^F

point
pointe^F

barb
ardillon^M

throat
gorge^F

bend
courbure^F

float tackle
bas^M *de ligne*^F

bobber
flotteur^M

swivel
émerillon^M

leader
avançon^M

sinker
plomb^M

snap
mousqueton^M

snelled fishhook
hameçon^M *monté*

spinner
cuiller^F

swivel
émerillon^M

treble fishhook
hameçon^M *triple*

split link
anneau^M *brisé*

blade
palette^F

clothing and accessories
vêtements^M *et*
accessoires^M

tackle box
boîte^F *à leurres*^M

creel
panier^M

fishing vest
veste^F *de pêche*^F

landing net
épuisette^F

waders
cuissardes^F

SPORTS AND GAMES

English Index

nave 285
navel 92, 94
navigation button 319
navigation key 327
navigation light 383, 393
Nazca Plate 27
Neapolitan coffee maker 181
neck 76, 83, 93, 94, 95, 101, 111, 167, 297, 301, 302, 303, 318
neck end 245
neck of femur 99
neck pad 486
neck roll 204
neck strap 458
neck support 525
neckhole 247
necklaces 264
necktie 245
nectarine 132
needle 36, 460
needle hub 460
needle-nose pliers 217
negative contact 410, 411
negative meniscus 419
negative plate 359
negative plate strap 359
negative region 410
negative terminal 359, 416, 417
negligee 256
neon lamp 217
neon tester 217
Nepal 453
Neptune 2, 3
nerve 114
nerve fiber 114
nerve termination 114
nerve, olfactory 117
nervous system 108
nervous system, central 109
nervous system, peripheral 108
nest of tables 202
net 487, 489, 491, 493, 495
net band 491
net judge 491
net support 493
Netherlands 449
nettle 127
network connection 198
network port 329
neurons 110
neutral conductor 198
neutral indicator 368
neutral line 416
neutral zone 484, 507
neutron 414
Nevis 449
New Caledonia 15
new crescent 5
New Guinea 15, 453
new moon 5
new shekel 440
New Zealand 15, 453
newborn children's clothing 260
newel post 191
Newfoundland Island 16
news items 313
newsgroup 335
newspaper 313
newspaper shop 437
newt 75
newton 426
next 328
next/fast-forward button 326

nib 312
Nicaragua 448
nictitating membrane 87
Niger 451
Niger River 20
Nigeria 451
night deposit box 443
nightgown 256
nightingale 80
nightshot button 320
nightwear 256
Nile 20
nimbostratus 42
nipple 92, 94, 113
nitric acid emission 48
nitrogen oxide emission 48
no. 8 482
nocking point 535
node 416
node of Ranvier 110
nonagon 429
nonbiodegradable pollutants 47
nonbreaking space 330
nonreusable residue waste 49
noodles 147
nori 123
normal vision 419
North 23
North America 14, 16, 34
North American Plate 27
North Korea 453
North Pole 21
north pole 416
North Sea 14, 18
North-Northeast 23
North-Northwest 23
Northeast 23
Northern hemisphere 21
Northern leopard frog 75
northern right whale 90
Northwest 23
Norway 450
Norwegian Sea 18
nose 82, 83, 94, 117, 392, 526, 534
nose landing gear 392
nose leather 87
nose of the quarter 240, 262
nose pad 273
nosing 191
nostril 74, 75, 76, 78, 83, 117
notation, musical 298
notch 244, 422, 473, 503
notched double-edged thinning scissors 270
notched edge 270
notched lapel 248
notched single-edged thinning scissors 270
note symbols 299
nozzle 12, 216, 219, 236
nubby tire 525
nuclear energy 408
nuclear energy, production of electricity 408
nuclear envelope 50, 66
nuclear fission 415
nuclear reactor 409
nuclear waste 48
nuclear whorl 73
nucleolus 50, 66, 112
nucleus 6, 50, 66, 110, 112, 414
nucleus splitting 415
number 473

number buttons 326
number key 328, 337
number plate 525
numbering machine 338
numeric keyboard 423
numeric keypad 331, 338
numeric lock 331
numeric lock key 331
nurse 464
nurses' lounge 465
nurses' station (ambulatory emergency) 463
nurses' station (major emergency) 462
nut 222, 223, 301, 302, 303
nutcracker 170
nutmeg 138
nutmeg grater 170
nuts 223
nylon thread 237

O

oak 64
oar 501
oasis 32, 36
oat flour 144
oats 61, 143
oats: panicle 61
Oberon 3
obituaries 313
object 421
object balls 502
objective 421
objective lens 8, 314, 327, 420
oblique fissure 105
oboe 306
oboes 295
observation deck 391
observation post 7
observation room 462, 465
observation window 13
observatory 7
obturator nerve 108
obtuse angle 428
occipital bone 99, 100
occipitalis 97
ocean 5, 24, 45
ocean floor 33
ocean ridges 34
ocean trenches 34
ocean weather station 38
Oceania 14, 15
Oceania and Polynesia 453
oceanic crust 26
oche 471
octave 298
octave mechanism 306
octopus 72, 157
octopus, morphology 72
odd pinnate 55
odometer 355
off-road motorcycle (dirtbike) 369
office 346, 374, 438, 439
office automation 312, 329
office building 381, 432, 435
office tower 435
official signature 441
officials' bench 507
offshore well 404
Ogen melon 135
ohm 426
oil 403
oil drain plug 360
oil pan 235, 360
oil pan gasket 360
oil pollution 48

oil pressure warning indicator 368
oil spill 48
oil terminal 381
oil warning light 355
okapi 84
okra 128
old crescent 5
old-fashioned glass 165
olecranon 99
olfactory bulb 117
olfactory mucosa 117
olfactory nerve 117
olfactory tract 117
olive oil 149
olives 128
Oman 452
Oman, Gulf 19
on-board computer 354
on-deck circle 474
on-off button 180
on-off indicator 269
on-off light 327
on-off switch 177, 180, 181, 206, 208, 209, 218, 269, 270, 271, 272, 314
on-off/volume 326
one 427
one hundred 427
one pair 468
one thousand 427
one-arm shoulder throw 499
one-bar shoe 241
one-person tent 529
one-storey house 289
one-way head 221
onion 124
online game 335
oolong tea 148
Oort cloud 2
Op-Ed article 313
open crate 162
open end wrench 223
open stringer 191
open strings 296
open-air terrace 387
open-face spinning reel 537
opening 243
opening, utensils 170
opera glasses 273
opera house 432
opera-length necklace 264
operating instructions 346
operating mask 459
operating room 464, 465
operating suite 464
operating table 464
operation keys 442, 443
operator's cab 397
operculum 74
ophthalmology room 463
opisthodomos 279
opposable thumb 91
optic chiasm 109
optic nerve 119
optical mouse 332
optical scanner 121
optical sensor 332
optical sorting 49
optician 437
optics 418
oral cavity 105, 106
oral hygiene center 272
oral irrigator 272
orange 134
orange, section 58
orangutan 91
orbicularis oculi 96

orbiculate 55
orbital-action selector 227
orbiter 12, 13
orchard 122
orchestra 278, 295
orchestra pit 292
orchid 56
order 285
ordinary die 468
oregano 142
organ 305
organ console 305
organ meat 154
Orinoco River 17
ornamental kale 126
ornamental tree 122, 182, 230
ornaments 299
ortho-cane 466
oscillating light 455
oscillating sprinkler 236
ostrich 81
ostrich egg 155
ottoman 201
outboard engine 385
outdoor leisure 528
outer bull 471
outer circle 515
outer core 26
outer lip 73
outer planets 2
outer ring 441
outer table 469
outer toe 78
outfield fence 475
outlet 361
output devices 333
output jack 303
output tray 333
outrigger 397, 400, 455
outside counter 240
outside linebacker 484
outside mirror 348, 362
outside mirror control 352
outside ticket pocket 244
outsole 240, 263
outwash plain 30
oval head 221
ovary 56, 112, 113
ovate 55
oven 164, 210
oven thermometer 171
over-blouse 255
overall standings scoreboard 496
overalls 254, 260, 261
overbed table 464
overcoat 248, 251
overflow 194, 195
overflow protection switch 214
overflow tube 196
overhead frame 401
overhead guard 396
overlay flooring 190
overpass 343, 344
oversized shirt 255
ovule 56
owl 81
ox 85
oxbow 32
oxbow lake 32
oxford shoe 240
oxygen outlet 464
oxygen pressure actuator 10
oxygenated blood 104
oyster 123
oyster fork 168
oyster knife 169
oysters, cupped Pacific 157
ozone layer 37

ENGLISH INDEX

Index français

B

INDEX FRANÇAIS